Microsoft® Word 2013

Step by Step

Joan Lambert
Joyce Cox

PUBLISHED BY
Microsoft Press
A Division of Microsoft Corporation
One Microsoft Way
Redmond, Washington 98052-6399

Library of Congress Control Number: 2012956091
ISBN: 978-0-7356-6912-3

Printed and bound in the United States of America.

Fourth Printing: July 2014

Microsoft Press books are available through booksellers and distributors worldwide. If you need support related to this book, email Microsoft Press Book Support at mspinput@microsoft.com. Please tell us what you think of this book at http://www.microsoft.com/learning/booksurvey.

Microsoft and the trademarks listed at http://www.microsoft.com/about/legal/en/us/IntellectualProperty/ Trademarks/EN-US.aspx are trademarks of the Microsoft group of companies. All other marks are property of their respective owners.

The example companies, organizations, products, domain names, email addresses, logos, people, places, and events depicted herein are fictitious. No association with any real company, organization, product, domain name, email address, logo, person, place, or event is intended or should be inferred.

This book expresses the author's views and opinions. The information contained in this book is provided without any express, statutory, or implied warranties. Neither the authors, Microsoft Corporation, nor its resellers, or distributors will be held liable for any damages caused or alleged to be caused either directly or indirectly by this book.

Acquisitions Editor: Rosemary Caperton
Editorial Production: Online Training Solutions, Inc.
Technical Reviewer: Rob Carr
Copyeditor: Kathy Krause
Indexer: Jan Bednarczuk
Cover: Microsoft Press Brand Team

Contents

PART 1

Basic Word documents

2   Enter, edit, and proofread text   51

3   Modify the structure and appearance of text   93

4 Organize information in columns and tables   139

5 Add simple graphic elements   169

6 Preview, print, and distribute documents   193

PART 2

Document enhancements

PART 3

Additional techniques

Introduction

Part of the Microsoft Office 2013 suite of programs, Microsoft Word 2013 is a sophisticated word-processing program that helps you quickly and efficiently author, format, and publish all the business and personal documents you are ever likely to need. *Microsoft Word 2013 Step by Step* offers a comprehensive look at the features of Word that most people will use most frequently.

Who this book is for

Microsoft Word 2013 Step by Step and other books in the *Step by Step* series are designed for beginning to intermediate-level computer users. Examples shown in the book generally pertain to small and medium-sized businesses but teach skills that can be used in organizations of any size. Whether you are already comfortable working in Word and want to learn about new features in Word 2013 or are new to Word, this book provides invaluable hands-on experience so that you can create and modify professional documents with ease.

How this book is organized

This book is divided into three parts. Part 1 teaches readers how to create, print, and distribute standard documents in Word 2013. Tutorials lead the reader through the process of creating document elements such as formatted text, columns, lists, tables, and simple graphics. Part 2 discusses ways of enhancing standard document content with diagrams, charts, and other visual elements; organizing and arranging content; and saving Word files in various formats. Part 3 delves into advanced techniques and tools that include creating reference elements, creating mail merge documents, collaborating on document creation, and customizing program functionality to fit the way you work. This three-part structure allows readers who are new to the program to acquire basic skills and then build on them, while readers who are comfortable with Word 2013 basics can focus on material that is of the most interest to them.

Chapter 1 contains introductory information that will primarily be of interest to readers who are new to Word or are upgrading from Word 2003 or an earlier version. If you have worked with a more recent version of Word, you might want to skip directly to Chapter 2.

This book has been designed to lead you step by step through all the tasks you're most likely to want to perform with Word 2013. If you start at the beginning and work your way through all the exercises, you will gain enough proficiency to be able to create and work with most types of Word documents. However, each topic is self-contained, so you can jump in anywhere to acquire exactly the skills you need.

Download the practice files

Before you can complete the exercises in this book, you need to download the book's practice files to your computer. These practice files can be downloaded from the following page:

http://aka.ms/Word2013sbs/files

IMPORTANT The Word 2013 program is not available from this website. You should purchase and install that program before using this book.

If you would like to be able to refer to the completed versions of practice files at a later time, you can save the practice files that you modify while working through the exercises in this book. If you save your changes and later want to repeat the exercise, you can download the original practice files again.

The following table lists the practice files for this book.

Chapter	File
Chapter 1: Explore Microsoft Word 2013	Prices.docx
	Procedures.docx
	Rules.docx
Chapter 2: Enter, edit, and proofread text	Brochure.docx
	Letter.docx
	Orientation.docx
	Regulations.docx
Chapter 3: Modify the structure and appearance of text	Association.docx
	BambooInformation.docx
	BambooStyled.docx
	Cottage.docx
	Guidelines.docx

Chapter	File
Chapter 4: Organize information in columns and tables	ConsultationA.docx
	ConsultationB.docx
	RepairCosts.docx
	RoomPlanner.docx
Chapter 5: Add simple graphic elements	AgendaDraft.docx
	Announcement.docx
	Authors.docx
	Joan.jpg
	Joyce.jpg
	OTSI-Logo.png
Chapter 6: Preview, print, and distribute documents	InfoSheetA.docx
	InfoSheetB.docx
	InfoSheetC.docx
	OfficeInfo.docx
Chapter 7: Insert and modify diagrams	Garden.jpg
	Neighborhood.docx
	Park.jpg
	Pond.jpg
	ServiceA.docx
	ServiceB.docx
	Woods.jpg
Chapter 8: Insert and modify charts	CottageA.docx
	CottageB.docx
	CottageC.docx
	Temperature.xlsx
Chapter 9: Add visual elements	AuthorsDraft.docx
	Flyer.docx
	MarbleFloor.jpg
	OTSI-Logo.png
	Welcome.docx
Chapter 10: Organize and arrange content	BambooInfo.docx
	DeliveryTruckPurchase.docx
	Loan.xlsx
	LoanComparisons.docx
	OfficeProcedures.docx

Chapter	File
Chapter 11: Create documents for use outside of Word	ParkingRules.docx
	WebPlanner.docx
Chapter 12: Link to information and content	Conductors.docx
	Conductors.pptx
	ProceduresFields.docx
	RulesBookmarks.docx
	Symphony.docx
	VisitorGuide.docx
Chapter 13: Reference content and content sources	BambooBibliography.docx
	BambooInfoA.docx
	BambooInfoB.docx
	ProceduresContents.docx
	RulesIndex.docx
Chapter 14: Work with mail merge	AnniversaryLetter.docx
	CustomerList.xlsx
	ThankYouEmail.docx
Chapter 15: Collaborate on documents	CompetitiveAnalysisA.docx
	CompetitiveAnalysisB.docx
	Loans.docx
	ProceduresRestricted.docx
	Service.docx
	ServiceCP.docx
	ServiceTA.docx
Chapter 16: Work in Word more efficiently	Agenda.docx
	AuthorsBlank.docx
	Bamboo.docx
	RoomFlyer.docx

Your companion ebook

With the ebook edition of this book, you can do the following:

- Search the full text
- Print
- Copy and paste

To download your ebook, please see the instruction page at the back of the book.

Get support and give feedback

The following sections provide information about getting help with this book and contacting us to provide feedback or report errors.

Errata

We've made every effort to ensure the accuracy of this book and its companion content. Any errors that have been reported since this book was published are listed on our Microsoft Press site, which you can find at:

http://aka.ms/Word2013sbs/errata

If you find an error that is not already listed, you can report it to us through the same page.

If you need additional support, email Microsoft Press Book Support at *mspinput @microsoft.com.*

Please note that product support for Microsoft software is not offered through the addresses above.

We want to hear from you

At Microsoft Press, your satisfaction is our top priority, and your feedback our most valuable asset. Please tell us what you think of this book at:

http://www.microsoft.com/learning/booksurvey

The survey is short, and we read every one of your comments and ideas. Thanks in advance for your input!

Stay in touch

Let's keep the conversation going! We're on Twitter at: *http://twitter.com/MicrosoftPress.*

Basic Word documents

Chapter at a glance

Identify

Identify new features of Word 2013, page 6

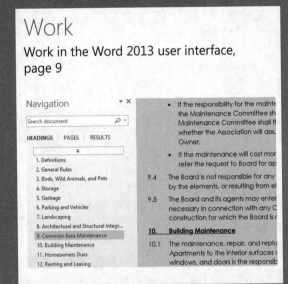

Work

Work in the Word 2013 user interface, page 9

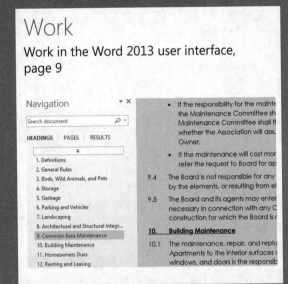

Navigate

Open, navigate, and close documents, page 31

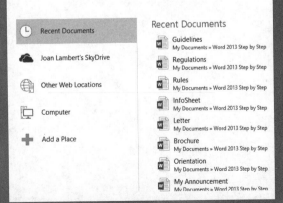

View

View documents in different ways, page 37

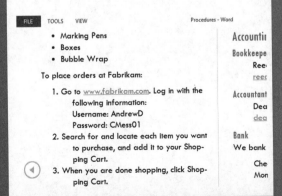

Explore Microsoft Word 2013

1

IN THIS CHAPTER, YOU WILL LEARN HOW TO

- Identify new features of Word 2013.

- Work in the Word 2013 user interface.

- Open, navigate, and close documents.

- View documents in different ways.

- Get help with Word 2013.

When you use a computer program to create, edit, and format text documents, you are performing a task known as word processing. Part of the Microsoft Office 2013 suite of programs, Microsoft Word 2013 is one of the most sophisticated word-processing programs available. By using Word, it is easy to efficiently create a wide range of business and personal documents, from the simplest letter to the most complex report. Word includes many desktop publishing features that you can use to enhance the appearance of documents so that they are visually appealing and easy to read.

You can use Word to:

- Create professional-looking documents that incorporate impressive graphics.

- Give documents a consistent look by applying styles and themes that control the font, size, color, and effects of text and the page background.

- Store and reuse pre-formatted elements such as cover pages and sidebars.

- Create personalized mailings to multiple recipients without repetitive typing.

- Make information in long documents accessible by compiling tables of contents, indexes, and bibliographies.

- Coauthor documents with team members.

- Safeguard documents by controlling who can make changes and the types of changes that can be made, as well as by removing personal and confidential information.

For many people, Word is the first Office program they will use. All the Office 2013 programs share a common working environment, called the user interface, so you can apply basic techniques that you learn in Word, such as those for creating and working with files, to other Office programs.

In this chapter, you'll learn about some of the different Word programs that are currently available so you can identify the one you are using. Then you'll get an overview of the new features in recent versions of Word to help you identify changes if you're upgrading from a previous version. You'll explore the program's user interface, and open, navigate, view, and close documents in various ways. Finally, you'll explore how to get help with the program.

PRACTICE FILES To complete the exercises in this chapter, you need the practice files contained in the Chapter01 practice file folder. For more information, see "Download the practice files" in this book's Introduction.

Office 2013 encompasses a wide variety of programs, including Microsoft Access 2013, Excel 2013, InfoPath 2013, Lync 2013, OneNote 2013, Outlook 2013, PowerPoint 2013, Publisher 2013, and Word 2013. Office is available in various editions that include different combinations of Office programs; you can also purchase most of the programs individually.

The programs in the Office suite are designed to work together to provide highly efficient methods of getting things done. You can install one or more Office programs on your computer. Some programs have multiple versions designed for different platforms. Although the core purpose of a program remains the same regardless of the platform on which it runs, the available functionality and the way you interact with the program might be different. We provide a brief description of the different Word 2013 programs here so that you can identify any differences between what appears on your screen and what's described in this book.

- **Word 2013 standard desktop installation** The program we work with and depict in images throughout this book is a desktop installation of Word 2013, meaning that we installed the program directly on our computers. The standard desktop installation has all the available Word functionality. It is available as part of the Office 2013 suite of programs, as a freestanding program, or as part of an Office 365 subscription that allows users to install the desktop programs from the Internet.

  TIP Office 365 is a cloud-based solution that provides a variety of products and services through a subscription licensing program. Depending on the subscription plan purchased, users will have access either to the full Word 2013 desktop installation and Word Web App or only to Word Web App.

- **Word 2013 RT** Tablet-style computers that run Windows RT (a version of Windows 8 that runs only on devices that use a type of processor called an ARM processor) come preloaded with Office Home & Student 2013 RT, which includes Word, Excel, Power-Point, and OneNote.

  The Office 2013 RT programs have the functionality of the full programs and also include a Touch Mode feature to help you work with the program and enter content by tapping the screen with your finger or with a tool such as a stylus. When Touch Mode is turned on, the user interface is slightly modified to simplify on-screen interactions, and an on-screen keyboard is readily available for text input. (You can simplify your interactions even further by attaching a keyboard and mouse to your Windows RT computer and interacting with Office in the usual manner.)

- **Word Web App** Word Web App may be available in your web browser when you are working with a document that is stored on a Microsoft SharePoint site or on a Microsoft SkyDrive. You can review and edit a document by using the Web App, which runs directly in your browser instead of on your computer. Web Apps are installed in the online environment in which you're working and are not part of the desktop version that you install directly on your computer. Word Web App is available as part of Office 365 and SharePoint Online subscriptions, and is free on SkyDrive storage sites.

  SEE ALSO For information about saving documents to SkyDrive and SharePoint sites, see "Starting, entering text in, and saving documents" in Chapter 2, "Enter, edit, and proofread text."

  Word Web App displays the contents of a document very much like the desktop application does. Although the Web App offers only a subset of the commands available in the full desktop application, it does provide the tools you need to edit, print, and share documents. Commands that are *not* available in Word Web App are those that control functionality, such as the commands for navigating by section or page; finding and replacing content; inserting fancy graphic elements; changing document design elements; controlling page breaks, line numbering, and hyphenation; arranging graphic elements on the page; working with reference elements; creating mail merge documents; using the research and language tools; working with comments and tracked changes; and working with multiple documents or document windows.

Both Word Web App and the desktop installation of the program might be available to you in the online environment. When viewing a document in the Web App, you can click the Edit Document menu and then choose the version you want to use by clicking Edit In Word or Edit In Word Web App. If you're editing a document in the Web App and find that you need more functionality than is available, and you have the full version of Word installed on your computer, you can click Open In Word to open the document in the full version.

Identifying new features of Word 2013

Word 2013 builds on previous versions to provide a powerful set of tools to meet all your word-processing needs. If you're upgrading to Word 2013 from a previous version, you're probably most interested in the differences between the old and new versions and how they will affect you, and want to find out about them in the quickest possible way. The following sections list new features you will want to be aware of, depending on the version of Word you are upgrading from. Start with the first section and work down to your previous version to get the complete picture.

If you are upgrading from Word 2010

If you have been using Word 2010, you might be wondering how Microsoft could have improved on what seemed like a pretty comprehensive set of features and tools. The new features introduced between Word 2010 and Word 2013 include the following:

- **Start screen** When you start Word without opening a specific document, the Start scree provides quick access to recent documents and and to document templates.

- **Cloud access** When you connect your Office or Word installation to a Microsoft account, you have the option of saving documents to your SkyDrive. After you save a document in a SkyDrive folder or other shared location, you and your colleagues can simultaneously work on one version of the document.

- **Previous location bookmark** When you close a document, Word marks the location where you were working. The next time you open the document (even on a different computer, if the document is saved in a shared location) a Resume Reading alert appears, to make it easy to return to that location.

- **Smart guides** When you place or move a graphic element on a page, on-screen guides appear to help you align the graphic with other page elements such as margins and paragraphs.

- **Read Mode** This view, which replaces the Full Screen Reading view, provides a simpler interface for reviewing documents.

- **Reply Comment** With this new feature you can place comments next to the text you're discussing so it's easy to track the conversation.

- **Present Online** Share your document with others even if they don't have Word. As you display the document on your screen, they can follow along in their browsers.

- **Live Layout** Text reflows instantly when you drag a photo, video, or shape to its new position. When you release the mouse button, your object and surrounding text stay where you want them.

- **PDF Reflow** When you open a PDF in Word, its paragraphs, lists, tables, and other content act just like Word content.

If you are upgrading from Word 2007

In addition to the features listed in the previous section, if you're upgrading from Word 2007, you'll want to take note of the following features that were introduced in Word 2010:

- **Backstage view** All the tools you need to work with your files, as opposed to their content, really are accessible from one location. You display the Backstage view by clicking the File tab, which replaces the Microsoft Office Button.

- **Customizable ribbon** The logical next step in the evolution of the command center that was introduced with Word 2007: create your own tabs and groups to suit the way you work.

- **Navigation pane** The replacement for the Document Map not only provides a means of navigating to any heading but also to any page or to any search term you enter.

- **Unsaved file recovery** Word preserves temporary versions of your unsaved files so that you can recover them if you need them.

- **Paste preview** No more trial and error when moving items to new locations. Preview what an item will look like in each of the available formats, and then pick the one you want.

- **Coauthoring** A team of authors can work simultaneously on a document stored in a SharePoint site document library or SkyDrive folder.

- **Language support** These days, more business is conducted internationally across language lines than ever before. Not only can you easily tailor the language of your working environment, but you can also use translation tools to collaborate with team members in other countries.

- **Graphics editing** After inserting a picture, you can edit it in multiple ways. In addition to changing color, brightness, and contrast, you can remove the background and, most exciting of all, apply artistic effects that make it appear like a watercolor, pencil drawing, or pastel sketch.

- **Text effects** WordArt has had a makeover. Not only can WordArt be used to create distinctive headlines, but its effects can be used on any text.

- **Screen shots and screen clippings** You no longer need to go outside of Word when you want to insert a screen image into a document. This capability is built into Word.

- **Improved SmartArt Graphics tool** You can include pictures in addition to text in your SmartArt diagrams.

If you are upgrading from Word 2003

In addition to the features listed in the previous sections, if you're upgrading from Word 2003, you'll want to take note of the new features that were introduced in Word 2007. The Word 2007 upgrade provided a more efficient working environment and included a long list of new and improved features, including the following:

- **The ribbon** No more hunting through menus, submenus, and dialog boxes. This interface organizes all the commands most people use most often, making them quickly accessible from tabs at the top of the program window.

- **Live Preview** Review the effect of a style, theme, or other formatting option before you apply it.

- **Building blocks** Think AutoText on steroids! Predefined building blocks include sets of matching cover pages, quote boxes, sidebars, and headers and footers.

- **Style sets and document themes** Quickly change the look of a document by applying a different style set or theme, previewing its effect before making a selection.

- **SmartArt Graphics tool** Use this awesome diagramming tool to create sophisticated diagrams with three-dimensional shapes, transparency, drop shadows, and other effects.

- **Improved charting** Enter data in a linked Excel worksheet and watch as the data is instantly plotted in the chart type of your choosing.

- **Document cleanup** Have Word check for and remove comments, hidden text, and personal information stored as properties before you declare a document final.

- **New file format** The Microsoft Office Open XML Formats reduce file size and help avoid loss of data.

Working in the Word 2013 user interface

The goal of the Microsoft Office working environment is to make working with Office documents, including Microsoft Word documents, Excel workbooks, PowerPoint presentations, Outlook email messages, and Access database tables, as intuitive as possible.

As with all Office 2013 programs, the most common way to start Word is from the Start screen (Windows 8) or the Start menu (Windows 7) that is displayed when you click at the left end of the Windows Taskbar. When you start Word without opening a specific document, a program starting screen appears, from which you can create a new document or open an existing one. Either way, when you're working with a document, it is displayed in a program window that contains all the tools you need to add and format content.

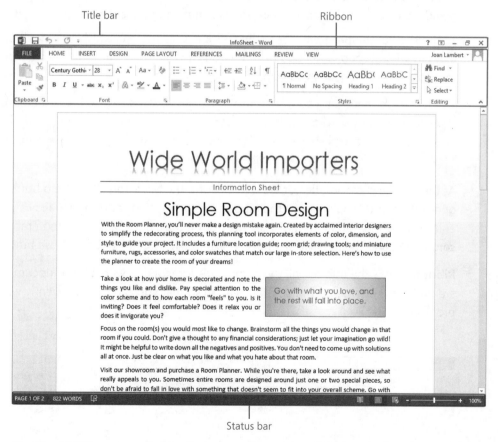

The Word 2013 program window, displaying a document and the standard program window elements.

Identifying program window elements

The program window contains the following elements:

- **Title bar** At the top of the program window, this bar displays the name of the active document and provides tools for managing the program and the program window.

Program icon   Document title   Help button

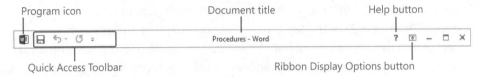

Quick Access Toolbar   Ribbon Display Options button

The title bar of a program window for an existing document.

At the left end of the title bar is the program icon, which you click to display commands to restore, move, size, minimize, maximize, and close the program window.

To the right of the program icon is the Quick Access Toolbar, which by default displays the Save, Undo, and Redo buttons. You can customize the Quick Access Toolbar to display any commands you want.

TIP You might find that you work more efficiently if you organize the commands you use frequently on the Quick Access Toolbar and then display it below the ribbon, directly above the workspace. For information, see "Customizing the Quick Access Toolbar" in Chapter 16, "Work in Word more efficiently."

At the right end of the title bar are five buttons: the Microsoft Word Help button that opens the Word Help window; the Ribbon Display Options button that allows you to entirely hide the ribbon, display only the ribbon tabs, or display the ribbon tabs and commands; and the familiar Minimize, Maximize/Restore Down, and Close buttons.

- **Ribbon** Below the title bar. all the commands for working with a Word document are gathered together in this central location so that you can work efficiently with the program.

Tabs   More button

Groups   Dialog box launcher   Collapse The Ribbon button

The ribbon, showing the Home tab.

TIP Don't be alarmed if your ribbon looks different from those shown in our screens. You might have installed programs that add their own tabs to the ribbon, or your screen settings might be different. For more information, see "Working with the ribbon" later in this chapter.

Across the top of the ribbon is a set of tabs. Clicking a tab displays an associated set of commands.

Commands related to managing Word and Word documents (rather than document content) are gathered together in the Backstage view, which you display by clicking the colored File tab located at the left end of the ribbon. Commands available in the Backstage view are organized on pages, which you display by clicking the page tabs in the colored left pane. You redisplay the document and the ribbon by clicking the Back arrow located above the page tabs.

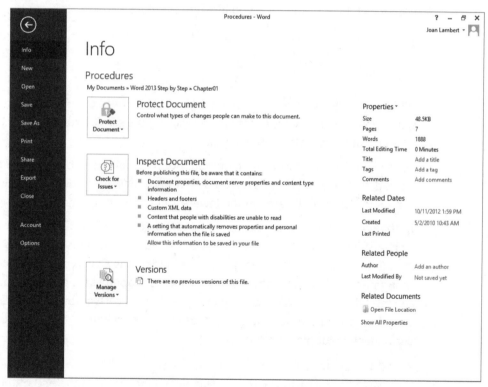

The Backstage view, where you can manage files and customize the program.

SEE ALSO For information about the functionality available in the Backstage view, see Chapter 6, "Preview, print, and distribute documents," Chapter 15, "Collaborate on documents," and Chapter 16, "Work in Word more efficiently."

Commands related to working with document content are represented as buttons on the remaining tabs of the ribbon. The Home tab, which is active by default, contains the commands most Word users will use most often. When a graphic element such as a picture, table, or chart is selected in a document, one or more *tool tabs* might appear at the right end of the ribbon to make commands related to that specific object easily accessible. Tool tabs are available only when the relevant object is selected.

TIP Some older commands no longer appear as buttons on the ribbon but are still available in the program. You can make these commands available by adding them to the Quick Access Toolbar. For more information, see "Customizing the Quick Access Toolbar" in Chapter 16, "Work in Word more efficiently."

On each tab, buttons representing commands are organized into named groups. You can point to any button to display a ScreenTip with the command name, a description of its function, and its keyboard shortcut (if it has one).

SEE ALSO For information about controlling the display and content of Screen-Tips, see "Changing default program options" in Chapter 16, "Work in Word more efficiently."

When a gallery contains more thumbnails than can be shown in the available ribbon space, you can display more content by clicking the scroll arrow or More button located on the right edge of the gallery.

Related but less common commands are not represented as buttons in a group. Instead, they're available in a dialog box or pane, which you display by clicking the dialog box launcher located in the lower-right corner of the group.

To the right of the groups on the ribbon is the Collapse The Ribbon button, which is shaped like a chevron. Clicking this button hides the groups of buttons but leaves the tab titles visible. When the groups are hidden, the Collapse The Ribbon button changes to the Pin The Ribbon button, which is shaped like a pushpin. You can click any tab title to temporarily display the groups, then click a ribbon command or click away from the ribbon to hide the groups again, or click the Pin The Ribbon button to permanently redisplay the groups.

KEYBOARD SHORTCUT Press Ctrl+F1 to unpin or pin the ribbon. For more information about keyboard shortcuts, see "Keyboard shortcuts" at the end of this book.

About buttons and arrows

Some buttons include an arrow, which may be integrated with or separate from the button. To determine whether a button and its arrow are integrated, point to the button to activate it. If both the button and its arrow are shaded, clicking the button displays options for refining the action of the button. If only the button or arrow is shaded when you point to it, clicking the button carries out its current default action. Clicking the arrow and then clicking the action you want carries out the action and assigns it to the button.

The Draw A Shape button has an integrated arrow;
the Insert An App button has a separate arrow.

- **Status bar** Across the bottom of the program window, this bar displays information about the current document and provides access to certain program functions.

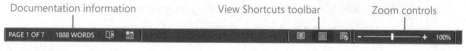

Documentation information   View Shortcuts toolbar   Zoom controls

The status bar.

By default, Word displays the Page Number, Word Count, Spelling And Grammar Check, and Macro Recording indicators at the left end of the status bar. Each of these indicators on the left displays at a glance the status of that feature; clicking any of these indicators displays the related pane or dialog box.

TIP Clicking the Macro Recording button allows you to review the macros embedded in a document. The subject of macros is beyond the scope of this book. For information, refer to Word Help.

At the right end of the status bar, Word displays by default the View Shortcuts, Zoom Slider, and Zoom Level controls. The View Shortcuts toolbar includes buttons for the three primary document content views. The Zoom Slider and Zoom Level controls enable you to adjust the magnification of the active document.

SEE ALSO For information about the various ways you can view document content, see "Viewing documents in different ways" later in this chapter. For information about customizing the status bar, see the sidebar "Customizing the status bar" in Chapter 16, "Work in Word more efficiently."

The goal of all these user interface features is to make working on a document as intuitive as possible. Commands for tasks you perform often are readily available, and even those you might use infrequently are easy to find.

When a formatting option has several choices available, they are often displayed in a gallery of images, called *thumbnails*, that provide a visual representation of each choice. When you point to a thumbnail in a gallery, the Live Preview feature shows you what the active content will look like if you click the thumbnail to apply the associated formatting.

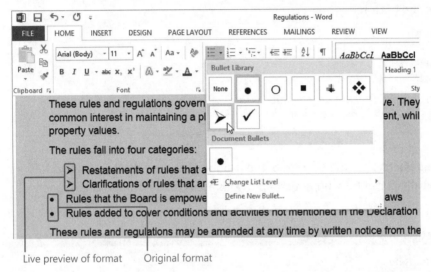

Live preview of format   Original format

Live Preview shows the effect on the active content of applying the format you are pointing to.

You can display the content of the active document in five views: Draft view, Outline view, Print Layout view, Read Mode view, and Web Layout view. All views are available from the View tab; Read Mode, Print Layout, and Web Layout views are available from the View Shortcuts toolbar on the status bar. You carry out most of the development work on a document in Print Layout view, which is the default.

Working with the ribbon

As with all Office 2013 programs, the goal of the ribbon is to make working with document content as intuitive as possible. The ribbon is dynamic, meaning that as its width changes, its buttons adapt to the available space. As a result, a button might be large or small, it might or might not have a label, or it might even change to an entry in a list.

For example, when sufficient horizontal space is available, the buttons on the Review tab are spread out, and you can review the commands available in each group.

The Review tab at 1024 pixels wide.

If you decrease the horizontal space available to the ribbon, small button labels disappear and entire groups of buttons might hide under one button that represents the entire group. Clicking the group button displays a list of the commands available in that group.

The Review tab at 660 pixels wide.

When the ribbon becomes too narrow to display all the groups, a scroll arrow appears at its right end. Clicking the scroll arrow displays the hidden groups.

The Review tab at 325 pixels wide.

The width of the ribbon depends on these three factors:

- **Program window width** Maximizing the program window provides the most space for the ribbon. To maximize the window, click the **Maximize** button, drag the borders of a non-maximized window, or drag the window to the top of the screen.

- **Screen resolution** Screen resolution is the size of your screen display expressed as pixels wide × pixels high. The greater the screen resolution, the greater the amount of information that will fit on one screen. Your screen resolution options are dependent on the display adapter installed in your computer, and on your monitor. Common screen resolutions range from 800 × 600 to 2560 × 1600. The greater the number of pixels wide (the first number), the greater the number of buttons that can be shown on the ribbon.

To change your screen resolution, first display the Screen Resolution control panel item by using one of the following methods:

- Right-click the Windows desktop, and then click **Screen Resolution**.

- Enter screen resolution in Windows 8 Search, and then click **Adjust screen resolution** in the **Settings** results.

- Open the **Display** control panel item, and then click **Adjust resolution**.

An easy way to do so is by right-clicking the Windows desktop, and then clicking Screen Resolution. On the Screen Resolution page, click the Resolution arrow, click or drag to select the screen resolution you want, and then click Apply or OK.

- **The magnification of your screen display** If you change the screen magnification setting in Windows, text and user interface elements are larger and therefore more legible, but fewer elements fit on the screen.

You can change the screen magnification from the Display control panel item.

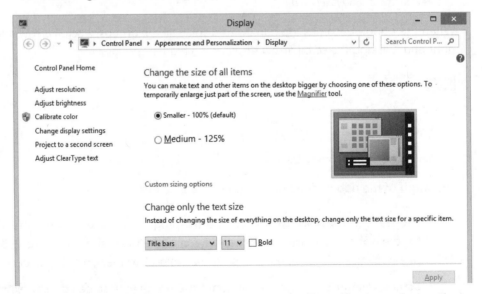

In the Display window, you can choose one of the standard magnification options or change the text size of specific elements.

You can open the Display window directly from Control Panel or by using one of the following methods:

- Right-click the Windows desktop, click **Personalize**, and then in the lower-left corner of the **Personalization** window, click **Display**.

- Enter display in Windows 8 Search, and then click **Display** in the **Settings** results.

To change the screen magnification to a magnification that is available in the Display window, click that option. To select another magnification, click the Custom Sizing Options link and then, in the Custom Sizing Options dialog box, click the magnification you want in the list or drag the ruler to change the magnification even more (the cursor changes to a pointer to indicate that you're dragging).

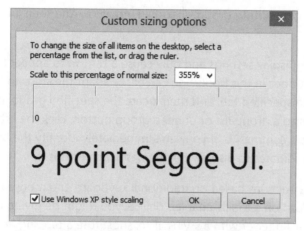

You can set the magnification as high as 500 percent by dragging the ruler in the Custom Sizing Options dialog box.

After you click OK in the Custom Sizing Options dialog box, the custom magnification is shown in the Display window along with any warnings about possible problems that might occur if you select that magnification. Click Apply in the Display window to apply the selected magnification.

Adapting exercise steps

The screen shots shown in this book were captured at a screen resolution of 1024 × 768, at 100 percent magnification. If your settings are different, the ribbon on your screen might not look the same as the one shown in this book. As a result, exercise instructions that involve the ribbon might require a little adaptation. Our instructions use this format:

- On the **Insert** tab, in the **Illustrations** group, click the **Chart** button.

If the command is in a list, our instructions use this format:

- On the **Home** tab, in the **Editing** group, click the **Find** arrow and then, in the **Find** list, click **Go To**.

If differences between your display settings and ours cause a button to appear differently on your screen than it does in this book, you can easily adapt the steps to locate the command. First click the specified tab, and then locate the specified group. If a group has been collapsed into a group list or under a group button, click the list or button to display the group's commands. If you can't immediately identify the button you want, point to likely candidates to display their names in ScreenTips.

In this book, we provide instructions based on traditional keyboard and mouse input methods. If you're using Word on a touch-enabled device, you might be giving commands by tapping with your finger or with a stylus. If so, substitute a tapping action any time we instruct you to click a user interface element. Also note that when we tell you to enter information in Word, you can do so by typing on a keyboard, tapping an on-screen keyboard, or even speaking aloud, depending on your computer setup and your personal preferences.

In this exercise, you'll start Word, create a sample document, and explore the functionality available from the ribbon and the Backstage view.

 SET UP You don't need any practice files to complete this exercise. Log on to your computer, but don't start Word. Then follow the steps.

1.   Start Word by following the steps appropriate to your operating system.

- If your computer is running Windows 7, on the **Start** menu, click **All Programs**, click **Microsoft Office**, and then click **Microsoft Word 2013**.

- If your computer is running Windows 8, click the program tile on the Windows Start screen or press the **Windows** key, enter word to display the **Search** pane, and then in the **Apps** search results list, click **Word 2013**.

Word starts and displays a list of recent documents in the left pane and document templates in the right pane.

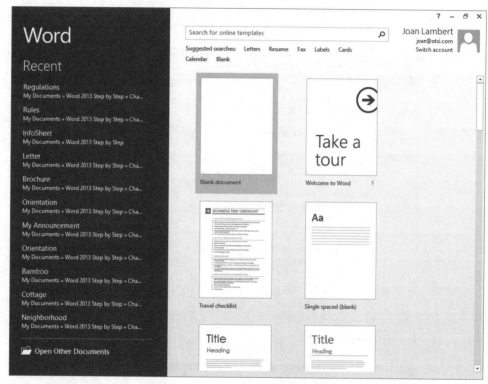

From the Word Start screen you can open an existing document or create a new one.

TROUBLESHOOTING Because the templates featured on the Start screen are dynamically updated to reflect seasonal offerings, the thumbnails on your Start screen might be different from ours.

2   Scroll through the list to review the currently featured templates. Then press the **Esc** key to create a new, blank document.

3   If the Word program window is not maximized, click the **Maximize** button near the right end of the title bar to maximize it now. Notice that the **Home** tab displays buttons related to working with document content, and that the buttons are organized in five groups: **Clipboard**, **Font**, **Paragraph**, **Styles**, and **Editing**.

4   Point to each button on the **Home** tab to display information about the button in a ScreenTip. Notice that some ScreenTips provide more information than the standard button name, keyboard shortcut, and description.

TROUBLESHOOTING If your ribbon shows the tab names but no buttons, or doesn't show the tabs at all, click the Ribbon Display Options button, and then click Show Tabs And Commands. Throughout this book, the exercise instructions assume that the ribbon is displayed unless we explicitly tell you to hide it.

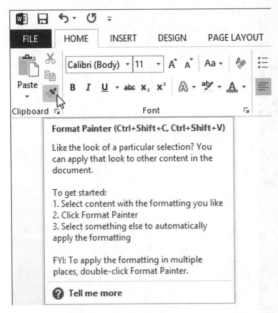

The ScreenTip for the Format Painter button displays the button's name, its keyboard shortcut, and its function.

TIP A button representing a command that cannot be performed on the selected document element is inactive (gray), but pointing to it still displays its ScreenTip.

5   On the scroll bar to the right of the thumbnails in the **Styles** group, click the down arrow to display the next row of paragraph style thumbnails.

6   At the bottom of the **Styles** scroll bar, click the **More** button to expand the entire **Styles** gallery.

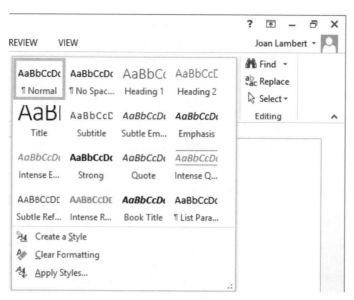

The expanded Styles gallery, showing the styles you can quickly apply to this document.

7   Press the **Esc** key to close the gallery without applying a style.

8   In the lower-right corner of the **Styles** group, click the **Styles** dialog box launcher to open the **Styles** pane. Notice that the pane displays a simple list of styles. If you're familiar with the styles in your document, you might find it more efficient to work with an unformatted list like this. If not, you can select the **Show Preview** button at the bottom of the pane to display visual previews of the styles in the same way that they appear in the **Styles** gallery.

9   Drag the **Styles** pane by its header to the right side of the program window, releasing the mouse button when the pane attaches to the edge of the window (this is called *docking*).

SEE ALSO For information about creating structure and ensuring consistency by using styles, see "Applying styles to text" in Chapter 3, "Modify the structure and appearance of text."

The Styles pane, showing the available styles and the style of the currently selected content.

New Style button

Style Inspector button

Manage Styles button

10 Click the **Close** button (the X) in the upper-right corner of the **Styles** pane to close the pane. Then click the **Insert** tab to display buttons related to all the items you can insert into a document. Familiarize yourself with the types of content you can insert into a document by reviewing the buttons in the 10 groups on this tab.

From the Insert tab, you can insert many different document and graphic elements.

11 Click the **Design** tab to display buttons related to the visual formatting of your document. Familiarize yourself with these formatting options by reviewing the buttons in the two groups on this tab.

From the Design tab, you can format thematic elements and apply visual effects to the document pages.

12 In the **Document Formatting** group, click the **Themes** button to expand the gallery of available themes.

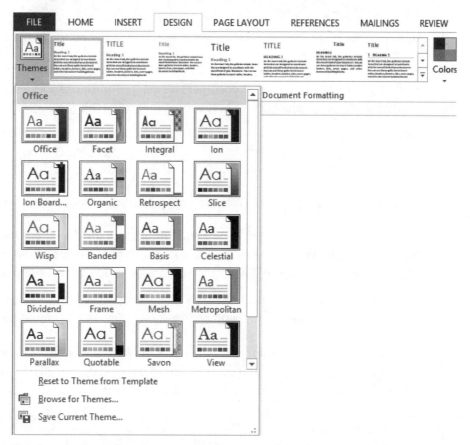

The theme controls the color scheme, fonts, and special effects applied to the text of a document.

13   In the **Page Background** group, click the **Page Color** button. In the **Page Color**
        gallery, point to each swatch in the top row of the **Theme Colors** palette. Notice
        that the page background changes to each color that you point to.

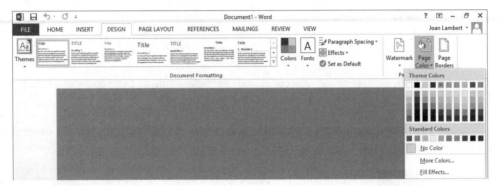

Formatting the page background doesn't affect the background of other colored page elements.

14   Press **Esc** to close the gallery. Then click the **Page Layout** tab to display buttons
        related to the physical layout of document elements. Familiarize yourself with these
        options by reviewing the buttons in the three groups on this tab.

From the Page Layout tab, you can format the physical layout of the document contents.

15   In the lower-right corner of the **Page Setup** group, click the dialog box launcher to
        open the **Page Setup** dialog box. Notice the three tabs at the top of this dialog box:
        Margins, **Paper**, and **Layout**. Clicking a tab displays a page of related options.

        SEE ALSO For information about using the Page Setup dialog box, see "Previewing
        and adjusting page layout" in Chapter 6, "Preview, print, and distribute documents."

16   Click **Cancel** to close the dialog box. Then click the **References** tab to display buttons
        related to reference information you can add to documents. Familiarize yourself with
        these options by reviewing the buttons in the six groups on this tab.

From the References tab, you can insert reference elements and compile reference tables.

TIP You will usually add references to longer documents, such as reports.

17   Click the **Mailings** tab to display buttons related to creating mass mailings. Familiarize yourself with these options by reviewing the buttons in the five groups on this tab.

From the Mailings tab, you can create mail merge letters, email messages, envelopes, labels, and other documents.

18   Click the **Review** tab to display buttons related to proofreading documents, working in other languages, adding comments, tracking and resolving document changes, and protecting documents. Familiarize yourself with these options by reviewing the buttons in the seven groups on this tab.

From the Review tab, you can proof and translate document contents, enter and review comments, track and review changes, compare multiple versions of a document, and protect a document from unauthorized changes.

19   Click the **View** tab to display buttons related to changing the view and other aspects of the display. Familiarize yourself with these options by reviewing the buttons in the five groups on this tab.

From the View tab, you can control the display of the document and of various Word elements, display and arrange multiple document windows, and work with macros.

Let's take a look at the Backstage view, where commands related to managing documents (such as creating, saving, and printing) are available.

20   Click the **File** tab to display the **Info** page of the **Backstage** view of Word 2013. The middle pane provides commands for controlling who can work on the document, removing properties (information that is associated with the document), and accessing document versions (older copies of the document that you saved or that Word automatically saved for you).

The right pane displays the associated properties, as well as dates of modification, creation, and printing, and who created and edited the document.

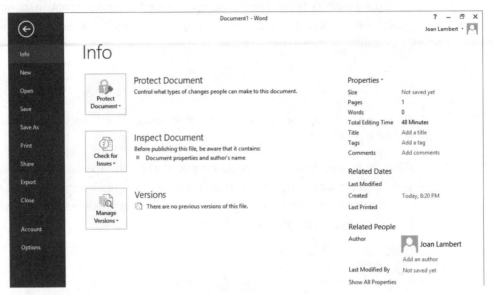

The Info page of the Backstage view provides commands for viewing and managing the behind-the-scenes information about a document.

TIP When you're coauthoring a shared document with other people, information about the people working in the document and ways of contacting them also appears on the Info page. For information about coauthoring, see "Coauthoring documents" in Chapter 15, "Collaborate on documents."

SEE ALSO For information about working with properties, see "Preparing documents for electronic distribution" in Chapter 6, "Preview, print, and distribute documents."

21 In the left pane, click the **New** page tab. Notice that the templates that were available on the Word Start screen are also available here. You can click links at the top of the page to locate additional templates online.

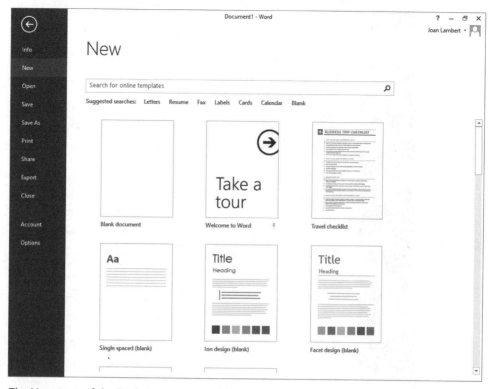

The New page of the Backstage view provides access to document templates saved locally (on your computer) and online.

TROUBLESHOOTING The thumbnails on your New page might be different from ours.

SEE ALSO For information about creating documents, see, "Starting, entering text in, and saving documents" in Chapter 2, "Enter, edit, and proofread text."

22 Click the **Open** page tab. This page displays locations from which you can open existing documents as well as a list of the documents you recently worked on. The content of the **Places** list varies based on your available resources. For example, if your organization has a SharePoint site, that location may be available in the list—if it isn't, you can click **Other Web Locations** to locate the site.

TIP By default, the Recent Documents list displays a maximum of 20 documents. You can change this number on the Advanced page of the Word Options dialog box.

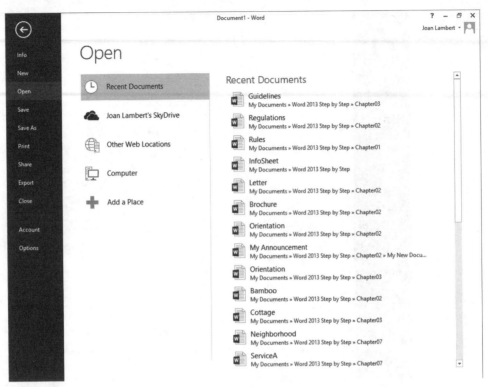

The Open page of the Backstage view provides links to locations from which you can open existing documents.

SEE ALSO For information about the Word Options dialog box, see "Changing default program options" in Chapter 16, "Work in Word more efficiently." For information about recovering unsaved documents, see the sidebar "Managing document versions" in Chapter 15, "Collaborate on documents."

23   In the **Open** dialog box, click **Cancel**. Click the **File** tab to return to the **Backstage** view, and then click the **Save As** page tab. (Because we haven't yet saved this file, the **Save** and **Save As** pages are identical.) Notice that the saving locations in the **Places** list on this page are the same as those on the **Open** page, with the exception of **Recent Documents**.

24   In the **Places** list, click **Computer**. In the right pane, Word provides a list of the folders on your computer in which you have recently saved documents. Selecting a folder in the **Recent Folders** list is an easy shortcut for locating a folder that you use frequently, and it's much simpler than having to browse through your computer's folder structure to find the location in which you want to save your document.

TIP When Computer is selected, clicking Browse in the right pane displays the Open dialog box. The first time you use this command, the Open dialog box displays the contents of your Documents library. If you display the dialog box again in the same Word session, it displays the contents of whatever folder you last used. To open a document from a different folder, use standard Windows techniques to navigate to the folder and then double-click the name of the document you want to work with.

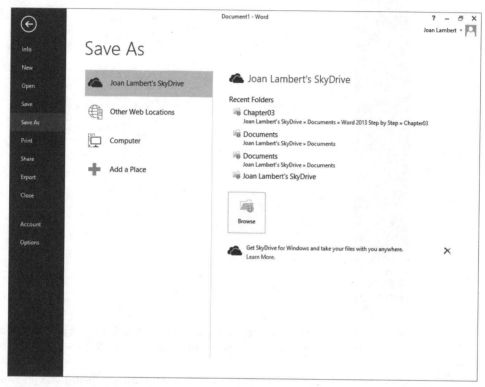

The Save As page of the Backstage view provides links to identify existing and new locations in which to save documents.

25   Display the **Print**, **Share**, and **Export** pages to get an overview of the functionality on these pages, which we discuss in depth in later chapters of this book. Then click the **Account** page tab to display information about your installation of Word 2013. Explore the options on this page.

SEE ALSO For information about printing, sharing, and exporting documents, see Chapter 6, "Preview, print, and distribute documents" and Chapter 11, "Create documents for use outside of Word."

Note that you can choose a decorative Office background (we don't show one in this book to avoid cluttering up the images, but you might want to use one) and connect to a variety of services.

The Account page of the Backstage view provides information about your installation or subscription as well as links to connect Word to a variety of internal and external services.

26 Click the **Options** page tab to open the **Word Options** dialog box, in which you can customize the way Word works to make it most efficient for your purposes. Briefly explore the pages of this dialog box to note the available options, which we cover in depth in later chapters.

> **SEE ALSO** For information about the Word Options dialog box, see "Changing default program options" in Chapter 16, "Work in Word more efficiently."

27 At the bottom of the **Word Options** dialog box, click **Cancel** to return to the current document with the **Home** tab active on the ribbon.

❌ CLEAN UP Leave the unsaved document open for the next exercise.

Opening, navigating, and closing documents

If Word isn't already running, you can start the program and simultaneously open an existing Word document from File Explorer by double-clicking the document's file name.

TIP In Windows 8, File Explorer has replaced Windows Explorer. Throughout this book, we refer to this browsing utility by its Windows 8 name. If your computer is running Windows 7, use Windows Explorer instead.

If Word is already running, from the Start page, select an existing document in the Recent pane, create a new document from a template, or click Open Other Documents to display the Backstage view. rom the New page of the Backstage view, create a blank document or a document based on a template, or click the Open page tab, select a location from the Places pane, and navigate to and select a file to open.

TIP Clicking a file name and then clicking the Open arrow displays a list of alternative ways in which you can open the document. To look through the document without making any changes, you can open it as read-only, or you can open an independent copy of the document. If you're concerned that a document might contain malicious content, you can open it in Protected view. Your computer can then display but not interact with the document. After an unexpected computer shutdown or other problem, you can tell Word to open the document and attempt to repair any damage.

If you open a document that is too long to fit entirely on the screen, you can bring off-screen content into view without changing the location of the cursor by using the vertical scroll bar that appears when you move the pointer.

- Click the scroll arrows to move up or down by one line.

- Click above or below the scroll box to move up or down one windowful.

- Drag the scroll box on the scroll bar to display the part of the document corresponding to the location of the scroll box. For example, dragging the scroll box to the middle of the scroll bar displays the middle of the document.

- Right-click the scroll bar and then click Scroll Here, Top, Bottom, Page Up, Page Down, Scroll Up, or Scroll Down.

If the document is too wide to fit on the screen, Word displays a horizontal scroll bar that you can use in similar ways to move from side to side.

You can also move around in a document by moving the cursor. To place the cursor in a specific location, you simply click there. You can also press keyboard shortcuts to move the cursor. For example, pressing the Home key moves the cursor to the left end of a line, and pressing Ctrl+Home moves it to the beginning of the document.

TIP The location of the cursor is displayed on the status bar. By default, the status bar tells you which page the cursor is on, but you can also display the cursor's location by section, line number, and column, and in inches from the top of the page. Simply right-click the status bar, and then click the option you want to display.

The following table lists ways to use your keyboard to move the cursor.

Cursor movement	Key or keyboard shortcut
Left one character	Left Arrow
Right one character	Right Arrow
Up one line	Up Arrow
Down one line	Down Arrow
Up one paragraph	Ctrl+Up Arrow
Down one paragraph	Ctrl+Down Arrow
Left one word	Ctrl+Left Arrow
To the beginning of the current line	Home
To the end of the current line	End
To the beginning of the document	Ctrl+Home
To the end of the document	Ctrl+End
To the top of the window	Alt+Ctrl+Page Up
To the bottom of the window	Alt+Ctrl+Page Down
Up one screen	Page Up
Down one screen	Page Down
To the beginning of the previous page	Ctrl+Page Up
To the beginning of the next page	Ctrl+Page Down
To a previous revision	Shift+F5
Immediately after opening, to where you were working when you last closed	Shift+F5

SEE ALSO For information about revisions, see "Tracking and managing document changes" in Chapter 15, "Collaborate on documents."

In a long document, you might want to move quickly among elements of a certain type; for example, from graphic to graphic. From the Go To page of the Find And Replace dialog box, you can select from a variety of browsing elements, including page, section, line, bookmark, comment, footnote, endnote, field, table, graphic, equation, object, and heading. You can also display the Navigation pane and move from heading to heading, from page to page, or to the next search result.

SEE ALSO For information about using the Navigation pane to search for specific content in a document, see "Finding and replacing text" in Chapter 2, "Enter, edit, and proofread text."

If more than one document is open, you can close the active document without exiting Word by clicking the Close button at the right end of the title bar. If only one document is open, clicking the Close button closes the document and also exits Word. To close the only open document but leave Word running, click Close in the Backstage view.

In this exercise, you'll open an existing document and explore various ways of moving around in it. Then you'll close the document.

➡ SET UP You need the Rules document located in the Chapter01 practice file folder to complete this exercise. With the unsaved document from the previous exercise open in Word, follow the steps.

1   From the **Open** page of the **Backstage** view, browse to the location where you saved the practice files for this book. Open the **Chapter01** folder and then double-click the **Rules** document to open it in a new instance of Word.

    TROUBLESHOOTING Don't worry if an information bar below the ribbon tells you that the document has been opened in Protected view. By default, Word opens any document that originates from the Internet or a potentially unsafe location, including email attachments, in Protected view. If you trust the file and want to work with it, click the Enable Editing button on the information bar.

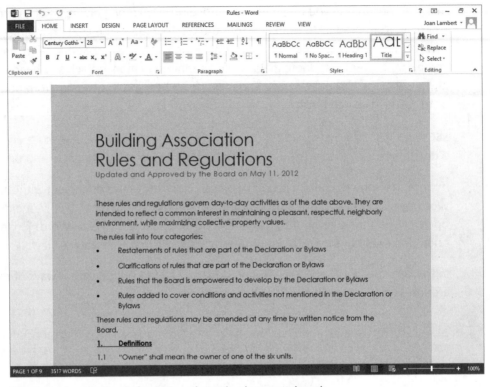

The status bar displays information about the document length.

2   In the second line of the document title, click at the right end of the paragraph to position the cursor.

3   Press the **Home** key to move the cursor to the beginning of the line.

4   Press the **Right Arrow** key six times to move the cursor to the beginning of the word **and**.

5   Press **Ctrl+Right Arrow** to move the cursor to the beginning of the word **Regulations**.

6   Press the **End** key to move the cursor to the end of the line.

7   Press **Ctrl+End** to move the cursor to the end of the document.

8   Press **Ctrl+Home** to move the cursor to the beginning of the document.

9   Right-click the center of the vertical scroll bar, and then click **Scroll Here** to move to the middle of the document.

10 Click above the scroll box on the scroll bar to change the view of the document by one windowful.

11 Drag the scroll box to the top of the scroll bar to display the beginning of the document. Note that the location of the cursor has not changed—only the part of the document that is visible.

12 On the **Home** tab, in the **Editing** group, click the **Find** arrow (not the button), and then click **Go To** to display the **Go To** page of the **Find and Replace** dialog box.

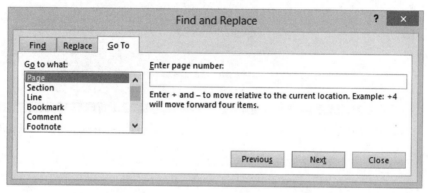

From the Go To page, you can move between specific types of content.

13 With **Page** selected in the **Go to what** list, enter 3 in the **Enter page number** dialog box, and then click **Go To** to move to the top of page 3. Then enter +3 in the **Enter page number** box, and click **Go To** to move to the top of page 6.

14 Scroll through the **Go to what** list to view the other types of document elements you can move among, and then click **Comment**. Notice that the input box title changes to **Enter reviewer's name**, and a list appears from which you can select a reviewer to move among that person's comments.

15 Close the **Find and Replace** dialog box, and then on the **View** tab, in the **Show** group, select the **Navigation Pane** check box to open the **Navigation** pane on the left side of the program window. Notice that **Headings** is selected at the top of the pane. The **Headings** page of the **Navigation** pane displays an outline of the headings in the document. The heading of the section containing the cursor is highlighted.

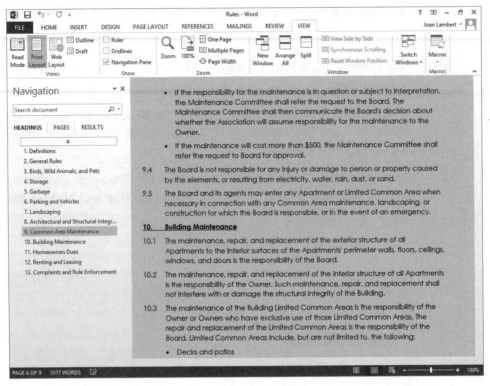

From the Navigation pane, you can move among headings, pages, or search results.

TIP The headings shown in the Navigation pane are based on headings formatted in the document by using styles. For information about creating structure and ensuring consistency by using styles, see "Applying styles to text" in Chapter 3, "Modify the structure and appearance of text."

16   In the **Navigation** pane, click the **Landscaping** heading to move the cursor directly to the selected heading.

17   At the top of the **Navigation** pane, click **Pages**. On the **Pages** page, scroll through the thumbnails to review the amount of visible detail, and then click the thumbnail for page **5** to move the cursor directly to the top of the selected page.

18   At the right end of the **Navigation** pane title bar, click the **Close** button (the X) to close the pane.

19   At the right end of the program window title bar, click the **Close** button to close the **Rules** document.

20 If **Document1** is not active, display that document. Click the **File** tab and then, in the Backstage view, click **Close**. If Word asks whether to save changes to this document, click **Don't Save**. Notice that when **Document1** closes, Word continues to run.

TROUBLESHOOTING In step 20, if you click the Close button at the right end of the title bar instead of clicking Close in the Backstage view, you'll close the open Word document and exit the Word program. To continue working, start Word again.

❌ CLEAN UP Leave Word running for the next exercise.

Viewing documents in different ways

In Word, you can display a document in a variety of views, each suited to a specific purpose. You switch the view by clicking the buttons in the Views group on the View tab, or those on the View Shortcuts toolbar in the lower-right corner of the program window.

- **Print Layout view** This view displays a document on the screen the way it will look when printed. You can review elements such as margins, page breaks, headers and footers, and watermarks.

- **Read Mode view** This view displays as much document content as will fit on the screen at a size that is comfortable for reading. In this view, the ribbon is replaced by one toolbar at the top of the screen with buttons for searching and navigating in the document. You can view comments, but you can't edit the document in this view.

- **Web Layout view** This view displays the document the way it will look when viewed in a web browser. You can review backgrounds and other effects. You can also review how text wraps to fit the window and how graphics are positioned.

- **Outline view** This view displays the structure of a document as nested levels of headings and body text, and provides tools for viewing and changing the hierarchy.

  SEE ALSO For information about displaying and modifying a document in Outline view, see "Reorganizing document outlines" in Chapter 10, "Organize and arrange content." For information about web documents, see "Creating and modifying web documents" in Chapter 11, "Create documents for use outside of Word."

- **Draft view** This view displays the content of a document with a simplified layout so that you can quickly enter and edit text. You cannot view layout elements such as headers and footers.

When you want to focus on the layout of a document, you can display rulers and gridlines to help you position and align elements. Simply select the corresponding check boxes in the Show group on the View tab. You can also adjust the magnification of the document by using the tools available in the Zoom group on the View tab or the Zoom Level button or Zoom Slider at the right end of the status bar. Clicking either the Zoom button or the Zoom Level button displays a dialog box in which you can select or type a percentage; or you can drag the Zoom Slider to the left or right or click the Zoom Out or Zoom In button on either side of the slider to change the percentage incrementally.

SEE ALSO For information about controlling document gridlines, see "Arranging objects on the page" in Chapter 10, "Organize and arrange content."

You are not limited to working with one document at a time. You can easily switch between open documents, and you can display more than one program window simultaneously. If you want to work with different parts of the same document, you can open the active document in a second window and display both, or you can split a single window into two panes and scroll through the content in each pane independently.

TIP At the right end of the View tab is the Macros group, which includes commands for viewing, recording, and pausing macros. A discussion of macros is beyond the scope of this book. If you are interested in finding out about them, search for *macros* in Word Help.

Not represented on the View tab is a feature that can be invaluable when you are fine-tuning the layout of a document. Clicking the Show/Hide ¶ button in the Paragraph group on the Home tab turns on and off the display of formatting marks and hidden characters. Formatting marks, such as tabs, paragraph marks, page breaks, and section breaks, control the layout of your document, and hidden characters provide the structure for behind-the-scenes processes, such as indexing. When you are developing a document, you might want to display these marks and characters.

KEYBOARD SHORTCUT Press Ctrl+* to turn on and off the display of formatting marks and hidden text. (You need to hold down the Shift key to activate the * key. So, in effect, you are pressing Ctrl+Shift+8.)

TIP You can format any text as hidden text by selecting it, clicking the Font dialog box launcher on the Home tab, selecting the Hidden check box, and clicking OK. When the Show/Hide ¶ button is active, hidden text is visible and is identified in the document by a dotted underline.

In this exercise, you'll first learn one more way of opening an existing document. You'll explore various ways that you can customize Print Layout view to make the work of developing documents more efficient. Then you'll switch to the other main views, noticing the differences so that you have an idea of which one is most appropriate for which task. Finally, you'll switch between open documents and view a document in multiple windows at the same time.

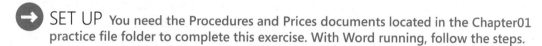 SET UP You need the Procedures and Prices documents located in the Chapter01 practice file folder to complete this exercise. With Word running, follow the steps.

1   On the **Open** page of the **Backstage** view, in the **Places** list, click **Computer**. Then in the **Recent Folders** list, click the **Chapter01** folder.

   TROUBLESHOOTING If the Chapter01 folder doesn't appear in the list, click the Browse button and locate the folder.

2   In the **Open** dialog box displaying the contents of the **Chapter01** folder, double-click the **Procedures** document to open it in the existing instance of Word.

3   With the document displayed in **Print Layout** view (the default view), scroll through the document.

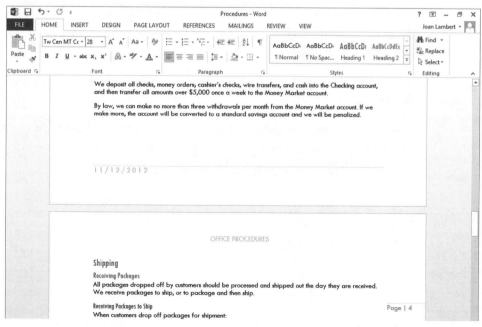

Document headers and footers are visible in Page Layout view when page breaks are displayed.

Notice that on all pages but the first, the printed document will have the title in the header at the top of the page, the page number in the right margin, and the date in the footer at the bottom of the page.

SEE ALSO For information about headers and footers, see "Inserting preformatted document parts" in Chapter 9, "Add visual elements."

4   Point to the gap between any two pages, and when the pointer changes to two opposing arrows, double-click the mouse button to hide the white space at the top and bottom of each page and the gray space between pages. Then scroll through the document again to review the change.

> We deposit all checks, money orders, cashier's checks, wire transfers, and cash into the Checking account, and then transfer all amounts over $5,000 once a week to the Money Market account.
>
> By law, we can make no more than three withdrawals per month from the Money Market account. If we make more, the account will be converted to a standard savings account and we will be penalized.
>
> **Shipping**
> **Receiving Packages**
> All packages dropped off by customers should be processed and shipped out the day they are received. We receive packages to ship, or to package and then ship.
>
> **Receiving Packages to Ship**   Page | 4
> When customers drop off packages for shipment:
>
> 1.   Ask for their name, and check the database to see if they already have an account with us. If it is an active company account, ask if they will be using a PO for payment.
> 2.   Ask if they have a preferred shipping company to use, the method of shipping (ground, air) and how quickly they need the package to arrive at its destination.

Hiding white space makes it quicker to scroll through a long document and easier to compare the content on two pages.

5   Point to the line that separates one page from the next and double-click to restore the space.

6   Press **Ctrl+Home** to move to the top of the document. At the right end of the status bar, click the **Zoom level** button, which currently indicates that the document is displayed at 100 percent, to open the **Zoom** dialog box.

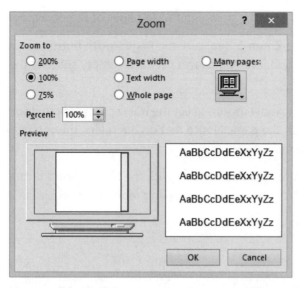

You can click a built-in zoom percentage or specify your own.

7   In the **Zoom** dialog box, click **Many pages**. Then click the monitor button, click the second page thumbnail in the top row, and click **OK** to change the magnification so that the two pages appear side by side. On the status bar, notice that the **Zoom level** and **Zoom slider** indicators change to reflect the new magnification.

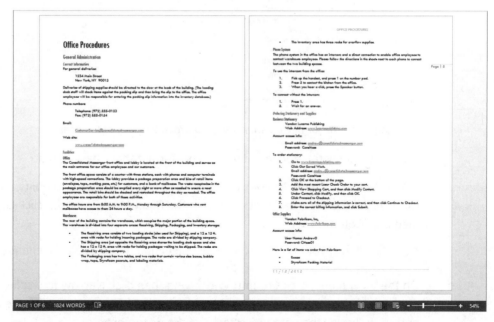

You can now scroll through the document two pages at a time.

8 Press **Page Down** to display the third and fourth pages of the document.

9 On the **View** tab, in the **Zoom** group, click the **Page Width** button to display only page **3**, at a magnification level that leaves very little empty space at the sides of the page.

10 On the **View** tab, in the **Show** group, select the **Ruler** check box to display rulers above and to the left of the page. Notice that on the rulers, the content area of the page is white and the margins are gray.

11 On the **Home** tab, in the **Paragraph** group, click the **Show/Hide ¶** button to make formatting marks such as spaces, tabs, and paragraph marks visible.

You can display the formatting marks that control the layout of the content.

Now let's display the document in a simple format that's easy to read.

12 On the **View Shortcuts** toolbar, click the **Read Mode** button to simplify the program window. On the **View** menu at the top of the **Read Mode** window, click **Layout**, and then click **Column Layout**.

> **TIP** If Column Layout is already selected, selecting it again will not change the layout.

13 On the **View** menu, click **Column Width**, and then click **Narrow** to display the document in two columns. Then on the right side of the window, click the **Forward** button to display the next two screens of the document.

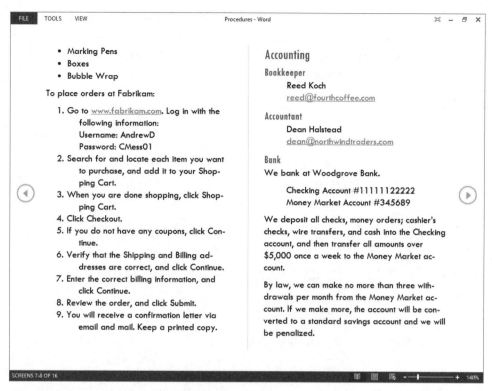

- Marking Pens
- Boxes
- Bubble Wrap

To place orders at Fabrikam:

1. Go to www.fabrikam.com. Log in with the following information:
   Username: AndrewD
   Password: CMess01
2. Search for and locate each item you want to purchase, and add it to your Shopping Cart.
3. When you are done shopping, click Shopping Cart.
4. Click Checkout.
5. If you do not have any coupons, click Continue.
6. Verify that the Shipping and Billing addresses are correct, and click Continue.
7. Enter the correct billing information, and click Continue.
8. Review the order, and click Submit.
9. You will receive a confirmation letter via email and mail. Keep a printed copy.

Accounting

Bookkeeper
Reed Koch
reed@fourthcoffee.com

Accountant
Dean Halstead
dean@northwindtraders.com

Bank
We bank at Woodgrove Bank.

Checking Account #11111122222
Money Market Account #345689

We deposit all checks, money orders; cashier's checks, wire transfers, and cash into the Checking account, and then transfer all amounts over $5,000 once a week to the Money Market account.

By law, we can make no more than three withdrawals per month from the Money Market account. If we make more, the account will be converted to a standard savings account and we will be penalized.

SCREENS 7-8 OF 16   140%

You cannot edit content in Read Mode view.

14   Investigate the options on the **Tools** menu and **View** menu. Notice that you can set the page color to **Sepia** or **Inverse** (white text on a black screen) if reading black text on a white screen bothers your eyes. Then on the **View** menu, click **Edit Document** to return to **Print Layout** view.

> **IMPORTANT** In previous versions of Word, clicking the Close button in the upper-right corner of the reading view (formerly known as Full Screen Reading view) returned you to the previous view so you could edit the document. In Word 2013, clicking the Close button in the upper-right corner of the window while in Read Mode view closes the document.

Now let's display the document as it will appear in a web browser.

15   Press **Ctrl+Home** to return to the beginning of the document. On the **View Shortcuts** toolbar, click the **Web Layout** button. Then scroll through the document. Notice that the text column fills the window, and there are no page breaks.

16   Press **Ctrl+Home** to return to the beginning of the document. On the **View** tab, in the **Views** group, click the **Draft** button, and then scroll through the document.

Notice that the basic content of the document appears without any extraneous elements, such as margins and headers and footers. Only the horizontal ruler is visible. The active area on the ruler indicates the width of the text column, dotted lines indicate page breaks, and scrolling is quick and easy.

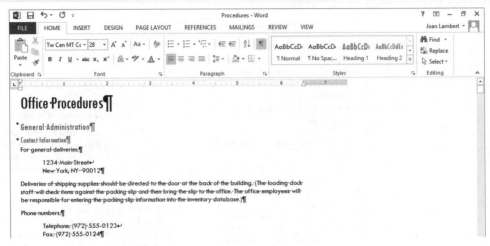

Draft view doesn't display graphic elements.

TROUBLESHOOTING If you have configured the style area pane to appear in Outline view and Draft view, it will be visible on the left side of the page. For information about using the style area pane, see "Reorganizing document outlines" in Chapter 10, "Organize and arrange content."

Now let's open a second document.

17   On the **Open** page of the **Backstage** view, in the left pane, click **Computer**. In the **Current Folder list**, click **Chapter01**. Then in the **Open** dialog box, double-click the **Prices** document to open it in its own program window.

Notice that the Prices document opens in Web Layout view; the last of the three main views (those available from the View Shortcuts toolbar) that you used. Word remembers this setting.

18   In the **Prices** document, on the **View Shortcuts** toolbar, click the **Print Layout** button. Notice that the telephone number in the body of the memo has a dotted underline, which indicates that it is formatted as hidden.

TIP The Show/Hide ¶ setting stays active in Word when you open or start another document. When you have multiple open documents, you can turn the setting on or off for each individual document.

19   On the **Home** tab, in the **Paragraph** group, click the **Show/Hide ¶** button to hide hidden text and formatting marks in this document. Notice that the telephone number is no longer visible.

20   On the **View** tab, in the **Window** group, click the **Switch Windows** button and then, in the list of open documents, click **Procedures** to redisplay the **Procedures** document. Notice that it is still in **Draft** view with formatting marks and hidden text turned on.

   TIP You can control the view and formatting marks for each window separately.

21   On the **View** tab, in the **Window** group, click the **Arrange All** button to resize the open windows and stack them one above the other. Notice that each window has a ribbon, so you can work with each document independently.

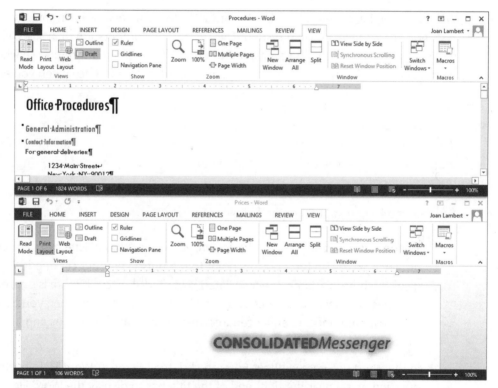

You can display more than one window at the same time.

   TIP The ribbons in each window take up a lot of screen space. To display more of each document, click the Collapse The Ribbon button in each window to hide all but the tab names.

22   At the right end of the **Procedures** title bar, click the **Close** button. If Word prompts you to save changes, click **Don't Save**. Notice that the **Prices** document window remains at half height.

23   At the right end of the **Prices** title bar, click the **Maximize** button to expand the window to fill the screen.

24   On the **View** tab, in the **Show** group, clear the **Ruler** check box to turn off the rulers.

❌ CLEAN UP Close the Prices document, but leave Word running for the next exercise.

Getting help with Word 2013

Whenever you have a question about Word 2013 that isn't answered in this book, your first recourse is the Word Help system. This system is a combination of articles, videos, and training tools and information available from the Office website for reference when you are online, and basic information stored on your computer for reference when you are offline.

TIP To switch between online and offline reference content, click the arrow to the right of Word Help and then click Word Help From Office.com or Word Help From Your Computer. You can print the information shown in the Help window by clicking the Print button on the toolbar. You can change the font size of the topic by clicking the Use Large Text button on the toolbar to the left of the Search Help box.

You can find Help resources in the following ways:

- To find out about an item on the screen, you can display a ScreenTip. For example, to display a ScreenTip for a button, point to the button without clicking it. The ScreenTip gives the button's name, the associated keyboard shortcut if there is one, and unless you specify otherwise, a description of what the button does when you click it. Some ScreenTips also include enhanced information such as instructions and links to related Help topics.

- In the Word program window, you can click the Microsoft Word Help button (the question mark) near the right end of the title bar to display the Word Help window.

- In a dialog box, you can click the Help button (also a question mark) near the right end of the dialog box title bar to open the Word Help window and display any available topics related to the functions of that dialog box.

In this exercise, you'll explore the Word Help window and search for information about printing and using SkyDrive.

SET UP You don't need any practice files to complete this exercise. With Word running, follow the steps.

1   Near the right end of the title bar, click the **Microsoft Word Help** button to open the **Word Help** window.

   KEYBOARD SHORTCUT Press F1 to display the Word Help window.

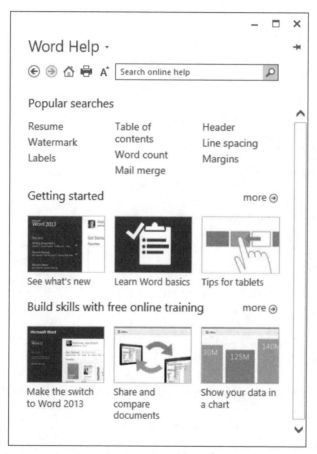

Your Help window might look different from this because the Office website is regularly updated.

2   At the top of the **Word Help** window, enter printing in the **Search** box and then click the **Search** button to display a list of topics related to printing Office documents. Click the **Print labels** link to display the corresponding article.

TIP Links to related articles are indicated by colored text. You can click section links that appear at the beginning of an article to move directly to that section of the article. You can click Show All at the beginning of an article to expand all collapsed sections of the article.

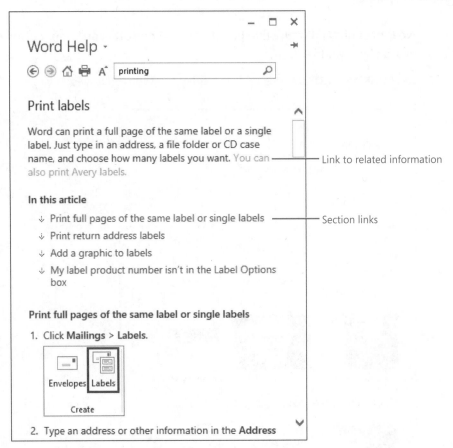

A typical Help article.

3   Jump to related information by clicking any link identified by colored text.

4   Enter SkyDrive in the **Search** box, and then press **Enter** to display topics related to the search term. In the results list, click **Share a document using SharePoint or SkyDrive** to display that topic.

5   At the left end of the toolbar, click the **Back** button to return to the topics you previously displayed. When you finish exploring, close the **Word Help** window by clicking the **Close** button in the upper-right corner.

❌ CLEAN UP If you are finished using Word for now, close the program window.

Key points

- The core functionality of Word 2013 remains the same regardless of the version of the program you are using. However, the available features and the way you interact with the program might be different in different versions.

- The Word user interface provides intuitive access to all the tools you need to develop a sophisticated document tailored to the needs of your audience.

- You can open more than one Word document, and you can view more than one document at a time, but only one document can be active at a time.

- It's easy to move the cursor by clicking in the text or by pressing keys and keyboard shortcuts.

- When you save a Word document, you specify its location on the Save As page of the Backstage view, and its name and file format in the Save As dialog box.

- You can view a document in a variety of ways, depending on your needs as you create the document and on the purpose for which you are creating it.

- The Word Help window gives you instant access to current information and training on most aspects of the program.

Chapter at a glance

Start

Start, enter text in, and save documents,
page 52

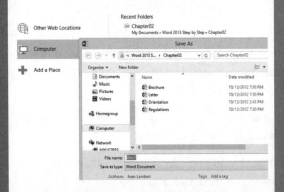

Modify

Modify text,
page 58

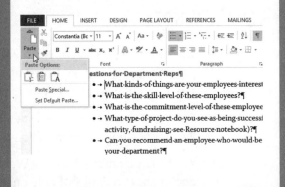

Find

Find and replace text,
page 68

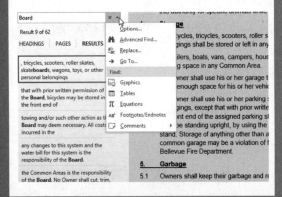

Correct

Correct spelling and grammatical errors,
page 86

Enter, edit, and proofread text

2

IN THIS CHAPTER, YOU WILL LEARN HOW TO

- Start, enter text in, and save documents.

- Modify text.

- Find and replace text.

- Fine-tune text.

- Correct spelling and grammatical errors.

Entering text into a Microsoft Word document is a simple matter of typing—whether on a traditional keyboard or an on-screen keyboard—or in some cases, writing (on a tablet) or speaking (into a microphone connected to your computer). However, even the most accurate typists occasionally make mistakes, also known as *typos* (for *typographical errors*), and the accuracy of handwritten or spoken entry may be even less dependable. Unless the documents you create are intended for no one's eyes but your own, you will want to ensure that they are not only correct but also professional. Word 2013 has several tools that make creating professional documents easy and efficient, whether you are a novice or experienced writer.

- **Editing tools** These tools provide quick-selection techniques and drag-and-drop editing to make it easy to move and copy text anywhere you want it.

- **Search tools** These tools can be used to locate and replace words, phrases, and special characters, either one at a time or throughout a document.

  SEE ALSO For information about using the search tools to find and replace formatting, see the sidebar "Finding and replacing formatting" in Chapter 3, "Modify the structure and appearance of text."

- **Research tools** These tools make it easy to find synonyms, look up information, and translate words and phrases.

- **AutoCorrect and Spelling And Grammar** These features make it easy to correct typos and grammatical errors before you share a document with others.

In this chapter, you'll be introduced to several of the new and improved features of Word 2013. You'll start by creating a blank document in which you will enter text. You'll edit the text in a document by inserting, deleting, copying, pasting, and moving it; and you'll learn about the options you have when relocating text. You'll find and replace words and phrases throughout a document and replace one phrase with another. Next, you'll look up the definition of a word, replace a word with a synonym, and locate translations for other words. You'll also personalize your AutoCorrect list and check the spelling and grammar of a document.

PRACTICE FILES To complete the exercises in this chapter, you need the practice files contained in the Chapter02 practice file folder. For more information, see "Download the practice files" in this book's Introduction.

Starting, entering text in, and saving documents

When you start Word 2013, you can open an existing document or create a new document. When you create a new document—either a blank document or one based on a populated template—a blinking cursor shows where the next character you enter will appear. When the cursor reaches the right margin, the word you are entering moves to the next line. You press the Enter key only to start a new paragraph, not a new line.

You can create a new document during a Word session from the New page of the Backstage view. The documents listed on the New page are based on templates, which are sets of formats that have been saved in such a way that you can use them as patterns for new documents. Some templates are installed on your computer with Office; many other templates are available online. To locate a template suitable for your purposes, enter a search phrase in the Search Online Templates box and then click the Start Searching button, or click a category in the Suggested Searches list below the box.

When you find a template you might want to use as the basis for your new document, clicking its thumbnail displays a preview and description of the document along with ratings provided by people who have downloaded the template. You can then click the Create button in the preview pane to create the document.

TIP Double-clicking a template thumbnail creates the document without first displaying it in the preview pane.

Each document you create is temporary, indicated by a file name such as Document1, until you save it. To save a document for the first time, you click the Save button on the Quick Access Toolbar or click Save in the Backstage view. Either action displays the Save As page of the Backstage view, where you can choose a storage location, assign a name, attach metadata tags, and specify a file type for the document.

When you choose a location on the Save As page, the Save As dialog box opens displaying that location in the Address bar at the top of the dialog box. If you want to save the document in a folder other than the one shown in the Address bar, you can click the arrow or chevrons in the Address bar or click locations in the Navigation pane on the left to display the folder you want. If you want to create a folder in which to store the document, you can click the New Folder button on the toolbar.

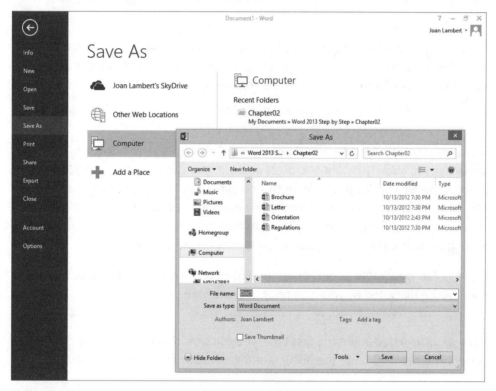

Saving a file from the Save As page of the Backstage view.

TROUBLESHOOTING If the Navigation pane is not open in the Save As dialog box, either click the Browse Folders link in the lower-left corner of the dialog box or click Organize on the toolbar, point to Layout, and then click Navigation Pane. (Only one of these options will be available.)

Saving files to SkyDrive

Whether you're working in a corporate environment or at home, you have the option of saving files to Microsoft SkyDrive. The SkyDrive location you save to might be part of your company's Microsoft SharePoint environment, or it might be a cloud-based storage location that is associated with your Microsoft account. Saving a file in either type of SkyDrive location provides the option of sharing the file with other people.

To save a document to SkyDrive, display the Save As page of the Backstage view, click your SkyDrive, and then specify the SkyDrive folder in which you want to save the file. If your SkyDrive doesn't already appear in the list of locations, click Add A Place, click SkyDrive, and then enter the credentials associated with the SkyDrive you want to access.

When you save a Word document to SkyDrive, you and other people with whom you share the document can work on it by using a local installation of Word or by using Word Web App, which is available in the SkyDrive environment.

SEE ALSO For information about Word Web App, see Chapter 1, "Explore Microsoft Word 2013."

Microsoft provides 7 gigabytes (GB) of free SkyDrive storage to Microsoft account holders. If you already have a Microsoft account, you can access your SkyDrive directly from any Office program, or from *skydrive.live.com*. If you don't yet have a Microsoft account, you can configure any existing email account as a Microsoft account at *signup.live.com*. (If you don't yet have an email account that you want to configure for this purpose, you can get a new account there too.)

SkyDrive Pro is available as part of a SharePoint 2013 environment, and your storage there will be managed by your company or SharePoint provider.

After you save a document the first time, you can save changes simply by clicking the Save button. The new version of the document then overwrites the previous version.

KEYBOARD SHORTCUT Press Ctrl+S to save the current document. For more information about keyboard shortcuts, see "Keyboard shortcuts" at the end of this book.

SEE ALSO For information about retrieving previous versions of documents, see the sidebar "Managing document versions" in Chapter 15, "Collaborate on documents."

If you want to save a separate version of a previously saved document, save the new version with a different name in the same location or with the same name in a different location. (You cannot store two files of the same type with the same name in the same folder.)

TIP By default, Word periodically saves the document you are working on in case the program stops responding or your computer shuts down unexpectedly. To adjust the time interval between automatic saves, display the Save page of the Word Options dialog box, specify the period of time in the Save AutoRecover Information Every scroll box, and then click OK.

In this exercise, you'll create a blank document, enter text, and save the document in a folder that you create.

SET UP You don't need any practice files to complete this exercise; just follow the steps.

1   If Word is not running, start Word and then double-click the **Blank document** thumbnail in the right pane of the **Start** screen to create a blank document temporarily named **Document1**. If Word is already running, double-click the **Blank document** thumbnail on the **New** page of the **Backstage** view to create a blank document.

    TROUBLESHOOTING If you have already created documents in your current Word session, the temporary file name will reflect the number of documents you've created and will not match the images shown in this exercise.

2   Because we won't be formatting the document content yet, click the **Unpin the ribbon** button to hide the groups so we can concentrate on the content.

    KEYBOARD SHORTCUT Press Ctrl+F1 to pin or unpin the ribbon.

3   With the cursor at the beginning of the new document, enter Parks Appreciation Day, and then press the **Enter** key to create a new paragraph.

4   Enter Help beautify our city by participating in the annual cleanup of Log Drift Park, Swamp Creek Park, and Tall Tree Park. Volunteers will receive a free T-shirt and barbeque lunch. Bring your own gardening tools and gloves, and be ready to have fun! Notice that you did not need to press **Enter** when the cursor reached the right margin, because the text automatically wrapped to the next line.

You press Enter at the end of each paragraph; the Word Wrap feature wraps each line within the paragraph.

TIP If a wavy line appears under a word or phrase, Word is flagging a possible error. For information about proofing errors, see "Correcting spelling and grammatical errors" later in this chapter.

5   Press **Enter**, and then enter The Park Service Committee is coordinating group participation in this event. If you are interested in spending time outdoors with family and friends while improving the quality of our parks, contact Nancy Anderson by email at nancy@adventure-works.com.

     Now let's save the new document.

6   On the **Quick Access Toolbar**, click the **Save** button to display the **Save As** page of the **Backstage** view. In the **Places** list, click the place where you saved the practice files for this book. Then in the right pane, click the **Browse** button to open the **Save As** dialog box. Notice that Word suggests the file name **Parks Appreciation Day** based on the current file content.

7   Using standard Windows techniques, navigate to the practice file folders. Then double-click the **Chapter02** practice file folder.

8   In the **Save As** dialog box, on the toolbar, click the **New folder** button to create a new folder. With the folder name selected for editing, enter My New Documents, and then press **Enter** once to save the folder name and once to open the folder.

9   In the **File name** box, click anywhere in **Parks Appreciation Day** to select it, and then replace the suggested name by typing My Announcement.

> **IMPORTANT** Programs that run on the Windows operating systems use file name extensions to identify different types of files. For example, the extension .docx identifies Word 2013 documents. Windows 7 and Windows 8 do not display these extensions by default, and you shouldn't enter them in the Save As dialog box. When you save a file, Word automatically adds whatever extension is associated with the file type selected in the Save As Type list.

10 Click **Save** to close the dialog box and save the **My Announcement** document in the **My New Documents** folder. Notice that the new file name appears on the program window's title bar.

11 Display the **Info** page of the **Backstage** view. Notice that the document's current location is shown below the file name.

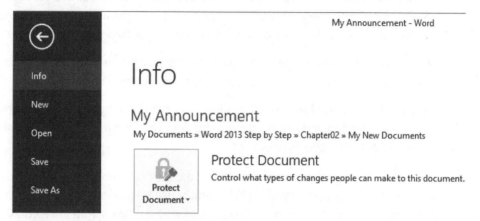

The Info page displays the current file location.

12 Click the **Save As** page tab. In the **Current Folder** list, click **My New Documents** to open the **Save As** dialog box to the current folder. In the **Address** bar of the **Save As** dialog box, to the left of **My New Documents**, click **Chapter02** to display the contents of the **Chapter02** practice file folder in which you created the **My New Documents** folder.

13 Click **Save** to save a separate copy of the **My Announcement** document in the **Chapter02** folder. You now have two versions of the document saved with the same name but in different folders.

SEE ALSO For information about saving a document in a different file format, see "Saving Word documents in other formats" in Chapter 11, "Create documents for use outside of Word." For information about working with the file properties that appear at the bottom of the Save As dialog box, see "Preparing documents for electronic distribution" in Chapter 6, "Preview, print, and distribute documents."

❌ CLEAN UP At the right end of the title bar, click the Close button to close the My Announcement document.

Document compatibility with earlier versions of Word

The Microsoft Office 2013 programs use file formats based on XML. By default, Word 2013 files are saved in the .docx format, which provides the following benefits:

- File size is smaller because files are compressed when saved, decreasing the amount of disk space needed to store the file, and the amount of bandwidth needed to send files in email, over a network, or across the Internet.

- Recovering at least some of the content of damaged files is possible because XML files can be opened in a text program such as Notepad.

- Security is greater because .docx files cannot contain macros, and personal data can be detected and removed from the file. (The .docm file format is designed for documents that contain macros.)

Word 2003 and earlier versions of Word used the .doc file format. You can open .doc files in Word 2013, but some Word 2013 features will be unavailable. When you open a file created in an earlier version of Word (even a .docx file created in Word 2010), the title bar displays *[Compatibility Mode]* to the right of the document name. You can work in Compatibility mode, or you can convert the document to Word 2013 format by clicking the Convert button on the Info page of the Backstage view, or by saving a copy of the document with Word Document as the file type.

If you work with people who are using a version of Word earlier than 2007, they can install the free Microsoft Office Compatibility Pack For Word, Excel, And PowerPoint File Formats from the Microsoft Download Center at *download.microsoft.com*. The Compatibility Pack doesn't provide additional functionality in the older program version but it does enable users to open .docx files in the older version of Word.

SEE ALSO For more information about file formats, see "Saving Word documents in other formats" in Chapter 11, "Create documents for use outside of Word."

Modifying text

You'll rarely write a perfect document that doesn't require any editing. You'll almost always want to add or remove a word or two, change a phrase, or move text from one place to another. Or you might want to edit a document that you created for one purpose so that you can use it for a different purpose. You can edit a document as you create it, or you can write it first and then revise it.

Inserting one document into another

Sometimes you'll want to insert the contents of one or more existing documents into another document. For example, you might want to compile 12 monthly reports into an annual report. It would be tedious to select and copy the text of each report and then paste it into the annual report document. Instead, you can have Word insert the existing documents for you. Here's how:

1   In the target document, position the cursor where you want to insert the existing document.

2   On the **Insert** tab, in the **Text** group, click the **Object** arrow (not the button) and then, in the list, click **Text from File**.

3   In the **Insert File** dialog box that opens, browse to the source file you want, and then double-click the file to insert its contents at the cursor.

Inserting text is easy; you click to position the cursor and then begin typing. Any existing text to the right of the cursor moves to make room for the new text.

Deleting text is equally easy. If you want to delete only one or a few characters, you can simply position the cursor and then press the Backspace or Delete key until the characters are all gone. Pressing Backspace deletes the character to the left of the cursor; pressing Delete deletes the character to the right of the cursor.

To delete more than a few characters efficiently, you need to know how to select text. Selected text appears highlighted on the screen. You can drag through a section of text to select it, or you can select specific items as follows:

- **Word** Double-click anywhere in the word. The word and the space immediately following it are selected, but not any punctuation following the word.

- **Sentence** Hold down the **Ctrl** key and then click anywhere in the sentence. Word selects all the characters in the sentence, from the first character through the space following the ending punctuation mark.

  TROUBLESHOOTING You cannot select a sentence by using this technique if other text is already selected. This activates the non-adjacent multi-selection functionality described at the end of this list.

- **Paragraph** Triple-click anywhere in the paragraph. Word selects the text of the paragraph and the paragraph mark.

- **Adjacent words, lines, or paragraphs** Position the cursor at the beginning of the text you want to select, hold down the **Shift** key, and then press the arrow keys to select one character or line at a time; hold down the **Shift** and **Ctrl** keys and press the arrow keys to select one word at a time; or click at the end of the text that you want to select.

- **Non-adjacent words, lines, or paragraphs** Make the first selection, and then hold down the **Ctrl** key while selecting the next text block.

TIP When you select content, Word displays the Mini Toolbar, from which you can quickly format the selection or perform other actions depending on the type of content you select. For information about applying formatting from the Mini Toolbar, see "Manually changing the look of characters" in Chapter 3, "Modify the structure and appearance of text." For information about turning off the display of the Mini Toolbar, see "Changing default program options" in Chapter 16, "Work in Word more efficiently."

As an alternative way of selecting, you can use an area of the document's left margin, called the *selection area*, to select items. When the mouse pointer is in the selection area, it changes to an arrow that points toward the upper-right corner of the page.

You can select specific items from the selection area as follows:

- **Line** Click in the selection area to the left of the line.

- **Paragraph** Double-click in the selection area to the left of the paragraph.

- **Entire document** Triple-click in the selection area.

  KEYBOARD SHORTCUT Press Ctrl+A to select all the content in the body of the document.

Parks Appreciation Day

Help beautify our city by participating in the annual cleanup of Log Drift Park, Swamp Creek Park, and Tall Tree Park. Volunteers will receive a free T-shirt and barbeque lunch. Bring your own gardening tools and gloves, and be ready to have fun!

The Park Service Committee is coordinating group participation in this event. If you are interested in spending time outdoors with family and friends while improving the quality of our parks, contact Nancy Anderson by email at nancy@adventure-works.com.

Clicking once in the selection area while the pointer is pointing toward the text selects the adjacent line.

After selecting the text you want to delete, press either Backspace or Delete.

TIP To release a selection, click anywhere in the window other than the selection area.

If you want to move or copy the selected text, you have three options:

- **Drag-and-drop editing** Use this feature, which is frequently referred to simply as *dragging*, when you need to move or copy text only a short distance—for example, within a paragraph. Start by using any of the methods described previously to select the text. Then point to the selection, hold down the mouse button, drag the text to its new location (indicated by a dotted vertical line), and release the mouse button. To copy the selection, hold down the **Ctrl** key while you drag.

- **Cut, Copy, and Paste buttons** Use this method when you need to move or copy text between two locations that you cannot display at the same time—for example, between pages or between documents. Select the text, and click the **Cut** or **Copy** button in the **Clipboard** group on the **Home** tab. (The cut or copied item is stored in an area of your computer's memory called the *Microsoft Office Clipboard*, hence the name of the group.) Then position the cursor in the new location and click the **Paste** button to insert the selection. If you click the **Paste** arrow instead of the button, Word displays options for pasting the selection.

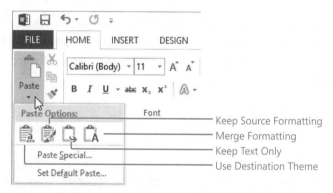

Word offers several different methods of pasting content.

The available buttons depend on the format of the cut or copied selection (the source) and the format of the place you're pasting it (the destination). Pointing to a button displays a preview of how the source content will look if you use that option to paste it at the current location.

SEE ALSO For more information about working with cut and copied content, see the sidebar "About the Clipboard" later in this chapter.

- **Keyboard shortcuts** When you're working with a traditional keyboard and mouse, or on a portable computer with an integrated mouse pad, it can be more efficient to press combinations of keyboard keys to cut, copy, and paste selections rather than to click buttons on the ribbon. The main keyboard shortcuts for editing tasks are shown in the following table.

Task	Keyboard shortcut
Cut	Ctrl+X
Copy	Ctrl+C
Paste	Ctrl+V
Undo	Ctrl+Z
Repeat/Redo	Ctrl+Y

Using a keyboard shortcut to cut or copy a selection stores the item on the Clipboard, just as if you had clicked the corresponding button.

TIP No matter which method you use, when you cut text, Word removes it from its original location. When you copy text, Word leaves the text in the original location and repeats it in the new location.

If you make a change to a document and then realize that you made a mistake, you can easily reverse the change. You can undo your last editing action by clicking the Undo button on the Quick Access Toolbar. To undo an earlier action, click the Undo arrow and then click that action in the list.

TIP Selecting an action from the Undo list undoes that action and all the editing actions you performed after that one. You cannot undo only one action other than the last one you performed.

If you make a change to a document and want to repeat that change elsewhere, you can click the Repeat button on the Quick Access Toolbar. If the last task you performed was to undo an action, the Repeat button is replaced by the Redo button. So if you change your mind about whatever you undid, you can click the Redo button to return the text to its previous state. You can't redo multiple actions by clicking them in a list as you can with the Undo button, but you can click the Redo button repeatedly until the text is restored to what you want.

KEYBOARD SHORTCUT Press Ctrl+Z to undo an action or Ctrl+Y to repeat or redo an action.

In this exercise, you'll edit the text in a document. You'll insert and delete text, undo the deletion, copy and paste a phrase, and move a paragraph.

→ SET UP You need the Orientation document located in the Chapter02 practice file folder to complete this exercise. Open the document in Print Layout view, and then follow the steps.

1   If the ribbon is unpinned (hidden), click the **Ribbon Display Options** button, and then click **Show Tabs and Commands**. If formatting symbols such as spaces and paragraph marks are not visible in the document, click the **Show/Hide ¶** button in the **Paragraph** group on the **Home** tab.

    KEYBOARD SHORTCUT Press Ctrl+* to turn on and off the display of formatting marks and hidden text.

2   In the second bullet point after **Project Goals**, double-click the word **natural** to select it, and then press **Backspace** to delete the selected word.

3   In the third bullet point, click to the left of the **a** in the word **and**, hold down the **Shift** and **Ctrl** keys, and then press the **Right Arrow** key twice to select the words **and motivate** and the following space.

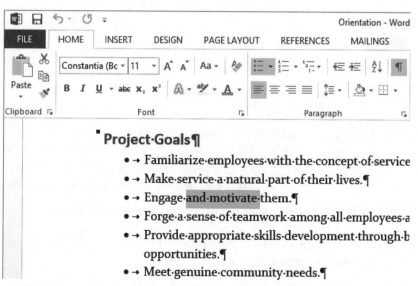

Pressing Shift+Ctrl+Right Arrow selects one word to the right.

4   Press **Delete** to delete the selection.

5   In the fourth bullet point, double-click the word **Forge**, and then replace it by entering **Build**. Notice that you don't have to enter a space after **Build**. Word inserts the space for you.

> **TIP** Word inserts and deletes spaces because the Use Smart Cut And Paste check box is selected on the Advanced page of the Word Options dialog box. For information about setting Word options, see "Changing default program options" in Chapter 16, "Work in Word more efficiently."

Now let's copy and move text by using the Clipboard.

6   At the bottom of page **1**, position the mouse pointer in the selection area to the left of the first bullet point after **Questions for Team Leaders**. Then click to select the paragraph.

7   On the **Home** tab, in the **Clipboard** group, click the **Copy** button to copy the selection to the Clipboard.

8   At the top of page **2**, click to the left of **What** in the first bullet point after **Questions for Department Reps**. Then in the **Clipboard** group, click the **Paste** arrow to expand the **Paste Options** menu. Notice that, because you're pasting a list item into a list, two of the three available buttons have list-related icons

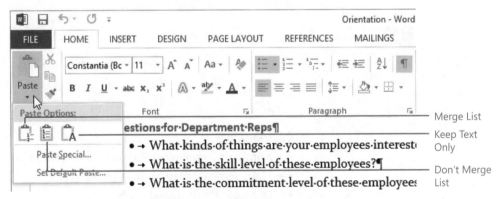

The Paste Options menu includes buttons representing pasting options.

9   Point to each of the paste option buttons to review how the source text will look with that paste option implemented.

10   Click the **Merge List** button to paste the copied bullet point into the second list and retain its formatting. Then click the **Paste Options** button that appears below and to the right of the inserted bullet point. Notice that most of the same paste options

that are available from the ribbon are also available from this menu; the **Merge List** button is selected to indicate the option that was applied.

- Questions·for·Department·Reps¶
  - • → **How·much·time·do·you·want/have·available·to·spend?¶**
  - • → What·kinds·of·things·are·your·employees·interested·in?¶
  - • → What·is·the·skill·level·of·these·employees?¶
  - • → What·is·the·commitment·level·of·these·employees?¶
  - • → What·type·of·project·do·you·see·as·being·successful·for·thes activity,·fundraising;·see·Resource·notebook)?¶

You can select paste options as part of the pasting process or after you paste the content.

TIP Notice that in the ScreenTip for each button, a single letter appears in parentheses after the button name. That single letter is the keyboard shortcut to invoke that paste option from this menu or from the mini Paste Options menu that appears when you paste any content into a document.

11   In the **Set Up Team** section, triple-click anywhere in the paragraph that begins **Explain the position's responsibilities** to select the entire paragraph.

12   In the **Clipboard** group, click the **Cut** button. Press the **Up Arrow** key to move to the beginning of the preceding paragraph, and then in the **Clipboard** group, click the **Paste** button to reverse the order of the two paragraphs.

TIP If you frequently edit documents, pressing Ctrl+X to cut, Ctrl+C to copy, and Ctrl+V to paste will probably become second nature to you. Feel free to use keyboard shortcuts in place of ribbon buttons while working through the exercises in this book.

13   On the **Quick Access Toolbar**, click the **Undo** arrow and then, in the **Undo** list, point to the third action (**Paste Merge List**). Notice that the text at the bottom of the list indicates that three actions will be undone if you click this list entry.

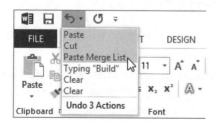

Selecting an action in the Undo list reverses that action and all subsequent actions you performed.

14   In the **Undo** list, click **Paste Merge List** to undo the previous cut-and-paste operation and the pasting of the copied text.

Now let's move text without using the Clipboard.

15   In the **Pre-Plan Project** section, position the pointer in the selection area adjacent to the bullet point that begins with **If some employee input**, and then double-click to select the paragraph.

16   Point to the selection, hold down the mouse button, and then drag the paragraph to the left of the word **If** at the beginning of the preceding bullet point. Release the mouse button to switch the order of the bullet points.

17   With the text still selected, press the **End** key to release the selection and move the cursor to the end of the paragraph.

18   Press the **Spacebar**, and then press **Delete** to delete the paragraph mark and merge the two bullet points.

- → If·some·employee·input,·select·a·few·projects·to·choose·from·or·outline·a·brainstorming· process.·|If·no·employee·input,·select·a·project.¶
- → What·tasks·will·be·involved·in·carrying·out·the·project?·Who·will·do·those·tasks?·(As· much·as·possible,·leave·room·for·employees·to·participate·in·planning·and·carrying·out· these·tasks.)¶
- → How·do·we·want·to·engage·the·skills·development·portion·of·this·project?·Avenues· include·reading·books·or·articles·about·the·population·being·helped,·asking· representatives·of·service·organizations·to·come·in·to·talk·to·the·team,·etc.·For·continuing· enrichment,·employees·can·keep·a·journal·of·progress,·create·a·poster·in·the·department,· make·periodic·reports,·update·graphs·and·charts,·etc.¶

Two bullets have been combined into one.

❌ CLEAN UP If you prefer to not show formatting symbols, turn them off. Then close the Orientation document, saving your changes if you want to.

TIP Another way to ensure consistency in your documents while also saving time is to use preformatted content objects called building blocks. Word 2013 comes with many built-in building blocks for formatted items such as cover pages, headers and footers, tables, and text boxes. You can also save your own building blocks. For more information, see "Inserting preformatted document parts" in Chapter 9, "Add visual elements" and "Creating custom building blocks" in Chapter 16, "Work in Word more efficiently."

About the Clipboard

You can view the items that have been cut or copied to the Clipboard by clicking the Clipboard dialog box launcher on the Home tab to display the Clipboard pane.

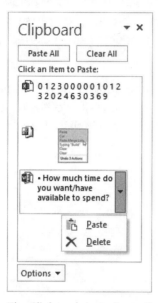

The Clipboard stores items that have been cut or copied from any Office program.

You can work with items stored on the Clipboard pane in the following ways:

- To paste an individual item at the cursor, click the item; or point to the item, click the arrow that appears, and then click **Paste**. To paste all the items stored on the Clipboard at the same location, click the **Paste All** button.

- To remove an item from the Clipboard, point to the item in the **Clipboard** pane, click the arrow that appears, and then click **Delete**. To remove all items from the Clipboard, click the **Clear All** button.

You can control the behavior of the Clipboard pane by clicking Options at the bottom of the pane and then clicking the display option you want.

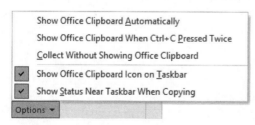

Clipboard display options.

Finding and replacing text

One way to ensure that the text in your documents is consistent and accurate is to use the Find feature to search for and review every occurrence of a particular word or phrase. For example, if you are responsible for advertising a trademarked product, you can search your marketing materials to check that every occurrence of the product's name is correctly identified as a trademark.

Clicking the Find button in the Editing group on the Home tab displays the Results page of the Navigation pane. As you enter characters in the search box at the top of the pane, Word highlights all occurrences of those characters in the document and displays them on the Results page.

KEYBOARD SHORTCUT Press Ctrl+F to display the Results page of the Navigation pane and activate the search box.

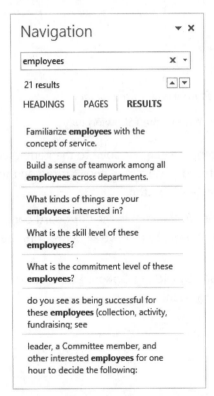

The Results page shows enough of the text surrounding the search term to identify its context.

When you point to a search result on the Results page, a ScreenTip displays the number of the page on which that result appears and the name of the heading preceding the search result. You can click a search result to move directly to that location in the document.

TIP The Results page of the Navigation pane allows you to continue editing your document as you normally would, while still having access to all the search results.

If you want to be more specific about the text you are looking for—for example, if you want to look for occurrences that match the exact capitalization of your search term—click the Search For More Things arrow at the right end of the search box in the Navigation pane and then click Advanced Find to display the Find page of the Find And Replace dialog box. Clicking More in the lower-left corner expands the dialog box to make additional search options available.

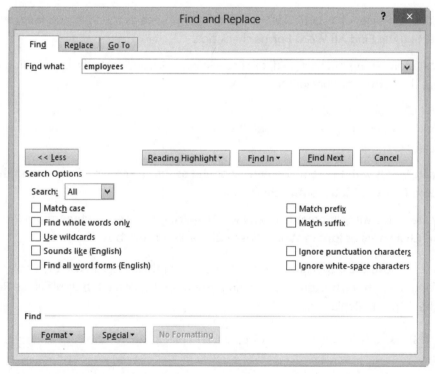

You can make a search more specific by using the criteria in the Search Options area of the Find page.

In the expanded dialog box, you can do the following:

- Guide the direction of the search by selecting **Down**, **Up**, or **All** from the **Search** list.

- Locate only text that matches the capitalization of the search term by selecting the **Match Case** check box.

- Exclude occurrences of the search term that appear within other words by selecting the **Find Whole Words Only** check box.

- Find two similar words, such as *effect* and *affect*, by selecting the **Use Wildcards** check box and then including one or more wildcard characters in the search term. The two most common wildcard characters are the following:

  - **?** Represents any single character in this location in the **Find What** text

  - ***** Represents any number of characters in this location in the **Find What** text

  TIP For a list of the available wildcards, select the Use Wildcards check box and then click Special.

- Find occurrences of the search text that sound the same but are spelled differently, such as *there* and *their*, by selecting the **Sounds Like** check box.

- Find occurrences of a particular word in any form, such as *try*, *tries*, and *tried*, by selecting the **Find All Word Forms** check box.

- Locate formatting, such as bold, or special characters, such as tabs, by selecting them from the **Format** or **Special** list.

  SEE ALSO For information about finding and replacing formatting, see the sidebar "Finding and replacing formatting" in Chapter 3, "Modify the structure and appearance of text."

- Locate words with the same beginning or end as the search term by selecting the **Match Prefix** or **Match Suffix** check box.

- Locate words with different hyphenation or spacing by selecting the **Ignore Punctuation Characters** or **Ignore White-Space Characters** check box.

If you want to substitute a specific word or phrase for another, you can use the Replace feature. Clicking the Replace button in the Editing group on the Home tab displays the Replace page of the Find And Replace dialog box.

KEYBOARD SHORTCUT Press Ctrl+H to display the Replace page of the Find And Replace dialog box.

TIP If the Navigation pane is open, you can click the Search For More Things arrow at the right end of the search box and then click Replace. The Find And Replace dialog box opens with the search term from the Navigation pane already in the Find What box.

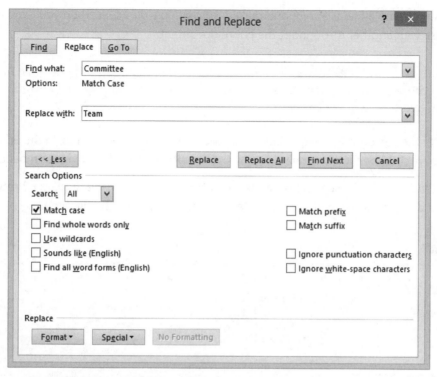

Correcting errors and inconsistencies is easy with the Replace feature.

For each instance of the search term that Word locates, you can click one of the following choices on the Replace page:

- **Replace** Replaces the selected occurrence with the text in the **Replace With** box and moves to the next occurrence

- **Replace All** Replaces all occurrences with the text in the **Replace With** box

  TIP Before clicking Replace All, ensure that the replacement is clearly defined. For example, if you want to change *trip* to *journey*, be sure to tell Word to find only the whole word *trip*; otherwise, *triple* could become *journeyle*.

- **Find Next** Finds the first occurrence or leaves the selected occurrence as it is and locates the next one

As on the Find page, clicking More displays the options you can use to carry out more complicated replacement operations. Note that the settings in the Search Options area apply to the search term and not to its replacement.

In this exercise, you'll find a phrase and make a correction to the text. Then you'll replace one phrase with another throughout the entire document.

SET UP You need the Regulations document located in the Chapter02 practice file folder to complete this exercise. Open the document, hide formatting marks if they are displayed, and then follow the steps.

1 With the cursor at the beginning of the document, on the **Home** tab, in the **Editing** group, click the **Find** button to display the **Results** page of the **Navigation** pane.

2 Enter Board in the search box. Notice that the **Navigation** pane displays 62 results, and every occurrence of the search term in the document is highlighted.

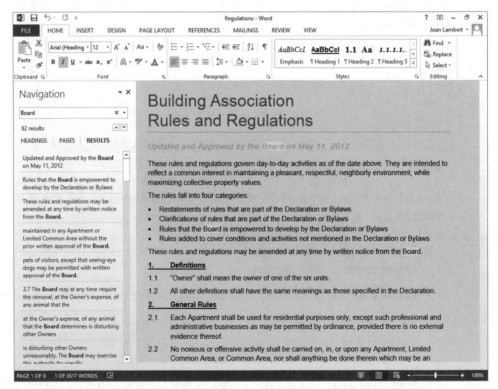

You can scroll through the document to scan the highlighted results or click each match in the Navigation pane to display its corresponding location in the document.

3 In the **Navigation** pane, click the **Next** button (the downward-pointing triangle) to move to the second and third search results. Then scroll through the document to show other highlighted results. Notice that on page **2**, in section **4**, Word has highlighted the **board** portion of **skateboards**.

You need to restrict the search to the whole word *Board*.

4   In the **Navigation** pane, click the **Search for more things** button to expand a menu of options for refining the search.

Search For More Things button

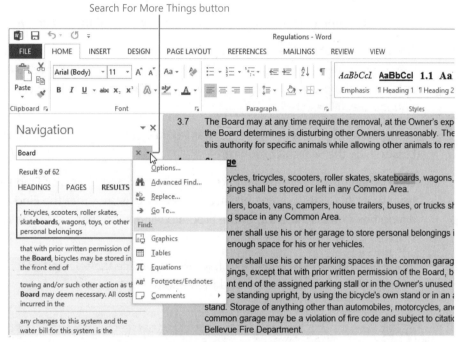

From this menu, you can locate specific types of objects and also refine text searches.

5   On the **Search for more things** menu, click **Options** to open the **Find Options** dialog box.

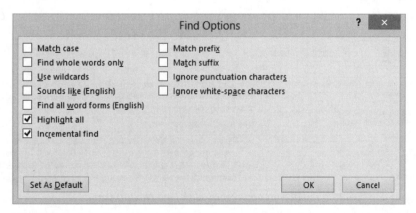

The Find Options dialog box contains most options for refining the current search, other than the style and special character options.

6   In the dialog box, select the **Match case** and **Find whole words only** check boxes, and then click **OK**. Enter Board in the search box again and scroll through the list of results. Notice that the word **skateboards** is no longer highlighted.

Now let's replace one word with another.

7   Press **Ctrl+Home** to move the cursor to the beginning of the document.

8   On the **Home** tab, in the **Editing** group, click **Replace** to open the **Find And Replace** dialog box with the **Replace** page active. Notice that the **Find What** box retains the entry from the previous search, and the **Match Case** and **Find Whole Words Only** options are still selected.

9   In the **Search Options** area, ensure that **Down** is selected in the **Search** list. Then click **Less** to hide the **Search Options** area.

10   Enter Association Board in the **Replace with** box, and then click **Find Next** to have Word highlight the first occurrence of **Board**. Notice that the **Find and Replace** dialog box moves to the top of the program window so that the search result is visible.

11   In the dialog box, click **Replace** to have Word replace the selected occurrence of **Board** with **Association Board** and then find the next occurrence.

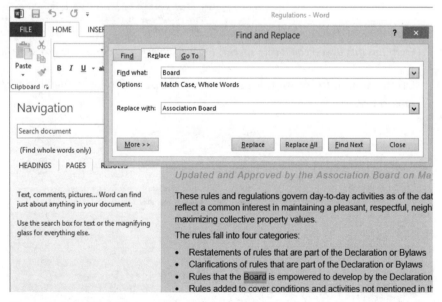

If you don't want to replace an occurrence, click Find Next to skip it.

12   Having tested the replacement process, click **Replace All**. Because you clicked this command partway through the document while performing a one-way search, Word tells you how many replacements it made from the starting point forward and asks whether to restart at the beginning.

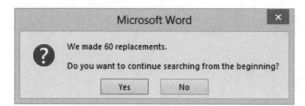

You can restart a one-way search or replace operation.

TROUBLESHOOTING If All is selected in the Search list, the Replace All operation will change the first instance of *Association Board* to *Association Association Board*. If a replace operation doesn't give you the results you want, close any open message boxes or dialog boxes and then use the Undo command to undo the replacement operations as necessary.

13   Click **No** to close the message box. Then close the **Find and Replace** dialog box.

❌ CLEAN UP Close the Navigation pane. Then close the Regulations document, saving your changes if you want to.

Fine-tuning text

Language is often contextual—you use different words and phrases in a marketing brochure than you would in a letter requesting immediate payment of an invoice or in an informal memo about a social gathering after work. To help ensure that you're using the words that best convey your meaning in any given context, you can look up definitions, synonyms, and antonyms of words from within a document by using the built-in proofing tools.

TROUBLESHOOTING Before you can look up the meaning of a word, you must first install a dictionary. Word will prompt you to do so if this is necessary.

You can install any of several free dictionaries from the Office Store. Your default dictionary then provides definitions when you use the Define or Thesaurus feature. To look up the definition of a word, right-click the word and then click Define; or click anywhere in the word and then click the Define button in the Proofing group on the Review tab.

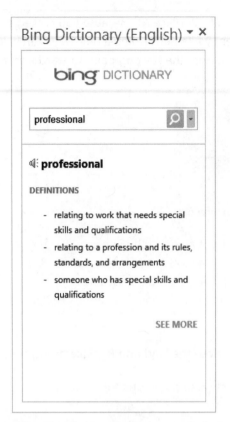

When the Dictionary pane is open, it displays definitions for whatever word you select in the document or enter in the search box at the top of the pane.

KEYBOARD SHORTCUT Press Ctrl+F7 to display definitions for the active word from the default dictionary.

To manage installed dictionaries, click in the upper-right corner of the definition pane (inside the frame below the pane title bar), click the arrow that appears, and then do any of the following:

- Click a dictionary name to change the dictionary.
- Click **Reload** to refresh the content of the **Dictionary** pane.
- Click **View Source** to view the HTML code that calls the displayed dictionary entry.
- Click **Lock** to dock the **Dictionary** pane to the program window. (You must unlock the pane before you can close it.)

Sometimes it's difficult to think of the best word to use in a specific situation. You can look up synonyms (words that have the same meaning) for a selected word by using the Thesaurus feature. To look up alternatives for a word, right-click the word, and then click Synonyms to display a list from which you can choose the one you want. Alternatively, you can select (or click anywhere in) the word and then click the Thesaurus button in the Proofing group on the Review tab. This opens the Thesaurus pane, displaying the selected word in the Search For box, synonyms for that word, and the most common dictionary definition.

If you install dictionaries for multiple languages, you can display definitions from other dictionaries by clicking the language list at the bottom of the pane and then clicking the language you want.

KEYBOARD SHORTCUT Press Shift+F7 to open the Thesaurus pane and display synonyms for the active word.

You can click a synonym to display its synonyms, and repeat that process until you find exactly the word you want. To replace the selected word with a synonym, point to your chosen synonym, click the arrow that appears, and then click Insert. If none of the suggested synonyms meet your requirements, the word you're using might not be the one you intend.

You can use built-in and online tools to translate words and phrases, or even entire documents, into other languages. You can access these tools by clicking the Translate button in the Language group on the Review tab and then, on the Translate menu, clicking the tool you want to use.

- **Mini Translator** Click **Mini Translator** on the **Translate** menu to turn this handy feature on or off (when it's on, its icon on the **Translate** menu appears selected). When the **Mini Translator** is turned on, you can point to a word or selected phrase to display a translation in the specified language. From the **Bilingual Dictionary** pane containing the translation, you can click the **Expand** button to display more information and options in the **Research** pane. You can also copy the translated word or phrase, or hear the original word or phrase spoken for you.

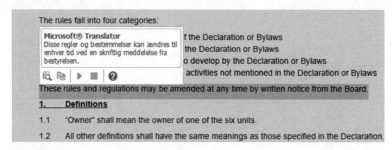

Using the Mini Translator is the quickest way to obtain the translation of a selection.

- **Online bilingual dictionary** To translate a selected word or phrase, click **Translate Selected Text** on the **Translate** menu and then, in the **Translation** area of the **Research** pane that appears, click the languages from and to which you want to translate. To obtain the translation of a word that does not appear in the text of a document, display the **Research** pane, enter the word in the search box, specify the languages you want, and then click the **Start Searching** button. Word consults the online bilingual dictionary for the selected language and displays the result.

The available translation options vary depending on the language selected.

- **Online machine translator** To translate an entire document, click **Translate Document** on the **Translate** menu. When Word displays a message that the document will be sent for translation by the Microsoft Translator service (which is free), click **Send**. The document and its translation then appear side by side in your web browser. You can modify the translation languages in the boxes at the top of the webpage, and point to any part of the translation to display the original text.

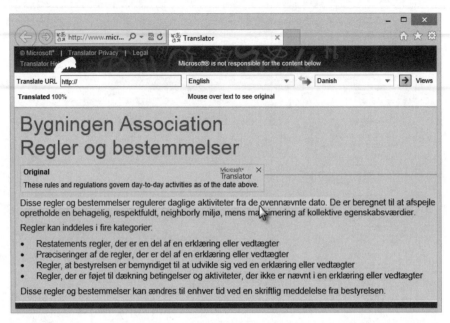

You can use the free Microsoft Translator service to translate a document into more than 40 languages.

To change the default language used by the Mini Translator or the online machine translator, click Choose Translation Language on the Translate menu. Then in the Translation Language Options dialog box, you can select different language pairs for each type of translator.

You can translate from and to many languages, including Arabic, Chinese, Greek, Hebrew, Italian, Japanese, Korean, Polish, Portuguese, Russian, Spanish, and Swedish.

In this exercise, you'll look up a word in the dictionary, replace a word with a synonym, and experiment with the Mini Translator.

SET UP You need the Brochure document located in the Chapter02 practice file folder to complete this exercise. Open the document, and then follow the steps.

1   We will first check whether a dictionary has been installed, because you will need one in order to complete the rest of the exercise. On the **Review** tab, in the **Proofing** group, click the **Define** button to open the **Dictionaries** pane. If a dictionary has not yet been installed, the pane displays a list of dictionaries that you can install from the Office Store.

If a dictionary has not yet been installed, options are listed here.

SEE ALSO For information about the Office Store, see the sidebar "Installing Office tools" later in this chapter.

2   If the **Dictionary** pane displays a definition, skip to step 4. Otherwise, in the **Dictionaries** pane, click the **Download** button below **Bing Dictionary** to install the dictionary.

3   When a dictionary has been installed, the **Dictionary** pane lists definitions for the word **simple** (the first word in the document). When the pane displays the definitions, close the pane.

Now let's find a synonym for a word.

4   In the second line of the first paragraph, double-click the word **acclaimed**.

5   On the **Review** tab, in the **Proofing** group, click the **Thesaurus** button to open the **Thesaurus** pane and display a list of synonyms for the word **acclaimed**. Scroll through the list of synonyms and notice that an antonym appears at the bottom of the list, so you can use the thesaurus to identify words that have the opposite meaning as well as those with similar meanings.

6   In the synonym list, below **much-admired**, click **commended**. Notice that the selected word replaces **acclaimed** in the search box at the top of the pane.

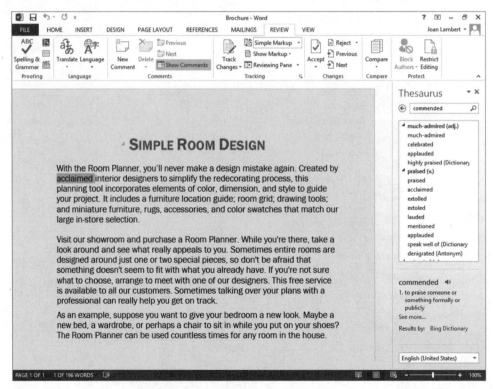

The Thesaurus pane now lists synonyms for and a definition of the word commended.

7   Point to the word **celebrated**, click the arrow that appears to its right, and then click **Insert** to replace the word **acclaimed** with **celebrated** in the document. Then close the **Thesaurus** pane.

Now let's translate a word.

8   In the **Language** group, click the **Translate** button, and then click **Choose Translation Language** to open the **Translation Language Options** dialog box.

9   In the **Choose Mini Translator language** area, click the **Translate to** arrow, and click **French (France)** in the list. Then click **OK** to close the dialog box.

10   In the **Language** group, click the **Translate** button, and then click **Mini Translator [French (France)]** to turn on the **Mini Translator**.

11   In the last paragraph of the document, point to the word **wardrobe**, and then move the pointer over the translucent box that appears above the word. Notice that the **Mini Translator** appears, showing two French translations for the word *wardrobe*: *armoire* and *garde-robe*.

12   In the **Mini Translator** box, click the **Expand** button to open the **Research** pane, which displays the settings for translating from English into French.

13   In the **Research** pane, in the **wardrobe** translation below **Bilingual Dictionary**, double-click the word **armoire** to select it.

14   Right-click the selection, and then click **Copy**.

15   In the document, double-click the word **wardrobe**.

16   Right-click the selection, and then point to (don't click) the **Keep Text Only** button below the **Paste Options** heading. Notice that Word displays a live preview of what the text will look like if you replace **wardrobe** with **armoire**.

17   Press the **Esc** key to close the shortcut menu and leave the word **wardrobe** in the text.

❌ CLEAN UP Close the Research pane, and turn off the Mini Translator by clicking Mini Translator on the Translate menu. Then close the Brochure document, saving your changes if you want to.

Installing Office tools

When you use the proofing tools in Word 2013, they are actually displaying results from a dictionary program (referred to as an *app*) that integrates with Word and connects to online resources. Many useful apps are available for Word and other Office programs, including dictionaries, fax services, maps, newsfeeds, and social connectors.

To manage apps from within Word, click the Apps For Office button in the Apps group on the Insert tab, and then in the Apps For Office window, click See All. Apps that are installed on your computer appear in the My Apps list. You can locate apps that are available for Word by clicking the Office Store button. Some apps can be installed from directly within Word (for example, you can install a dictionary app from the Dictionaries pane, the Spelling pane, or the Thesaurus pane).

If you no longer want to use an app, display the Apps For Office window and then click the Manage My Apps link in the upper-right corner of the window. This signs you in to the Office website using the Microsoft account associated with your Office installation and displays your personal My Apps For Office And SharePoint page. Select an app on this page, and then click Hide to make the app unavailable.

Viewing document statistics

Word displays information about the size of a document at the left end of the status bar. To show the number of words in only part of the document, such as a few paragraphs, simply select that part. You can review more statistics and specify the content to include in the statistics in the Word Count dialog box, which you open by clicking the Word Count indicator on the status bar or the Word Count button in the Proofing group on the Review tab.

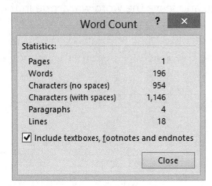

In addition to counting pages and words, Word counts characters, paragraphs, and lines.

Modifying spelling and grammar checking settings

Word saves your responses to suggested spelling and grammar changes with the document. If you choose to ignore a flagged error, the error will not be reflagged when you run the spelling and grammar checker again.

You can specify the behavior of the spelling and grammar checker on the Proofing page of the Word Options dialog box. In the Writing Style list, you can specify whether the spelling and grammar checker also checks for style issues such as sentence structure, unclear phrasing, and wordiness. (Yes, it's your own personal editor!) To specify the types of errors that the spelling and grammar checker flags, click the Settings button to the right of the Writing Style list. Not all grammar and style issues are examined by default.

The default grammar options in Word 2013 are different from those in earlier versions of Word. It's a good idea to check these settings before you start.

To check the spelling and grammar of a document from scratch, click the Recheck Document button on the Proofing page of the Word Options dialog box.

Correcting spelling and grammatical errors

In the days of handwritten and typewritten documents, people might have tolerated a typographical or grammatical error or two because correcting such errors without creating a mess was difficult. Word-processing programs such as Word have built-in spelling and grammar checkers, so now documents that contain these types of errors are likely to reflect badly on their creators.

TIP Although Word can help you eliminate misspellings and grammatical errors, its tools are not infallible. You should always read through your document to catch any problems that the Word tools can't detect—for example, homonyms such as *their*, *there*, and *they're*.

Word provides these three tools to help you with the chore of eliminating spelling and grammar errors:

- **AutoCorrect** This feature corrects common spelling and grammatical errors, replaces text codes with mathematical symbols, and automatically applies formatting based on text cues. AutoCorrect has a built-in list of frequently misspelled words and their correct spellings. If you frequently misspell a word that AutoCorrect doesn't change, you can add it to the list in the **AutoCorrect** dialog box. If you deliberately enter a word that is on the **AutoCorrect** list and don't want to accept the AutoCorrect change, you can reverse the correction by clicking the **Undo** button before you enter anything else, or by pointing to the bar that appears below the word and then clicking **Undo**.

- **Error indicators** Word indicates possible spelling errors with red wavy underlines, possible grammatical errors with green wavy underlines, and possible formatting errors with blue wavy underlines. You can right-click an underlined word or phrase to display suggested corrections and links to proofing resources.

- **Spelling and grammar checker** To check the spelling or grammar of selected text or the entire document, click the **Spelling & Grammar** button in the **Proofing** group on the **Review** tab. Word then works its way through the selection or the document and displays the **Spelling** pane or **Grammar** pane if it encounters a potential error.

  KEYBOARD SHORTCUT Press F7 to start checking the spelling and grammar from your current location in the document.

  The pane that appears displays an explanation of the likely problem and suggests corrections. You can implement a suggestion by double-clicking it.

The buttons in the Spelling pane reflect the type of error found.

In this exercise, you'll change an AutoCorrect setting and add a word to the AutoCorrect list. Then you'll review and correct the spelling and grammar in a document and add terms to the custom dictionary.

 SET UP You need the Letter document located in the Chapter02 practice file folder to complete this exercise. Open the document, and then follow the steps.

1   In the last line of the first paragraph, click immediately to the left of **negative** and then enter corresponding, followed by a space. Notice that when you press the **Spacebar**, the AutoCorrect function changes **coresponding** to **corresponding**.

2   In the **Backstage** view, click **Options** to display the **Word Options** dialog box, and then click the **Proofing** page tab.

3   At the top of the **Proofing** page, click the **AutoCorrect Options** button to display the **AutoCorrect** page of the **AutoCorrect** dialog box.

A selected check box indicates a category of error that AutoCorrect will automatically correct.

TIP You can clear the check box of any error category you don't want to automatically change. For example, if you don't want AutoCorrect to capitalize the first letter that follows a period, clear the Capitalize First Letter Of Sentences check box.

4   In the **Replace** box, enter avalable. Notice that Word scrolls through the list below the box to show the entry that is closest to what you entered.

5   Press the **Tab** key to move the cursor to the **With** box, and then enter available.

6   Click **Add** to add the entry to the correction list, click **OK** to close the **AutoCorrect** dialog box, and then click **OK** to close the **Word Options** dialog box.

7   Position the cursor at the end of the second paragraph, press the **Spacebar**, and then enter Sidney will not be avalable May 10-14. Notice that the misspelled word **avalable** changes to **available** as soon as you enter the space following the word.

Now let's correct one of the misspellings Word has identified.

8   In the first paragraph, right-click **sorces**, the first word with a red wavy underline, to have Word list possible correct spellings for this misspelled word.

As you know, operating an import business in the global arena requires careful consideration of current economic and environmental conditions, as well as of political issues that could affect our ability to maintain a viable business. When we select our product sorces, we strive to not only to improve the local economy but to to ensure the preservation of fragil complex balancing act, but we are commited to maximizing our positive imp no negative impacts.

| sources |
| sores |
| scores |
| forces |
| source's |
| Ignore All |
| Add to Dictionary |
| Hyperlink... |
| New Comment |

This is an exciting and challenging venture, and we wood like to invite you t office to discuss your needs with our purchasing agent Cristina Potra. You m through our main number at (925) 555-0167, through email at cristina@wideworldimporters.com, or by regular mail at our corporate addre

In the meantime, here is a packet of informational material that includes a lis suppliers, a travel manual used by our purchasing agents in the field, and our which outlines our commitment to supporting grass-root businesses such as (

The shortcut menu also lists actions you might want to carry out, such as adding the word to the dictionary.

SEE ALSO For information about the hyperlink option on the shortcut menu, see "Linking to external resources" in Chapter 12, "Link to information and content."

9   In the list, click **sources** to insert the correctly spelled word.

TIP Word's grammar checker helps identify phrases and clauses that don't follow traditional grammatical rules, but it's not always accurate. It's easy to get in the habit of ignoring green wavy underlines. However, it's wise to scrutinize them all to be sure that your documents don't contain any embarrassing mistakes.

Now let's check the spelling and grammar of the entire document.

10   Press **Ctrl+Home** to move to the beginning of the document. On the **Review** tab, in the **Proofing** group, click the **Spelling & Grammar** button to open the **Spelling** pane. Notice that the duplicated word **to** is highlighted in the first paragraph of the document, and the **Spelling** pane indicates that the word is repeated.

TROUBLESHOOTING If the errors we mention don't appear to be in the practice file, display the Proofing page of the Word Options dialog box, , and then in the When Correcting Spelling And Grammar In Word area, click Recheck Document. Click Yes to reset the spelling and grammar checkers, and then click OK.

erating an import business in the global arena requires careful consideration of
and environmental conditions, as well as of political issues that could affect
ntain a viable business. When we select our product sources, we strive to not
he local economy but to to ensure the preservation of fragile ecologies. It is a
g act, but we are commited to maximizing our positive impacts while causing
cts.

g and challenging venture, and we wood like to invite you to visit our corporate
/our needs with our purchasing agent Cristina Potra. You may contact Cristina
number at (925) 555-0167, through email at
rldimporters.com, or by regular mail at our corporate address.

here is a packet of informational material that includes a list of products and
manual used by our purchasing agents in the field, and our mission statement,
r commitment to supporting grass-root businesses such as Contoso.

Word highlights the duplicate word in the document.

11   In the **Spelling** pane, click **Delete** to delete the second instance of **to** and move to
the next word that Word does not recognize, **commited**.

12   With **committed** selected in the suggestions box, click **Change** to correct the
error and display the next possible error, which is marked as a grammar error. The
document author has used the wrong form of a word that has multiple spellings.

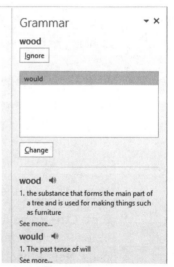

erating an import business in the global arena requires careful consideration of
and environmental conditions, as well as of political issues that could affect
ntain a viable business. When we select our product sources, we strive to not
he local economy but to ensure the preservation of fragile ecologies. It is a
g act, but we are committed to maximizing our positive impacts while causing
cts.

g and challenging venture, and we wood like to invite you to visit our corporate
/our needs with our purchasing agent Cristina Potra. You may contact Cristina
number at (925) 555-0167, through email at
rldimporters.com, or by regular mail at our corporate address.

here is a packet of informational material that includes a list of products and
manual used by our purchasing agents in the field, and our mission statement,
r commitment to supporting grass-root businesses such as Contoso.

The Grammar pane displays the definitions of the original word and the suggested replacement.

13   In the **Grammar** pane, click **Change** to replace the selected word and display the
next possible error—the purchasing agent's last name. Because Cristina's full name is
likely to come up often in correspondence from this company, let's add **Potra** to the
custom dictionary so that Word doesn't flag it as an error in the future.

14   Near the top of the **Spelling** pane, below **Potra**, click the **Add** button. Word adds
      the name to the dictionary and displays a message indicating that it has finished
      checking the spelling and grammar of the document.

Word might suggest replacements that do not appear in the dictionary.

15   Click **OK** to close the message box.

   TIP The grammar checker doesn't always catch awkward phrasing. For example,
   note the unmarked error ("to not only to") in the second sentence of the first
   paragraph of the Letter document. It's a good example of why you should always
   proofread your documents (or have someone else do it for you).

❌ CLEAN UP Close the Letter document, saving your changes if you want to.

Key points

- You create simple Word documents by selecting a template and entering text at
  the cursor.

- You can drag text from one location in a document to another.

- You can cut or copy text and paste it elsewhere in the same document or in a
  different document. Cut and copied text is stored on the Clipboard.

- Undo one action or the last several actions you performed by clicking the Undo button (or its arrow) on the Quick Access Toolbar. Click the Redo button if you change
  your mind again.

- You can find each occurrence of a word or phrase and replace it with another.

- Rely on AutoCorrect to correct common misspellings. Correct other spelling and
  grammatical errors as you enter text, or by checking the entire document in one pass.

Chapter at a glance

Style

Apply styles to text,
page 94

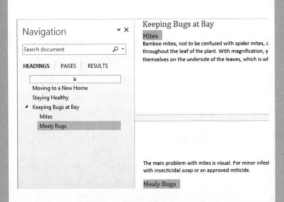

Color

Change a document's theme,
page 102

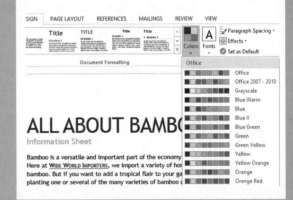

Format

Manually change the look of characters,
page 108

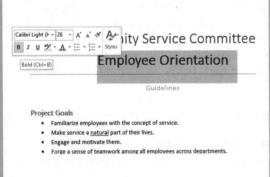

List

Create and modify lists,
page 130

1. Each Apartment shall be used for residential purposes only, except such professional and administrative businesses as may be permitted by ordinance, provided there is no external evidence thereof.
2. No noxious or offensive activity shall be carried on, in, or upon any Apartment, Limited Common Area, or Common Area; nor shall anything be done therein which may be an annoyance or nuisance to other resident.
3. No sports, activities, or games, whether organized or unorganized, that might cause damage to buildings, grounds, facilities, structures, or vehicles, or that are an annoyance or nuisance, shall be played in any Limited Common Area or Common Area.
4. No Owner shall keep any animal within his or her Apartment for any purpose other than as a pet. The number of cats and/or dogs any Owner may keep is limited to the following:
   - Two small dogs
   - Two cats
   - One cat and one small dog
5. No large dogs are allowed, either as pets of Owners or as pets of visitors.
   a. Seeing-eye dogs may be permitted with written approval of the Board.
   b. The Board reserves the right to make exceptions to this rule.
6. All pets must reside within their Owners' Apartments.
7. Owners may keep other types of small pets that are confined to aquariums or cages.
8. Pets must be on a leash when in the Common Area.

Modify the structure and appearance of text

3

IN THIS CHAPTER, YOU WILL LEARN HOW TO

- Apply styles to text.

- Change a document's theme.

- Manually change the look of characters.

- Manually change the look of paragraphs.

- Create and modify lists.

The appearance of your documents helps to convey their message. Microsoft Word 2013 can help you develop professional-looking documents whose appearance is appropriate to their contents. You can easily format words and paragraphs so that key points stand out and the structure of your document is clear. You can also change the look of major elements within a document by applying predefined sets of formatting called *styles*, and you can change the look of selected text by applying predefined combinations called *text effects*. In addition, you can change the fonts, colors, and effects throughout a document with one click by applying a theme.

In this chapter, you'll first experiment with built-in styles and text effects, and then you'll change the theme applied to a document. You'll change the look of individual words, and then you'll change the indentation, alignment, and spacing of individual paragraphs. You'll also add borders and shading to make paragraphs stand out. Finally, you'll create and format both bulleted and numbered lists.

PRACTICE FILES To complete the exercises in this chapter, you need the practice files contained in the Chapter03 practice file folder. For more information, see "Download the practice files" in this book's Introduction.

Applying styles to text

You don't have to know much about character and paragraph formatting to be able to format your documents in ways that will make them easier to read and more professional looking. With a couple of mouse clicks, you can easily change the look of words, phrases, and paragraphs by using styles. More importantly, you can structure a document by applying styles that are linked to outline levels. In doing so, you build a document outline that is reflected in the Navigation pane and can be used to create a table of contents.

SEE ALSO For information about tables of contents, see "Creating and modifying tables of contents" in Chapter 13, "Reference content and content sources."

Styles can include character formatting (such as font, size, and color), paragraph formatting (such as line spacing and outline level), or a combination of both. Styles are stored in the template that is attached to a document. By default, blank new documents are based on the Normal template. The Normal template includes a standard selection of styles that fit the basic needs of most documents. These styles include nine heading levels, various text styles including those for multiple levels of bulleted and numbered lists, index and table of contents entry styles, and many specialized styles such as those for hyperlinks, quotations, placeholders, captions, and other elements.

By default, Word makes the most common predefined styles available in the Styles gallery on the Home tab.

The Styles gallery in a new, blank document based on the Normal template.

Styles can be used for multiple purposes: to affect the appearance of the content, to build a document outline, and to tag content as a certain type so that you can easily locate it.

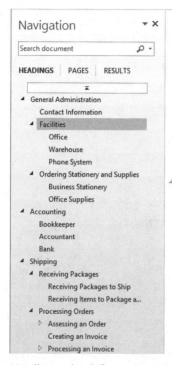

Heading styles define a document's outline.

Styles stored in a template are usually based on the Normal style and use only the default body and heading fonts associated with the document's theme, so they all go together well. For this reason, formatting document content by using styles produces a harmonious effect. After you apply styles from the current style set, you can easily change the look of the entire document by switching to a different style set, which associates different formatting rules with the same styles. So if you have applied the Heading 1 style to a paragraph, you can change its formatting simply by changing the style set.

SEE ALSO For information about document theme elements, see "Changing a document's theme," later in this chapter.

Style sets are available from the Document Formatting menu on the Design tab.

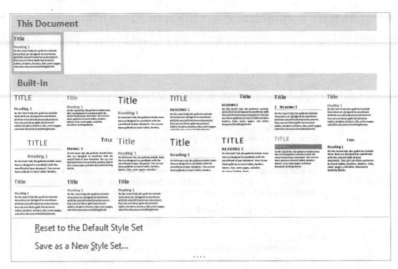

Pointing to a style set in the gallery displays a live preview of the effects of applying that style set to the entire document.

TIP Style sets provide a quick and easy way to change the look of an existing document. You can also modify style definitions by changing the template on which the document is based. For more information about styles and templates, see "Creating custom styles and templates" in Chapter 16, "Work in Word more efficiently."

In this exercise, you'll experiment with the styles in the Normal template and change the look of a document by switching to a different style set.

→ SET UP You need the BambooInformation document located in the Chapter03 practice file folder to complete this exercise. Open the document in Print Layout view, and then follow the steps.

1 Scroll through the document to gain an overview of its contents. Notice that the document begins with a centered title and subtitle, and there are several headings throughout.

2 Display the **Navigation** pane. Notice that the **Headings** page of the **Navigation** pane does not reflect the headings in the document.

3 On the **Home** tab, click the **Styles** dialog box launcher to display the **Styles** pane. If it floats above the page, drag it by its title bar to the right edge of the program window to dock it.

4　If necessary, change the zoom level of the page to fit the page content between the **Navigation** pane and the **Styles** pane.

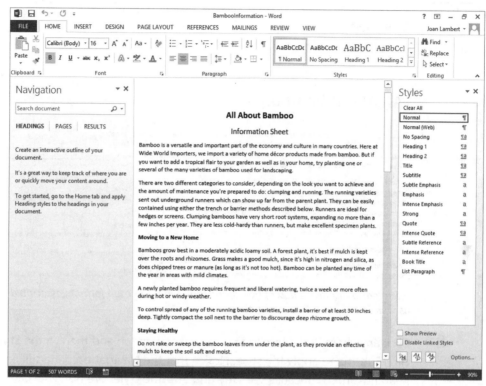

You're ready to build a document structure by applying styles.

TIP Squiggly lines indicating possible grammatical errors might appear below some words in this document. You can remove them by right-clicking each word and then clicking Ignore.

5　Click anywhere in the document title, **All About Bamboo**, and then click in the first heading, **Moving to a New Home**. In the **Styles** pane, notice that each of these paragraphs is styled as **Normal**. Because the document headings do not have heading styles applied to them, they do not appear in the **Navigation** pane.

6　Click again in the document title and then, in the **Styles** pane, click **Title** to apply the style. Notice that Word applies the style to the entire paragraph even if you haven't selected it.

7　In the **Styles** pane, point to the **Title** style.

A ScreenTip displays a description of the font and paragraph formats associated with the style, as well as the base style information.

8   Click anywhere in the **Information Sheet** paragraph and then, in the **Styles** pane, click **Subtitle** to apply the style. Notice that the **Navigation** pane still contains no headings. This is because the **Title** and **Subtitle** styles are not associated with outline levels.

9   Select the bold heading **Moving to a New Home**. In the **Styles** pane, point to the **Heading 1** style to display a description of the style. Notice that the paragraph description includes **Outline Level: Level 1** to indicate that paragraphs with this style appear at the first level of an outline.

10   In the **Styles** gallery, point to the **Heading 1** style to display a live preview of the selected text with that style. Notice the different result of pointing to the style in the **Styles** gallery and in the **Styles** pane.

11   In the **Styles** gallery or in the **Styles** pane, click **Heading 1** to apply the style. Notice that the selected heading also appears in the **Navigation** pane.

Document headings provide not only an outline structure and formatting; you can also use them to collapse entire sections. This is a nifty new feature in Word 2013. Let's try it.

12   In the document, point to the heading to display a downward-angled gray triangle to its left. Then click the gray triangle to hide the content that follows the heading.

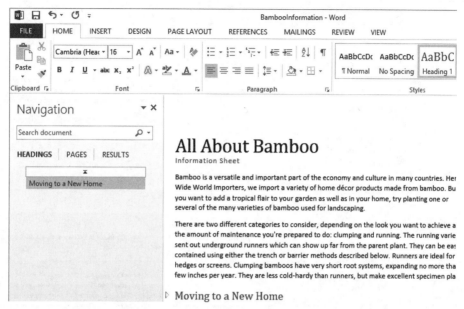

The gray triangle changes to a right-facing white triangle to indicate that content is hidden.

13   Click in the text above the heading. Notice that the white triangle remains visible to the left of the heading to indicate that content associated with the heading is hidden.

14   Click the white triangle to the left of the heading to display the hidden document content.

15   Select **Staying Healthy**, and click the **Heading 1** style to apply it. Then select **Keeping Bugs at Bay** and on the **Quick Access Toolbar**, click the **Repeat** button to apply the same style to the selected text. This is a technique you can use to quickly apply multiple instances of a style.

KEYBOARD SHORTCUT Press Ctrl+Y to repeat the previous action. For more information about keyboard shortcuts, see "Keyboard shortcuts" at the end of this book.

16   Display the page so that both underlined headings are visible. Select **Mites**, press and hold the **Ctrl** key, and then select **Mealy Bugs**. With both headings selected, click **Heading 2** in the **Styles** gallery or **Styles** pane to simultaneously apply the style to both selections.

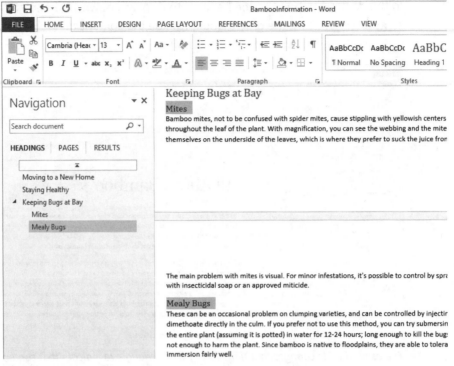

Applying multiple heading styles creates a multilevel outline in the Navigation pane.

17 Notice that **Heading 3** now appears in the **Styles** pane. The **Normal** template contains many more headings than are currently displayed in the **Styles** pane or **Styles** gallery. At the bottom of the **Styles** pane, click **Options** to open the **Style Pane Options** dialog box. Notice that **Show next heading when previous level is used** is selected by default; this is the setting that caused **Heading 3** to appear in the **Styles** pane after you applied the **Heading 2** style.

Let's look at the many styles that are available for use in this document.

18 In the **Style Pane Options** dialog box, click the **Select styles to show** arrow. Notice that you can display all styles, all styles that are in the document template, all styles that are currently being used, or a selection of "recommended" styles.

SEE ALSO For more information about working with styles and the Styles pane, see "Creating custom styles and templates" in Chapter 16, "Work in Word more efficiently."

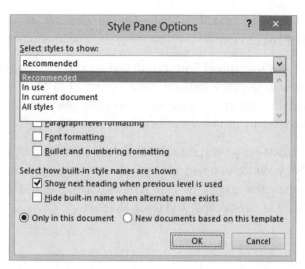

You can choose to display any of four categories of styles in the Styles pane.

19 In the **Select styles to show** list, click **All styles**. In the **Select how list is sorted** list, click **Alphabetical**. Then in the **Style Pane Options** dialog box, click **OK** to display the full list of available styles in the **Styles** pane.

> **TIP** To add any style from the Styles pane to the Styles gallery, point to the style name, click the arrow that appears, and then click Add To Style Gallery.

20 Scroll through the **Styles** pane to view the wide range of available styles, and point to any that interests you to display a description. Notice that many of the built-in styles are intended for specific uses, such as the **Index** and **TOC** (table of contents) styles.

21 In the **Navigation** pane, just above the headings, click the **Jump to the beginning** button to return to the document title.

Now we'll apply some character styles to the document content, so we can see how they change when we change the style set.

22 In the first paragraph of the document, select the company name **Wide World Importers**. In the **Styles** group, click the **More** button to expand the **Styles** gallery, and then click the **Intense Reference** thumbnail to apply the style.

23 In the second paragraph, near the end of the first sentence, select the word **clumping** and apply the **Emphasis** style. Then, at the end of the sentence, apply the same style to the word **running**. Notice that the application of these character styles does not affect the **Navigation** pane contents.

24 Close the **Navigation** pane and the **Styles** pane. On the **View** tab, in the **Zoom** group, click **Multiple Pages** to display both pages of the document in the window.

25 On the **Design** tab, in the **Document Formatting** gallery, point to each of the style sets in the **Built-In** area to display a live preview of the effect of applying that style set. Notice how the style set affects the appearance of the headings and text to which you applied styles, and also how it affects the document length.

26 In the **Document Formatting** gallery, click the **Basic (Elegant)** thumbnail. Then on the **View** tab, click **Page Width** to have a closer look at the changes. Notice that the selected style set formats the font of the **Title** style as uppercase, and the font of the **Intense Reference** style as "small caps" and underlined.

ALL ABOUT BAMBOO

Information Sheet

Bamboo is a versatile and important part of the economy and culture in many countries. Here at WIDE WORLD IMPORTERS, we import a variety of home décor products made from bamboo. But if you want to add a tropical flair to your garden as well as in your home, try planting one or several of the many varieties of bamboo used for landscaping.

There are two different categories to consider, depending on the look you want to achieve and the amount of maintenance you're prepared to do: *clumping* and *running*. The running varieties sent out underground runners which can show up far from the parent plant. They can be easily contained using either the trench or barrier methods described below. Runners are ideal for hedges or screens. Clumping bamboos have very short root systems, expanding no more than a few inches per year. They are less cold-hardy than runners, but make excellent specimen plants.

You can control the case of text by applying a style.

✖ CLEAN UP Close the BambooInformation document, saving your changes if you want to.

Changing a document's theme

Every document you create is based on a template, and the look of the template is controlled by a theme. The theme is a combination of coordinated colors, fonts, and effects that visually convey a certain tone. To change the look of a document, you can apply a different theme by clicking the Themes button in the Document Formatting group on the Design tab, and then making a selection in the Themes gallery.

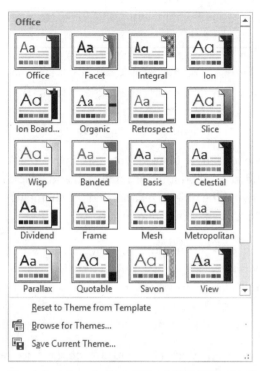

The default installation of Word 2013 offers 21 themes to choose from.

If you like the background elements of one theme but not the colors or fonts, you can mix and match theme elements. First apply the theme that most closely resembles the look you want, and then select colors and fonts from the Theme Colors and Theme Fonts galleries in the Document Formatting group.

In addition to colors and fonts, you can control more subtle elements such as paragraph spacing and visual effects that are associated with a theme.

If you create a combination of theme elements that you would like to be able to use with other documents, you can save the combination as a new theme. By saving the theme in the default Document Themes folder, you make the theme available in the Themes gallery. However, you don't have to store custom themes in the Document Themes folder; you can store them anywhere on your hard disk, on removable media, or in a network location. To use a theme that is stored in a different location, click Browse For Themes at the bottom of the Themes menu, locate the theme you want in the Choose Theme Or Themed Document dialog box, and then click Open to apply that theme to the current document.

By default, Word applies the Office theme to all new, blank documents. In Word 2013, the Office theme uses a primarily blue palette, the Calibri font for body text, and Calibri Light for headings. You can make a different theme the default by applying the theme you want and then clicking Set As Default in the Document Formatting group.

In this exercise, you'll apply a theme to an existing document and change the colors and fonts. Then you'll save the new combination as a custom theme.

 SET UP You need the BambooStyled document located in the Chapter03 practice file folder to complete this exercise. Open the document, and then follow the steps.

1   On the **Design** tab, in the **Document Formatting** group, click the **Themes** button to display the **Themes** menu.

2   Point to each thumbnail in turn to display a live preview of the theme. (Scroll through the gallery so that you can explore all the themes.)

3   In the **Themes** gallery, click **Facet** to change the colors and fonts to those defined for that theme. Notice that the font and character formatting controlled by the styles and style set you applied to the document in the previous exercise do not change; the title and first-level headings remain uppercase.

4   In the **Document Formatting** group, click the **Colors** button to display the **Colors** menu.

5   Point to any color palette that interests you to preview its effects on the document. Notice that the first color in each palette is applied to the **Title** and **Intense Reference** styles, and different shades of the third color are applied to the **Subtitle**, **Heading 1**, and **Heading 2** styles. Each color in the palette has a specific role assigned to it.

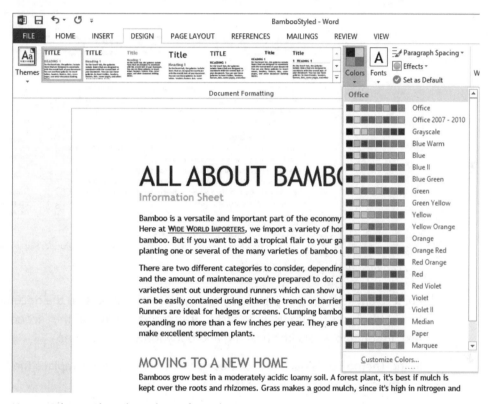

You can change the color palette of any theme.

6   In the **Theme Colors** gallery, click the **Orange** palette. The selected colors replace the **Facet** colors, but nothing else in the document changes.

7   In the **Document Formatting** group, click the **Fonts** button to display the **Theme Fonts** menu.

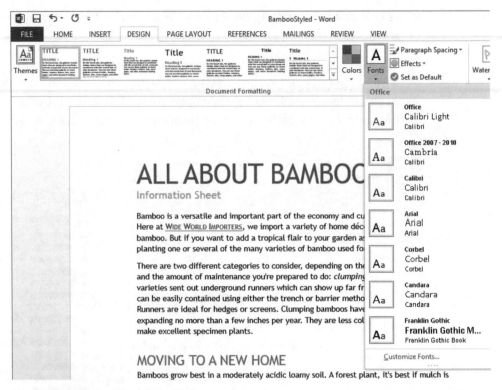

You can modify the theme by applying any font set.

8   Point to any font set that interests you to preview its effects on the document. Each font set includes two fonts—the first is used for headings and the second for body text. In some font sets, the heading and body fonts are the same.

9   In the **Theme Fonts** gallery, click **Georgia**. The selected fonts replace the **Facet** fonts, but the colors and style elements remain the same.

Now that you've made some changes to the theme, let's save the modified theme so you can reuse it on other documents.

10   In the **Document Formatting** group, click the **Themes** button, and then at the bottom of the menu, click **Save Current Theme** to display the contents of the **Document Themes** folder in the **Save Current Theme** dialog box.

11   In the **File name** box, replace the suggested name with My Theme, and then click **Save**.

12 Display the **Themes** menu. Notice that it now includes a **Custom** area that contains your theme.

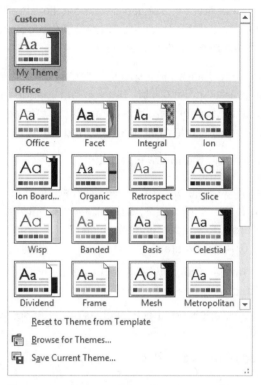

You can apply your custom theme to any document.

13 Click away from the menu to close it without making a selection.

⊗ CLEAN UP Close the BambooStyled document, saving your changes if you want to.

TIP If you want to delete the custom theme you created in this topic, open File Explorer, navigate to the Document Themes folder, and delete the My Theme file, or, in Word, display the Themes menu, right-click your custom theme, and click Delete. Note that the second method removes the theme choice from the gallery but does not remove the theme file from your Themes folder.

Manually changing the look of characters

Word 2013 makes changing the look of content in a styled document almost effortless. But styles and themes can't do everything. To be able to precisely control the look of your text, you need to know how to manually change individual elements.

When you enter text in a document, it is displayed in a specific font. By default, the font used for text in a new blank document is 11-point Calibri, but you can change the font of any element at any time. The available fonts vary from one computer to another, depending on the programs installed. Common fonts include Arial, Verdana, and Times New Roman.

You can vary the look of a font by changing the following attributes:

- **Size** Almost every font comes in a range of sizes, which are measured in points from the top of letters that have parts that stick up (ascenders), such as h, to the bottom of letters that have parts that drop down (descenders), such as p. A point is approximately 1/72 of an inch (about 0.04 centimeters).

- **Style** Almost every font has a range of font styles. The most common are regular (or plain), italic, bold, and bold italic.

- **Effects** Fonts can be enhanced by applying effects, such as underlining, small capital letters (small caps), or shadows.

- **Color** A palette of coordinated colors is available, and you can also specify custom colors.

- **Character spacing** You can alter the spacing between characters by pushing them apart or squeezing them together.

Although some attributes might cancel each other out, they are usually cumulative. For example, you might use a bold font style in various sizes and various shades of green to make words stand out in a newsletter. Collectively, the font and its attributes are called *character formatting*.

You apply character formatting from one of three locations:

- **Mini Toolbar** Several common formatting buttons are available on the Mini Toolbar that appears when you select text.

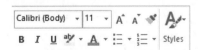

The Mini Toolbar appears temporarily when you select text, becomes transparent when you move the pointer away from the selected text, and then disappears entirely.

- **Font group on the Home tab** This group includes buttons for changing the font and most of the font attributes you are likely to use.

The Font group.

- **Font dialog box** Less-commonly applied attributes such as small caps and special underlining are available from the Font dialog box, which you display by clicking the Font dialog box launcher.

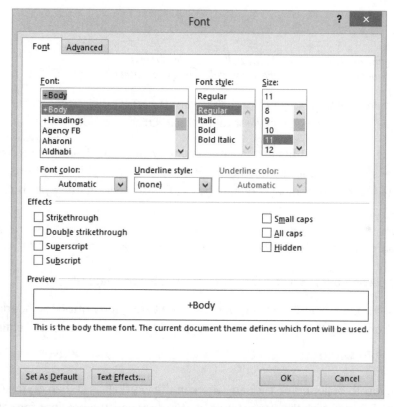

Most font attributes are set from the Font page of the dialog box, except character spacing and OpenType attributes, which are set on the Advanced page.

In addition to applying character formatting to change the look of characters, you can apply predefined text effects to a selection to add more zing. Clicking the Text Effects And Typography button in the Font group on the Home tab displays a gallery of effects matched to the current theme colors.

You can apply any predefined effect in the gallery to selected text,
or you can click options below the gallery and define a custom effect.

These effects are dramatic, so you'll probably want to restrict their use to document titles and similar elements to which you want to draw particular attention.

In this exercise, you'll format the text in a document by changing its font, style, size, color, and character spacing. You'll experiment with highlighting and apply text effects. Then you'll return selected text to its original condition by clearing some formatting you no longer want.

 SET UP You need the Guidelines document located in the Chapter03 practice file folder to complete this exercise. Open the document, and then follow the steps.

1   In the second bullet point, click anywhere in the word **natural**.

2   On the **Home** tab, in the **Font** group, click the **Underline** button to underline the word containing the cursor. Notice that you did not have to select the entire word.

    KEYBOARD SHORTCUT Press Ctrl+U to underline the active word or selection.

3   In the fourth bullet point, click anywhere in the word **all**, and then on the **Quick Access Toolbar**, click the **Repeat** button. Word repeats the previous formatting command. Again, although you did not select the entire word, it is now underlined.

    KEYBOARD SHORTCUT Press Ctrl+Y to repeat the previous command.

4   In the same bullet point, click anywhere in the word **across**. In the **Font** group, click the **Underline** arrow and then click **Thick underline** (the third option) to apply a thick underline to the word. Then click the next word, **departments**, and click the **Underline** button (not the arrow). Notice that the thick underline has now been assigned to the **Underline** button.

    TIP You can choose an underline style and color from the Underline gallery or from the Font dialog box.

5   Select the **Employee Orientation** heading, and leave the pointer in place to display the **Mini Toolbar**.

6   On the **Mini Toolbar**, click the **Bold** button to apply bold formatting to the heading. Notice that the active buttons on the **Mini Toolbar** and in the **Font** group on the **Home** tab indicate the attributes applied to the selection.

    KEYBOARD SHORTCUT Press Ctrl+B to make the active word or selection bold.

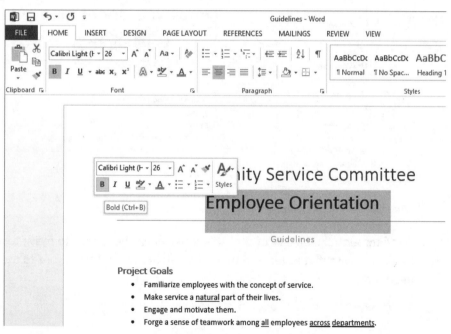

The ribbon reflects the settings in the Mini Toolbar.

7   On the **Mini Toolbar**, click the **Format Painter** button.

    TIP The Format Painter button is available in the Clipboard group on the Home tab.

8   Move the pointer into the selection area to the left of the **Guidelines** subtitle, and click the mouse button to apply the formatting of **Employee Orientation** to **Guidelines**.

9   With **Guidelines** selected, on the **Home** tab, in the **Font** group, click the **Font** arrow to expand the **Font** gallery.

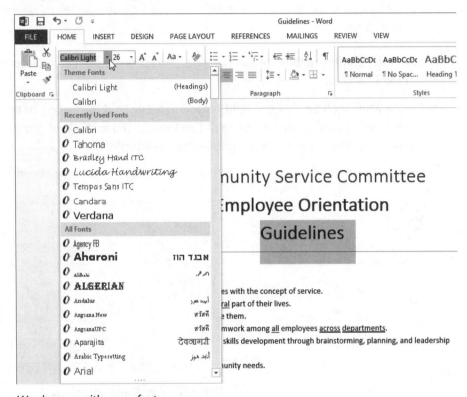

Word comes with many fonts.

10 Scroll through the gallery of available fonts, press the letter **I** to move to the fonts beginning with that letter, and then click **Impact** to apply that font to the **Guidelines** heading.

TROUBLESHOOTING If Impact is not available, select any heavy font that catches your attention.

11 In the **Font** group, click the **Font Size** arrow, and then in the list, click **20**. The size of the heading text decreases to 20 points.

TIP You can increase or decrease the font size in set increments by clicking the Increase Font Size or Decrease Font Size buttons in the Font group or on the Mini Toolbar, or by pressing Ctrl+> or Ctrl+<.

Next we'll apply some font formatting that isn't available from the ribbon.

12 With **Guidelines** still selected, click the **Font** dialog box launcher to open the **Font** dialog box.

> **KEYBOARD SHORTCUT** Press Ctrl+Shift+F to display the Font dialog box.

13 On the **Font** page, in the **Effects** area, select the **Small caps** check box.

14 Click the **Advanced** tab to display character spacing and typographic features.

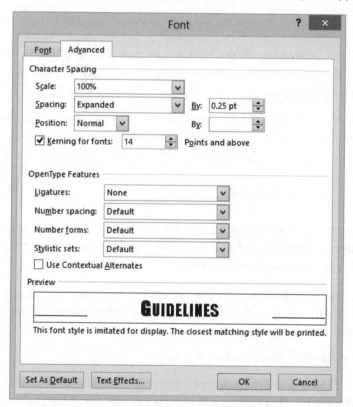

The Spacing option is currently set to Expanded.

TIP OpenType is a common scalable computer font format that incorporates options to enhance the font's ability to support advanced typographic capabilities and render multiple languages gracefully.

15   To the right of the **Spacing** list, in the **By** box, select **0.25 pt** and enter 10 pt (the *pt* stands for *points*). Then click **OK**. In the document, press the **Home** key to release the selection. Notice that the manually formatted text appears in small capital letters with the spacing between the characters expanded by 10 points.

Community Service Committee
Employee Orientation
G U I D E L I N E S

You can expand and contract the spacing between letters to create different effects.

16   Select **Employee Orientation**. In the **Font** group, click the **Font Color** arrow, and then in the **Theme Colors** palette, click the top green swatch (**Green, Accent 6**) to change the color of the selected words.

> **TIP** To apply the Font Color button's current color, you can simply click the button (not its arrow). If you want to apply a color that is not shown in the Theme Colors or Standard Colors palette, click More Colors. In the Colors dialog box, click the color you want in the honeycomb on the Standard page, or click the color gradient or enter values for a color on the Custom page.

17   Select **Community Service Committee**. In the **Font** group, click the **Text Effects and Typography** button and then, in the gallery, point to each of the thumbnails to preview its effect on the selected heading.

18   Below the gallery, click **Outline**, and then in the **Theme Colors** palette, click the **Green, Accent 6** square to outline the letters in the same color you applied to **Employee Orientation**.

This is interesting, but let's get a little fancier.

19   Click the **Text Effects and Typography** button, click **Shadow**, and then click **Shadow Options** to display the **Text Effects** page of the **Format Text Effects** pane.

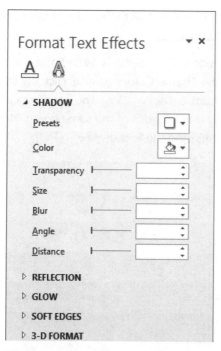

The Format Text Effects pane includes the Text Fill & Outline page and the Text Effects page.

20   In the **Shadow** settings, click the **Presets** button, and then in the **Outer** section of the **Presets** gallery, click the thumbnail at the right end of the top row.

21   Click the **Color** button, and then in the **Theme Colors** palette, click the bottom green swatch (**Green, Accent 6, Darker 50%**) to create a dark green shadow.

22   At the top of the **Format Text Effects** pane, click the **Text Fill & Outline** button to display that page. Then click the **Text Fill** heading to expand those settings.

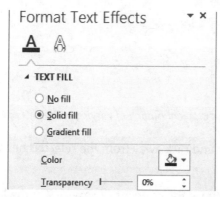

You can format characters with a solid or gradient fill.

23   With **Solid fill** selected, click the **Color** button, and then in the **Theme Colors** palette, click the top green swatch (**Green, Accent 6**).

24   Click the **Text Outline** heading to expand those settings. With **Solid line** selected, click the **Color** button, and then in the **Theme Colors** palette, click the second green swatch from the bottom (**Green, Accent 6, Darker 25%**). You have now applied three text effects to the selected text using three shades of the same green. Notice that there are many other options for formatting the text outline.

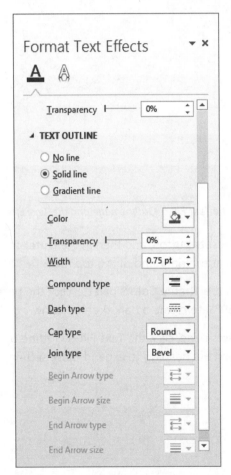

You can format characters with a solid or gradient outline of varying widths.

25   Close the **Format Text Effects** pane and click away from the selected heading to review the effects of your changes.

26   In the first bullet point, select the phrase **the concept of service**. On the **Mini Toolbar**, click the **Text Highlight Color** arrow, and click the **Bright Green** swatch in

the top row. The selected phrase is now highlighted in green, and the **Text Highlight Color** button shows bright green as its active color.

TIP If you click the Text Highlight Color button without first making a selection, the shape of the mouse pointer changes to a highlighter that you can drag across text. Click the button again, or press Esc, to turn off the highlighter.

27 In the fifth bullet point, double-click the word **brainstorming**. Hold down the **Ctrl** key, double-click **planning**, and then double-click **leadership**.

28 In the **Font** group, click the **Change Case** button, and then click **UPPERCASE**.

KEYBOARD SHORTCUT Press Shift+F3 to change the case of the selected text. Press Shift+F3 multiple times to move through the case options (Sentence case, UPPER-CASE, lowercase, and Capitalize Each Word). Note that the options vary based on the selected text. If the selection ends in a period, Word does not include the Capitalize Each Word option in the rotation. If the selection does not end in a period, Word does not include Sentence case in the rotation.

29 In the document, click away from the bullet point to release the selection and review the results. The selected words now appear in all capital letters.

Community Service Committee
Employee Orientation
GUIDELINES

Project Goals
- Familiarize employees with the concept of service.
- Make service a natural part of their lives.
- Engage and motivate them.
- Forge a sense of teamwork among all employees across departments.
- Provide appropriate skills development through BRAINSTORMING, PLANNING, and LEADERSHIP opportunities.
- Meet genuine community needs.

Instead of retyping, you can have Word change the case of words.

TIP To remove all styles and formatting other than highlighting from selected text, click the Clear Formatting button in the Font group. To remove only manually applied formatting (and not styles) press Ctrl+Spacebar. To remove highlighting, select the highlighted text and then in the Text Highlight Color menu, click No Color.

❌ CLEAN UP Close the Guidelines document, saving your changes if you want to.

Character formatting and case considerations

The way you use case and character formatting in a document can influence its visual impact on your readers. Used judiciously, case and character formatting can make a plain document look attractive and professional, but excessive use can make it look amateurish and detract from the message. For example, using too many fonts in the same document is the mark of inexperience, so don't use more than two or three.

Bear in mind that lowercase letters tend to recede, so using all uppercase (capital) letters can be useful for titles and headings or for certain kinds of emphasis. However, large blocks of uppercase letters are tiring to the eye.

TIP Where do the terms *uppercase* and *lowercase* come from? Until the advent of computers, individual characters made of lead were assembled to form the words that would appear on a printed page. The characters were stored alphabetically in cases, with the capital letters in the upper case and the small letters in the lower case.

Manually changing the look of paragraphs

A paragraph is created by entering text and then pressing the Enter key. A paragraph can contain one word, one sentence, or multiple sentences. You can change the look of a paragraph by changing its indentation, alignment, and line spacing, as well as the space before and after it. You can also put borders around it and shade its background. Collectively, the settings you use to vary the look of a paragraph are called *paragraph formatting*.

In Word, you don't define the width of paragraphs and the length of pages by defining the area occupied by the text; instead you define the size of the white space—the left, right, top, and bottom margins—around the text. You click the Margins button in the Page Setup group on the Page Layout tab to define these margins, either for the whole document or for sections of the document.

SEE ALSO For information about setting margins, see "Previewing and adjusting page layout" in Chapter 6, "Preview, print, and distribute documents." For information about sections, see "Controlling what appears on each page" in the same chapter.

Although the left and right margins are set for a whole document or section, you can vary the position of the paragraphs between the margins. The quickest way to indent a paragraph from the left is to click the Increase Indent button; clicking the Decrease Indent button has the opposite effect.

TIP You cannot increase or decrease the indent beyond the margins by using the Increase Indent and Decrease Indent buttons. If you do need to extend an indent beyond the margins, you can do so by setting negative indentation measurements in the Paragraph dialog box.

Another way to control the indentation of lines is by dragging markers on the horizontal ruler to indicate where each line of text starts and ends. You can set four individual indent markers for each paragraph:

- **First Line Indent** The paragraph's first line of text begins at this marker.

- **Hanging Indent** The paragraph's second and subsequent lines of text begin at this marker at the left end of the ruler.

- **Left Indent** The left side of the paragraph aligns with this marker.

- **Right Indent** The paragraph text wraps when it reaches this marker at the right end of the ruler.

You display the horizontal and vertical rulers by selecting the Ruler check box in the Show group on the View tab.

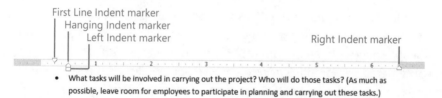

You can manually change a paragraph's indentation by moving the indent markers on the horizontal ruler.

Setting a right indent indicates where the lines in a paragraph should end, but sometimes you might want to specify where only one line should end. For example, you might want to break a title after a specific word to make it look balanced on the page. You can end an individual line by inserting a text wrapping break (more commonly known as a *line break*). After positioning the cursor where you want the break to occur, click the Breaks button in the Page Setup group on the Page Layout tab, and then click Text Wrapping. Word indicates the line break with a bent arrow (visible when hidden formatting symbols are shown). Inserting a line break does not start a new paragraph, so when you apply paragraph formatting to a line of text that ends with a line break, the formatting is applied to the entire paragraph, not only to that line.

KEYBOARD SHORTCUT Press Shift+Enter to insert a line break.

You can also determine the positioning of a paragraph between the left and right margins by changing its alignment. There are four paragraph alignment options:

- **Align Left** Aligns each line of the paragraph at the left margin, with a ragged right edge

    KEYBOARD SHORTCUT Press Ctrl+L to left-align a paragraph.

- **Center** Aligns the center of each line in the paragraph between the left and right margins, with ragged left and right edges

    KEYBOARD SHORTCUT Press Ctrl+E to center-align a paragraph.

- **Align Right** Aligns each line of the paragraph at the right margin, with a ragged left edge

    KEYBOARD SHORTCUT Press Ctrl+R to right-align a paragraph.

- **Justify** Aligns each line between the margins and modifies the spacing within the line to create even left and right edges

    KEYBOARD SHORTCUT Press Ctrl+J to justify a paragraph.

TIP If you know that you want to create a centered paragraph, you don't have to type the text and then align the paragraph. You can use the Click And Type feature to create appropriately aligned text. Move the pointer to the center of a blank area of the page, and when the pointer's shape changes to an I-beam with centered text attached, double-click to insert the cursor in a centered paragraph. Similarly, you can double-click at the left edge of the page to enter left-aligned text and at the right edge to enter right-aligned text.

You can align lines of text in different locations across the page by using tab stops. The easiest way to set tab stops is to use the horizontal ruler. By default, Word sets left-aligned tab stops every half inch (1.27 centimeters). To set a custom tab stop, start by clicking the Tab button located at the left end of the ruler until the type of tab stop you want appears.

The tab options.

You have the following options:

- **Left Tab** Aligns the left end of the text with the tab stop
- **Center Tab** Aligns the center of the text with the tab stop
- **Right Tab** Aligns the right end of the text with the tab stop
- **Decimal Tab** Aligns the decimal point in the text (usually a numeric value) with the tab stop
- **Bar Tab** Draws a vertical line at the position of the tab stop

After selecting the type of tab stop you want to set, simply click the ruler where you want the tab stop to be. Word then removes any default tab stops to the left of the one you set.

The ruler displays the custom tab stops for the selected paragraph.

To change the position of an existing custom tab stop, drag it to the left or right on the ruler. To delete a custom tab stop, drag it away from the ruler. Or, if you find it too difficult to "grab" the tab stops on the ruler, you can set, clear, align, and format tab stops from the Tab dialog box, which you open by clicking the Tabs button at the bottom of the Paragraph dialog box. You might also work from this dialog box if you want to use tab leaders—visible marks such as dots or dashes connecting the text before the tab with the text after it. For example, tab leaders are useful in a table of contents to carry the eye from the text to the page number.

To align the text to the right of the cursor with the next tab stop, press the Tab key. The text is then aligned on the tab stop according to its type. For example, if you set a center tab stop, pressing Tab moves the text so that its center is aligned with the tab stop.

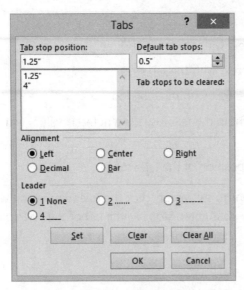

You can specify the alignment and tab leader for each tab.

To make it obvious where one paragraph ends and another begins, you can add space between them. There are several methods for adjusting paragraph spacing within a document:

- To set the spacing for all paragraphs in a document, choose from the **Paragraph Spacing** options in the **Document Formatting** group on the **Design** tab.

Each paragraph spacing option controls space around and within the paragraph.

- To set the spacing for only selected paragraphs, adjust the **Spacing Before** and **Spacing After** settings in the **Paragraph** group on the **Page Layout** tab.

- To make a quick adjustment to selected paragraphs, click the paragraph spacing commands on the **Line And Paragraph Spacing** menu that is available in the **Paragraph** group on the **Home** tab.

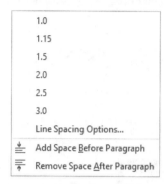

You can set internal line spacing or add or remove external space from this menu.

When you want to make several adjustments to the alignment, indentation, and spacing of selected paragraphs, it is sometimes quicker to use the Paragraph dialog box than to click buttons and drag markers. Clicking the Paragraph dialog box launcher on either the Home tab or the Page Layout tab opens the Paragraph dialog box.

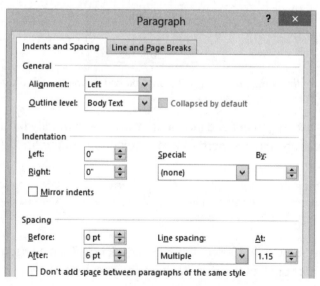

The Indents And Spacing page of the Paragraph dialog box.

You can do a lot with the options in the Paragraph dialog box, but to make a paragraph really stand out, you might want to put a border around it or shade its background. (For real drama, you can do both.) Clicking the Border arrow in the Paragraph group on the Home tab displays a menu of border options. You can select a predefined border from the Borders menu, or click Borders And Shading at the bottom of the menu to display the Borders And Shading dialog box, in which you can select the style, color, width, and location of the border.

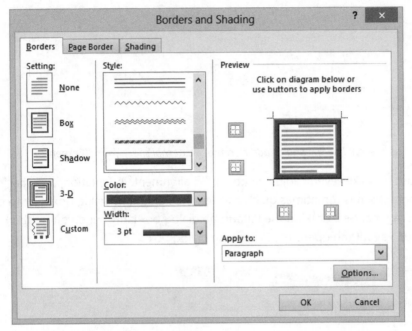

You can customize many aspects of the border. By clicking Options you can set the specific distance between the paragraph text and border.

In this exercise, you'll change text alignment and indentation, insert and modify tab stops, modify paragraph and line spacing, and add borders and shading to paragraphs.

SET UP You need the Cottage document located in the Chapter03 practice file folder to complete this exercise. Open the document, click the Show/Hide ¶ button to turn on the display of formatting marks, and then follow the steps.

1   On the **View** tab, in the **Show** group, select the **Ruler** check box. Then adjust the zoom level to display most or all of the paragraphs in the document.

TIP In the following steps, we give measurements in inches. If you're using a different measurement unit, you can substitute approximate measurements in those units. If you want to change the measurement units Word uses, display the Advanced page of the Word Options dialog box. Then in the Display area, click the units you want in the Show Measurements In Units Of list, and click OK.

First we'll modify the paragraph formatting.

2   Select the first two paragraphs (**Welcome!** and the next paragraph). Then on the **Home** tab, in the **Paragraph** group, click the **Center** button to center the lines between the margins.

TIP When applying paragraph formatting, you don't have to select the entire paragraph.

3   In the second paragraph, click to the left of **your**. Then on the **Page Layout** tab, in the **Page Setup** group, click the **Breaks** button, and click **Text Wrapping**. Notice that Word inserts a line break character and moves the part of the paragraph that follows that character to the next line.

The bent arrow after cottage indicates that you have inserted a line break.

SEE ALSO For information about page and section breaks, see "Controlling what appears on each page" in Chapter 6, "Preview, print, and distribute documents."

4   Click anywhere in the third paragraph, and then on the **Home** tab, in the **Paragraph** group, click the **Justify** button. Word inserts space between the words in the lines of the paragraph so that the edges of the paragraph are flush against both the left and right margins.

5   With the cursor still in the third paragraph, on the horizontal ruler, drag the **Left Indent** marker (the rectangle at the left margin) to the **0.5** inch mark. The **First Line Indent** and **Hanging Indent** markers (the triangles) move with the **Left Indent** marker.

6   At the right end of the ruler, drag the **Right Indent** marker (the triangle at the right margin) to the **6** inch mark. The paragraph is now indented a half inch in from each of the side margins.

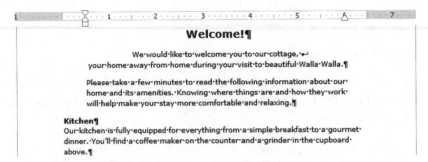

Left and right indents are often used to make paragraphs such as quotations stand out.

7   Click in the **Be careful** paragraph, and then in the **Paragraph** group, click the **Increase Indent** button.

Now we'll override the default tab stops.

8   Select the **Pillows**, **Blankets**, **Towels**, and **Dish towels** paragraphs. Ensure that the **Left Tab** marker is active at the top of the vertical ruler (if it's not, click the tab stop marker until the **Left Tab** stop appears), click the ruler at the **2** inch mark to insert a custom left-aligned tab at that location on the ruler and void the default tab stops prior to that location.

9   In the **Pillows** paragraph, click to the left of **There**, press **Backspace** to delete the space, and then press the **Tab** key to align the description with the tab stop. Repeat the process to insert tabs in each of the next three paragraphs. The part of each paragraph that follows the colon is now aligned at the 2-inch mark, producing more space than you need.

10   Select the four paragraphs containing tabs, and on the ruler, drag the custom **Left Tab** stop from the **2** inch mark to the **1.25** inch mark.

TROUBLESHOOTING If your attempts to drag the tab stop result in placing an additional tab stop on the ruler, drag the extra tab stop away from the ruler to delete it.

11   With the four paragraphs still selected, on the ruler, drag the **Hanging Indent** marker to the tab stop at the **1.25** inch mark (the **Left Indent** marker moves with it) to cause the second line of the paragraphs to start in the same location as the first line. Then press **Home** to release the selection so you can review the results.

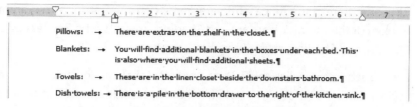

You can use hanging indents to create table-like effects.

12 At the bottom of the document, select the three paragraphs containing dollar amounts. At the top of the vertical ruler, click the **Tab** button three times to display the **Decimal Tab** button, and then click the ruler at the **3 inch** mark.

13 In each of the three paragraphs, replace the space to the left of the dollar sign with a tab to align the prices on the decimal points.

Next, we'll adjust the line spacing.

14 Select the **Pillows** paragraph, hold down the **Ctrl** key, and then select the **Blankets**, **Towels**, **Limousine winery tour**, and **In-home massage** paragraphs.

15 On the **Home** tab, in the **Paragraph** group, click the **Line and Paragraph Spacing** button, and then click **Remove Space After Paragraph**. Then press the **Home** key to review the results. Now only the last paragraphs of the two lists have extra space after them.

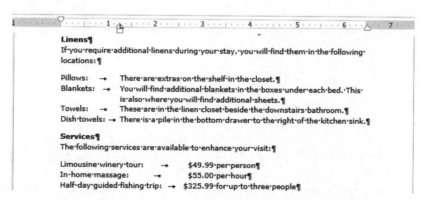

Removing space from between list paragraphs makes them easier to read.

And finally, we'll apply paragraph borders.

16 Move to the top of the document, and click anywhere in the **Please take a few minutes** paragraph. On the **Home** tab, in the **Paragraph** group, click the **Border** arrow, and then click **Outside Borders**.

17   Click anywhere in the **Be careful** paragraph, click the **Border** arrow, and then at the bottom of the list, click **Borders and Shading** to display the **Borders** page of the **Borders and Shading** dialog box.

18   In the **Setting** area, click the **3-D** icon to select that border style. Scroll through the **Style** list and click the fourth style from the bottom (the wide gradient border). Then click the **Color** arrow, and in the top row of the **Theme Colors** palette, click the **Red, Accent 2** swatch.

TIP If you want only one, two, or three sides of the selected paragraphs to have a border, click the buttons surrounding the image in the Preview area to remove the border from the other sides.

19   In the **Borders and Shading** dialog box, click the **Shading** tab.

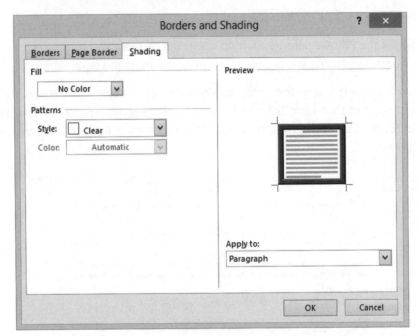

You can use the options on this page to format the background of the selected paragraph.

20   Click the **Fill** arrow, and then in the **Theme Colors** palette, click the lightest-colored square in the red column (**Red, Accent 2, Lighter 80%**). Then click **OK** to close the **Borders and Shading** dialog box. A border surrounds the paragraph, and a light red color fills its background. The border stretches all the way to the right margin.

21   To achieve a more balanced look, on the **Page Layout** tab (not the **Home** tab), in the **Paragraph** group, enter .5" in the **Right** box and press **Enter**. Then on the **Home** tab, in the **Paragraph** group, click the **Center** button. The paragraph is now centered between the page margins and within its surrounding box.

22   In the **Paragraph** group, click the **Show/Hide ¶** button to hide the formatting marks to better display the results of your work.

Welcome!

We would like to welcome you to our cottage,
your home away from home during your visit to beautiful Walla Walla.

Please take a few minutes to read the following information about our home and its amenities. Knowing where things are and how they work will help make your stay more comfortable and relaxing.

Kitchen
Our kitchen is fully equipped for everything from a simple breakfast to a gourmet dinner. You'll find a coffee maker on the counter and a grinder in the cupboard above.

Be careful when using the hot water—very hot!

Spill something on the glass cooktop? Please use the special cleaner under the sink to remove the spill before your next use.

Dining room
Our cozy dining room table expands into a round table that will seat eight. Just use the stools from the kitchen for those larger gatherings.

Den
The downstairs sitting area is a relaxing place to watch TV or a movie or listen to music after a day out. You'll find board games in the cupboard.

Linens
If you require additional linens during your stay, you will find them in the following locations:

Pillows:	There are extras on the shelf in the closet.
Blankets:	You will find additional blankets in the boxes under each bed. This is also where you will find additional sheets.
Towels:	These are in the linen closet beside the downstairs bathroom.
Dish towels:	There is a pile in the bottom drawer to the right of the kitchen sink.

Services
The following services are available to enhance your visit:

Limousine winery tour:	$49.99 per person
In-home massage:	$55.00 per hour
Half-day guided fishing trip:	$325.99 for up to three people

A combination of a border and shading really makes text stand out. Don't overdo it!

❌ CLEAN UP Close the Cottage document, saving your changes if you want to.

Finding and replacing formatting

In addition to searching for words and phrases in the Find And Replace dialog box, you can use the dialog box to search for a specific character format, paragraph format, or style, and replace it with a different one.

SEE ALSO For information about finding and replacing text, see "Finding and replacing text" in Chapter 2, "Enter, edit, and proofread text."

To search for a specific format and replace it with a different format:

1   On the **Home** tab, in the **Editing** group, click the **Replace** button to display the **Replace** tab of the **Find and Replace** dialog box, and then click **More** to expand the dialog box.

    KEYBOARD SHORTCUT Press Ctrl+H to display the Replace tab of the Find And Replace dialog box.

2   With the cursor in the **Find what** box, in the **Replace** section, click **Format**, and on the **Format** menu, click either **Font** to open the **Find Font** dialog box, **Paragraph** to open the **Find Paragraph** dialog box, or **Style** to open the **Find Style** dialog box.

3   In the dialog box, click the format or style you want to find, and then click **OK**.

4   Click in the **Replace With** text box, click **Format**, click **Font**, **Paragraph**, or **Style**, click the format or style you want to substitute for the original format or style, and then click **OK**.

5   Click **Find Next** to search for the first occurrence of the format or style, and then click **Replace** to replace that one occurrence or **Replace All** to replace every occurrence.

Creating and modifying lists

Lists are paragraphs that start with a character and are formatted with a hanging indent so that the characters stand out on the left end of each list item. Fortunately, Word takes care of the formatting of lists for you. You simply indicate the type of list you want to create. When the order of items is not important—for example, for a list of people or supplies—a bulleted list is the best choice. And when the order is important—for example, for the steps in a procedure—you will probably want to create a numbered list.

You can format an existing set of paragraphs as a list or create the list as you enter information into the document.

To format a new list item as you enter content, start the paragraph as follows:

- **Bulleted list** Enter * (an asterisk) at the beginning of a paragraph, and then press the **Spacebar** or the **Tab** key before entering the list item text.

- **Numbered list** Enter 1. (the number 1 followed by a period) at the beginning of a paragraph, and then press the **Spacebar** or the **Tab** key before entering the list item text.

When you start a list in this fashion, Word automatically formats it as a bulleted or numbered list. When you press Enter to start a new item, Word continues the formatting to the new paragraph. Typing items and pressing Enter adds subsequent bulleted or numbered items. To end the list, press Enter twice; or click the Bullets arrow or Numbering arrow in the Paragraph group on the Home tab, and then in the library, click None.

TIP If you want to start a paragraph with an asterisk or number but don't want to format the paragraph as a bulleted or numbered list, click the AutoCorrect Options button that appears after Word changes the formatting, and then in the list, click the appropriate Undo option. You can also click the Undo button on the Quick Access Toolbar.

If you want to create a list that has multiple levels, start off by creating the list in the usual way. Then when you want the next list item to be a level lower (indented more), press the Tab key at the beginning of that paragraph, before you enter the lower-level list item text. If you want the next list item to be a level higher (indented less), press Shift+Tab at the beginning of the paragraph. In the case of a bulleted list, Word changes the bullet character for each item level. In the case of a numbered list, Word changes the type of numbering used, based on a predefined numbering scheme.

If you create a set of paragraphs containing a series of items and then decide you want to turn the set into a list, you can select the paragraphs and then click the Bullets, Numbering, or Multilevel List button in the Paragraph group on the Home tab.

After you create a list, you can modify, format, and customize the list as follows:

- You can move items around in a list, insert new items, or delete unwanted items. If the list is numbered, Word automatically updates the numbers.

- You can modify the indentation of the list by dragging the indent markers on the horizontal ruler. You can change both the overall indentation of the list and the relationship of the first line to the other lines.

  SEE ALSO For information about paragraph indentation, see "Manually changing the look of paragraphs" earlier in this chapter.

- For a bulleted list, you can sort list items into ascending or descending order by clicking the **Sort** button in the **Paragraph** group on the **Home** tab.

- For a bulleted list, you can change the bullet symbol by clicking the **Bullets** arrow in the **Paragraph** group and making a selection from the **Bullets** gallery. You can also define a custom bullet (even a picture bullet) by clicking **Define New Bullet**.

- For a numbered list, you can change the number style by clicking the **Numbering** arrow in the **Paragraph** group and making a selection from the **Numbering** gallery. You can also define a custom style by clicking **Define New Number Format**.

- For a numbered list, you can start a list or part of a list at a predefined number by clicking **Set Numbering Value** in the **Numbering** gallery and then entering the number you want in the **Set Numbering** Value dialog box.

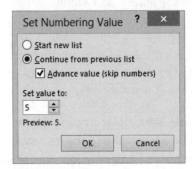

You can start or restart a numbered list at any number.

- For a multilevel list, you can change the numbering pattern or bullets by clicking the **Multilevel List** button in the **Paragraph** group and then clicking the pattern you want, or you can define a custom pattern by clicking **Define New Multilevel List**.

In this exercise, you'll create a bulleted list and a numbered list and then modify the lists in various ways.

SET UP You need the Association document located in the Chapter03 practice file folder to complete this exercise. Open the document, display formatting marks and rulers, and then follow the steps.

1 Select the first four paragraphs below **The rules fall into four categories**, and then on the **Home** tab, in the **Paragraph** group, click the **Bullets** button to format the selected paragraphs as a bulleted list.

2 With the paragraphs still selected, in the **Paragraph** group, click the **Bullets** arrow to display the **Bullets** menu.

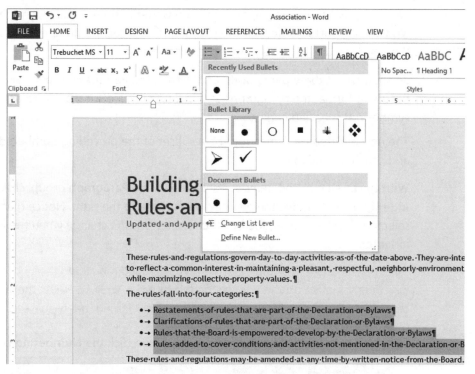

The Bullets menu offers several predefined bullet choices.

3   In the **Bullets** gallery, point to each bullet character under **Bullet Library** to display a live preview in the document, and then click the bullet composed of four diamonds to change the bullet character that begins each item in the selected list.

4   Select the two paragraphs below the **Definitions** heading, and then in the **Paragraph** group, click the **Numbering** button to number the selected paragraphs sequentially.

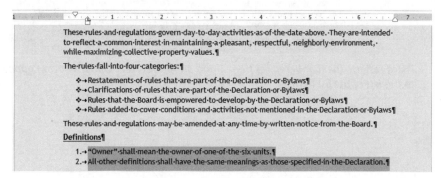

You can choose the bullet characters and numbering style that suit your document.

5   Select the first four paragraphs below the **General Rules** heading, and then click the **Numbering** button to format the paragraphs as a second numbered list. Notice that the new list starts with the number **1**.

6   Select the next three paragraphs, and then in the **Paragraph** group, click the **Bullets** button to format the paragraphs as a bulleted list. Notice that Word uses the bullet symbol you specified earlier.

The new bulleted list is meant to be a subset of the preceding numbered list item and should be indented.

7   With the three bulleted items still selected, in the **Paragraph** group, click the **Increase Indent** button to move the bulleted paragraphs to the right. Notice that because you selected a custom bullet, the bullet character doesn't change when the list items are indented.

TIP You can also adjust the indent level of a selected bulleted list by dragging the Left Indent marker on the ruler to the left or right. You can adjust the space between the bullets and their text by dragging only the Hanging Indent marker.

8   Select the remaining three paragraphs, and then click the **Numbering** button.

Word restarts the numbered list from 1 and an AutoCorrect Options button appears temporarily to the left of the list items.

You want the numbered list to continue the sequence of the previous numbered list.

9   Click the **AutoCorrect Options** button, and then click **Continue Numbering**.

> **TROUBLESHOOTING** If the AutoCorrect Options button disappears, right-click the number preceding the No Large Dogs list item, and then click Continue Numbering.

10 In the **No large dogs** numbered item, click to the left of **Seeing**, press **Enter**, and then press **Tab**. Notice that Word first creates a new number **6** item and renumbers all subsequent items. However, when you press **Tab** to make this a second-level item, Word changes the **6** to an **a**, indents the item, and restores the original numbers to the subsequent items.

11 Press the **End** key, and then press **Enter** to start a new list item. Enter The Board reserves the right to make exceptions to this rule.

12 Press **Enter**, and then press **Shift+Tab**. In the new first-level item, enter All pets must reside within their Owners' Apartments. Notice that the **General Rules** list is now organized hierarchically.

General·Rules¶
1.→Each·Apartment·shall·be·used·for·residential·purposes·only,·except·such·professional·and·administrative·businesses·as·may·be·permitted·by·ordinance,·provided·there·is·no·external·evidence·thereof.¶
2.→No·noxious·or·offensive·activity·shall·be·carried·on,·in,·or·upon·any·Apartment,·Limited·Common·Area,·or·Common·Area;·nor·shall·anything·be·done·therein·which·may·be·an·annoyance·or·nuisance·to·other·resident.¶
3.→No·sports,·activities,·or·games,·whether·organized·or·unorganized,·that·might·cause·damage·to·buildings,·grounds,·facilities,·structures,·or·vehicles,·or·that·are·an·annoyance·or·nuisance,·shall·be·played·in·any·Limited·Common·Area·or·Common·Area.¶
4.→No·Owner·shall·keep·any·animal·within·his·or·her·Apartment·for·any·purpose·other·than·as·a·pet.·The·number·of·cats·and/or·dogs·any·Owner·may·keep·is·limited·to·the·following:¶
❖→Two·small·dogs¶
❖→Two·cats¶
❖→One·cat·and·one·small·dog¶
5.→No·large·dogs·are·allowed,·either·as·pets·of·Owners·or·as·pets·of·visitors.·¶
a.→Seeing-eye·dogs·may·be·permitted·with·written·approval·of·the·Board.¶
b.→The·Board·reserves·the·right·to·make·exceptions·to·this·rule.¶
6.→All·pets·must·reside·within·their·Owners'·Apartments.¶
7.→Owners·may·keep·other·types·of·small·pets·that·are·confined·to·aquariums·or·cages.¶
8.→Pets·must·be·on·a·leash·when·in·the·Common·Area.¶

Word takes the work out of creating hierarchical lists.

13 Select the three bulleted paragraphs, and then in the **Paragraph** group, click the **Sort** button to open the **Sort Text** dialog box.

Formatting text as you type

The Word list capabilities are only one example of the program's ability to intuit how you want to format an element based on what you type. You can learn more about these and other AutoFormatting options by exploring the AutoCorrect dialog box, which you can open from the Proofing page of the Word Options dialog box.

The AutoFormat As You Type page shows the options Word implements by default, including bulleted and numbered lists.

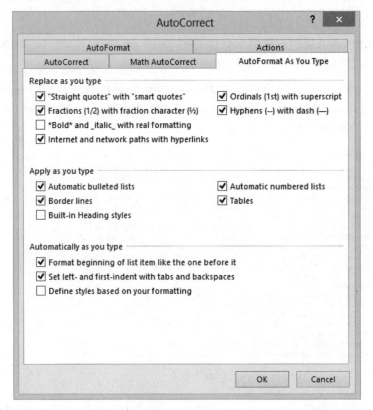

You can select and clear options to control automatic formatting behavior.

One interesting option in this dialog box is Border Lines. When this check box is selected, typing three consecutive hyphens (-) or three consecutive underscores (_) and pressing Enter draws a single line across the page. Typing three consecutive equal signs (=) draws a double line, and typing three consecutive tildes (~) draws a zigzag line.

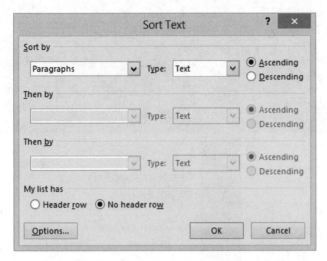

You can sort list items in ascending or descending order.

14   With the **Ascending** option selected, click **OK** to reorder the bulleted list items in ascending alphabetical order.

❌ CLEAN UP Close the Association document, saving your changes if you want to.

Key points

- Styles and style sets make it simple to apply combinations of character and paragraph formatting to give your documents structure and a professional look.

- The same document can look very different depending on the theme applied to it. Colors, fonts, and effects can be combined to create just the look you want.

- You can format characters with an almost limitless number of combinations of font, size, font style, and effect. For best results, resist the temptation to use more than a handful of combinations.

- You can change the look of paragraphs by varying their indentation, spacing, and alignment and by setting tab stops and applying borders and shading. Use these formatting options judiciously to create a balanced, uncluttered look.

- Bulleted and numbered lists are a great way to present information in an easy-to-read, easy-to-understand format. If the built-in bulleted and numbered formats don't provide what you need, you can define your own formats.

Chapter at a glance

Organize

Present information in columns,
page 140

you. Is it inviting? Does it feel comfortable? Does it relax you or does it invigorate you?

Focus on the room(s) you would most like to change. Brainstorm all the things you would change in that room if you could. Don't give a thought to any financial considerations; just let your imagination go wild! It might be helpful to write down all the negatives and positives. You don't need to come up with solutions all at once. Just be clear on what you like and what you hate about that room.

Visit our showroom and purchase a Room Planner. While you're there, take a look around and see what really appeals to you. Sometimes entire rooms

This is where the fun begins! Start changing things around a bit. Move the furniture, add different colors, and watch the room come together! Here's where you can tell if that rich red rug you saw in the showroom enhances or overwhelms your room. What about that overstuffed chair that caught your eye? Place a furniture or accessory shape, and then color it. Does it look great or is it too jarring? Change the color... does that help? Don't forget about the walls. Try different colors to see the effect on the room overall.

When you're sure you have the right look and feel, take a break. Put the planner away and sleep

planner for a little m tweaking. If you are sure, tak look around the store one m catches your eye. Then m your purchases. You're alm there!

NOTE: If you decided to pa your room, do that before y new pieces are delivered. Yc want to start enjoying your r room as soon as your purcha arrive.

After a few weeks, ask your whether the room is as grea you thought it would be. Doe achieve the look and feel v were after? You have 30 day fall in love with our furnit and accessories, so if you disappointed in any way,

Create

Create tabbed lists,
page 147

Consultation Fee Schedule

Location	Discount Applies	Hourly Rate
In home	No	$50.00
Phone	Yes	$35.00
In store	Yes	$40.00

In-Home Trip Charge

Distance	Fee
0-5 miles	No charge
6-10 miles	$5.50
11-20 miles	$7.00
21-50 miles	$10.00
Over 50 miles	$20.00

Present

Present information in tables,
page 149

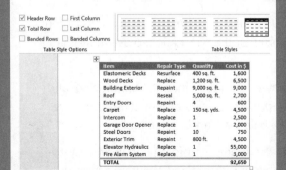

Format

Format tables,
page 161

☑ Header Row	☑ First Column
☑ Total Row	☐ Last Column
☐ Banded Rows	☐ Banded Columns

Table Style Options

Table Styles

Item	Repair Type	Quantity	Cost in $
Elastomeric Decks	Resurface	400 sq. ft.	1,600
Wood Decks	Replace	1,200 sq. ft.	6,500
Building Exterior	Repaint	9,000 sq. ft.	9,000
Roof	Reseal	5,000 sq. ft.	2,700
Entry Doors	Repaint	4	600
Carpet	Replace	150 sq. yds.	4,500
Intercom	Replace	1	2,500
Garage Door Opener	Replace	1	2,000
Steel Doors	Repaint	10	750
Exterior Trim	Repaint	800 ft.	4,500
Elevator Hydraulics	Replace	1	55,000
Fire Alarm System	Replace	1	3,000
TOTAL			**92,650**

Organize information in columns and tables

4

IN THIS CHAPTER, YOU WILL LEARN HOW TO

- Present information in columns.

- Create tabbed lists.

- Present information in tables.

- Format tables.

Information in documents is most commonly presented as paragraphs of text. To make a text-heavy document more legible, you can arrange the text in two or more columns, or you can display information in a table. For example, flowing text in multiple columns is a common practice in newsletters, flyers, and brochures; and presenting information in tables is common in reports.

When you need to present facts and figures in a document, using a table is often more efficient than describing the data in a paragraph, particularly when the data consists of numeric values. Tables make the data easier to read and understand. A small amount of data can be displayed in simple columns separated by tabs, which creates a *tabbed list*. A larger amount of data, or more complex data, is better presented in a table, which is a structure of rows and columns, frequently with row and column headings.

In this chapter, you'll first create and modify columns of text. Then you'll create a simple tabbed list. Finally, you'll create tables from scratch and from existing text, and format a table in various ways.

PRACTICE FILES To complete the exercises in this chapter, you need the practice files contained in the Chapter04 practice file folder. For more information, see "Download the practice files" in this book's Introduction.

Presenting information in columns

By default, Microsoft Word 2013 displays text in one column that spans the width of the page between the left and right margins. You can specify that text be displayed in two, three, or more columns to create layouts like those used in newspapers and magazines. When you format text to flow in columns, the text fills the first column on each page and then moves to the top of the next column. When all the columns on one page are full, the text moves to the next page. You can manually indicate where you want the text within each column to end.

> **IMPORTANT** Assistive devices such as screen readers do not always correctly process text that is arranged in columns. Consider the limitations of these devices if you intend for your document to meet accessibility requirements.

The Columns gallery in the Page Setup group on the Page Layout tab displays several standard options for dividing text into columns. You can choose one, two, or three columns of equal width or two columns of unequal width. If the standard options don't suit your needs, you can specify the number and width of columns. The number of columns is limited by the width and margins of the page. Each column must be at least a half inch (or 0.27 centimeter) wide.

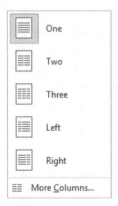

The Columns gallery displays the predefined column options.

No matter how you set up the columns initially, you can change the layout or column widths at any time.

You can format an entire document or a section of a document in columns. When you select a section of text and format it in columns, Word inserts *section breaks* at the beginning and end of the selected text to delineate the area in which the columnar formatting is applied. Within the columnar text, you can insert *column breaks* to specify where you want to end one column and start another. Section breaks and column breaks are visible when you display hidden formatting marks in the document.

SEE ALSO For information about formatting marks, see "Viewing documents in different ways" in Chapter 1, "Explore Microsoft Word 2013."

TIP You can format the content within a specific section of a document independently of other sections. For example, you can place a wide table in its own section and format the page orientation of that section as landscape to accommodate the wider table. For more information about sections, see "Controlling what appears on each page" in Chapter 6, "Preview, print, and distribute documents."

You apply character and paragraph formatting to columnar text in the same way you do to any other text. Here are some formatting tips for columnar text:

- When presenting text in columns, you can justify the paragraphs to give the page a clean and organized appearance.

  SEE ALSO For information about justifying paragraphs, see "Manually changing the look of paragraphs" in Chapter 3, "Modify the structure and appearance of text."

- To more completely fill columns with text and lessen the amount of white space within a line, you can have Word hyphenate the text and break longer words into syllables.

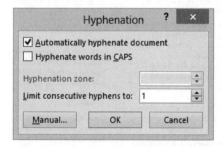

When hyphenating a document, you can specify whether you want to allow stacked hyphens at the ends of consecutive lines of a paragraph.

In this exercise, you'll lay out the text in one section of a document in columns. You'll justify and hyphenate the text in the columns, and change the column spacing. You'll then break a column at a specific location.

SET UP You need the RoomPlanner document located in the Chapter04 practice file folder to complete this exercise. Open the document, display formatting marks and the rulers, and then follow the steps.

1 Select the paragraphs that are between the empty paragraph marks—from the paragraph that begins with **Take a look** through the paragraph that ends with **credit cards**.

   TIP If you want to format an entire document with the same number of columns, you can simply click anywhere in the document—you don't have to select the text.

2 On the **Page Layout** tab, in the **Page Setup** group, click the **Columns** button, and then in the **Columns** gallery, click **Three** to flow the selected text into three columns.

3 Press **Ctrl+Home** to return to the top of the document. Notice that a section break precedes the columns.

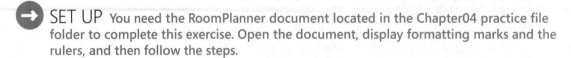

Simple·Room·Design¶

With·the·Room·Planner,·you'll·never·make·a·design·mistake·again.·Created·by·acclaimed·interior· designers·to·simplify·the·redecorating·process,·this·planning·tool·incorporates·elements·of·color,· dimension,·and·style·to·guide·your·project.·It·includes·a·furniture·location·guide;·room·grid;·drawing· tools;·and·miniature·furniture,·rugs,·accessories,·and·color·swatches·that·match·our·large·in·store· selection.·Here's·how·to·use·the·planner·to·create·the·room·of·your·dreams!¶

¶···Section·Break·(Continuous)···

Take·a·look·at·how·your· home·is·decorated·and·note· the·things·you·like·and· dislike.·Pay·special·attention· to·the·color·scheme·and·to· how·each·room·"feels"·to· you.·Is·it·inviting?·Does·it· feel·comfortable?·Does·it· relax·you·or·does·it· invigorate·you?¶

Focus·on·the·room(s)·you· would·most·like·to·change.· Brainstorm·all·the·things·you· would·change·in·that·room· if·you·could.·Don't·give·a· thought·to·any·financial· considerations;·just·let·your· imagination·go·wild!·It·might·

love,·and·the·rest·will·fall· into·place.¶

Take·your·Room·Planner· home·and·get·to·work!· Adjust·the·planner·so·that·it· models·the·room· dimensions.·Don't·forget·to· place·the·windows·and· doors.·Arrange·the·furniture· placeholders·to·mirror·how· your·room·is·currently·set· up.·Add·the·current·colors,· too.¶

This·is·where·the·fun·begins!· Start·changing·things·around· a·bit.·Move·the·furniture,· add·different·colors,·and·

design·for·a·day·or·two.· Then·review·it·again.·Does·it· still·look·perfect,·or·is· something·not·quite·right?· You·might·need·to·"live"· with·the·new·plan·for·a·few· days,·especially·if·you've· made·big·changes.·When· everything·feels·just·right·to· you,·you're·ready·for·the· next·big·step!¶

Come·back·to·the·store.· Look·again·at·the·pieces·you· liked·during·your·last·visit· and·see·if·you·still·love· them.·If·you're·not·quite· sure,·go·back·to·your· planner·for·a·little·more·

A continuous section break changes the formatting of the subsequent text but keeps it on the same page.

Now let's align the content with the column edges to make it easier to read.

4   Click at the beginning of the first paragraph after the heading (the paragraph that begins with **With the Room Planner**). Then press **Shift+Ctrl+End** to select the content from that point to the end of the document.

5   On the **Home** tab, in the **Paragraph** group, click the **Justify** button. Notice that Word adjusts the spacing between words to align all the paragraphs in the document with both the left and right margins.

KEYBOARD SHORTCUT Press Ctrl+J to justify paragraphs. For more information about keyboard shortcuts, see "Keyboard shortcuts" at the end of this book.

There is too much white space between the columns; let's widen the columns so more content fits within each.

6   Scroll through the document to display the section break and columns, and then click anywhere in the first column to display the column margins on the horizontal ruler.

On the ruler, the indent markers show the indentation of the active column.

TIP If the rulers aren't turned on, select the Ruler check box in the Show group on the View tab.

7   On the **Page Layout** tab, at the bottom of the **Columns** gallery, click **More Columns** to open the **Columns** dialog box. Notice that the spacing between columns is set to the default distance of a half inch.

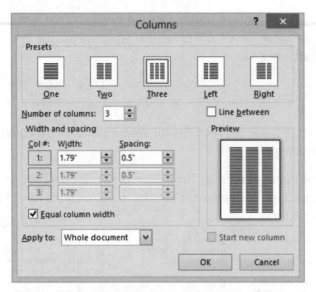

Because the Equal Column Width check box is selected, you can adjust the width and spacing of only the first column.

TIP To separate the columns with vertical lines, select the Line Between check box. If you need to fit a greater amount of content on a page, you can decrease the space between columns and insert a vertical line to more clearly denote the separation.

8   In the **Width and spacing** area, in the **Spacing** box for column **1**, enter or select **0.2"**. Notice that the **Spacing** measurement for column **2** also changes to **0.2"**, and the width of all three columns increases to **1.99"**. The columns in the **Preview** thumbnail reflect the new settings.

9   Click the **Apply to** arrow. Notice that you can choose to apply the change to the entire section, the entire document, or from the current cursor location to the end of the document.

10   In the **Apply to** box, click **This section**. Then click **OK** to apply the changes to the columns in the document.

Take a look at how your home is decorated and note the things you like and dislike. Pay special attention to the color scheme and to how each room "feels" to you. Is it inviting? Does it feel comfortable? Does it relax you or does it invigorate you?¶

Focus on the room(s) you would most like to change. Brainstorm all the things you would change in that room if you could. Don't give a thought to any financial considerations; just let your imagination go wild! It might be helpful to write down all the negatives and positives. You don't need to come up with

to place the windows and doors. Arrange the furniture placeholders to mirror how your room is currently set up. Add the current colors, too.¶

This is where the fun begins! Start changing things around a bit. Move the furniture, add different colors, and watch the room come together! Here's where you can tell if that rich red rug you saw in the showroom enhances or overwhelms your room. What about that overstuffed chair that caught your eye? Place a furniture or accessory shape, and then color it. Does it look

Come back to the store. Look again at the pieces you liked during your last visit and see if you still love them. If you're not quite sure, go back to your planner for a little more tweaking. If you are sure, take a look around the store one more time to see if anything else catches your eye. Then make your purchases. You're almost there!¶

NOTE: If you decided to paint your room, do that before your new pieces are delivered. You'll want to start enjoying your new room as soon as your purchases arrive.¶

Wider columns display more content and generally look neater on the page.

11 In the **Page Setup** group, click the **Hyphenation** button, and then click **Automatic** to hyphenate the text of the document.

Let's make the note stand out from the surrounding text.

12 In the third column, click anywhere in the **NOTE** paragraph.

13 On the horizontal ruler, drag the **Hanging Indent** marker for the third column one mark (0.125 in.) to the right to offset the note from the surrounding text by indenting all but the first line of the paragraph.

Take a look at how your home is decorated and note the things you like and dislike. Pay special attention to the color scheme and to how each room "feels" to you. Is it inviting? Does it feel comfortable? Does it relax you or does it invigorate you?¶

Focus on the room(s) you would most like to change. Brainstorm all the things you would change in that room if you could. Don't give a thought to any financial considerations; just let your imagination go wild! It might be helpful to write down all the negatives and positives. You don't need to come up with solutions all at once. Just be clear on what you like and what you hate about that room.¶

Visit our showroom and purchase a Room Planner. While

to place the windows and doors. Arrange the furniture placeholders to mirror how your room is currently set up. Add the current colors, too.¶

This is where the fun begins! Start changing things around a bit. Move the furniture, add different colors, and watch the room come together! Here's where you can tell if that rich red rug you saw in the showroom enhances or overwhelms your room. What about that overstuffed chair that caught your eye? Place a furniture or accessory shape, and then color it. Does it look great or is it too jarring? Change the color...does that help? Don't forget about the walls. Try different colors to see the effect on the room overall.¶

Come back to the store. Look again at the pieces you liked during your last visit and see if you still love them. If you're not quite sure, go back to your planner for a little more tweaking. If you are sure, take a look around the store one more time to see if anything else catches your eye. Then make your purchases. You're almost there!¶

NOTE: If you decided to paint your room, do that before your new pieces are delivered. You'll want to start enjoying your new room as soon as your purchases arrive.¶

After a few weeks, ask yourself whether the room is as great as you thought it would be. Does it achieve the look and feel you were after? You have 30 days to fall in love with our furniture

You can change the indentation of individual paragraphs within a column.

14 Scroll through the document to display the bottom of page **1**. In the first column on page **1**, click at the beginning of the **Take your Room Planner home** paragraph.

15 In the **Page Setup** group, click the **Breaks** button, and then click **Column** to insert a column break and move the text that follows to the top of the second column.

16 At the bottom of the third column on page **1**, click at the beginning of the **If you're not sure** paragraph, and then on the **Quick Access Toolbar**, click the **Repeat Insertion** button to insert another column break and move the text that follows to the top of the first column on page **2**.

KEYBOARD SHORTCUT Press Ctrl+Y to repeat the previous action.

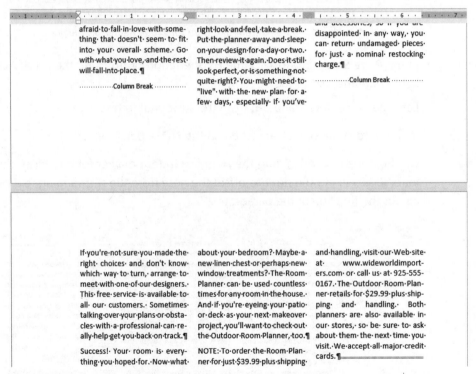

Consider manually breaking columns to even out the text at the end of a page.

❌ CLEAN UP Close the RoomPlanner document, saving your changes if you want to.

Creating tabbed lists

If you have a relatively small amount of data to present, you might choose to display it in a tabbed list, which arranges text in simple columns separated by tabs. You can align the text within the columns by using left, right, centered, or decimal tab stops.

SEE ALSO For more information about setting tab stops, see "Manually changing the look of paragraphs" in Chapter 3, "Modify the structure and appearance of text."

When entering text in a tabbed list, inexperienced Word users have a tendency to press the Tab key multiple times to align the columns of the list with the default tab stops. If you do this, you have no control over the column widths, and changing the text between two tabs might misalign the next section of text. To be able to fine-tune the columns, you need to set custom tab stops rather than relying on the default ones.

When setting up a tabbed list, enter the text and press Tab only once between the items that you want to appear in separate columns. Apply any necessary formatting so that you can accurately set the column width. Then set the custom tab stops. Set left, right, centered, and decimal tab stops to control the alignment of the column content, or set a bar tab to visually separate list columns with a vertical line. By setting the tabs in order from left to right, you can check the alignment of the text within each column as you go.

TIP It's more efficient to make all character and paragraph formatting changes to the text before setting tab stops. Otherwise, you might have to adjust the tab stops after applying the formatting.

In this exercise, you'll enter text separated by tabs, format the text, and then set custom tab stops to create a tabbed list.

➜ SET UP You need the ConsultationA document located in the Chapter04 practice file folder to complete this exercise. Open the document, display formatting marks and the rulers, and then follow the steps.

1   Press **Ctrl+End** to move the cursor to the blank line at the end of the document.

2   Enter Location, press **Tab**, enter Discount Applies, press **Tab**, enter Hourly Rate, and then press **Enter**.

3   Add three more lines to the list by typing the following text, pressing the **Tab** and **Enter** keys where indicated. The tab characters push the items to the next default tab stop, but because some items are longer than others, they do not line up.

In home **Tab No Tab** $50.00 **Enter**
Phone **Tab Yes Tab** $35.00 **Enter**
In store **Tab Yes Tab** $40.00 **Enter**

In a tabbed list, it's important to press the Tab key only one time between columns.

4   Select the first line of the tabbed list, and then on the **Mini Toolbar** that appears, click the **Bold** button to format the items as the column headings.

KEYBOARD SHORTCUT Press Ctrl+B to apply bold.

5   Select all four lines of the tabbed list, including the headings.

6   On the **Page Layout** tab, in the **Paragraph** group, in the **Indent** area, enter or select 0.5" in the **Left** box.

7   In the **Paragraph** group, in the **Spacing** area, enter or select 0 pt in the **After** box.

8   Click the **Tab** button at the top of the vertical ruler until the **Center Tab** button is active. (You will probably have to click only once.) Then click the **2.5** inch mark on the horizontal ruler to set a center-aligned tab stop and center the items in the second column of the tabbed list at that position.

9   Click the **Tab** button one time to activate the **Right Tab** button.

10   With the **Right Tab** button active, click the horizontal ruler at the **4.5** inch mark to set a right-aligned tab stop and right-align the items in the third column of the tabbed list at that position.

11   Press **Home** to move the cursor to the beginning of the tabbed list, and then hide the formatting marks to display the results. Notice that the tabbed list now resembles a simple table.

     KEYBOARD SHORTCUT Press Ctrl+* to toggle the display of formatting marks.

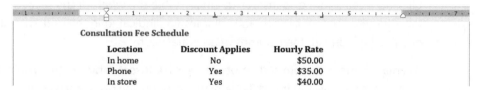

Consultation Fee Schedule

Location	Discount Applies	Hourly Rate
In home	No	$50.00
Phone	Yes	$35.00
In store	Yes	$40.00

You have created a simple table-like layout with just a few clicks.

✖ CLEAN UP Close the ConsultationA document, saving your changes if you want to.

Presenting information in tables

A table is a structure of vertical columns and horizontal rows. Each column and each row can be identified by a heading, although some tables have only column headings or only row headings. The box at the junction of each column and row is a *cell* in which you can store data (text or numeric information).

You can create tables in a Word document in the following ways:

- To create a blank table of up to 10 columns and eight rows, click **Table** on the **Insert** tab. This displays the **Insert Table** gallery and menu. The gallery is a simple grid that represents columns and rows of cells. Pointing to a cell in the grid outlines the cells that would be included in a table created by clicking that cell and displays a live preview of the prospective table.

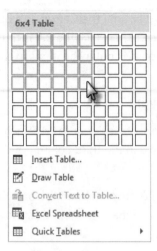

The intended table dimensions (expressed as columns x rows) are shown in the gallery header.

Clicking a cell in the grid inserts an empty table the width of the text column. The table has the number of rows and columns you indicated in the grid, with all the rows one line high and all the columns of an equal width.

- To create a more customized empty table, click **Insert Table** on the **Insert Table** menu. This displays the **Insert Table** dialog box, in which you can specify the number of columns and rows and the width of the table and its columns.

You can create a custom-width table from the Insert Table dialog box.

- To create a less clearly defined empty table, click **Draw Table** on the **Insert Table** menu. This displays a pencil with which you can draw cells directly in the Word document to create a table. The cells you draw connect by snapping to a grid, but you have some control over the size and spacing of the rows and columns. After drawing a base table, you can erase parts of it that you don't want and adjust the table, column, and row size by using tools on the **Layout** tool tab for tables.

You can draw a table directly on the page.

TIP When drawing a table, you can display the rulers or gridlines to help guide you in placing the lines. For more information about rulers, see "Viewing documents in different ways" in Chapter 1, "Explore Microsoft Word 2013." For information about controlling document gridlines, see "Arranging objects on the page" in Chapter 10, "Organize and arrange content."

IMPORTANT Assistive devices such as screen readers can usually access content in tables created by using the Insert Table command, but not in manually drawn tables. Consider the limitations of these devices if you intend for your document to meet accessibility requirements.

SEE ALSO For information about drawing tables, see "Using tables to control page layout" in Chapter 10, "Organize and arrange content."

- To present data that already exists in the document (either as regular text or as a tabbed list) as a table, select the data and then click **Convert Text to Table** on the **Insert Table** menu. (Conversely, you can convert the active table to regular text by clicking **Convert to Text** in the **Data** group on the **Layout** tool tab.)

- To create a table by entering data in a Microsoft Excel worksheet, click **Excel Spreadsheet** on the **Insert Table** menu. Enter the data you want in the spreadsheet that appears in the document—you can use Excel features such as functions and formulas to create or manipulate the data. Format the data in Excel as you want it to appear in Word. Then click in the document outside the spreadsheet window to insert a table-like snapshot of the data. You can modify the data by double-clicking the table and editing the content of the spreadsheet that opens.

IMPORTANT Inserting Excel spreadsheet content does not create a Word table, it creates only a snapshot of the Excel content. You cannot work with the content in Word or use any of the table tools we discuss in this chapter.

Tables appear in the document as a set of cells, usually delineated by borders or gridlines. (In some Quick Tables, borders and gridlines are turned off.) Each cell contains an end-of-cell marker, and each row ends with an end-of-row marker.

TROUBLESHOOTING Two separate elements in Word 2013 are named *gridlines*, and both can be used in association with tables. From the Show group on the View tab, you can display the *document gridlines* with which you can position content on the page. From the Table group on the Layout tool tab, you can display the *table gridlines* that define the cells of a table.

When you point to a table, a move handle appears in its upper-left corner and a size handle in its lower-right corner. When the cursor is in a table, two Table Tools tabs—Design and Layout—appear on the ribbon.

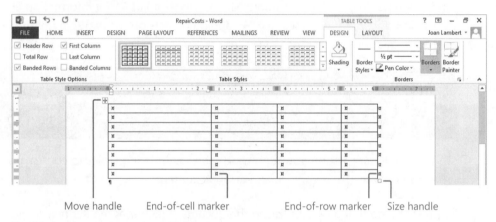

Move handle   End-of-cell marker   End-of-row marker   Size handle

A table has its own controls and tool tabs.

TIP The end-of-cell markers and end-of-row markers are identical in appearance, and are visible only when you display formatting marks in the document. The move handle and size handle appear only in Print Layout view and Web Layout view.

After you create a table in Word, you can enter data (such as text, numbers, or graphics) into the table cells. You can move and position the cursor by pressing the Tab key or the arrow keys, or by clicking in a table cell. Pressing the Tab key moves the cursor to the next cell; pressing Shift+Tab moves the cursor to the previous cell. Pressing Tab when the cursor is in the last cell of a row moves the cursor to the first cell of the next row. Pressing Tab when the cursor is in the last cell of the last row adds a new row to the table and moves the cursor to the first cell of that row.

You can modify a table's structure by changing the size of the table, changing the size of one or more columns or rows, or adding or removing rows, columns, or individual cells.

TIP To change a table's structure, you often need to select the entire table or a specific column or row. The simplest way to select an entire table is to point to or click in the table so that the move handle appears, and then click the move handle. To select a specific element, position the cursor in the table, column, or row, click the Select button in the Table group on the Layout tool tab, and then click the table element you want. Alternatively, you can point to the top edge of a column or left edge of a row and, when the pointer changes to an arrow, click to select the column or row.

The basic methods for manipulating a table or its contents are as follows:

- **Insert rows or columns** A new feature in Word 2013 makes it easier than ever to insert a single row or column in an existing table. Simply point to the left edge of the table where you want to insert a row, or to the top of the table where you want to insert a column. A gray insertion indicator labeled with a plus sign appears as you approach a possible insertion point (after any existing row or column). When the insertion indicator turns blue, click to insert the row or column where indicated.

Item	Repair Type	Quantity	Cost in $
Elastomeric Decks	Resurface	400 sq. ft.	1,600
Wood Decks	Replace	1,200 sq. ft.	6,500
Building Exterior	Repaint	9,000 sq. ft.	9,000
Roof	Reseal	5,000 sq. ft.	2,700
Entry Doors	Repaint	4	600
Carpet	Replace	150 sq. yds.	4,500
Intercom	Replace	1	2,500
Garage Door Opener	Replace	1	2,000
Steel Doors	Repaint	10	750
Exterior Trim	Repaint	800 ft.	4,500
Elevator Hydraulics	Replace	1	55,000
Fire Alarm System	Replace	1	3,000
TOTAL			92,650

Inserting a row or column now takes only one click.

To insert one or more rows or columns, select the same number of existing rows or columns adjacent to the location where you want to insert them. On the **Mini Toolbar** that appears, click **Insert** and then click **Insert Above**, **Insert Below**, **Insert Left**, or **Insert Right**. If the **Mini Toolbar** doesn't appear, on the **Layout** tool tab, in the **Rows & Columns** group, click the **Insert Above**, **Insert Below**, **Insert Left**, or **Insert Right** button.

- **Insert cells** To insert one or more cells in a table, select the number of cells you want to insert adjacent to the location where you want to insert them, click the **Rows & Columns** dialog box launcher to open the **Insert Cells** dialog box, and then specify the direction to move adjacent cells to accommodate the new cells.

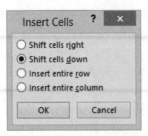

When inserting less than a full row or column you must specify the movement of the surrounding cells.

- **Delete table elements** Select one or more rows, columns, or cells. On the **Mini Toolbar** that appears, or in the **Rows & Columns** group, click **Delete**, and then click **Delete Cells**, **Delete Columns**, **Delete Rows**, or **Delete Table**.

Item	Repair Type	Quantity	Cost in $
Elastomeric Decks	Resur		
Wood Decks	Repla		
Building Exterior	Repai		
Roof	Resea		
Entry Doors	Repaint	4	600
Carpet	Replace	150 sq. yds.	4,500
Intercom	Replace	1	2,500
Garage Door Opener	Replace	1	2,000
Steel Doors	Repaint	10	750
Exterior Trim	Repaint	800 ft.	4,500
Elevator Hydraulics	Replace	1	55,000
Fire Alarm System	Replace	1	3,000
TOTAL			92,650

Calibri · 10 · A˄ A˅ ≔ · ⅗≣ · 田· 田· Insert Delete

- Delete Cells...
- Delete Columns
- Delete Rows
- Delete Table

You can now insert or delete table elements from the Mini Toolbar.

- **Resize an entire table** Point to the table, and then drag the size handle that appears in its lower-right corner. Hold down the **Shift** key while dragging the size handle to maintain the original aspect ratio of the table.

- **Resize a single column or row** Drag the right border of a column to the left or right to manually set the width, or double-click the border to adjust it to the narrowest width that fits its content. Drag the bottom border of a row up or down to manually set the height, or use the commands in the **Cell Size** group on the **Layout** tool tab to manage column width and row height.

- **Move a table** Point to the table, and then drag the move handle that appears in its upper-left corner to a new location, or use the **Cut** and **Paste** commands in the **Clipboard** group on the **Home** tab to move the table.

- **Merge cells** Create cells that span multiple columns or rows by selecting the cells you want to merge and clicking the **Merge Cells** button in the **Merge** group on the

Layout tool tab. For example, to center a title in the first row of a table, you can merge all the cells in the row to create one merged cell that spans the table's width.

- **Split cells** Divide one cell into multiple cells by clicking the **Split Cells** button in the **Merge** group on the **Layout** tool tab and then specifying the number of columns and rows into which you want to divide the cell.

- **Sort information** Click the **Sort** button in the **Data** group on the **Layout** tool tab to sort the rows in ascending or descending order by the data in any column. For example, in a table that has the column headings **Name**, **Address**, **ZIP Code**, and **Phone Number**, you can sort on any one of those columns to arrange the information in alphabetical or numerical order.

Performing calculations in tables

When you want to perform calculations with the numbers in a Word table, you can create a formula that uses a built-in mathematical function. You construct a formula by using the tools in the Formula dialog box, which you display by clicking the Formula button in the Data group on the Layout tool tab.

A formula consists of an equal sign (=), followed by a function name (such as SUM), followed by parentheses containing the location of the cells you want to use for the calculation. For example, the formula =SUM(Left) totals the cells to the left of the cell containing the formula.

To use a function other than SUM in the Formula dialog box, you click the function you want in the Paste Function list. You can use built-in functions to perform a number of calculations, including averaging (AVERAGE) a set of values, counting (COUNT) the number of values in a column or row, or finding the maximum (MAX) or minimum (MIN) value in a series of cells.

Although formulas commonly refer to the cells above or to the left of the active cell, you can also use the contents of specified cells or constant values in formulas. To use the contents of a cell, you enter the cell address in the parentheses following the function name. The cell address is a combination of the column letter and the row number—for example, A1 is the cell at the intersection of the first column and the first row. A series of cells in a row can be addressed as a range consisting of the first cell and the last cell separated by a colon, such as A1:D1. For example, the formula =SUM(A1:D1) totals the values in row 1 of columns A through D. A series of cells in a column can be addressed in the same way. For example, the formula =SUM(A1:A4) totals the values in column A of rows 1 through 4.

In this exercise, you'll work with two tables. First you'll create an empty table, modify the table layout, enter text in the table cells, and perform a calculation in the table by using a formula. Then you'll create a second table by converting an existing tabbed list, and modify the table to fit its contents.

➡ SET UP You need the ConsultationB document located in the Chapter04 practice file folder to complete this exercise. Open the document, display formatting marks and the rulers, and then follow the steps.

1 Click to the left of the second blank paragraph below **Please complete this form**. On the **Insert** tab, in the **Tables** group, click the **Table** button. Then in the **Insert Table** gallery, point to (don't click) the cell that is five columns to the right and five rows down from the top to preview the effect of creating the table in the document.

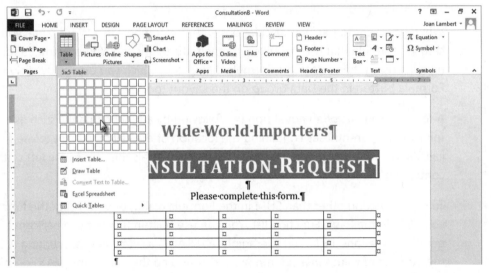

You can preview the table with the number of columns and rows you have specified.

2 Click the cell to create a blank table consisting of five columns and five rows, with the cursor located in the first cell. Because the table is active, Word displays the **Design** and **Layout** tool tabs.

3 In the selection area to the left of the table, point to the first row of the table, and then click once to select the five cells in the row. On the **Layout** tool tab, in the **Merge** group, click the **Merge Cells** button to combine the five cells into one cell.

4 With the merged cell selected, in the **Alignment** group, click the **Align Center** button. The end-of-cell marker moves to the exact center of the merged cell to indicate that its content will be centered both horizontally and vertically.

5   Click in the merged cell, and then enter Consultation Estimate. The table now
    appears to have a title.

Consultation Estimate¤					¤
¤	¤	¤	¤	¤	¤
¤	¤	¤	¤	¤	¤
¤	¤	¤	¤	¤	¤
¤	¤	¤	¤	¤	¤

Merged cells are often used for table titles and column headings.

6   Enter Type in the first cell in the second row, and then press **Tab**.

7   Enter Location, Consultant, Hourly Rate, and Total, pressing **Tab** after each entry
    to create a row of column headings. Pressing **Tab** after the **Total** heading moves the
    cursor to the first cell of the third row.

8   Select the column heading row, and then on the **Mini Toolbar**, click the **Bold** button.

9   In the third row, enter Window treatments, In home, Patrick Hines, $50.00, and
    $50.00, pressing **Tab** after each entry to enter a complete row of data.

    Now we'll merge some cells to create Subtotal and Total rows.

10 Select the last two rows of the table. On the **Mini Toolbar**, click the **Insert** button,
    and then click **Insert Below** to add two rows to the end of the table.

11 In the last row of the table, select the first four cells. On the **Layout** tool tab, in
    the **Merge** group, click the **Merge Cells** button to combine the selected cells
    into one cell.

12 In the merged cell, enter Subtotal. Then in the **Alignment** group, click the **Align
    Center Right** button to move the word to the right edge of the cell.

13 Press **Tab** twice to create a new row with the same formatting as the **Subtotal** row.

Consultation Estimate¤					¤
Type¤	**Location**¤	**Consultant**¤	**Hourly Rate**¤	**Total**¤	¤
Window treatments¤	In home¤	Patrick Hines¤	$50.00¤	$50.00¤	¤
¤	¤	¤	¤	¤	¤
¤	¤	¤	¤	¤	¤
¤	¤	¤	¤	¤	¤
Subtotal¤				¤	¤
				¤	¤

When you add a new row, it has the same format as the one it is based on.

4

14   Enter Add trip charge, press Tab two times, and then enter Total.

Next we'll have Word calculate the Subtotal.

15   Click in the cell to the right of **Subtotal**. On the **Layout** tool tab, in the **Data** group, click the **Formula** button to open the **Formula** dialog box, which already contains a simple formula for adding the amounts in the rows above the cell.

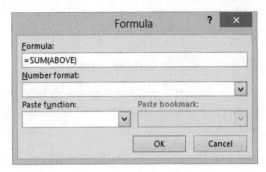

You can easily create a formula to calculate a value in a table.

16   In the **Formula** dialog box, click **OK** to enter the formula in the **Subtotal** cell and display the formula results, **$50.00**.

17   Click in the last cell of the table, and repeat the previous two steps to enter the same formula in the **Total** cell. When you click **OK**, notice that the formula result (**$50.00**) doesn't include the numbers that are included in the previous formula.

18   In the cell to the right of **Add trip charge**, enter **$10.00**. In the **Total** cell, right-click the formula results, and then click **Update Field** to recalculate the results. Hide formatting marks to display the results.

Consultation Estimate				
Type	**Location**	**Consultant**	**Hourly Rate**	**Total**
Window treatments	In home	Patrick Hines	$50.00	$50.00
			Subtotal	$50.00
			Add trip charge	$10.00
			Total	$60.00

You can enter mathematical formulas in even a simple table like this one.

Now we'll create a table by using a different method.

19   Scroll to the end of the document, and under the **In-Home Trip Charge** heading, select all the rows of the tabbed list beginning with **Distance** and ending with **$20.00**.

20 On the **Insert** tab, in the **Tables** group, click the **Table** button, and then click **Convert Text to Table** to open the **Convert Text to Table** dialog box, which already displays the number of columns and rows corresponding to the selected list.

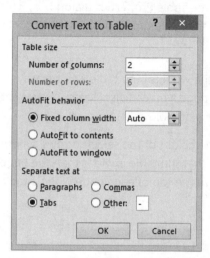

You can cleanly convert content that is separated by paragraph marks, tabs, commas, or any single character that you specify.

21 Verify that the **Number of columns** box displays **2**, and then click **OK** to reformat the tabbed list as a table with two columns and six rows.

22 Point to the top of the **Distance** column. When the pointer changes to a thick downward-pointing arrow, click and drag to the right to select the two columns.

23 Point to the right border of the table. When the pointer changes to two opposing arrows, double-click the border to resize the columns to fit their longest entries. Click away from the table to release the selection and display the results.

In-Home Trip Charge

Distance	Fee
0-5 miles	No charge
6-10 miles	$5.50
11-20 miles	$7.00
21-50 miles	$10.00
Over 50 miles	$20.00

It's simple to convert a tabbed list to a tidy table.

TIP You can also adjust the column width by changing the Table Column Width setting in the Cell Size group on the Layout tool tab.

❌ CLEAN UP Close the ConsultationB document, saving your changes if you want to.

Other table layout options

You can control many aspects of a table in the Table Properties dialog box, which you display by clicking the Properties button in the Table group on the Layout tool tab. You can set the following options:

- On the **Table** page, you can specify the width of the table and the way it interacts with the surrounding text. From this page, you can also access border and shading options, including the internal margins of table cells.

- On the **Row** page, you can specify the height of the selected rows, whether rows can break across pages (in the event that the table is wider than the page), and whether the header row is repeated at the top of each page when a table is longer than one page.

  TIP The Repeat As Header Row option applies to the entire table rather than the selected row. The option is available only when the cursor is in the top row of the table. Selecting this option helps readers of a document to more easily interpret data in multi-page tables. It also allows assistive devices such as screen readers to correctly interpret the table contents.

- On the **Column** page, you can set the width of each column.

- On the **Cell** page, you can set the width of selected cells and the vertical alignment of text within them. Click the **Options** button on this page to set the internal margins and text wrapping of individual cells.

- On the **Alt Text** page, you can enter text that describes what the table is about. Alt text may be displayed when a table can't be displayed on the page, or when the document is read aloud by an assistive device to a person who has a visual impairment. Including alt text or a table caption improves the accessibility of the table.

  TIP You can also control cell width, alignment, and margins by using the settings in the Cell Size and Alignment groups on the Layout tool tab.

Formatting tables

Manually formatting a table to best convey its data can be a process of trial and error. With Word 2013, you can quickly get started by applying one of the table styles available in the Table Styles gallery on the Design tool tab. The table styles include a variety of borders, colors, and other attributes that give the table a very professional appearance.

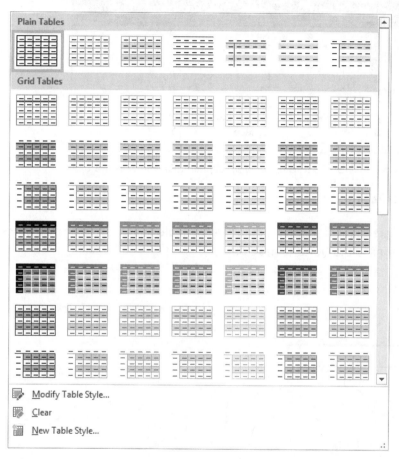

In Word 2013, the Table Styles gallery is divided into sections for plain tables, grid tables, and list tables.

If you want to control the appearance of a table more precisely, you can use the commands on the Design and Layout tool tabs to format the table elements. You can also separately format the table content. As you saw in the previous exercise, you can apply character formatting to the text in tables just as you would to regular text, by clicking buttons on the Mini Toolbar and in the Font, Paragraph, or Quick Styles groups on the Home tab.

Quick Tables

In addition to inserting empty tables, you can insert any of the available Quick Tables, which are predefined tables of formatted data that you can replace with your own information. Built-in Quick Tables include a variety of calendars and simple tables.

The Greek alphabet

Letter name	Uppercase	Lowercase	Letter name	Uppercase	Lowercase
Alpha	A	α	Nu	N	ν
Beta	B	β	Xi	Ξ	ξ
Gamma	Γ	γ	Omicron	O	o
Delta	Δ	δ	Pi	Π	π
Epsilon	E	ε	Rho	P	ρ
Zeta	Z	ζ	Sigma	Σ	σ
Eta	H	η	Tau	T	τ
Theta	Θ	θ	Upsilon	Y	υ
Iota	I	ι	Phi	Φ	φ

The Quick Tables gallery includes a selection of predefined tables such as this one.

To create a Quick Table:

1   On the **Insert** tab, in the **Tables** group, click the **Table** button, and then click **Quick Tables** to expand the **Quick Tables** gallery.

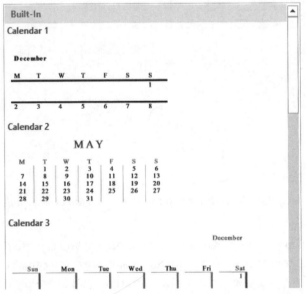

The predefined Quick Tables can be a convenient starting point.

2   Scroll through the gallery, noticing the types of tables that are available, and then click the one you want.

City or Town	Point A	Point B	Point C	Point D	Point E
Point A	—				
Point B	87	—			
Point C	64	56	—		
Point D	37	32	91	—	
Point E	93	35	54	43	—

By default, the Matrix Quick Table includes row and column headings, placeholder data, and no summary data, such as totals.

3   Modify content and apply formatting to tailor the **Quick Table** to your needs.

City or Town	Point A	Point B	Point C	Point D	Point E
Point A	—	87	64	37	93
Point B	87	—	56	32	35
Point C	64	56	—	91	54
Point D	37	32	91	—	43
Point E	93	35	54	43	—

You can easily customize a Quick Table.

You can also save a modified Quick Table, or any customized table, to the Quick Tables gallery. Saving a table saves both the table structure and the table content to the gallery. You can then easily insert an identical table into any document.

To save a table to the Quick Tables gallery:

1   Select the table by using the table selector or the commands in the **Table** group on the **Layout** tool tab.

2   On the **Insert** tab, in the **Tables** group, click the **Table** button, click **Quick Tables**, and then click **Save Selection to Quick Tables Gallery**.

3   In the **Create new Building Block** dialog box, assign a name to the table, and then click **OK**.

When you exit Word, save the Building Blocks template when Word prompts you to do so, to ensure that the table will be available in the Quick Tables gallery for future use.

SEE ALSO For information about building blocks, see "Inserting preformatted document parts" in Chapter 9, "Add visual elements."

In this exercise, you'll first apply a table style to a table. Then you'll format a table row and column. You'll also apply character and paragraph formatting to various cells so that the table's appearance helps the reader understand its data.

→ SET UP You need the RepairCosts document located in the Chapter04 practice file folder to complete this exercise. Open the document, hide formatting marks and the rulers, and then follow the steps.

1   Click anywhere in the table, and then on the **Design** tools tab, point to each thumbnail in the first row of the **Table Styles** gallery to display a live preview of the style.

2   In the **Table Style Options** group, select the **Header Row** and **Total Row** check boxes. In the **Table Styles** gallery, notice that the table style thumbnails change to reflect special formatting applied to the top and bottom rows.

3   In the **Table Styles** group, click the **More** button to expand the gallery of available table styles. Scroll through the gallery and preview styles that you like. Notice that the gallery is divided into three sections: **Plain Tables**, which have very little formatting; **Grid Tables**, which include vertical separators between columns; and **List Tables**, which don't include vertical column separators.

4   When you finish exploring, click the second thumbnail in the third row of the **List Tables** section (**List Table 3 – Accent 1**) to format the table to match the thumbnail. Notice that the selected thumbnail moves to the visible row of the **Table Style** gallery on the ribbon.

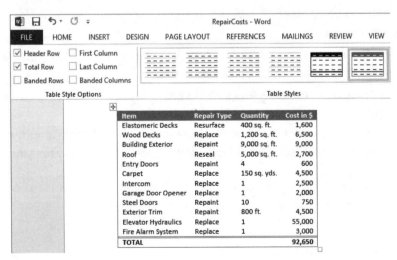

This table style applies formatting to the header and total rows and to the table text.

5 On the **Design** tool tab, select the **First Column** check box to change the formatting applied to the first column. With the selected table style, the text of the first column becomes bold. Let's make the first column content stand out even more.

6 Expand the **Table Styles** gallery and notice that the thumbnails now show special formatting applied to the first column. Point to various thumbnails to preview the styles on the table. Then click the second thumbnail in the fifth row of the **Grid Tables** section (**Grid Table 5 Dark - Accent 1**) to apply the style.

TIP If the first row of your table has several long headings that make it difficult to fit the table on one page, you can turn the headings sideways. Simply select the heading row and click the Text Direction button in the Alignment group on the Layout tool tab.

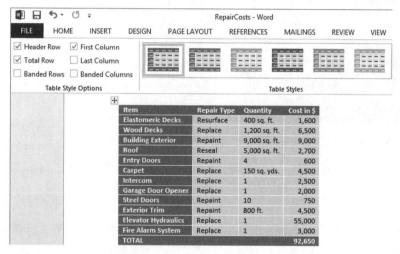

You can apply formatting to specific table elements by selecting them in the Table Style Options groups.

The new style emphasizes the first row but makes it difficult to delineate between the items and the Item column header. Let's make two changes to fix that.

7 Select the first and last rows of the table. On the **Design** tool tab, in the **Borders** group, click the **Line Weight** arrow, and then click **1 ½ pt** to select a thicker border.

8 In the Borders group, click the **Borders** arrow and click **Top Border**. Then click the **Borders** arrow and click **Bottom Border** to set off the header and total rows from the surrounding text.

9   In the table, select the list of items, from **Elastomeric Decks** through **Fire Alarm System** (select only the entries in the first column and not the associated information). In the **Table Styles** group, click the **Shading** arrow and then in the **Theme Colors** palette, click the third swatch under the currently selected color (**Blue, Accent 1, Lighter 40%**).

10   On the **Home** tab, in the **Font** group, click the **Font Color** arrow, and then click **Automatic**. In the **Font** group, click the **Bold** button. Then click away from the table to display the results.

Item	Repair Type	Quantity	Cost in $
Elastomeric Decks	Resurface	400 sq. ft.	1,600
Wood Decks	Replace	1,200 sq. ft.	6,500
Building Exterior	Repaint	9,000 sq. ft.	9,000
Roof	Reseal	5,000 sq. ft.	2,700
Entry Doors	Repaint	4	600
Carpet	Replace	150 sq. yds.	4,500
Intercom	Replace	1	2,500
Garage Door Opener	Replace	1	2,000
Steel Doors	Repaint	10	750
Exterior Trim	Repaint	800 ft.	4,500
Elevator Hydraulics	Replace	1	55,000
Fire Alarm System	Replace	1	3,000
TOTAL			92,650

You can customize aspects of a table style to meet your needs.

TIP If you will need to use this formatted table with different data in the future, you can save it as a Quick Table.

❌ CLEAN UP Close the RepairCosts document, saving your changes if you want to.

Key points

- To vary the layout of a document, you can divide text into columns. You can control the number of columns, the width of the columns, and the space between the columns.

- To clearly present a simple set of data, you can use tabs to create a tabbed list, with custom tab stops controlling the width and alignment of columns.

- You can create a table from scratch, or convert existing text to a table. You can control the size of the table and its individual structural elements.

- By using the built-in table styles, you can quickly apply professional-looking cell and character formatting to a table and its contents.

- You can enhance a table and its contents by applying text attributes, borders, and shading.

4

Chapter at a glance

Decorate

**Insert and modify pictures,
page 170**

Joan has worked in the training and certificatic
OTSI, Joan is responsible for guiding the transl
requirements into useful, relevant, and measu

Clip

**Insert screen clippings,
page 178**

Draw

**Draw and modify shapes,
page 180**

Add

**Add WordArt text,
page 185**

Take your Room Planner home and get to work! Adjust the planner so that it models the room dimensions. Don't forget to place the windows and doors. Arrange the furniture placeholders to mirror how your room is currently set up. Add the current colors, too.

This is where the fun begins! Start changing things around a bit. Move the furniture, add different colors, and watch the room come together! Here's where you can tell if that rich red rug you saw in the show-room enhances or overwhelms your room. What about that overstuffed chair that caught your eye? Place a furniture or accessory shape, and then color it. Does it look great or is it too jarring? Change the color... does that help? Don't forget about the walls. Try different colors to see the effect on the room overall.

When you're sure you have the right look and feel, take a break. Put the planner away and sleep on your design for a day or two. Then review it again. Does it still look perfect, or is something not quite right? You might need to "live" with the new plan for a few days, especially if you've made big changes. When everything feels just right to you, you're ready for the next big step!

Come back to the store. Look again at the pieces you liked during your last visit and see if you still love them. If you're not quite sure, go back to your planner for a little more tweaking. If you are sure, take a look around the store one more time to see if anything else catches your eye. Then make your purchases. You're almost there!

Add simple graphic elements

IN THIS CHAPTER, YOU WILL LEARN HOW TO

- Insert and modify pictures.
- Insert screen clippings.
- Draw and modify shapes.
- Add WordArt text.

Many documents that you create in Microsoft Word 2013 contain only text. Others might benefit from the addition of graphic elements to reinforce their concepts, to grab the reader's attention, or to make them more visually appealing. These graphic elements can include a wide variety of objects and effects, including:

- **Pictures** These objects are created outside of Word—photographs from digital cameras, clip art images, or files created by using a computer graphics program. No matter what the origin of the picture, you can change its size and its position in relation to other content after you insert it in the Word document. You can make additional changes to most types of pictures from within Word, such as cropping the picture or embellishing it by applying artistic effects.

- **Drawing objects** These objects are created within Word—text boxes, WordArt text, diagrams, charts, shapes, and other such objects. As with pictures, you can size, move, and format drawing objects from within Word.

  SEE ALSO For information about diagrams, see Chapter 7, "Insert and modify diagrams." For information about charts, see Chapter 8, "Insert and modify charts."

In this chapter, you'll first insert and modify pictures in a document. Then you'll insert screen clippings and shapes. Finally, you'll have a bit of fun with WordArt.

PRACTICE FILES To complete the exercises in this chapter, you need the practice files contained in the Chapter05 practice file folder. For more information, see "Download the practice files" in this book's Introduction.

Inserting and modifying pictures

You can insert digital photographs or pictures created in almost any program into a Word document. You specify the source of the picture you want to insert by clicking one of these two buttons, which are located in the Illustrations group on the Insert tab:

- **Pictures** Click this button to insert a picture that is saved as a file on your computer, on a network drive, or on a device (such as a digital camera) that is connected to your computer.

- **Online Pictures** Click this button to insert a royalty-free clip art image from Office.com, a web search result from Bing, or an image stored on your Microsoft SkyDrive or another online source.

  SEE ALSO For information about clip art, see the sidebar "About online pictures and video clips" later in this chapter.

After you insert a picture in a document, you can modify the image by using commands on the Format tool tab, which is displayed only when an object is selected.

The Format tool tab for pictures.

- The **Adjust** group contains commands that enable you to change the picture's brightness and contrast, recolor it, apply artistic effects to it, and compress it to reduce the size of the document containing it.

- The **Picture Styles** group offers a wide range of picture styles that you can apply to a picture to change its shape and orientation, as well as add borders and picture effects.

- The **Arrange** group contains commands for specifying the relationship of the picture to the page and to other elements on the page.

  SEE ALSO For information about using the commands in the Arrange group, see "Arranging objects on the page" in Chapter 10, "Organize and arrange content."

- You can use the commands in the **Size** group for cropping and resizing pictures.

In this exercise, you'll insert a couple of photographs and resize and crop them. You'll modify one of them and then copy the modifications to the other one. Then you'll insert an illustration and apply an artistic effect to it.

SET UP You need the Authors document, the Joan and Joyce photographs, and the OTSI-Logo image located in the Chapter05 practice file folder to complete this exercise. Open the Authors document, display the rulers, and then follow the steps.

1 Scroll through the document to the section with the heading **Joyce Cox**. Click to the left of the **Joyce has over 30 years' experience** paragraph, press the **Enter** key to create a blank paragraph, and then press the **Up Arrow** key to position the cursor in the new paragraph.

2 On the **Insert** tab, in the **Illustrations** group, click the **Pictures** button to display the **Insert Picture** dialog box. In the dialog box, navigate to the **Chapter05** practice file folder, and double-click the **Joyce** picture to insert the picture at the cursor. Notice that the picture is selected. Handles surround the picture, a **Layout Options** button appears to its right, and the **Format** tool tab appears on the ribbon.

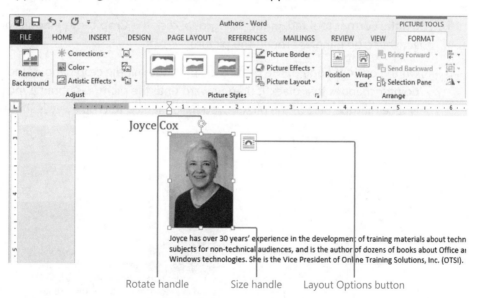

When you select a picture, the tools for managing it become active.

TROUBLESHOOTING If Word inserts a frame the size of the picture but displays only a sliver of the picture itself, the line spacing must be reset to accommodate the picture. To correct this problem, click the Paragraph dialog box launcher, and in the Paragraph dialog box, change the Line Spacing setting to Single.

TIP In this exercise, you insert pictures in blank paragraphs. By default, Word inserts pictures in line with text, meaning that Word increases the line spacing to accommodate the picture. If you were to enter text adjacent to the picture, the bottom of the picture would align with the bottom of the text on the same line. After you insert a picture, you can change its position and the way text wraps around it by using the options on the Layout Options menu or in the Arrange group on the Format tool tab.

SEE ALSO For more information about positioning objects and wrapping text around them, see "Adding WordArt text" later in this chapter and "Arranging objects on the page" in Chapter 10, "Organize and arrange content."

3   Point to the size handle in the lower-right corner of the picture. When the pointer changes to a double-headed arrow, drag up and to the left until the right side of the picture aligns with the **1.75** inch mark on the horizontal ruler. Because the aspect ratio of the picture is locked, the height and width change proportionally

TIP You can fine-tune the size of a graphic by adjusting the Shape Height and Shape Width settings in the Size group on the Format tool tab.

4   On the **Format** tool tab, in the **Size** group, click the **Crop** button (not its arrow) to activate crop handles around the picture.

5   On the bottom edge of the picture, point to the middle crop handle, and when the pointer changes to a black T, drag upward until the picture is about 1 inch high. Notice that the part of the picture you have marked to crop away is shaded.

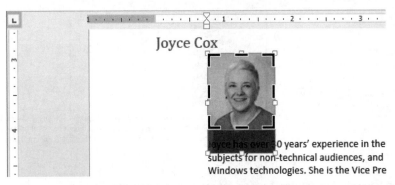

When you release the mouse, the text moves to indicate its position after the crop.

TIP You can check the new dimensions of the picture in the Size group on the Format tool tab before you commit to the crop.

6   Click away from the picture (or click the **Crop** button again) to complete the process.

TIP In addition to cropping a picture manually, you can click the Crop arrow and select from various options, including having Word crop a picture to fit a shape you select, cropping to a precise aspect ratio, filling an area with a picture, or fitting a picture to an area.

Now we'll insert and format a second picture.

7   Scroll through the document to the section with the heading **Joan Lambert**. Click to the left of the **Joan has worked** paragraph, press **Enter** to create a blank paragraph, and then press the **Up Arrow** key to position the cursor in the new paragraph.

8   On the **Insert** tab, in the **Illustrations** group, click the **Pictures** button and then, in the **Insert Picture** dialog box, double-click the **Joan** picture to insert it in the blank paragraph.

9   On the **Format** tool tab, in the **Size** group, enter or select **1"** in the **Shape Width** box.

10 Click the **Crop** arrow, click **Aspect Ratio**, and then click **1:1** to place a square set of crop handles in the center of the picture. Drag the picture down behind the crop handles so the entire head and shoulders are visible, and click the **Crop** button to complete the cropping process.

11 With the picture still selected, in the **Adjust** group, click the **Color** button to expand the gallery of color choices.

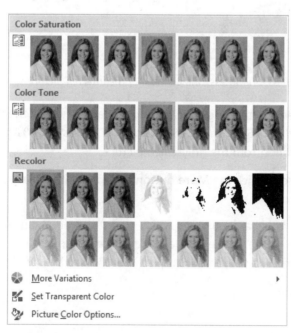

You can change the saturation and tone, as well as recolor the picture.

12   On the **Color** menu, below **Recolor**, click the second thumbnail in the first row (**Grayscale**) to convert the picture color to shades of gray.

13   In the **Adjust** group, click the **Corrections** button to display the picture correction options.

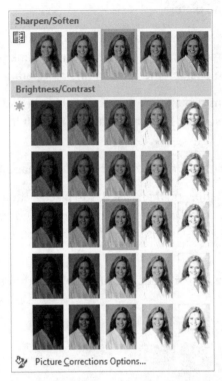

You can change the sharpness, brightness, and contrast of the inserted picture.

14   On the **Corrections** menu, in the **Brightness/Contrast** category, click the third thumbnail in the fourth row (**Brightness: 0% (Normal) Contrast: +20%**) to remove some of the gray overtones from the grayscaled picture.

15   In the **Picture Styles** group, click the **More** button to expand the gallery of available picture styles.

TIP To move a picture within a document, simply drag it to where you want it. To copy a picture, hold down the Ctrl key while you drag, releasing first the mouse button and then the Ctrl key. (If you release Ctrl first, Word will move the picture instead of copying it.)

You can apply frames, shadows, glows, and three-dimensional effects from the Picture Styles gallery.

5

16   Point to each thumbnail in the **Picture Styles** gallery to preview the effect on the selected picture (scroll down the page if necessary to display the picture and gallery at the same time). Notice that the relationship of the text to the picture changes depending on the style you select.

17   In the **Picture Styles** gallery, click the third thumbnail in the third row (**Center Shadow Rectangle**) and then click away from the picture to display the effect.

Joan Lambert

Joan has worked in the training and certification industry for over 15 years. As President of OTSI, Joan is responsible for guiding the translation of technical information and requirements into useful, relevant, and measurable training and certification tools.

This picture style gives the impression that the picture is indented from the left edge of the page.

18   Click the **Joan** picture to select it, and then on the horizontal ruler, drag the **Left Indent** marker to the left to align the picture with the paragraph that follows it.

19   With the **Joan** picture still selected, on the **Home** tab, in the **Clipboard** group, click the **Format Painter** button. Then click the **Joyce** picture to copy the grayscale format, color corrections, and picture style from one picture to the other.

Now we'll insert and format a third image.

20   Scroll through the document to the section with the heading **Online Training Solutions, Inc. (OTSI)**. Click to the left of the **OTSI specializes** paragraph, press **Enter**, and then press the **Up Arrow** key.

21   On the **Insert** tab, in the **Illustrations** group, click the **Pictures** button. Then in the **Insert Picture** dialog box, double-click the **OTSI-Logo** graphic.

22   With the logo selected, on the **Format** tool tab, in the **Adjust** group, click the **Artistic Effects** button.

23   In the **Artistic Effects** gallery, point to each thumbnail to preview its effect on the logo, and then click the third thumbnail in the first row (**Pencil Grayscale**). Click away from the picture to display the logo's new hand-drawn effect.

Joyce Cox

Joyce has over 30 years' experience in the development of training materials about technical subjects for non-technical audiences, and is the author of dozens of books about Office and Windows technologies. She is the Vice President of Online Training Solutions, Inc. (OTSI).

As President of and principal author for Online Press, she developed the Quick Course series of computer training books for beginning and intermediate adult learners. She was also the first managing editor of Microsoft Press, an editor for Sybex, and an editor for the University of California.

Online Training Solutions, Inc. (OTSI)

You can use artistic effects to make pictures look like paintings, sketches, cutouts, and more.

❌ CLEAN UP Close the Authors document, saving your changes if you want to.

About online pictures and video clips

Clicking the Online Pictures button in the Illustration group on the Insert tab displays the Insert Pictures window. From this window you can search for a royalty-free clip art image on the Microsoft Office website, search for a published image on the Internet by using Bing Image Search, or browse your SkyDrive for an image.

If you want to dress up a document with a graphic but you don't have a suitable picture, you can use any of the clip art images available from the Microsoft Office website without requesting permission from the clip art creator. Clip art available from Office.com includes illustrations and photographs that are free to use and available without any copyright restrictions.

Using Bing Image Search returns images that are published on the Internet but that might be otherwise copyrighted. If you want to use one of these images in any public way, you must check the copyright information associated with the image.

If you want to insert a video clip (more likely in a Microsoft PowerPoint presentation but also possible in a document), click Online Video in the Media group on the Insert tab to open a Bing Video Search window. Entering a search term in this window returns matching videos that have been posted on the Internet. As with the Bing Image Search results, these are not necessarily copyright-free.

When you search any of these sources, results matching your search term are displayed in the window. You can point to an image or video clip and click the View Larger button to display a larger version.

When you view a larger version of a video clip, a Play button appears on the image; you can click the Play button to play the entire video (including any associated audio) in the window. Click an image or video clip to select it for insertion; to select multiple images or video clips, hold down the Ctrl or Shift key and select the other items you want. Then click the Insert button to insert the selected item or items in your document.

TIP If you already know the web address (embed code) of the video you want to insert—for example, if you want to insert a video that you previously posted on YouTube, you can enter the embed code for the video in the Insert Video window.

After you insert an image or video clip, you can format its appearance by using the tools on the Format tool tab for pictures.

Inserting screen clippings

These days, many people rely on the Internet as a source of the information they use in their daily lives. Sometimes that information is presented in a graphic that would be useful in a Word document. Word 2013 includes a screen clipping tool that you can use to capture an image of anything that is visible on your computer screen. You simply display the content you want to include in a document, open the document, and click the Screenshot button in the Illustrations group on the Insert tab. You can then insert a screen clipping in one of two ways:

- Clicking a window thumbnail in the **Screenshot** gallery inserts a picture of that window into the document at the cursor.

- Clicking **Screen Clipping** below the gallery enables you to drag across the part of the screen you want to capture, so that only that part is inserted as a picture into the document.

In this exercise, you'll insert a screen clipping from a website into a document.

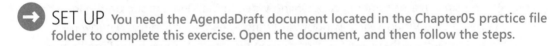 SET UP You need the AgendaDraft document located in the Chapter05 practice file folder to complete this exercise. Open the document, and then follow the steps.

1   Press **Ctrl+End** to move to the end of the document, below the **Directions to the Bellevue Library** heading. Then minimize the program window.

2   Start your web browser, and display a website from which you want to capture a screen clipping. For this example, we used a map showing the location of a public library. You might want to display a map of the location of your office or a local landmark.

3   When the content you want to capture is displayed in your web browser, switch to the **AgendaDraft** document. Then on the **Insert** tab, in the **Illustrations** group, click the **Screenshot** button. On the **Screenshot** menu, the **Available Windows** gallery displays currently open windows.

Available Windows

Screen Clipping

You can capture and insert a screen shot of an open window by clicking it in the gallery.

4   On the **Screenshot** menu, click **Screen Clipping** to minimize the program window and apply a translucent white layer over the entire screen.

TIP If you change your mind about capturing the screen clipping, press the Esc key to remove the white layer.

5   Drag to select the area of the webpage you want. When you release the mouse button, Word inserts the screen clipping into the document at the cursor.

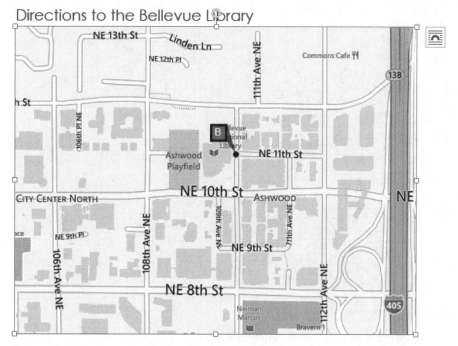

Directions to the Bellevue Library

You can format the screen clipping just as you would any other picture.

CLEAN UP Close the AgendaDraft document, saving your changes if you want to.

Drawing and modifying shapes

If you want to add visual interest and impact to a document but you don't need anything as fancy as a picture or a clip art image, you can draw a shape. Shapes can be simple, such as lines, circles, or squares; or more complex, such as stars, hearts, and arrows.

To draw a shape directly on the page (Word's default setting), you click the Shapes button in the Illustrations group on the Insert tab, and then click the shape you want.

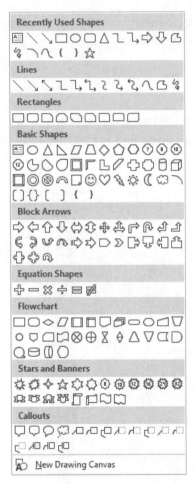

The Shapes menu includes a wide variety of shapes.

After selecting the shape you want, you can do one of the following:

- Click the document to insert the selected shape at the default size and aspect ratio.

- Drag across the page to create a drawing the size and shape you want.

When you finish drawing the shape, it is automatically selected. Later, you can select the shape by clicking it. While the shape is selected, you can move and size it, and you can modify it by using commands on the Format tool tab to do the following:

- Change the shape to a different shape.

- Change the style, fill color, outline, and effects assigned to the shape, including the three-dimensional aspect, or perspective, from which you are observing the shape.

  TIP If you change the attributes of a shape—for example, its fill color and border weight—and you want all the shapes you draw from now on in the same document to have those attributes, right-click the shape, and then click Set As Default Shape.

- Specify the position of the shape on the page, and the way text wraps around the shape.

  TIP You can manually position a shape by dragging it, or you can select it and press the arrow keys on your keyboard to move the shape in small increments.

- Control the order of the shape in a stack of shapes.

- Specify the shape's alignment and angle of rotation.

- Precisely control the size of the shape.

  TIP You can manually change the size and shape of an object by dragging its handles.

You can right-click a shape and click Add Text to place a cursor in the center of the shape. After you enter the text, you can format it with the commands in the WordArt Styles group and control its direction and alignment with the commands in the Text group.

If you build a picture by drawing individual shapes, you can group them so that they act as one object. If you move or size a grouped object, the shapes retain their positions in relation to each other. To break the bond, you ungroup the object.

5

If your picture consists of more than a few shapes, you might want to draw the shapes on a drawing canvas instead of directly on the page. The drawing canvas keeps the parts of the picture together, helps you position the picture, and provides a framelike boundary between your picture and the text on the page. To open a drawing canvas, you click New Drawing Canvas at the bottom of the Shapes menu. You can then draw shapes on the canvas in the usual ways. At any time, you can size and move the drawing canvas and the shapes on it as one unit.

TIP If you prefer to always use the drawing canvas when creating pictures with shapes, display the Backstage view, click Options, and in the Word Options dialog box, click Advanced. Then in the Editing Options area, select the Automatically Create Drawing Canvas When Inserting AutoShapes check box, and click OK.

In this exercise, you'll draw two shapes and a text box on a drawing canvas to create a logo. Next, you'll change the style of the shapes and the color of the text box. Then you'll move and resize the canvas.

 SET UP You don't need any practice files to complete this exercise. Open a blank document, display the rulers, and then follow the steps.

1   On the **Insert** tab, in the **Illustrations** group, click the **Shapes** button. At the bottom of the **Shapes** menu, click **New Drawing Canvas** to insert a drawing canvas and display the **Format** tool tab for drawings.

2   On the **Format** tool tab, in the **Insert Shapes** group, click the **Shapes** button, and then in the **Block Arrows** category, click the first shape in the second row (**Curved Right Arrow**).

3   Point to the upper-left corner of the drawing canvas, and then drag down and to the right to draw an arrow about 1.5 inches tall and 1.5 inches wide. When you finish drawing, the arrow is selected, as indicated by the handles around it.

   TIP To draw a shape with equal height and width, such as a square or circle, hold down the Shift key while you drag, and then release the mouse button before releasing the Shift key.

4   In the **Size** group, set the **Height** and **Width** to precisely **1.5"**.

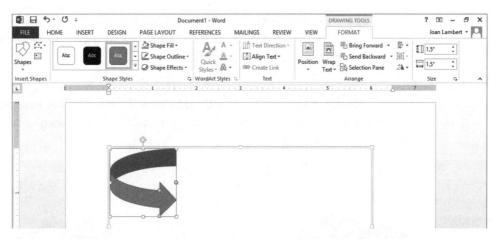

You can drag handles to rotate the arrow, change its size, and change its shape.

5   Hold down the **Ctrl** key and drag the arrow shape to the upper-right corner of the
    drawing canvas. First release the mouse button and then release the **Ctrl** key to
    create a copy of the arrow shape.

6   In the **Arrange** group, click the **Rotate Objects** button, and then click **Flip Horizontal**
    to rotate the copy of the arrow so that it points to the left.

7   In the **Insert Shapes** group, click the **Draw Text Box** button, and drag to draw a text
    box between the arrows. In the text box, enter What goes around comes around.

    Now we'll group the shapes together and apply formatting to the group and its indi-
    vidual elements.

8   With the text box still selected, hold down the **Shift** key, and then click the left arrow
    and the right arrow to select all three shapes. Handles around each shape indicate
    that they are all selected individually.

9   In the **Arrange** group, click the **Group Objects** button, and then click **Group** to group
    the three shapes as one object.

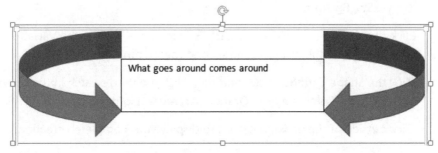

One set of handles appears around a grouped object.

10   In the **Shape Styles** group, click the **More** button to expand the **Shape Styles** gallery, and then click the third thumbnail in the last row (**Intense Effect – Orange, Accent 2**) to apply the style to all the grouped shapes.

11   Select the text in the text box. Use the commands on the **Home** tab, in the **Font** group, to format the text as **18-point Bold Comic Sans MS**. In the **Paragraph** group, click the **Center** button. Then click the page outside of the drawing canvas to release the selection and display the results.

> **KEYBOARD SHORTCUT** Press Ctrl+E to center the paragraph. For more information about keyboard shortcuts, see "Keyboard shortcuts" at the end of this book.

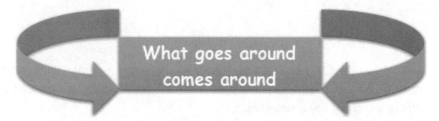

You can format a grouped object as a whole, or format individual shapes within the object.

12   Click the shape to select it. On the **Format** tool tab, in the **Size** group, click the **Width** down arrow until the drawing canvas is as narrow as it can be without the text wrapping to a third line.

13   Point to the sizing handle in the middle of the bottom border of the drawing canvas frame, and drag upward until the drawing canvas is just tall enough to contain the grouped shape.

14   Drag the sizing handle in the middle of the right border of the drawing canvas to the left until the drawing canvas is just wide enough to contain the grouped shape.

15   With the drawing canvas selected, in the **Shape Styles** group, click the **Shape Fill** arrow, and then click the third swatch in the top row of the **Theme Colors** palette, (**Gray-25%, Background 2**).

16   Click the **Shape Fill** arrow again, click **Gradient**, and then in the **Variations** category, click the second thumbnail in the second row (**From Center**).

17   Click the **Shape Outline** arrow, and then click the third swatch in the orange column of the **Theme Colors** palette (**Orange, Accent 2, Lighter 60%**).

18   Click outside of the drawing canvas to display your completed creation.

You can format the drawing canvas or leave it blank.

TIP If you were creating this object in the context of a document that contained text, you would now use the commands in the Arrange group to position and wrap text around the shape. For information about text wrapping, see "Arranging objects on the page" in Chapter 10, "Organize and arrange content."

✖ CLEAN UP Close the document, saving it if you want to.

Adding WordArt text

WordArt provides a method for applying a series of effects to text with one click. The 15 default WordArt styles included with Word 2013 combine outlines, fills, shadows, reflections, glow effects, beveled edges, and three-dimensional rotation to create text that really gets your attention. You can apply a default WordArt style, modify the effects of that style, or build a combination of effects from scratch.

WordArt differs from simple formatting in that text formatted as WordArt becomes an object that you can position anywhere on a page. Although the WordArt object is attached to the paragraph that contained the cursor when you created it, you can move it independently of the text, even positioning it in front of the text if you want.

To convert existing text into WordArt, select the text, click the Insert WordArt button in the Text group on the Insert tab, and then click a text style in the WordArt gallery. (The WordArt text styles are the same as the text effects available in the Text Effects gallery in the Font group on the Home tab.).

To insert a new WordArt object, click the Insert WordArt button, click the text style you want, and then enter your text in the text box that appears. You can edit the text, adjust the character formatting in the usual ways, and change the text style of a WordArt object at any time.

SEE ALSO For information about character formatting, see "Manually changing the look of characters" in Chapter 3, "Modify the structure and appearance of text." For information about text effects, see "Applying styles to text" in the same chapter.

When a WordArt object is selected, the Format tool tab appears on the ribbon. You can use the commands on this tab to further format the WordArt object. For example, you can add effects such as shadows and depth to create a three-dimensional appearance, change the fill and outline colors, and change the text direction and alignment. You can also position the WordArt object in any of several predefined locations on the page, as well as specify how other text should wrap around the object.

TIP Don't go too wild with WordArt formatting. Many WordArt styles and text effects require quite a bit of trial and error to produce a tidy effect.

In this exercise, you'll insert a new WordArt object, modify it, and then position it on the page. Then you'll change the way it relates to the text on the page.

➡ SET UP You need the Announcement document located in the Chapter05 practice file folder to complete this exercise. Open the document, and then follow the steps.

1   On the **Insert** tab, in the **Text** group, click the **Insert WordArt** button, and in the gallery, click the last thumbnail in the second row (**Fill – Olive Green, Accent 3, Sharp Bevel**) to insert a generic WordArt object with that text effect at the cursor.

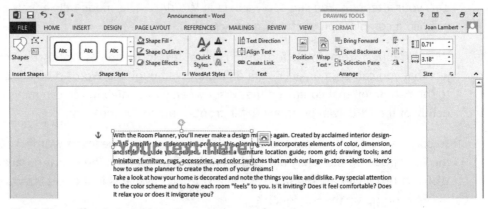

The full text effect isn't visible until you click away from the text.

TIP The object anchor and Layout Options button are visible whenever a WordArt object is selected. You can ignore them for now.

SEE ALSO For information about anchoring objects, see "Arranging objects on the page" in Chapter 10, "Organize and arrange content."

2   Select **Your text here**, and then enter The Room Planner.

TIP WordArt objects can accommodate multiple lines. Simply press Enter if you want to start a new line.

3   Click the border of the WordArt object to select it, and then change the zoom level to display the whole page in the program window.

4   On the **Format** tool tab, in the **Arrange** group, click the **Position** button to display the available text wrapping options.

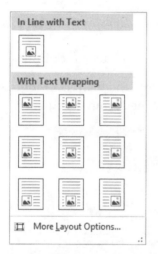

You control the position of the WordArt object in relation to the surrounding text.

5   Point to each thumbnail in turn to preview where that option will place the WordArt object. Then in the **With Text Wrapping** area, click the second thumbnail in the second row (**Position in Middle Center with Square Text Wrapping**) to move the WordArt object to that location on the page.

6   In the **Arrange** group, click the **Wrap Text** button to display the **Wrap Text** menu.

You can control the text wrapping independently of the position of the WordArt object.

7   Point to each option in turn to preview its effects, and then click **Tight**.

8   In the **Arrange** group, click the **Wrap Text** button, and then click **More Layout Options** to display the **Text Wrapping** page of the **Layout** dialog box.

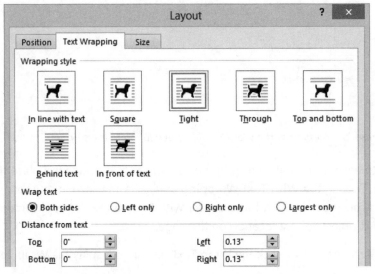

If you know what kind of text wrapping you want, you can select it on this page of the dialog box, but you can't preview it.

9   In the **Distance from text** area, change the **Left** and **Right** settings to **0.3"**, and then click **OK**. The text outside the box is no longer encroaching on the box.

10   On the **Format** tool tab, in the **Shape Styles** group, click the **More** button to expand the **Shape Styles** gallery. Then click the fourth thumbnail in the fourth row (**Subtle Effect – Olive Green, Accent 3**).

11   Press **Ctrl+Home** to display the formatted WordArt object.

This simple text banner is a stylish alternative to a traditional title.

12   If you want, experiment with combinations of the styles and formatting available on the **Format** tab. For example, you might want to try some of the **Text Effects** options, such as the path and warp effects available in the **Transform** gallery.

CLEAN UP Close the Announcement document, saving your changes if you want to.

Formatting the first letter of a paragraph as a drop cap

Many books, magazines, and reports begin the first paragraph of a section or chapter by using an enlarged, decorative capital letter. Called a dropped capital, or simply a *drop cap*, this effect can be an easy way to give a document a finished, professional look.

When you format a paragraph to start with a drop cap, Word inserts the first letter of the paragraph in a text box and formats its height and font in accordance with the Drop Cap options.

With the Room Planner, you'll never make a design mistake again. Created by acclaimed interior designers to simplify the redecorating process, this planning tool incorporates elements of color, dimension, and style to guide your project. It includes a furniture location guide; room grid; drawing tools; and miniature furniture, rugs, accessories, and color swatches that match our large in-store selection. Here's how to use the planner to create the room of your dreams!

By default, the letter is the same font face as the rest of the paragraph and the height of three lines of text.

Word 2013 has two basic drop-cap styles:

- **Dropped** The letter is embedded in the original paragraph.

- **In margin** The letter occupies its own column, and the remaining paragraph text is moved to the right.

To format the first letter of a paragraph as a drop cap:

1   Click anywhere in the paragraph.
2   On the **Insert** tab, in the **Text** group, click the **Add a Drop Cap** button and then click the drop cap style you want to apply.

To change the font, height, or distance between the drop cap and the paragraph text, click Drop Cap Options on the Drop Cap menu, and then format the options in the Drop Cap dialog box.

If you want to apply the drop cap format to more than the first letter of the paragraph, add the drop cap to the paragraph, click to the right of the letter in the text box, and enter the rest of the word or text that you want to make stand out. If you do this, don't forget to delete the word from the beginning of the paragraph!

Inserting symbols

Some documents require characters not found on a standard keyboard. These characters might include the copyright (©) or registered trademark (®) symbols, currency symbols (such as € or £), Greek letters, or letters with accent marks. Or you might want to add arrows (such as ì or ë) or graphic icons (such as (or Q). Word gives you easy access to a huge array of symbols that you can easily insert into any document.

Like graphics, symbols can add visual information or eye appeal to a document. However, they are different from graphics in that they are characters associated with a particular font.

TIP You can insert some common symbols by typing a keyboard combination. For example, if you enter two consecutive dashes followed by a word and a space, Word changes the two dashes to a professional-looking em-dash—like this one. (This symbol gets its name from the fact that it was originally the width of the character *m*.) To use these keyboard shortcuts, display the Backstage view, click Options, and on the Proofing page of the Word Options dialog box, click AutoCorrect Options. On the AutoCorrect page of the AutoCorrect dialog box, ensure that the Replace Text As You Type check box is selected, and then select or clear check boxes in the Replace Text As You Type area of the AutoFormat As You Type page. You can review many of the available shortcuts on the Special Characters page of the Symbol dialog box.

5

Key points

- You can insert illustrations created with most graphics programs, as well as digital photos, into a Word document.

- A background color, texture, pattern, or picture can really give a document pizzazz, but be careful that it doesn't overwhelm the text.

- Word comes with predefined building blocks that quickly add graphic elements to a document.

- By using WordArt, you can easily add fancy text to a document and then format and position it for the best effect.

Chapter at a glance

Preview

Preview and adjust page layout,
page 194

Control

Control what appears on each page,
page 200

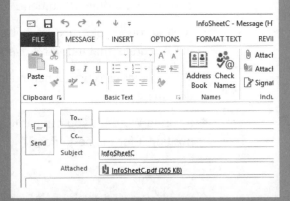

Prepare

Prepare documents for electronic
distribution, page 206

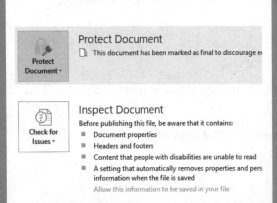

Distribute

Print and send documents,
page 212

Preview, print, and distribute documents

6

IN THIS CHAPTER, YOU WILL LEARN HOW TO

- Preview and adjust page layout.
- Control what appears on each page.
- Prepare documents for electronic distribution.
- Print and send documents.

When you finish developing a document, you'll often want to distribute either a printed version or an electronic version. Before committing the document to paper, you should check that the pages are efficiently laid out and that there are no glaring problems, such as headings that print on separate pages from their text. Microsoft Word 2013 provides several tools you can use to manipulate how much text appears on each page and to control page layout. When you are ready to print, you can control precisely how many copies and what parts of your document appear on paper.

If you intend to distribute your document electronically, Word provides tools for ensuring that the document doesn't contain unresolved revisions, hidden text, or identifying information that you might not want to send out. It also provides tools for indicating that a document is final and ready to distribute, and makes it easy to send the document by using email.

In this chapter, you'll first preview a document and make some adjustments to improve its presentation. Then you'll look at the options available for controlling page breaks and learn about problems that might occur. You'll inspect a document for confidential information and finalize it for electronic distribution. Finally, you'll print and email a document.

PRACTICE FILES To complete the exercises in this chapter, you need the practice files contained in the Chapter06 practice file folder. For more information, see "Download the practice files" in this book's Introduction.

Previewing and adjusting page layout

Working on your document in the default Print Layout view means that you always know how the document content will appear on the printed page. While you're working in the document, you can use the commands in the Page Setup group on the Page Layout tab to adjust the margins and the direction of the page (the *page orientation*) to best suit your content and delivery method. If you're planning to deliver the document at a page size other than the default, you can format the document to display and print correctly by changing the paper size.

Although the layout of each page is visible in Print Layout view, it's also a good idea to preview the whole document before you print it. This gives you more of a high-level overview of the document than when you're working directly in the content. Previewing is essential for multipage documents but is helpful even for one-page documents. You can preview a document by displaying the Print page of the Backstage view and then page through the document displayed in the right pane. This view shows exactly how each page of the document will look when printed on the specified printer.

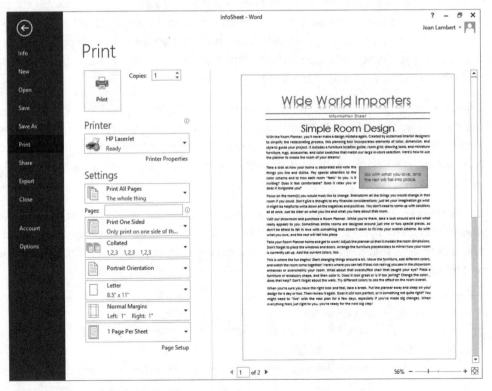

The Print page of the Backstage view.

If you don't like what appears in the preview pane of the Print page, you don't have to leave the Backstage view to make adjustments. The left pane of the Print page provides access to many of the commands that are available in the Page Setup group on the Page Layout tab, allowing you to change the following document settings while previewing their effect on the printed page:

- **Orientation** You can switch the direction in which a page is laid out on the paper. The default orientation is Portrait, in which the page is taller than it is wide. You can set the orientation to Landscape, in which the page is wider than it is tall.

- **Paper size** You can switch to one of the sizes available for the selected printer by making a selection from a list.

- **Margins** Changing the margins of a document changes where information can appear on each page. You can select one of Word's predefined sets of top, bottom, left, and right margins, or set custom margins.

  TIP All the pages of a document have the same orientation and margins unless you divide the document into sections. Then each section can have independent orientation and margin settings. For more information about sections, see "Controlling what appears on each page" later in this chapter.

To configure multiple print layout settings in one place, or to configure settings for only specific sections of the document, click Page Setup on the Print page (or click the Page Setup dialog box launcher on the Page Layout tab) to open the Page Setup dialog box, in which you can configure additional options.

SEE ALSO We work with the Page Setup dialog box in the next exercise.

When you have the settings as you want them, click the large Print button at the top of the Print page to send the document to the printer.

In this exercise, you'll preview a document, change the orientation, and adjust the margins.

 SET UP You need the InfoSheetA document located in the Chapter06 practice file folder to complete this exercise. Open the document, and then follow the steps.

> **IMPORTANT** The exercises in this chapter require that you have a printer installed. On a default installation of Windows 8 or Windows 7 and Office 2013, the Fax, Microsoft XPS Document Writer, and Send To OneNote 2013 options will appear in your Printers list. You can complete the following exercise by using one of those options or an actual local or network printer connection.

1   Display the **Backstage** view, and in the left pane, click the **Print** page tab to display the print options and the document preview. Notice that the page navigator below the preview pane indicates that the document will print on two pages, and the preview pane does not display the shaded background of the document because the shading will not be printed.

    KEYBOARD SHORTCUT Press Ctrl+P to display the Print page of the Backstage view. For more information about keyboard shortcuts, see "Keyboard shortcuts" at the end of this book.

2   In the lower-right corner of the preview pane, click the **Zoom Out** button until the two pages of the document are displayed side by side in the preview pane.

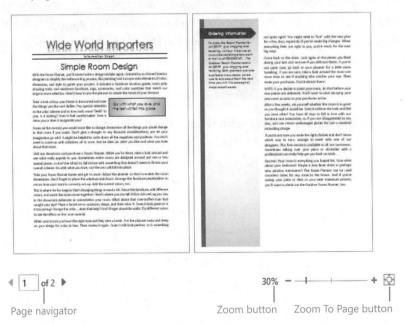

You can select a specific zoom level or number of pages to display.

TIP If you want to preview a multipage document as it will look when printed on both sides of the page and bound, add a blank page or a cover page to the beginning of the document before previewing it.

3   In the **Settings** area of the **Print** page, click **Normal Margins** to display the **Margins** menu. This is the same menu that appears when you click the **Margins** button in the **Page Setup** group on the **Page Layout** tab.

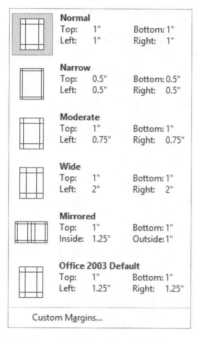

You can select from predefined margin settings, or you can set your own.

4   On the **Margins** menu, click **Wide**. Notice that the change is immediately reflected in the preview pane, and the page navigator indicates that the document now has three pages.

5   In the page navigator, click the **Next Page** button two times to display the new third page.

6   At the bottom of the left pane of the **Print** page, click the **Page Setup** link to display the **Margins** page of the **Page Setup** dialog box. Notice that selecting **Wide** margins on the **Print** page set the **Left** and **Right** margins to 2 inches.

7   In the **Orientation** area, click **Landscape**. Notice that the settings in the **Margins** area change so that **Top** and **Bottom** are now set to **2** inches and **Left** and **Right** are set to **1** inch. This change is also reflected in the **Preview** area of the dialog box.

8   In the **Multiple pages** list, click **Mirror margins** to indicate that you want to set margins for facing pages. Notice that the **Preview** area changes to display two pages and the **Left** and **Right** margin labels change to **Inside** and **Outside**.

9   In the **Margins** area, click or type to set the **Inside** margin to 2".

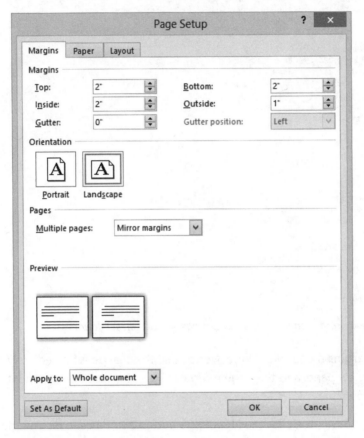

The Mirror Margins setting is a good choice when you plan to print and bind a double-sided document.

10   In the **Page Setup** dialog box, click the **Paper** tab and then the **Layout** tab, and notice the available options on those pages. Then click **OK** to return to the **Print** page of the **Backstage** view. In the **Settings** area and preview pane, notice the effect of the changes that you made in the **Page Setup** dialog box.

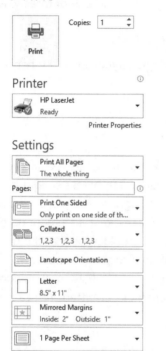
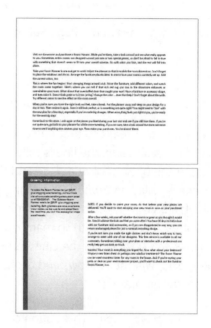

6

You can significantly change the appearance of a document while preparing it for print.

11   Experiment with other print settings to see what is available for your installed printer.

❌ CLEAN UP Close the InfoSheetA document, saving your changes if you want to.

TIP By default, hidden text does not print with the document. If you want to print the hidden text as well as the non-hidden text, select the Print Hidden Text check box in the Printing Options area of the Display page of the Word Options dialog box.

Controlling what appears on each page

When a document includes more content than will fit between its top and bottom margins, Word creates a new page by inserting a *soft page break* (a page break that moves if the preceding content changes). If you want to break a page in a place other than where Word would normally break it, you can insert a manual page break in one of three ways:

- Click **Page Break** in the **Pages** group on the **Insert** tab.
- Click **Breaks** in the **Page Setup** group on the **Page Layout** tab, and then click **Page**.
- Press **Ctrl+Enter**.

TIP As you edit the content of a document, Word changes the location of the soft page breaks, but not of any manual page breaks that you insert.

If a paragraph breaks so that most of it appears on one page but its last line appears at the top of the next page, the line is called a *widow*. If a paragraph breaks so that its first line appears at the bottom of one page and the rest of the paragraph appears on the next page, the line is called an *orphan*. These single lines of text can make a document hard to read, so by default, Word specifies that a minimum of two lines should appear at the top and bottom of each page. As with so many other aspects of the program, however, you have control over this setting. On the Line And Page Breaks page of the Paragraph dialog box, you can specify whether widows and orphans are controlled or permitted. You can also change the following options:

- **Keep with next** This option controls whether Word will break a page between the paragraph and the following paragraph.
- **Keep lines together** This option controls whether Word will break a page within the paragraph.
- **Page break before** This option controls whether Word will break a page before the paragraph.

TIP You can apply these options to individual paragraphs, or you can incorporate them into the styles you define for document elements such as headings. For information about styles, see "Creating custom styles and templates" in Chapter 16, "Work in Word more efficiently."

When you want to format part of a document differently from the rest, for example with page layout settings that are different from the surrounding text, you do so by inserting section breaks above and below it. A common example of this is when you need to print a wide table on a page with a Landscape orientation within a report that has a Portrait page orientation.

TIP Formatting selected text in columns automatically inserts section breaks. For more information, see "Presenting information in columns" in Chapter 4, "Organize information in columns and tables."

You insert a section break by clicking Breaks in the Page Setup group on the Page Layout tab and then selecting from the following section types:

- **Next Page** Starts the following section on the next page
- **Continuous** Starts a new section without affecting page breaks
- **Even Page** Starts the following section on the next even-numbered page
- **Odd Page** Starts the following section on the next odd-numbered page

When hidden formatting marks are displayed, a section break appears in Print Layout view as a double-dotted line from the preceding paragraph mark to the margin, with the words *Section Break* and the type of section break in the middle of the line.

TIP To remove a page or section break, click at the left end of the break, or select the break, and then press the Delete key.

In this exercise, you'll insert page and section breaks and ensure that the pages break in logical places.

 **SET UP** You need the OfficeInfo document located in the Chapter06 practice file folder to complete this exercise. Open the document, display formatting marks, and then follow the steps.

1   Scroll through the document, noticing any awkward page breaks, such as a topic or list that starts close to the bottom of a page.

   TIP If you drag the scroll box in the scroll bar, Word displays the current page number in a ScreenTip.

   First we'll configure some common settings for all the document elements.

2   On the **Home** tab, in the **Editing** group, click the **Select** button, and then click **Select All**.

   KEYBOARD SHORTCUT Press Ctrl+A to select all content in the document.

3   Click the **Paragraph** dialog box launcher, and then in the **Paragraph** dialog box, click the **Line and Page Breaks** tab. Because different settings have been applied to different paragraphs in the document, all the check boxes contain small black squares.

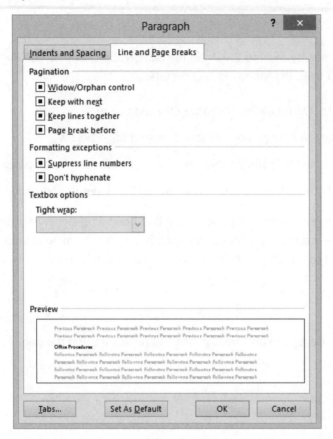

Filled check boxes indicate that the setting is not the same for all selected content.

4   Double-click each check box to clear it. (Clicking once inserts a check mark; clicking twice clears it.)

5   Click the **Keep lines together** check box twice to select it, and then click **OK** to ensure that none of the paragraphs will be broken across two pages. Then press **Home** to release the selection and return to the beginning of the document.

·Office Procedures¶

- · General Administration¶
- · Contact Information¶
- · For general deliveries:¶
  - 1234 Main Street↵
    New York, NY ·90012¶
- · Deliveries of shipping supplies should be directed to the door at the back of the building. (The loading · dock staff will check items against the packing slip and then bring the slip to the office. The office · employees will be responsible for entering the packing slip information into the inventory database.)¶
- · Phone numbers:¶
  - Telephone: (972) 555-0123↵
    Fax: (972) 555-0124¶

The small black square to the left of each paragraph indicates that the Keep Lines Together option is selected for that paragraph.

Now we'll adjust the way content breaks across individual pages.

6   Click to position the cursor at the left end of the **Warehouse** heading (be careful not to click the triangle that collapses the content below the heading).

7   On the **Insert** tab, in the **Pages** group, click the **Page Break** button to move the **Warehouse** heading and the following text to the next page.

   KEYBOARD SHORTCUT Press Ctrl+Enter to insert a page break.

8   Near the bottom of page **2**, select **To order stationery** and the eight list items that follow, and then display the **Line and Page Breaks** page of the **Paragraph** dialog box.

9   In the **Pagination** area, leave the **Keep lines together** check box selected, select the **Keep with next** check box, and then click **OK** to move the list introduction and steps to the beginning of the next page with the remainder of the list.

   TIP By selecting Keep With Next instead of inserting a page break, you allow the content to move from page to page as long as it stays with the following paragraph.

10   In the middle of page **3**, select all the bulleted list items. On the **Page Layout** tab, in the **Page Setup** group, click the **Columns** button, and then click **Two** to enclose the bulleted list items inside section breaks and put all the list items on one page.

TIP By this point you have probably noticed that it's important to set manual page breaks and layout options from the beginning of a document to the end, because each change you make affects the content from that point forward.

11   At the bottom of page **5** and top of page **6**, select the heading **What is the payment method?** and the paragraph and first three bulleted list items that follow the heading.

12   Display the **Line and Page Breaks** page of the **Paragraph** dialog box, select the **Keep with next** check box, and then click **OK** to move the heading and table introduction to the beginning of the next page.

13   At the bottom of page **6**, click at the left end of the **Shipping Quick Reference** heading.

14   On the **Page Layout** tab, in the **Page Setup** group, click the **Breaks** button, and then below the **Section Breaks** heading, click **Next Page** to create a new section.

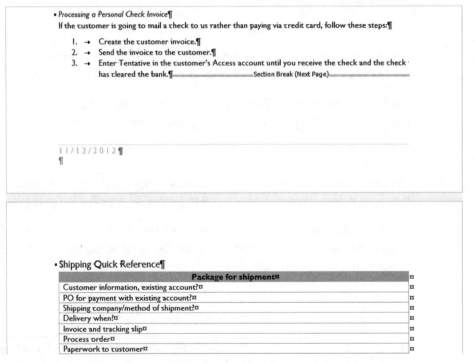

The heading and table move to the next page, after the section break indicator.

15   Display page **7** and ensure that the cursor is in the **Shipping Quick Reference** heading. On the **Page Layout** tab, in the **Page Setup** group, click the **Margins** button and then click **Wide** to make the table narrower to better fit its content.

Finally, we'll configure the header and footer in accordance with the changes we've made to the content.

16   On the **Insert** tab, in the **Header & Footer** group, click the **Header** button, and then click **Edit Header**.

Notice that on the **Header & Footer Tools Design** tab, in the **Navigation** group, the **Link to Previous** button is selected. This indicates that this section has inherited the header and footer settings of the preceding section. Because the preceding section has no header or footer on its first page, this one doesn't either.

SEE ALSO For more information about headers and footers, see "Inserting preformatted document parts" in Chapter 9, "Add visual elements."

17   On the **Design** tool tab, in the **Options** group, clear the **Different First Page** check box to add the header to this page.

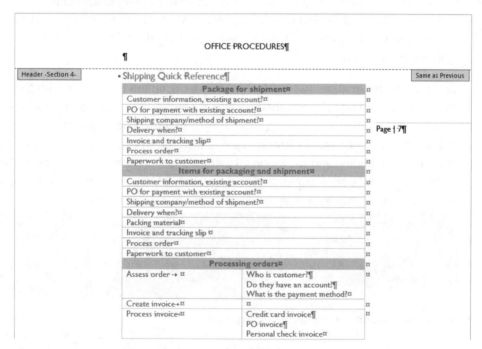

You might have to adjust the header and footer settings after creating a new section.

18   Click the **Close Header and Footer** button.

❌ CLEAN UP Close the OfficeInfo document, saving your changes if you want to.

Preparing documents for electronic distribution

When a document is complete, you can distribute it in two ways: printed on paper or electronically. When you distribute a printed document, only the printed information is visible to the reader. When you distribute a document electronically, you should ensure that no confidential information is attached to the file and that it can be viewed by the people to whom you are sending it.

Many documents go through several revisions, and some are scrutinized by multiple reviewers. During this development process, documents can accumulate information that you might not want in the final version, such as the names of people who worked on the document, the time spent working on the document, and comments that reviewers have added to the file. There might also be hidden tracked changes. This extraneous information is not a concern if the final version is to be delivered as a printout. However, it has become very common to deliver documents electronically, making this information available to anyone who wants to read it.

Some of the information that is attached to the document is available with the document properties on the Info page of the Backstage view. You can change or remove some types of information from this page and more from either the Document Panel or the Properties dialog box. However, Word provides a tool called the *Document Inspector* that automates the process of finding and removing all extraneous and potentially confidential information. After you run the Document Inspector, a summary of its search results is displayed, and you have the option of removing all the items found in each category.

> **IMPORTANT** By default, Word 2013 is configured to remove certain personal properties when saving a document. If you want to change this setting, display the Trust Center page of the Word Options dialog box, click Trust Center Settings, and then on the Privacy Options page of the Trust Center dialog box, clear the Remove Personal Information From File Properties On Save check box. Then click OK in each of the open dialog boxes to save the setting.

Word also includes two other finalizing tools:

- **Accessibility Checker** Identifies document elements and formatting that might be difficult for people with certain kinds of disabilities to read or for assistive devices such as screen readers to access

- **Compatibility Checker** Identifies formatting and features not supported in earlier versions of Word

After you remove extraneous information and overcome accessibility and compatibility issues, you can mark a document as final, so that other people know that they should not make changes to this released document.

In this exercise, you'll inspect a document, remove confidential information, and mark it as final.

SET UP You need the InfoSheetB document located in the Chapter06 practice file folder to complete this exercise. Open the document, and then follow the steps.

1   Display the **Backstage** view, which opens by default to the **Info** page. The **Properties** section lists properties that have been saved with the file. Some of the information, including the name of the author, was attached to the file by Word. Other information, such as the title, was added by a user.

Properties ˅

Size	30.5KB
Pages	2
Words	822
Total Editing Time	95 Minutes
Title	Simple Room Design
Tags	information sheet; inf...
Comments	Finalize before distribu...

Related Dates

Last Modified	Today, 6:30 PM
Created	10/30/2012 10:18 PM
Last Printed	

Related People

Author
 Joyce Cox

 Joan Lambert

Add an author

Last Modified By   Joan Lambert

Related Documents

Open File Location

Show All Properties

Some of the properties attached to the sample document.

2   Click the **Properties** button, and then in the list, click **Advanced Properties** to open the **Properties** dialog box for this document. On the **General** page of the dialog box are properties maintained by Word.

3   Click the **Summary** tab to display additional identifying information on this page.

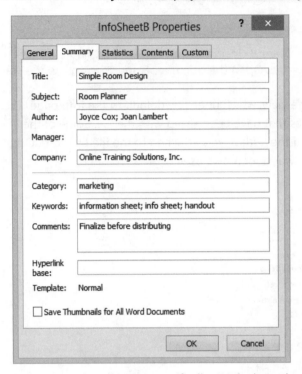

Properties such as these are specifically attached to a document.

TIP To make a document easier to find, you can add tags in the Properties area of the Info page or keywords in the Properties dialog box.

4   Click **Cancel** to close the **Properties** dialog box.

5   In the **Inspect Document** area of the **Info** page, click the **Check for Issues** button, and then click **Inspect Document** to open the **Document Inspector** dialog box, listing the items that will be checked.

TROUBLESHOOTING If Word prompts you to save changes to the file, click Yes.

6   Without changing the default selections in the **Document Inspector** dialog box, click **Inspect** to view the **Document Inspector** report on the presence of the properties you viewed earlier, as well as headers and footers, and possibly custom XML data.

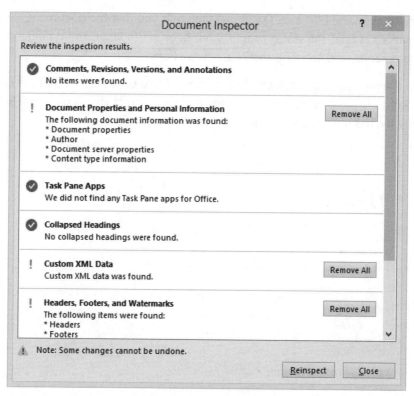

Not visible in the image are the results for Invisible Content and Hidden Text; neither was found.

7　To the right of **Document Properties and Personal Information**, click **Remove All**.

8　If custom XML data was found, click the **Remove All** button in that section.

> **IMPORTANT** Do not click the Remove All button to the right of Headers, Footers, And Watermarks. You can choose to retain content identified by the Document Inspector if you know that it is appropriate for distribution.

9　In the **Document Inspector** dialog box, click **Reinspect**, and then click **Inspect** to verify the removal of the properties and XML data.

10　Close the **Document Inspector** dialog box and display the **Info** page of the **Backstage** view. Notice that the **Properties** area displays only properties related to the file, and not those that are attached to the document.

11　In the **Protect Document** area of the **Info** page, click the **Protect Document** button, and then click **Mark As Final**. A message tells you that the document will be marked as final and then saved.

12   In the message box, click **OK**. A message tells you that the document has been marked as final, the status property has been set to **Final**, and typing, editing commands, and proofing marks are turned off.

13   In the message box, click **OK**. The document title bar indicates that the document is read-only (no changes can be saved), and the **Protect Document** area indicates that the file has been marked as final.

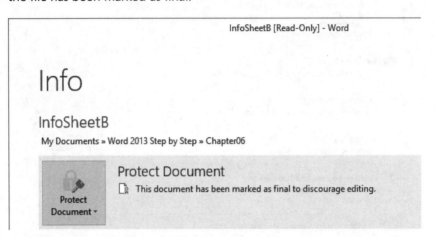

InfoSheetB [Read-Only] - Word

Info

InfoSheetB

My Documents » Word 2013 Step by Step » Chapter06

Protect Document

This document has been marked as final to discourage editing.

Protect Document ▾

The Info page reminds people that the file is final.

14   Click the **Return** button (the arrow) above the **Backstage** view page tabs to return to the document. Notice that only the ribbon tabs are visible; the commands are hidden.

15   Click the **Insert** tab to temporarily expand it, and notice that all the buttons are inactive (dimmed). Then click away from the tab to contract it. Word displays an information bar, notifying you that the document has been marked as final.

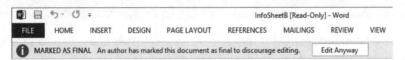

InfoSheetB [Read-Only] - Word

FILE   HOME   INSERT   DESIGN   PAGE LAYOUT   REFERENCES   MAILINGS   REVIEW   VIEW

MARKED AS FINAL An author has marked this document as final to discourage editing.   Edit Anyway

The information bar discourages people from making casual changes.

TIP If you really want to make changes to the document, you can click the Edit Anyway button on the information bar to remove the Final designation and read-only protection from the file.

❌ CLEAN UP Close the InfoSheetB document, saving your changes if you want to.

Digitally signing documents

When you create a document that will be circulated to other people in electronic form (by sending the file in an email message or posting it for other people to access), you might want to attach a digital signature, which is an electronic stamp of authentication. The digital signature confirms the origin of the document and indicates that no one has tampered with the document since it was signed. The digital signature remains valid until changes are made to the document.

To add a digital signature to a Word document:

1 On the **Info** page of the **Backstage** view, click the **Protect Document** button, and then click **Add a Digital Signature** to open the **Sign** dialog box.

TROUBLESHOOTING If a digital ID is not installed on your computer, the Get A Digital ID message box will open. You can click Yes in the message box to connect to the Microsoft website and from there to a Microsoft partner site from which you can get a digital ID.

2 In the **Commitment Type** list, click the entry to indicate whether you created, approved, or created and approved the document.

3 In the **Purpose for signing this document** box, enter the reason that you are attaching the digital signature to the document.

4 To attach specific details to your digital signature, click the **Details** button and enter your name, title, and the address of the document production location in the **Additional Signing Information** dialog box. Then click **OK**.

5 To display additional information about the document you're signing and the source information stored with the signature, click the **See additional information** link.

6 When you finish providing and reviewing signature information, click **Sign**. If Word prompts you to verify that you want to use the current digital certificate, click **Yes**.

The document is marked as final, the status property is set to Final, and typing, editing commands, and proofing marks are turned off. Flags on the Info page indicate that the document has been signed. Anyone who wants to edit the document must first acknowledge and dismiss the digital signature.

Printing and sending documents

When you're ready to distribute your document to other people, you can do so either by printing it on paper or by sending it electronically. You can also distribute the document in other formats, present it online, or post it to a blog. We discuss those options in Chapter 11, "Create documents for use outside of Word."

When you are ready to print a document, you display the Print page of the Backstage view, and then, to print one copy on the current printer with the settings shown, you simply click the Print button.

TIP You can add the Quick Print button to the Quick Access Toolbar and then print a document with the default settings by simply clicking the button. For more information, see "Customizing the Quick Access Toolbar" in Chapter 16, "Work in Word more efficiently."

From the Settings area of the Print page, you can specify what part of the document is printed and whether markup (tracked changes) is indicated in the printed document. In addition, you have the option of printing the following information instead of the document content:

- Document properties
- Tracked changes
- Styles
- AutoText entries
- Custom shortcut keys

You can choose to print a multipage document on one or both sides of the paper. If your printer supports double-sided printing, you have the option of flipping the double-sided page on the long edge or the short edge (depending on how you plan to bind and turn the document pages).

IMPORTANT Some of the settings on the Print page of the Backstage view are dependent on the functionality supported by your printer. These settings may vary when you select a different device in the Printer list.

You can choose to print multiple copies of a document and whether to print collated pages (all pages of each copy together) or uncollated pages (all copies of each page together).

Finally, you have the option of specifying the number of pages to print per sheet of paper, up to 16. You can use this option to print a booklet with two pages per sheet that will be folded in the middle. You might also use this option to save paper when you're printing a long document, but bear in mind that as the number of pages per sheet increases, the size of the content printed on the page decreases.

TIP If your printer has multiple paper trays or a manual paper feeder, you can select the paper source you want to use, on the Paper page of the Page Setup dialog box.

If you prefer to send the document electronically, and you have configured Microsoft Outlook 2013 to connect to an email account, you can do so directly from within Word. You can send the document as a Word file, or if you want to ensure that the document content is displayed to the recipient exactly as you intend, you can send it as a PDF file or an XPS file. If you have a subscription to an online fax service, you can also send the document over the Internet to a fax machine. The beauty of all these options is that you can perform them directly from within Word without starting another program, using another device, or even getting up from your chair.

Share

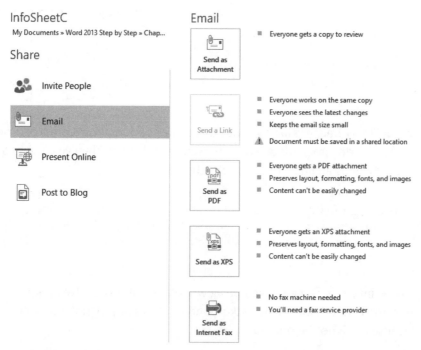

If your file is saved on a Microsoft SkyDrive or Microsoft SharePoint site, the Send A Link option will also be available.

Clicking Send As Attachment opens a message window with the current document already attached as a .docx file. All you have to do is enter the email addresses of anyone you want to receive the message and its attachment. If you want, you can modify the subject line, which contains the name of the document you're sending.

Similarly, you can click Send As PDF or Send As XPS to attach a version of the document saved in the corresponding file format.

In addition to sending a document as an email attachment from within Word, if you have signed up with an Internet fax service provider, you can send the document as a fax. Although the exact terms vary from one provider to another, these services let you send and receive faxes from your computer without needing a fax machine or dedicated fax line. After establishing an Internet fax service account, you can send the current document as a fax by clicking Send As Internet Fax on the Share page. You then follow the procedure specified by your fax service provider.

TIP If you do not sign up with an Internet fax service provider before clicking Send As Internet Fax, a message box appears. Clicking OK opens a webpage where you can choose a fax service provider.

In this exercise, you'll first become familiar with the printer options. You'll print part of a document and send the document as an email message attachment. Then you'll send a PDF version of the document as an email message attachment.

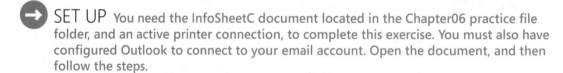 SET UP You need the InfoSheetC document located in the Chapter06 practice file folder, and an active printer connection, to complete this exercise. You must also have configured Outlook to connect to your email account. Open the document, and then follow the steps.

1 Display the **Print** page of the **Backstage** view. Notice that this is a two-page document. The colored document background is not displayed in the preview pane, because it will not be printed.

2 In the **Printer** area, click the active printer to display the list of installed printers.

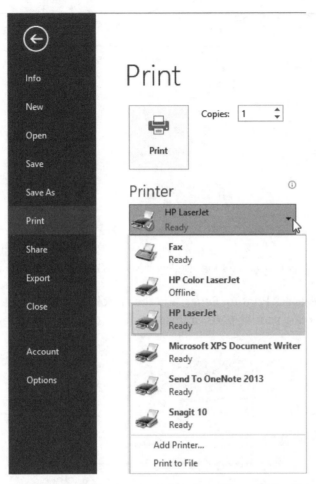

Programs to which you can print, such as Microsoft OneNote, might be installed here as well as local and network printers.

TIP You can manage these programs and printers from the Devices And Printers control panel item.

3 In the **Printer** list, click the printer to which you want to send the document. Notice that the options available on the **Print** page might change when you select a different printer.

4 Point to the **Information** icon in the upper-right corner of the **Printer** area, or to the selected printer name, to display a ScreenTip that contains printer status information.

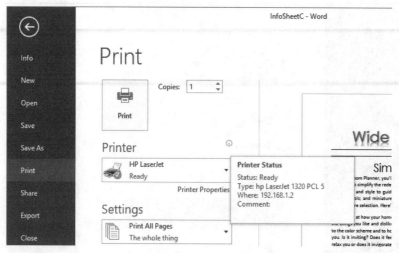

The printer status information includes the installed driver and connection information.

5   In the **Settings** area, click **Print All Pages**, and then scroll through the list to review the options for printing specific parts of the document, or document information.

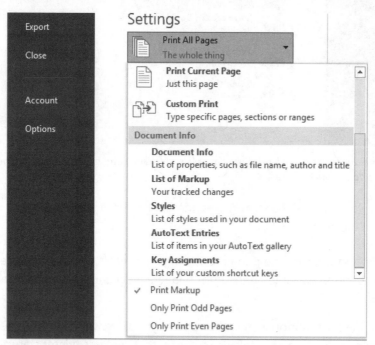

You can choose to print all or part of a document, or to print information that is stored with the document.

6   In the list, click **Custom Print**, and then in the **Pages** box, enter 2.

7   In the **Copies** box at the top of the page, enter 2. Then click the **Print** button to print two copies of the second page of the document on the selected printer and return to the document.

Now let's send the document as an email message attachment.

8   Display the **Share** page of the **Backstage** view. In the **Share** area, click **Email**, and then in the **Email** area, click **Send as Attachment** to open a message window.

TROUBLESHOOTING If Outlook isn't already running, Word starts it before generating the email message. Enter your password if you are prompted to do so.

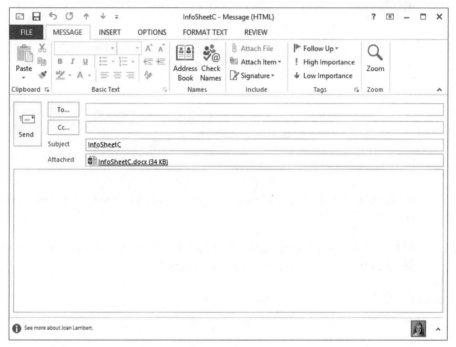

Word enters the name of the document in the Subject line and attaches the document to the message.

SEE ALSO For information about the many fabulous features of Outlook 2013, refer to *Microsoft Outlook 2013 Step by Step* by Joan Lambert and Joyce Cox (Microsoft Press, 2013).

9   In the **To** box, enter your own email address. Then in the message header, click the **Send** button to send the message to yourself.

> **TIP** When working in the message window, you are working in Outlook, not in Word. You can attach other files to the email message, set message options, and format the message content just as you would in an email message you create from scratch.

Finally, let's send a PDF version of the document as an email message attachment.

10   Display the **Share** page of the **Backstage** view. In the **Share** area, click **Email**, and then in the **Email** area, click **Send as PDF** to open a message window.

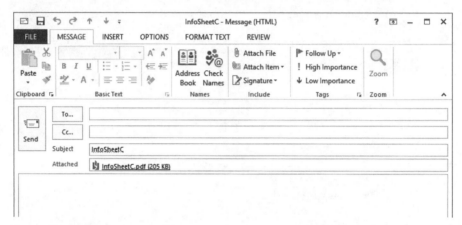

Word creates a PDF version of the document and attaches it to the message without saving it to your hard drive.

11   In the **To** box, enter your own email address. Then in the message header, click the **Send** button to send the message to yourself.

✖ CLEAN UP Close the InfoSheetC document.

Key points

- You should always preview a document before printing it. You can efficiently preview a document and perform most page layout commands from the Print page of the Backstage view.

- You can use line break options, page breaks, and section breaks to ensure that document content is readable.

- Before distributing a document electronically, you can use the Document Inspector to remove information that you don't want other people to see. You can use the Accessibility Checker and Compatibility Checker to ensure that your document content is available to recipients who aren't using the same system as you.

- You can print a document to a local or network printer, and configure the printer settings, from the Print page of the Backstage view.

- You can send a document as an attachment to an email message from the Share page of the Backstage view. When sending a document, you can send the original document file or, if you want to ensure that the document is displayed to recipients exactly as you have laid it out, you can have Word create and send a PDF file or XPS file.

6

Document enhancements

Chapter at a glance

Create
Create diagrams,
page 224

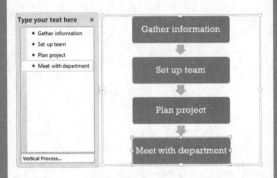

Modify
Modify diagrams,
page 231

Illustrate
Create picture diagrams,
page 239

Insert and modify diagrams

7

IN THIS CHAPTER, YOU WILL LEARN HOW TO

- Create diagrams.

- Modify diagrams.

- Create picture diagrams.

Diagrams are graphics that convey information. Business documents often include diagrams to clarify concepts, describe processes, and show hierarchical relationships. Microsoft Word 2013 includes a powerful diagramming feature called SmartArt that you can use to create diagrams directly in your documents. By using ready-made yet dynamic diagram templates, you can produce sophisticated results tailored to your needs.

SmartArt diagrams can illustrate many different types of concepts. Although graphic in nature, SmartArt diagrams are merely visual containers for information stored as bulleted lists. You can also incorporate pictures and other images to create truly spectacular, yet divinely professional, diagrams.

In this chapter, you'll insert a diagram into a document and specify its size and position. Then you'll change the diagram's layout, visual style, and color theme. Finally, you'll use a diagram to arrange pictures in a document.

PRACTICE FILES To complete the exercises in this chapter, you need the practice files contained in the Chapter07 practice file folder. For more information, see "Download the practice files" in this book's Introduction.

Creating diagrams

When you need your document to clearly illustrate a concept such as a process, cycle, hierarchy, or relationship, the powerful SmartArt Graphics tool is available to help you create a dynamic, visually appealing diagram. By using predefined sets of sophisticated formatting, you can almost effortlessly put together any of the following diagrams:

- **List** These diagrams visually represent lists of related or independent information—for example, a list of items needed to complete a task, including pictures of the items.

- **Process** These diagrams visually describe the ordered set of steps that are required to complete a task—for example, the steps for getting a project approved.

- **Cycle** These diagrams represent a circular sequence of steps, tasks, or events, or the relationship of a set of steps, tasks, or events to a central, core element—for example, the looping process for continually improving a product based on customer feedback.

- **Hierarchy** These diagrams illustrate the structure of an organization or entity—for example, the top-level management structure of a company.

- **Relationship** These diagrams show convergent, divergent, overlapping, merging, or containment elements—for example, how using similar methods to organize your email, calendar, and contacts can improve your productivity.

- **Matrix** These diagrams show the relationship of components to a whole—for example, the product teams in a department.

- **Pyramid** These diagrams illustrate proportional or interconnected relationships—for example, the amount of time that should ideally be spent on different phases of a project.

- **Picture** These diagrams rely on pictures instead of text to create one of the other types of diagrams—for example, a process picture diagram with photographs showing the recession of glaciers in Glacier National Park. Picture diagrams are a subset of the other categories but are also available from their own category so that you can easily locate diagram layouts that support images.

To create a SmartArt diagram in Word 2013, you begin by selecting the type of diagram you want to create from the Choose A SmartArt Graphic dialog box. The categories are not mutually exclusive, meaning that some diagrams appear in more than one category.

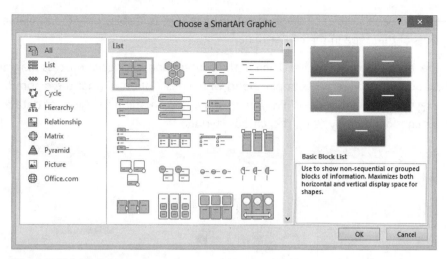

Word 2013 includes more SmartArt templates than previous versions of Word.

After you choose a layout, Word inserts the basic diagram into the document and displays the associated list format in the Text pane, into which you can enter information. You can enter more or less information than is required by the original diagram; most diagrams support a range of entries (although a few are formatted to support only a specific number of entries). You can insert and modify text either directly in the diagram shapes or in the associated Text pane. Depending on the diagram type, the text appears in or adjacent to its shapes.

In this exercise, you'll create a simple diagram, add text, adjust the diagram size, and specify the diagram's position in relation to the document text and page margins.

SET UP You need the ServiceA document located in the Chapter07 practice file folder to complete this exercise. Open the document, and then follow the steps.

1   Click to position the cursor at the left end of the **Gather Information** heading.

2   On the **Insert** tab, in the **Illustrations** group, click the **SmartArt** button to display all the available SmartArt graphic layouts in the **Choose a SmartArt Graphic** dialog box.

    KEYBOARD SHORTCUT Press Alt+N+M to open the Choose A SmartArt Graphic dialog box. For more information about keyboard shortcuts, see "Keyboard shortcuts" at the end of this book.

3   In the left pane, click each diagram category in turn to display only the available layouts of that type in the center pane.

4   In the left pane, click **Process**. Then in the center pane, click each process diagram layout in turn to view an example, along with a description of what the diagram best conveys, in the right pane. While you are exploring, imagine the types of data that you might diagram by using the various layouts.

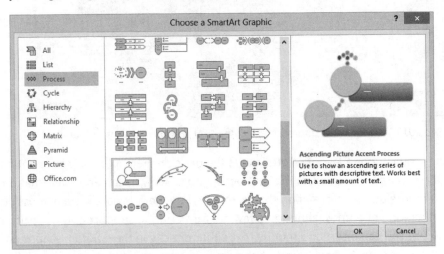

Diagrams that include spaces for pictures have "Picture" in the layout name.

TIP The diagram element colors shown in the preview pane are representational only. SmartArt diagrams that you insert into a document will take on the current theme colors of that document.

5   When you finish exploring, click the second thumbnail in the seventh row (**Vertical Process**), and then click **OK** to insert the process diagram at the cursor.

TIP Depending on your screen resolution, there might be a description of the Vertical Process diagram at the bottom of the Text pane. If your Text pane looks like the one in our graphic, you can point to Vertical Process to display the description in a ScreenTip.

TROUBLESHOOTING If the Text pane is not open, click the chevron on the left side of the diagram frame to open it. You can also display and hide the Text pane by clicking the Text Pane button in the Create Graphic group on the Design tool tab.

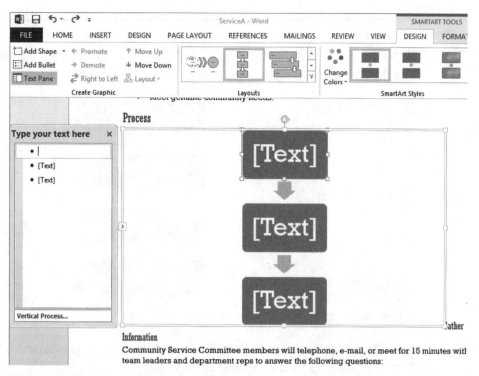

Three text placeholders appear in the diagram shapes and in the adjacent Text pane, where the text placeholders are formatted as a bulleted list.

Now we'll enter content into the diagram.

6   With the cursor in the first bulleted item in the **Text** pane, enter the following: Gather information. Then press the **Down Arrow** key to move the cursor to the next placeholder. Notice that as you enter letters in the bulleted list, they appear in the corresponding diagram shape.

> **TROUBLESHOOTING** Be sure to press the Down Arrow key. If you press the Enter key, you'll add a new bullet, and if you press the Tab key, you'll change the current first-level bullet into a second-level bullet.

7   Enter Set up team in the second bulleted list item, press the **Down Arrow** key, and then enter Plan project in the third bulleted list item.

> **TIP** For a clean look, don't enter any punctuation at the end of the text in diagram shapes.

8   With the cursor at the end of the third bulleted item in the **Text** pane, press **Enter** to extend the bulleted list and add a new shape to the diagram. Then enter Meet with department. Notice that the diagram shapes adjust to accommodate the new entry, and the text in all the shapes resizes so that the longest entry fits.

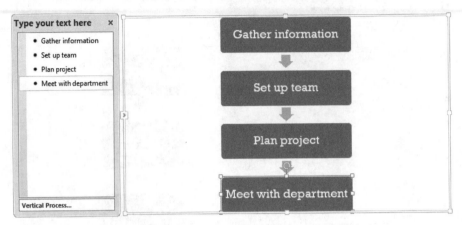

You can easily add more shapes and levels to the diagram.

9   In the **Text** pane, click the **Close** button. Notice that the diagram is awkwardly located and surrounded by a lot of white space.

Next we'll resize the diagram and specify how text flows around it.

10   On the right side of the diagram frame, point to the sizing handle (the square), and when the pointer changes to a double-headed arrow, drag to the left until the frame is approximately as wide as the shapes within the diagram.

TROUBLESHOOTING If you drag further to the left, the diagram shapes resize to fit the new space. If this happens, drag a bit back to the right. The final width should be approximately 2.5 inches.

TIP You can also resize the diagram frame by selecting it and then entering the size you want in the Height and Width boxes in the Size group on the Format tool tab.

11   When you release the mouse button, the **Layout Options** button appears to the right of the diagram frame. Click the **Layout Options** button to expand the menu.

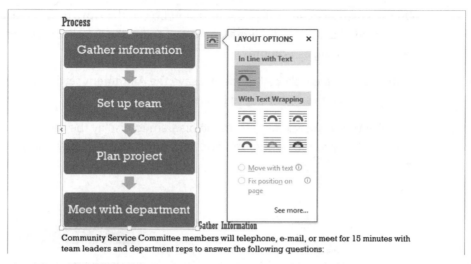

The diagram is anchored to the Gather Information heading and moves with it.

12 On the **Layout Options** menu, in the **With Text Wrapping** area, click the first thumbnail (**Square**) to move the text that follows the graphic to its right side.

TIP Layout options are also available from the Wrap Text menu in the Arrange group on the Format tool tab. For information about text wrapping, see "Arranging objects on the page" in Chapter 10, "Organize and arrange content."

13 On the **Layout Options** menu, click the **See more** link.

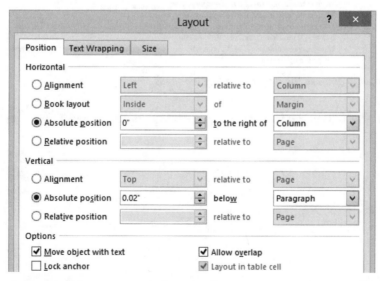

Options on this page control where the diagram appears relative to other document elements.

14   On the **Position** page of the **Layout** dialog box, in the **Horizontal** area, click **Alignment**. Then click the **Alignment** arrow, and in the list, click **Right**. Leave the **relative to** setting as **Column**.

15   In the **Vertical** area, click **Alignment**. Leave the **Alignment** setting as **Top**, and change the **relative to** setting to **Line**.

16   Click **OK** and then click away from the diagram to display the results. The diagram now sits neatly to the right of the text, to support the content without interrupting its flow.

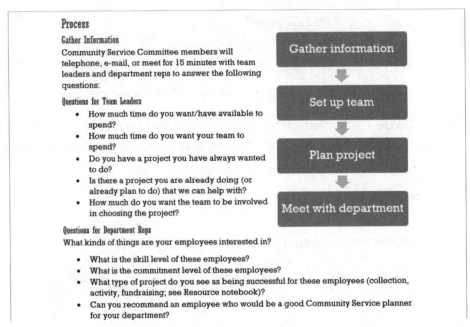

You can align and size the diagram to fit your needs.

❌ CLEAN UP Close the ServiceA document, saving your changes if you want to.

Modifying diagrams

After you create a diagram and add the text you want to display in it, you might find that the diagram layout you originally selected doesn't precisely meet your needs. You can easily change to a different diagram layout without losing any of the information you entered in the diagram. If a particular layout doesn't support the amount of information that is associated with the diagram, the extra text will be hidden but not deleted and will be available when you choose another layout that does support that amount of text.

When you have the layout you want to use, you can add and remove shapes and edit the text of the diagram by making changes in the Text pane. You can also customize the diagram by using the options on the SmartArt Tools tabs.

You can make changes such as the following by using the commands on the Design tool tab:

- Add shading and three-dimensional effects to all the shapes in a diagram.

- Change the color scheme.

- Add shapes and change their hierarchy.

    TIP You can remove a shape and its text by selecting it in the diagram or in the Text pane and then pressing the Delete key. You can also rearrange shapes by dragging them.

You can customize individual shapes in the following ways by using the commands on the Format tool tab:

- Change an individual shape—for example, you can change a square into a star.

- Apply a built-in shape style.

- Change the color, outline, or effect of a shape.

- Change the style of the shape's text.

The Live Preview feature displays the effects of these changes before you apply them. If you apply changes and then decide you preferred the original version, you can click the Reset Graphic button in the Reset group on the Design tool tab to return to the unaltered diagram layout.

7

In this exercise, you'll change a diagram's layout, style, and colors. Then you'll change the shape and color of one of its elements and customize copies of the diagram.

➡ SET UP You need the ServiceB document located in the Chapter07 practice file folder to complete this exercise. Open the document, and then follow the steps.

1 Scroll through the document and change the zoom level if necessary so that the diagram is visible in the lower-right corner of the program window.

2 Click a blank area inside the diagram frame (not one of the shapes) to activate the diagram and the associated tool tabs.

> TROUBLESHOOTING Be sure to click a blank area away from any shapes. If handles appear around a shape in the diagram, that shape is selected, either for editing or for manipulation, instead of the diagram as a whole.

3 On the **Design** tool tab, in the **Layouts** group, click the **More** button to expand the **Layouts** gallery. This view of the gallery displays only the available **Process** diagram layouts because the current diagram layout is from the **Process** category.

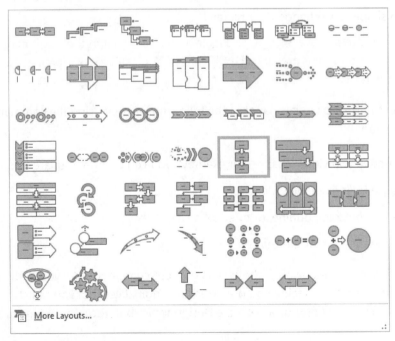

You can easily switch to another layout in the same category.

TIP If a gallery has a sizing handle (three dots) in its lower-right corner, as this one does, you can drag the handle upward to reduce the height of the gallery. You can then display more of the document and the gallery at the same time.

4   Point to each thumbnail in the **Layouts** gallery to preview the diagram with that layout. Because changing the layout does not change the width of the diagram frame, some of the horizontal layouts create a very small diagram. Notice that some of the layouts (such as those in the last row of the gallery) treat the diagram entries differently than others, and some don't support all seven entries.

5   In the **Layouts** gallery, click the third thumbnail in the fifth row (**Basic Bending Process**) to change the diagram to two columns with arrows indicating the process flow.

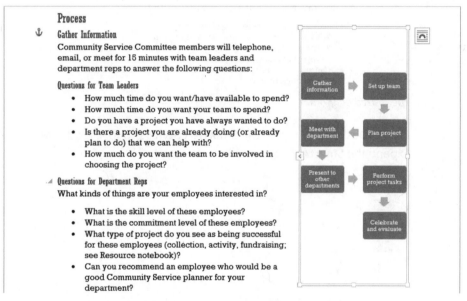

The Basic Bending Process diagram.

6   Point to the sizing handle on the left side of the diagram frame (the left edge of the **Text Pane** button), and when the pointer changes to a two-headed arrow, drag the frame to the left until the diagram occupies about half the page width. When you release the mouse button, the shapes in the diagram expand to fill the resized frame.

7   Drag the sizing handle on the bottom of the diagram frame up so that the diagram ends just above the **Questions for Department Reps** heading.

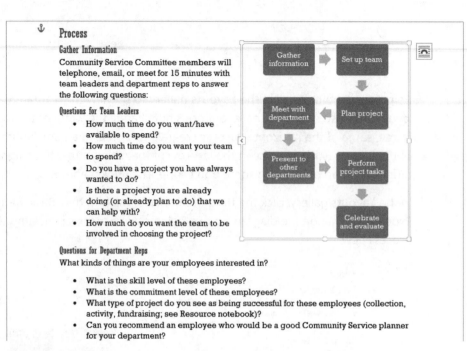

Process

Gather Information

Community Service Committee members will telephone, email, or meet for 15 minutes with team leaders and department reps to answer the following questions:

Questions for Team Leaders

- How much time do you want/have available to spend?
- How much time do you want your team to spend?
- Do you have a project you have always wanted to do?
- Is there a project you are already doing (or already plan to do) that we can help with?
- How much do you want the team to be involved in choosing the project?

Questions for Department Reps

What kinds of things are your employees interested in?

- What is the skill level of these employees?
- What is the commitment level of these employees?
- What type of project do you see as being successful for these employees (collection, activity, fundraising; see Resource notebook)?
- Can you recommend an employee who would be a good Community Service planner for your department?

The resized diagram.

8   On the **Design** tool tab, in the **SmartArt Styles** group, click the **More** button to expand the **SmartArt Styles** gallery.

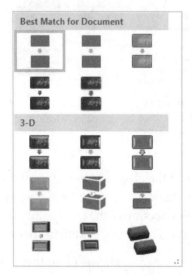

You can apply two-dimensional or three-dimensional styles.

9   In the gallery, point to each style, noticing the changes to your diagram. Then in the **3-D** area, click the third thumbnail in the first row (**Cartoon**).

10   In the **SmartArt Styles** group, click the **Change Colors** button to display a gallery of color variations based on the current document theme colors.

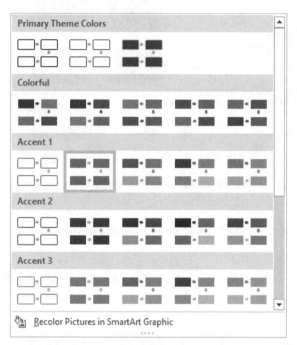

SmartArt graphics use theme colors to ensure that they blend in with the document.

11   Preview a few color combinations, and then in the **Colorful** area, click the second thumbnail (**Colorful Range - Accent Colors 2 to 3**) to apply the selected color range to the diagram shapes. Then click away from the diagram to display the results.

Process

Gather Information

Community Service Committee members will telephone, email, or meet for 15 minutes with team leaders and department reps to answer the following questions:

Questions for Team Leaders

- How much time do you want/have available to spend?
- How much time do you want your team to spend?
- Do you have a project you have always wanted to do?
- Is there a project you are already doing (or already plan to do) that we can help with?
- How much do you want the team to be involved in choosing the project?

Applying a style and changing the colors gives the diagram a modern look.

Now that we've applied a unified color scheme to the diagram, we'll emphasize an individual shape by changing its characteristics.

12 In the upper-left corner of the diagram, click the **Gather information** shape (not its text) to select it.

13 On the **Format** tool tab, in the **Shape Styles** group, click the **Shape Fill** button, and then in the **Standard Colors** palette, click the first color swatch (**Dark Red**) to change the color of the selected diagram shape.

14 In the **Shape Styles** group, click the **Shape Effects** button, click **Glow**, and then in the **Glow Variations** area, click the first thumbnail in the third row (**Orange, 11pt glow, Accent color 1**). Click away from the diagram to display the results.

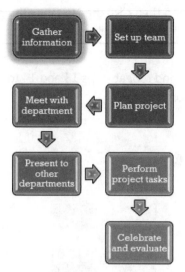

The shape that corresponds with the heading to the left of the diagram is now accentuated with a different shape and color.

Next we'll make unique versions of the diagram corresponding to the steps of the illustrated process.

15 Click a blank area of the diagram to select it. Then on the **Home** tab, in the **Clipboard** group, click the **Copy** button.

KEYBOARD SHORTCUT Press Ctrl+C to copy the active element.

16 Scroll to page **2**, click to the left of the **Set up team** heading, and in the **Clipboard** group, click the **Paste** button to paste a copy of the diagram into the document.

17 On the **Layout Options** menu, click the **See more** link to display the **Position** tab of the **Layout** dialog box. Set the horizontal alignment to **Right relative to Column** and the vertical alignment to **Top relative to Line**. Then click **OK**.

18 Select the **Gather information** shape (not its text). In the **Shape Styles** group, click the **Shape Fill** button, and then in the **Theme Colors** palette, click the first color swatch under the maroon swatch (**Dark Red, Accent 2, Lighter 80%**).

TIP In step 11 we chose the Accent Colors 2 To 3 color scheme. The color specified in step 18 is a lighter shade of the selected starting color.

TROUBLESHOOTING Although the color we chose in step 13 and the Accent 2 color of this theme are both named Dark Red, they are not the same color. Be sure to use the Standard Colors palette for step 13 and the Theme Colors palette for step 18.

19   On the **Shape Effects** menu, click **Glow**, and then click the **No Glow** thumbnail. The shape corresponding to the previous heading is now muted to show that it has already been discussed.

20   Click the **Set up team** shape (not its text), and repeat steps 13 and 14 to highlight the shape that corresponds to the adjacent topic.

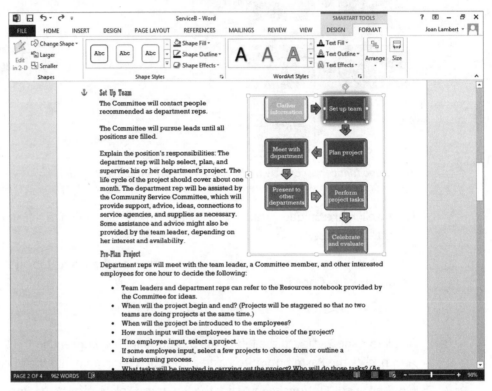

The highlighted shape reflects the heading to the left, and the previous topic is a muted color.

21   If you want, repeat steps 15 through 20 to insert a customized copy of the diagram adjacent to each of the remaining headings in the **Process** section.

TIP Sometimes headings appear too close together, or a heading might appear too close to the bottom of the page, to accommodate a series of diagrams neatly. In that case, insert a page break before each heading to move it to a new page before inserting the diagram.

CLEAN UP Close the ServiceB document, saving your changes if you want to.

Creating picture diagrams

The SmartArt Graphics tool that comes with Word 2013 includes diagram layouts that are specifically designed to hold pictures. You can use these diagrams for business uses such as creating organization charts with pictures, names, and titles, or for personal uses such as creating a page of family photographs.

In this exercise, you'll create a page of photographs. You'll size and position the photographs and then enter and format accompanying captions.

SET UP You need the Neighborhood document and the Garden, Park, Pond, and Woods pictures located in the Chapter07 practice file folder to complete this exercise. Open the document, and then follow the steps.

1 On the **View** tab, click the **One Page** button to display the entire document in the program window.

2 Click anywhere in the **Enjoy the Neighborhood!** heading, and then press the **Down Arrow** key to position the cursor in the blank paragraph below the heading.

3 On the **Insert** tab, in the **Illustrations** group, click the **SmartArt** button. In the left pane of the **Choose a SmartArt Graphic** dialog box, click **Picture**. Then in the middle pane, double-click the first thumbnail in the first row (**Accented Picture**) to insert the template for the selected diagram at the cursor.

The Accented Picture diagram, ready for you to enter pictures and captions.

4   Click a blank area inside the diagram frame to select the diagram. On the **Format** tool tab, click the **Size** group button and set the **Height** to **5.75"** and the **Width** to **9"** to change the size of the frame.

   TIP You don't have to enter the inch marks; Word will add them for you. After you enter a Size setting, press Enter or click outside the box to implement the change.

5   Click a blank area of the biggest shape to select it. Display the **Size** settings and set the **Height** to **5"** and the **Width** to **8"** to change the size of the shape. Then drag the shape down and to the left until it sits in the lower-left corner of the diagram frame.

6   Click a blank area of the top circle, press and hold the **Ctrl** key, and then click the middle and bottom circles. In the **Size** settings, click the arrows in the **Height** and **Width** boxes to increase both settings to **1.7"**.

   TROUBLESHOOTING Don't enter the sizes; use the arrows. Sometimes the shapes don't hold precise measurements when you enter them directly.

7   With the three circles selected, drag them to the right edge of the frame. Press the arrow keys on the keyboard for more precise positioning if necessary.

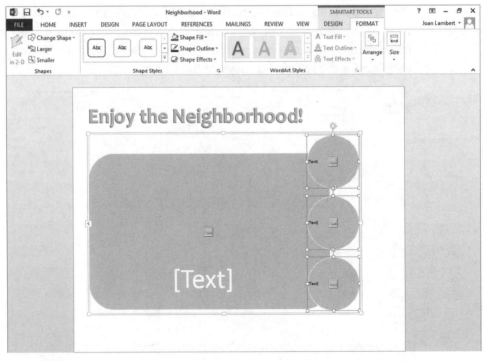

The picture placeholders have been sized and positioned to fit the available space.

8   In the large diagram shape, click the **Insert Picture** icon to open the **Insert Pictures** window. Notice that you can insert pictures from a variety of sources.

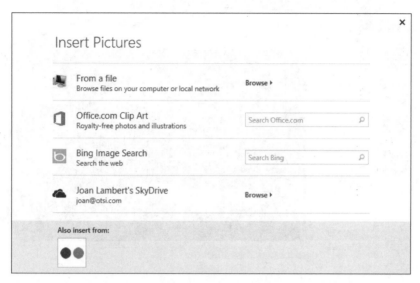

The Insert Pictures window provides access to local and online resources.

9   In the **From a file** area, click **Browse**. In the **Insert Picture** dialog box, navigate to the **Chapter07** practice file folder, and then double-click the **Park** picture.

10 Repeat steps 8 and 9 to insert the **Garden** picture in the top circle, the **Pond** picture in the middle circle, and the **Woods** picture in the bottom circle.

11 Click a blank area of the diagram to select it, and then on the **Design** tool tab, in the **Create Graphic** group, click the **Text Pane** button. Notice that the **Text** pane displays a thumbnail of each picture next to the bullet point representing the text in that shape.

12 In the **Text** pane, replace the placeholder bullet points with Park, Garden, Pond, and Woods to enter the captions on the diagram in the position and format specified by the diagram template.

The pictures now have captions, although they're a bit clunky.

13   Click any entry in the **Text** pane. On the **Home** tab, in the **Editing** group, click **Select**, and then click **Select All** to select all the labels.

14   On the **Home** tab, in the **Font** group, click the **Text Effects and Typography** button and then click the first thumbnail in the third row of the gallery (**Fill – Black, Text 1, Outline - Background 1, Hard Shadow - Background 1**).

15   In the **Font** group, in the **Font** list, click **Candara**, and in the **Font Size** list, click **36**.

16   In the **Paragraph** group, click the **Center** button. Then close the **Text** pane.

17   Make any additional changes to the document that you'd like to create a balanced look. We set a custom left margin of 1.25" and added a shadow effect to each of the shapes.

The final picture diagram.

✖ CLEAN UP Close the Neighborhood document, saving your changes if you want to.

Key points

- You can easily create a sophisticated diagram to convey a process or the relationship between hierarchical elements.

- Diagrams are dynamic illustrations that you can customize to produce precisely the effect you are looking for.

- You can use a picture diagram to neatly lay out pictures on a page.

Chapter at a glance

Insert

Insert charts,
page 246

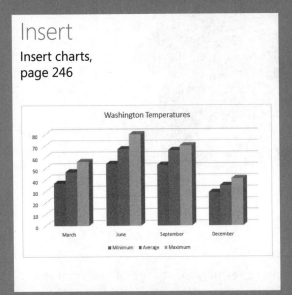

Modify

Modify charts,
page 250

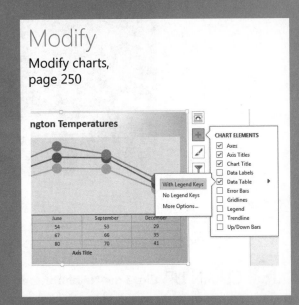

Use

Use existing data in charts,
page 259

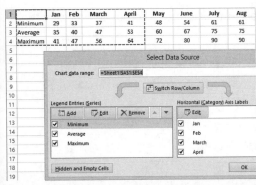

Insert and modify charts 8

IN THIS CHAPTER, YOU WILL LEARN HOW TO

- Insert charts.

- Modify charts.

- Use existing data in charts.

You'll often find it helpful to reinforce the argument you are making in a document with facts and figures. When it's more important for your audience to understand trends than identify precise values, you can use a chart to present numerical information in visual ways.

You can create simple or elaborate charts from data that is stored in a Microsoft Excel 2013 workbook. If your final deliverable is a document rather than a workbook, you can create a chart in Excel and insert it into the document, or you can create a chart from within Microsoft Word 2013 and either enter new data or reference existing data. The chart takes on the visual formatting associated with the design template that is attached to the document and blends in with the rest of the document content.

In this chapter, you'll add a chart to a document and modify its appearance by changing its chart type, style, and layout, as well as the color of some elements. Then you'll recreate the chart by plotting data stored in an existing Excel worksheet.

IMPORTANT The exercises in this chapter assume that you have Excel 2013 installed on your computer. If you do not have this version of Excel, the steps in the exercises won't work as described.

PRACTICE FILES To complete the exercises in this chapter, you need the practice files contained in the Chapter08 practice file folder. For more information, see "Download the practice files" in this book's Introduction.

Inserting charts

When you create a new chart from within a Word document, Word and Excel work together to provide some pretty fancy functionality. A generic chart appears in the document, and a worksheet containing the sample data opens in Excel. You can then edit the sample data to create the chart that you want. You don't have to save the Excel file; Word maintains its data with the document and it is available to you whenever you want to update it.

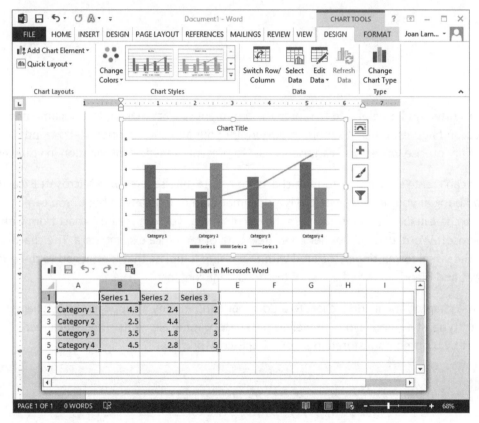

A sample chart plotted from the data in its associated Excel worksheet.

TIP You can open the worksheet associated with a chart by clicking the chart and then clicking the Edit Data button in the Data group on the Design tool tab.

The Excel worksheet is composed of rows and columns of cells that contain values, which in charting terminology are called *data points*. Collectively, a set of data points is called a *data series*. As with Word tables, each worksheet cell is identified by an address consisting of its column letter and row number—for example, A2 is the first cell in the second row. A range of cells is identified by the address of the cell in the upper-left corner and the address of the cell in the lower-right corner, separated by a colon—for example, A2:D5 is the range of cells from the first cell in the second row to the fourth cell in the fifth row.

To customize the chart, you replace the sample data in the Excel worksheet with your own data. Because the Excel worksheet is linked to the chart, when you change the values in the worksheet, the chart changes as well. To enter a value in a cell, you click the cell to select it, or move to the cell by pressing the Tab key or arrow keys, and then enter the data. You can select an entire column by clicking the column header—the shaded box containing a letter at the top of each column—and an entire row by clicking the row header—the shaded box containing a number to the left of each row. You can select the entire worksheet by clicking the Select All button—the box at the junction of the column and row headers.

In this exercise, you'll insert a generic chart into a document, replace the sample data in the associated worksheet, and then group the data appropriately.

→ SET UP You need the CottageA document located in the Chapter08 practice file folder to complete this exercise. Open the document, and then follow the steps.

1   Press **Ctrl+End** to move to the end of the document.

2   On the **Insert** tab, in the **Illustrations** group, click the **Chart** button.

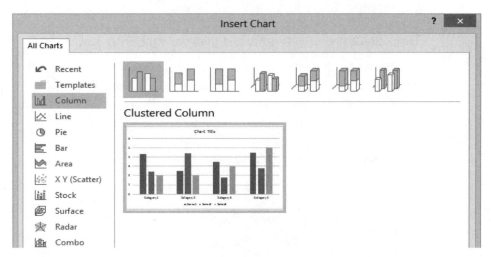

In the Insert Chart dialog box, you can select from several chart types and their variations.

3   In the left pane of the **Insert Chart** dialog box, click each of the categories to review the types of charts you can create in Word. Then return to the **Column** category.

4   In the gallery at the top of the right pane, click the fourth thumbnail (**3-D Clustered Column**) to preview that chart type, and then click **OK** to insert the generic three-dimensional clustered column chart at the end of the document and open the associated Excel worksheet.

5   Click the **Select All** button in the upper-left corner of the Excel worksheet, and then press the **Delete** key to delete the sample data in the worksheet, so that the worksheet is blank. The columns in the sample chart in the document disappear, leaving only the colored guides.

6   Click the second cell in row **1** (cell **B1**), enter March, and then press the **Tab** key to enter the heading (in the worksheet and on the chart) and move to the next cell.

7   In cells **C1** through **E1**, enter June, September, and December, pressing **Tab** after each entry to move to the next cell. When you enter **December**, notice that it is outside of the colored guides and does not appear on the chart in the document.

8   Point to the blue handle in the lower-right corner of cell **D5**, and when the pointer changes to a diagonal double-headed arrow, drag it one cell to the right and one cell up so that the chart data is defined as cells **A1:E4**.

> **TIP** If you were entering a sequential list of months, you could enter *January* and then drag the fill handle in the lower-right corner of the cell to the right to fill subsequent cells in the same row with the names of the months.

9   Click cell **A2**, enter Minimum, and then press the **Enter** key.

> **KEYBOARD SHORTCUT** Press Enter to move down in the column (or to the beginning of a data entry series) or Shift+Enter to move up. Press Tab to move to the right in the same row or Shift+Tab to move to the left. For more information about keyboard shortcuts, see "Keyboard shortcuts" at the end of this book.

10   In cells **A3** and **A4**, enter Average and Maximum.

	A	B	C	D	E	F	G	H	I
				Chart in Microsoft Word					
1		March	June	September	December				
2	Minimum								
3	Average								
4	Maximum								
5									

The row and column headings for your chart.

11   Point to the border between the headers of columns **A** and **B**, and when the pointer changes to a double-headed arrow, double-click to adjust the width of the column to the left of the border to fit the entries in the column.

12   Select columns **B** through **E** by dragging through their headers. Then point to the border between any two selected columns, and double-click to adjust the width of all the selected columns to fit their cell entries.

13   In cell **B2**, enter 37, and press **Tab**. Notice that a corresponding column appears in the chart.

14   In cells **C2** through **E2**, enter 54, 53, and 29, pressing **Tab** to move from cell to cell. After you enter the last number, press **Enter**. Notice that cell **B3** becomes active.

15   Enter the following data into the chart worksheet, noticing as you enter data that the chart columns and scale change to reflect the data:

	B	C	D	E
3	47	67	66	35
4	56	80	70	41

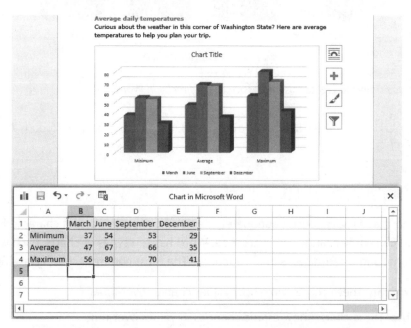

The data series in the columns (the months) are plotted by the categories in the rows (Minimum, Average, and Maximum).

16   In the **Chart in Microsoft Word** window, click the **Close** button. Notice that the temperatures on the chart are grouped by category rather than by month.

17   In the document, click a blank area of the chart to select it. Then on the **Design** tool tab, in the **Data** group, click **Switch Row/Column** to group the temperatures more logically by month.

18   On the chart, click **Chart Title** to select that element, enter Washington Temperatures, and then click a blank area of the page to display the results.

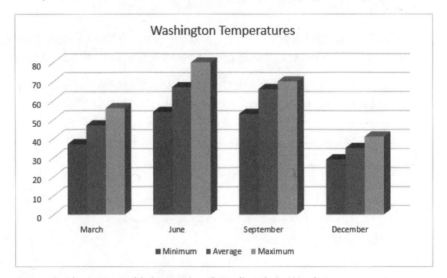

It was simple to create this impressive chart directly in Word.

❌ CLEAN UP Close the CottageA document, saving your changes if you want to.

Modifying charts

If you find that a chart doesn't adequately depict the most important characteristics of your data, you can easily change the chart type. Word has ten types of charts, each with two-dimensional and three-dimensional variations. The most common chart types include:

- **Column** These charts show how values change over time.
- **Line** These charts show erratic changes in values over time.
- **Pie** These charts show how parts relate to the whole.
- **Bar** These charts show the values of several items at one point in time.

Having settled on the most appropriate chart type, you can modify the chart as a whole or change any of its elements, such as the following:

- **Chart area** This is the entire area within the chart frame.

- **Plot area** This is the rectangular area bordered by the axes.

- **Axes** These are the lines along which the data is plotted. The x-axis shows the categories, and the y-axis shows the data series, or values. (Three-dimensional charts also have a z-axis.)

- **Labels** These identify the data along each axis.

- **Data markers** These graphically represent each data point in each data series.

- **Legend** This is a key that identifies the data series.

- **Chart title** This title identifies the chart purpose and frequently takes the form of a short explanation of the data displayed.

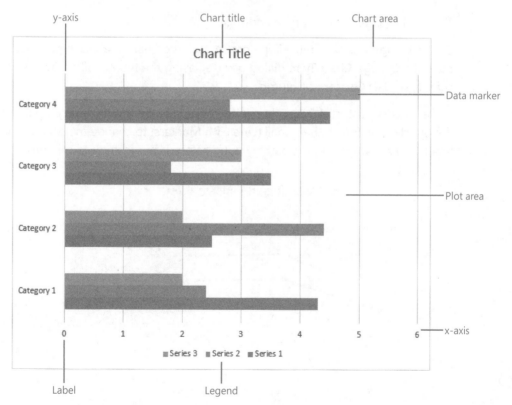

The main elements of a chart.

8

To modify a specific element, you first select it by clicking it, or by clicking its name in the Chart Elements box in the Current Selection group on the Format tool tab. You can then modify the element by clicking the buttons on the Design and Format tool tabs.

If you make extensive modifications, you can save the customized chart as a template so that you can plot similar data in the future without having to repeat all the changes.

In this exercise, you'll modify the appearance of a chart, and then save it as a template.

 SET UP You need the CottageB document located in the Chapter08 practice file folder to complete this exercise. Open the document, and then follow the steps.

1   Scroll to the end of the document to display the chart. Click the chart area to activate it and display the **Chart Tools** tabs.

    TROUBLESHOOTING Be sure to click a blank area inside the chart frame. Clicking any of the chart elements will activate that element, not the chart as a whole.

    First we'll change the chart type and style.

2   On the **Design** tool tab, in the **Type** group, click the **Change Chart Type** button to open the **Change Chart Type** dialog box displaying the thumbnail of the current chart type, **3-D Clustered Column**.

3   In the category list, click **Line**. Then in the gallery at the top of the right pane, double-click the fourth thumbnail (**Line with Markers**) to change the column chart to a line chart, which depicts data by using colored lines instead of columns.

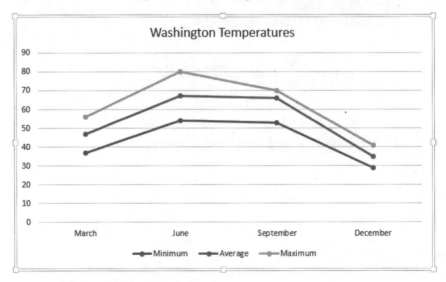

The temperature data plotted as a line chart.

4   In the document, to the right of the chart, click the **Chart Styles** button. Notice that you can choose **Style** or **Color** at the top of the window that opens to display a gallery of options.

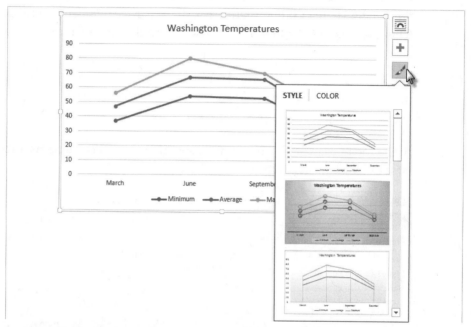

You can quickly switch to a different chart area or data marker style for the same chart type.

TIP You can also access the available styles from the Chart Styles gallery by clicking the More button in the Chart Styles group.

5   In the **Style** gallery, point to each of the thumbnails to preview that chart style in the document. Then click the second thumbnail (**Style 2**) to change the data markers to circles displaying the actual data points.

Now we'll change the color of the plot area and data series.

6   In the **Chart Styles** pane, click **Color** to display the **Colorful** and **Monochromatic** palettes of color options based on the current theme. Scroll through the gallery and notice that the **Monochromatic** palette offers color gradients that go from dark to light and from light to dark, so you can use a color effect that is appropriate to your data.

7   At the bottom of the **Monochromatic** palette, click the light-to-dark purple gradient (**Color 15**). Then click the **Chart Styles** button to close the gallery.

8　Point to an area of the chart between the axes that contains the data markers, and when a ScreenTip indicates that you are pointing to the plot area, click to select it.

9　On the **Format** tool tab, in the **Shape Styles** group, click the **Shape Fill** arrow, and then in the **Theme Colors** palette, click the first swatch under the orange swatch (**Orange, Accent 6, Lighter 80%**) to distinguish the plot area from the rest of the chart.

> **TIP** To change several aspects of the plot area, right-click the area and then click Format Plot Area to open the Format Plot Area pane, from which you can change the fill and border and apply shadow, glow, soft-edge, and three-dimensional effects.

10　At the top of the **Current Selection** group, click the **Chart Elements** arrow to display a list of the elements of the current chart.

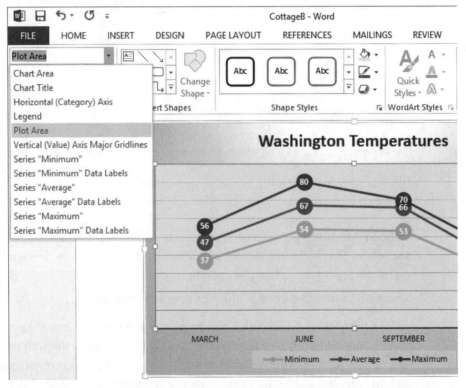

You can select a chart element by clicking it in the chart or by selecting it from the list.

11   In the **Chart Elements** list, click **Series "Maximum"** to select the data points of the top line on the chart.

12   In the **Current Selection** group, click the **Format Selection** button to display the **Series Options** page of the **Format Data Series** pane.

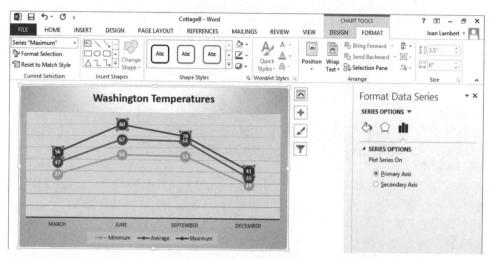

The Format Data Series pane displays the formatting options for whatever chart element is selected.

13   At the top of the **Format Data Series** pane, click the **Fill and Line** button (the bucket) to display the **Line** options.

14   Click the **Outline color** button, and then in the **Standard Colors** palette, click the **Green** swatch.

15   Near the top of the pane, click **Marker** to display the **Marker Options**, **Fill**, and **Border** categories.

16   In the **Fill** category, click **Solid Fill**. Click the **Fill Color** button, and then in the **Standard Colors** palette, click the **Green** swatch.

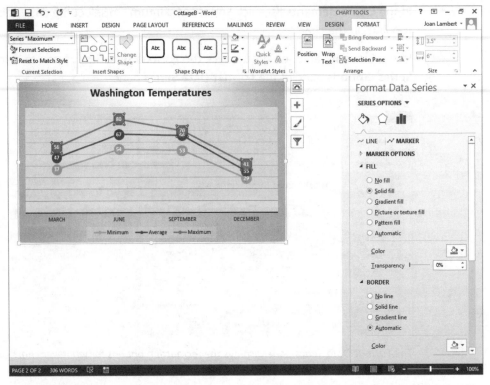

The Maximum temperature data series is now represented by the color green, both on the chart and in the legend.

17 Close the **Format Data Series** pane and click a blank part of the chart area to release the data series. Then to the right of the chart, click the **Chart Elements** button.

Next, we'll change the chart elements that are displayed.

18 In the **Chart Elements** list, clear the **Data Labels**, **Gridlines**, and **Legend** check boxes to remove those elements from the chart. Then select the **Axis Titles** and **Data Table** check boxes, and click the arrow that appears to the right of **Data Table** to verify that the **With Legend Keys** option is selected.

TIP You can display specific sets of chart elements by choosing a preformatted layout from the Quick Layouts gallery on the Design tool tab.

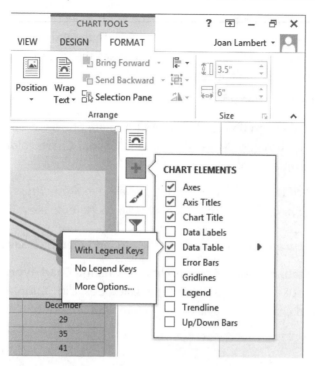

You can display or hide chart elements from this list.

19 Click the **Chart Elements** button to close the list. You've completely changed the presentation of your data with only a few clicks.

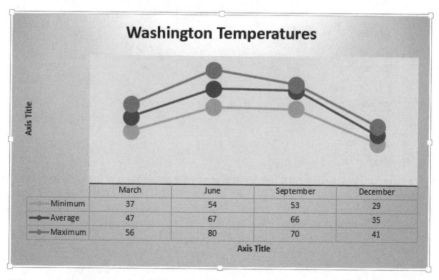

	March	June	September	December
Minimum	37	54	53	29
Average	47	67	66	35
Maximum	56	80	70	41

When you don't have a lot of data, displaying a datasheet can clarify without adding clutter.

20   In the chart, click the **Axis Title** placeholder on the left to select it, and then enter Degrees F to replace the placeholder text. Then replace the **Axis Title** placeholder on the bottom with Month. Notice that you can replace the text even though only the placeholder, and not the text, is selected.

Finally, we'll save the chart element as a template.

21   Right-click the chart area and then click **Save As Template** button to open the **Save Chart Template** dialog box and display the contents of your **Charts** folder, which is a subfolder of your **Templates** folder.

> **TROUBLESHOOTING** If the Charts folder is not displayed in the Address bar, navigate to the C:\Users\<*user name*>\AppData\Roaming\Microsoft\Templates\Charts folder.

22   Enter My Temperature Chart in the **File name** box, and then click **Save**.

23   On the **Design** tool tab, in the **Type** group, click the **Change Chart Type** button, and then in the left pane of the **Change Chart Type** dialog box, click **Templates** to verify that your customized chart is now available as a template.

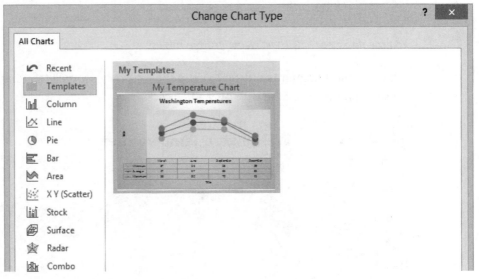

In the future, you can click the custom template to create a chart with the same layout and formatting.

24   In the **Change Chart Type** dialog box, click **Cancel** to close the dialog box without creating a new chart.

❌ CLEAN UP Close the CottageB document, saving your changes if you want to.

Using existing data in charts

If the data you want to plot as a chart in Word already exists in a Microsoft Access database, an Excel worksheet, or a Word table, you can copy the data from its source program and paste it into the chart worksheet.

In this exercise, you'll copy data stored in an Excel worksheet into a chart's worksheet and then expand the plotted data range so that the new data appears in the chart.

➡ SET UP You need the CottageC document and the Temperature workbook located in the Chapter08 practice file folder to complete this exercise. Open the document, and then follow the steps.

1   Scroll to the end of the document to display the chart, and then click a blank part of the chart area to display the **Chart Tools** tabs.

2   On the **Design** tool tab, in the **Data** group, click the **Edit Data** arrow and then in the list click **Edit Data in Excel 2013** to display the chart data in an Excel worksheet.

3   In the Excel window, display the **Open** page of the **Backstage** view. In the left pane of the **Open** page, click **Computer**, and then in the right pane, click the **Browse** button. In the **Open** dialog box, navigate to the **Chapter08** practice file folder, and double-click the **Temperature** workbook to open it in a new Excel window.

4   In the **Temperature** workbook, on the **View** tab, in the **Window** group, click the **Arrange All** button. Then in the **Arrange Windows** dialog box, click **Horizontal**, and click **OK** to arrange the **Temperature** worksheet above the chart data worksheet so that both are visible at the same time.

8

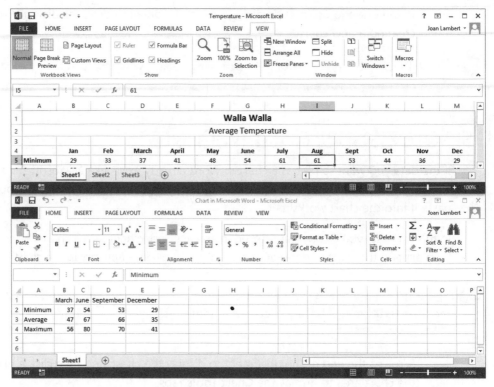

Displaying two worksheets at the same time makes it easy to copy data between them.

5   In the **Temperature** workbook, position the worksheet to display both cell **B4** and cell **M7**. Click cell **B4**, hold down the **Shift** key, and then click cell **M7** to select the range **B4:M7**.

6   In the **Temperature** workbook, on the **Home** tab, in the **Clipboard** group, click the **Copy** button.

KEYBOARD SHORTCUT Press Ctrl+C to copy the selected content to the Microsoft Office Clipboard.

7   Click the title bar of the **Chart in Microsoft Word** workbook to activate it, click cell **B1**, and then on the **Home** tab, in the **Clipboard** group, click the **Paste** button to paste the copied data into the chart data worksheet.

KEYBOARD SHORTCUT Press Ctrl+V to paste the most recent contents from the Clipboard.

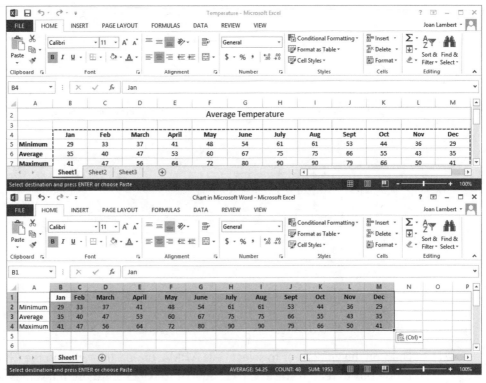

The copied data will be plotted in the chart.

8 Close the **Temperature** workbook. Maximize the chart workbook and click cell **A1** to release the selection. Now you need to specify that the new data should be included in the chart.

9 Switch to the **CottageC** document and click a blank part of the chart area. On the **Design** tool tab, in the **Data** group, click the **Select Data** button to activate the chart worksheet and open the **Select Data Source** dialog box. Drag the **Select Data Source** dialog box so that the worksheet data is visible.

TIP You can also import data into your chart from a text file, webpage, or other external source, such as Microsoft SQL Server. To import data, first display the associated Excel worksheet. Then on the Excel Data tab, in the Get External Data group, click the button for your data source, and navigate to the source. For more information, refer to Excel Help.

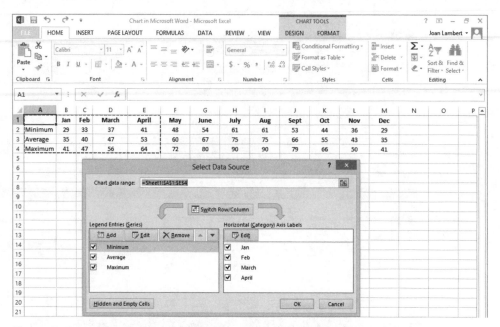

You can enter a data range in the dialog box or select the data on the worksheet.

10   Drag on the worksheet to select cells **A1:M4**, or edit the range in the **Chart data range** box to read =Sheet1!$A$1:$M$4 to tell Excel to use the values in **A1:M4** on **Sheet1** of the associated worksheet. (The **$** symbols ensure that only that range of cells will be used as the source of the chart's data. **Sheet1** is the name defined for the worksheet on the sheet tab at the bottom of the Excel program window.)

11   In the **Select Data Source** dialog box, click **OK**, and then close the chart worksheet to display the updated chart. Notice that you are not prompted to save the chart worksheet as a file.

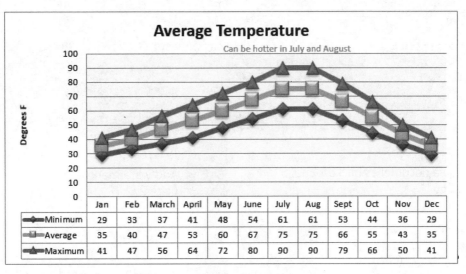

	Jan	Feb	March	April	May	June	July	Aug	Sept	Oct	Nov	Dec
Minimum	29	33	37	41	48	54	61	61	53	44	36	29
Average	35	40	47	53	60	67	75	75	66	55	43	35
Maximum	41	47	56	64	72	80	90	90	79	66	50	41

The chart depicts a range of temperatures throughout the year.

❌ CLEAN UP Close the CottageC document, saving your changes if you want to.

Key points

8

- A chart is often the most efficient way to present numeric data with at-a-glance clarity.

- You can select the type of chart and change the appearance of its elements until it clearly conveys key information.

- Existing data in a Word table, Excel workbook, Access database, or other structured source can easily be copied and pasted into the associated chart worksheet, eliminating time-consuming typing.

Chapter at a glance

Decorate

Change a document's background,
page 266

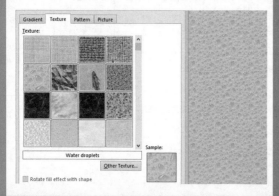

Mark

Add watermarks,
page 272

Certified Applications Specialist (MCAS) Instructor, a Microsoft Certified Technology
Specialist (MCTS), and the author of more than two dozen books about Windows and Office
(for Windows and Mac).

Joyce Cox

Joyce Cox has over 30 years' experience in the development of training materials about
technical subjects for non-technical audiences, and is the author of dozens of books about
Office and Windows technologies. She is the Vice President of Online Training Solutions, Inc.

As President of and principal author for Online Press, she developed the Quick Course series
of computer training books for beginning and intermediate adult learners. She was also the
first managing editor of Microsoft Press, an editor for Sybex, and an editor for the University
of California.

Online Training Solutions, Inc. (OTSI)

OTSI specializes in the design, creation, and production of Office and Windows training
products for office and home computer users. For more information about OTSI, visit

www.otsi.com

Reuse

Insert preformatted document parts,
page 276

[Sidebar Title]
[Sidebars are great for calling out important points from your text or adding additional info for quick reference, such as a schedule. They are typically placed on the left, right, top or bottom of the page. But you can easily drag them to any position you prefer. When you're ready to add your content, just click here and start typing.]

If you're not sure you made the right choices and don't know which way to turn, arrange to meet with one of our designers. This free service is available to all our customers. Sometimes talking over your plans or obstacles with a professional can really help get you back on track.

Success! Your room is everything you hoped for. Now what about your bedroom? Maybe a new linen chest or perhaps new window treatments? The Room Planner can be used countless times for any room in the house. And if you're eyeing your patio or deck as your next makeover project, you'll want to check out the Outdoor Room Planner, too.

NOTE: To order the Room Planner for just $39.99 plus shipping and handling, visit our website at www.wideworldimporters.com or call us at 925-555-0167. The Outdoor Room Planner retails for $29.99 plus shipping and handling. Both planners are also available in our stores, so be sure to ask about them the next time you visit. We accept all major credit cards.

Calculate

Build equations,
page 288

Services
The following services are available to enhance your visit:

Limousine winery tour:	$49.99 per person
In-home massage:	$55.00 per hour
Guided fishing trips	
Full-day base cost:	$575.00 for up to three people
Half-day base cost:	$325.00 for up to three people
Each additional person:	

$$(p - 3) * \frac{b}{3}$$

where p is the total number of
people and b is the base cost

Add visual elements

9

IN THIS CHAPTER, YOU WILL LEARN HOW TO

- Change a document's background.

- Add watermarks.

- Insert preformatted document parts.

- Build equations.

We have looked at some of the more common graphic elements you can add to a document, such as pictures, diagrams, and charts. These elements reinforce concepts or make a document more attention grabbing or visually appealing. You can also improve the appearance of a document by using other types of visual elements, such as the following:

- **Backgrounds** You can apply a variety of backgrounds to the pages of your document, including plain colors, gradients, textures, patterns, and pictures.

- **Watermarks** You can provide information without distracting from the document content by adding text or graphic watermarks to the page background of a document.

- **Building blocks** You can draw attention to specific information and add graphic appeal by incorporating ready-made graphic building blocks (also called *Quick Parts*) into a document. These building blocks are combinations of drawing objects (and sometimes pictures) in a variety of formatting styles that you can select to insert elements such as cover pages, quotations pulled from the text (called *pull quotes*), and sidebars. You can also create your own building blocks.

In this chapter, you'll first experiment with page backgrounds, and then create text and picture watermarks. You'll add three types of building blocks to a document. Finally, you'll build a simple equation.

PRACTICE FILES To complete the exercises in this chapter, you need the practice files contained in the Chapter09 practice file folder. For more information, see "Download the practice files" in this book's Introduction.

Changing a document's background

Whether you're creating a document that will be printed, viewed on a computer, or published on the Internet and viewed in a web browser, you can make your document stand out by adding a background color, texture, picture, or border to the document pages.

SEE ALSO For information about creating documents for the web, see "Creating and modifying web documents" in Chapter 11, "Create documents for use outside of Word."

When it comes to backgrounds, the trick is to not overdo it. The effects should be subtle enough that they do not interfere with the text or other elements on the page or make the document difficult to read.

In this exercise, you'll first apply a solid background color to every page. Then you'll create a two-color gradient across the pages. You'll fill the pages with one of the textures that comes with Word and then fill them with a picture. Finally, you'll put a border around every page.

 SET UP You need the MarbleFloor picture located in the Chapter09 practice file folder to complete this exercise. Open a blank document, turn off the rulers and formatting marks, and then follow the steps.

1   On the **View** tab, in the **Zoom** group, click the **One Page** button to display the whole page in the program window.

2   On the **Design** tab, in the **Page Background** group, click the **Page Color** button. On the **Page Color** menu, in the **Theme Colors** palette, click the second swatch under the main green swatch (**Green, Accent 6, Lighter 60%**) to change the document background to the selected color.

3   On the **Page Color** menu, click **Fill Effects** to open the **Fill Effects** dialog box.

4   In the **Colors** area, select the **Two colors** option. Leave **Color 1** set to green. Click the **Color 2** arrow, and in the **Theme Colors** palette, click the third swatch under the main orange swatch (**Orange, Accent 2, Lighter 40%**). The **Variants** and **Sample** areas change to show various combinations of the two colors.

5   In the **Shading styles** area, click each option in turn and observe the effects in the **Variants** and **Sample** areas. Notice that some shading styles have only two variants. Then click **Diagonal down**.

6   In the **Variants** area, click the lower-left option to preview its effect. Then click **OK** to change the document background to match the sample.

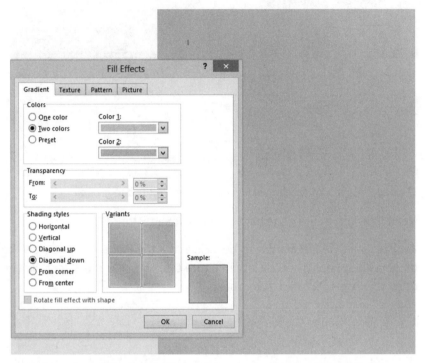

You can configure fill effects with multiple colors and in a variety of directions.

Now let's format the page background with a texture fill.

7   Redisplay the **Fill Effects** dialog box. Click the **Texture** tab to display the 24 texture fill options that come with Word.

8   Scroll through the gallery to familiarize yourself with the available textures. Click the first texture swatch in the second row (**Water droplets**), and then click **OK** to format the page background with the texture. Notice that the texture swatch has been configured to repeat seamlessly across the page.

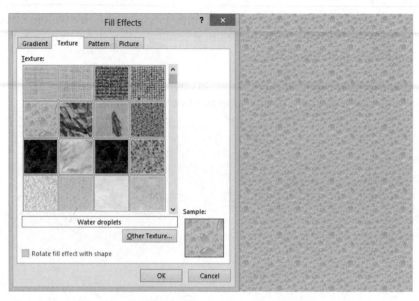

The page with the Water Droplets texture applied to the background.

Next, let's format the page background with a picture fill.

9 Redisplay the **Fill Effects** dialog box. First click the **Pattern** tab to view the available pattern fill options. Then click the **Picture** tab, and click the **Select Picture** button to open the **Insert Pictures** dialog box.

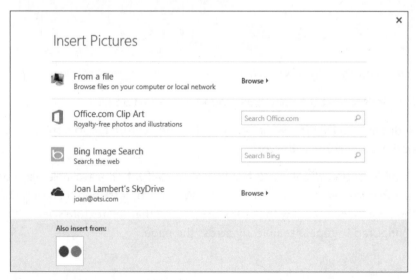

You can select a background picture from your computer, network location, or an online source.

TIP You can insert background pictures from the Texture tab or from the Picture tab with slightly different results. Inserting an image from the Texture tab adds it to the Texture gallery.

10   In the **From a file** area of the **Insert Pictures** dialog box, click **Browse**. In the **Select Picture** dialog box that opens, browse to the **Chapter09** practice file folder and double-click the **MarbleFloor** image. Then in the **Fill Effects** dialog box, click **OK** to change the page background to display a blurred picture of the marble floor in the Doge's Palace in Venice.

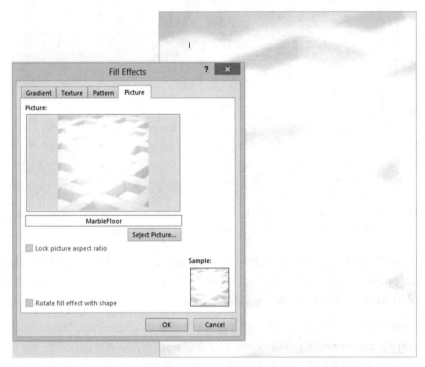

The page with the MarbleFloor picture applied to the background.

TIP Word fills the page with as much of the picture as will fit. If one copy of the picture does not completely fill the page, Word inserts another copy, effectively "tiling" the image. If the picture is particularly large, only a portion of it will be visible.

Finally, let's add a border to the page.

11   In the **Page Background** group, click the **Page Borders** button to display the **Page Border** page of the **Borders and Shading** dialog box.

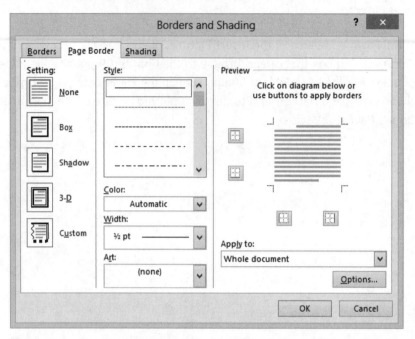

The Page Border page is identical to the Borders page from which you format paragraph borders, except that an Art option is available for page borders.

12   In the **Setting** area of the **Borders and Shading** dialog box, click **Box**. Then click the **Color** arrow, and in the **Theme Colors** palette, click the fourth swatch under the main gold swatch, (**Gold, Accent 4, Darker 25%**).

13   Scroll through the **Style** list, clicking any line style option you like to apply it to the page in the **Preview** pane. When you find a style you like, click **OK**. We chose a triple border near the bottom of the list.

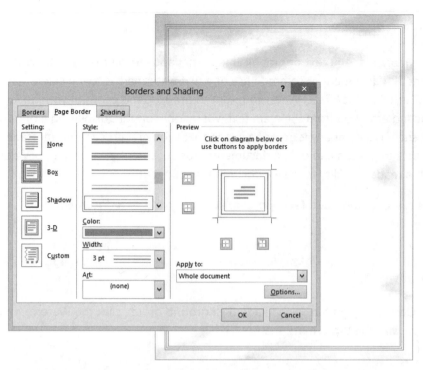

The blank page with a border applied on top of the background picture.

14   On the **Insert** tab, in the **Pages** group, click **Page Break**, and then scroll to display the new second page. Notice that the background options are applied to all pages of the document.

KEYBOARD SHORTCUT Press Ctrl+Enter to insert a page break. For more information about keyboard shortcuts, see "Keyboard shortcuts" at the end of this book.

✕ CLEAN UP Close the document, saving it if you want to.

9

Adding watermarks

A watermark is a faint text or graphic image that appears on the page behind the main content of a document. A common use of a text watermark is to indicate a status such as *DRAFT* or *CONFIDENTIAL*. When you want to dress up the pages of your document without distracting attention from the main text, you might consider displaying a graphic watermark, such as a company logo or an image that subtly reinforces your message. Watermarks are visible in printed and online documents, but because they are faint, they don't interfere with the readers' ability to view a document's main text.

In this exercise, you'll add text and graphic watermarks to a document.

 SET UP You need the AuthorsDraft document and the OTSI-Logo image located in the Chapter09 practice file folder to complete this exercise. Open the document, and then follow the steps.

1   On the **Design** tab, in the **Page Background** group, click the **Watermark** button to display the **Watermark** menu.

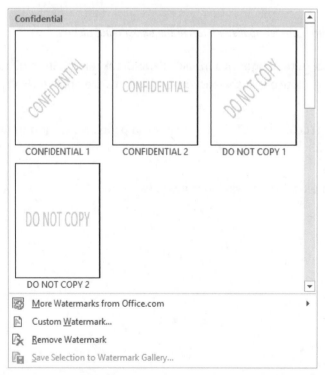

You can use a predefined watermark or click Custom Watermark to define your own.

2   Scroll through the watermark galleries, noticing the available options. Clicking any of these options inserts the specified watermark in light gray on every page of the current document.

3   At the bottom of the menu, click **Custom Watermark** to open the **Printed Watermark** dialog box. Then click **Text watermark**.

In this dialog box, you can specify a custom picture or text watermark.

4   Click the **Text** arrow, and then in the list, click **DRAFT**.

5   Click the **Color** arrow, and then in the **Theme Colors** palette, click the main purple swatch (**Purple, Accent 4**).

6   With the **Semitransparent** check box and **Diagonal** layout option selected, click **OK** to insert the watermark diagonally across the page and close the dialog box.

> **TIP** Watermarks are so named because the process of creating one on an actual sheet of paper is done by using water. A well-created watermark appears to be more part of the paper than of the content.

9

About the Authors

Joan Lambert

Joan has worked in the training and certification industry for over 15 years. As President of OTSI, Joan is responsible for guiding the translation of technical information and requirements into useful, relevant, and measurable training and certification tools.

Joan is a Microsoft Certified Office Master, a Microsoft Certified Trainer (MCT), a Microsoft Certified Applications Specialist (MCAS) Instructor, a Microsoft Certified Technology Specialist (MCTS), and the author of more than two dozen books about Windows and Office (for Windows and Mac).

Joyce Cox

Joyce has over 30 years' experience in the development of training materials about technical subjects for non-technical audiences, and is the author of dozens of books about Office and Windows technologies. She is the Vice President of Online Training Solutions, Inc.

As President of and principal author for Online Press, she developed the Quick Course series of computer training books for beginning and intermediate adult learners. She was also the first managing editor of Microsoft Press, an editor for Sybex, and an editor for the University of California.

Online Training Solutions, Inc. (OTSI)

OTSI specializes in the design, creation, and production of Office and Windows training products for office and home computer users. For more information about OTSI, visit

www.otsi.com

The text watermark is faint enough that the document text is still legible, but bold enough to be noticed.

Next let's insert a picture watermark.

7   Redisplay the **Printed Watermark** dialog box. Click **Picture watermark**, and then click **Select Picture** to open the **Insert Pictures** dialog box.

8   In the **From a file** area of the **Insert Pictures** dialog box, click **Browse**. In the **Insert Picture** dialog box that opens, browse to the **Chapter09** practice file folder and double-click the **OTSI-Logo** image to insert the image's file path in the **Printed Watermark** dialog box.

9   In the **Printed Watermark** dialog box, click the **Scale** arrow and then, in the list, click **200%**.

10 With the **Washout** check box selected, click **Apply** to insert the watermark in the document but leave the dialog box open. Drag the dialog box by its title bar until the watermark is displayed.

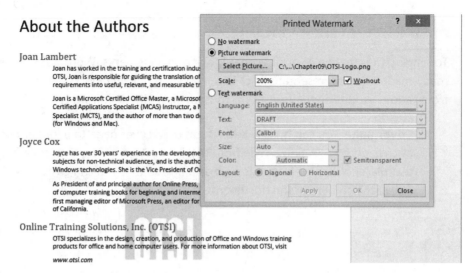

About the Authors

Joan Lambert

Joan has worked in the training and certification industry for over 15 years. As President of OTSI, Joan is responsible for guiding the translation of technical information and requirements into useful, relevant, and measurable training and certification tools.

Joan is a Microsoft Certified Office Master, a Microsoft Certified Trainer (MCT), a Microsoft Certified Applications Specialist (MCAS) Instructor, a Microsoft Certified Technology Specialist (MCTS), and the author of more than two dozen books about Windows and Office (for Windows and Mac).

Joyce Cox

Joyce has over 30 years' experience in the development of training materials about technical subjects for non-technical audiences, and is the author of dozens of books about Office and Windows technologies. She is the Vice President of Online Training Solutions, Inc. (OTSI).

As President of and principal author for Online Press, she developed the Quick Course series of computer training books for beginning and intermediate adult learners. She was also the first managing editor of Microsoft Press, an editor for Sybex, and an editor for the University of California.

Online Training Solutions, Inc. (OTSI)

OTSI specializes in the design, creation, and production of Office and Windows training products for office and home computer users. For more information about OTSI, visit

www.otsi.com

You can adjust the size of a picture watermark, but you can't change its angle.

Let's make the watermark larger.

11   In the **Printed Watermark** dialog box, click in the **Scale** box, drag to select **200%**, and enter **400%** to replace the existing setting. Then click **OK** to change the watermark size and close the dialog box.

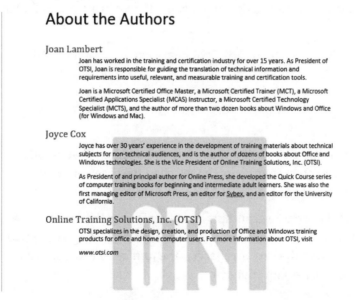

The picture watermark adds visual interest without obscuring the text.

❌ CLEAN UP Close the AuthorsDraft document, saving your changes if you want to.

Inserting preformatted document parts

To simplify the creation of professional-looking text elements, Word 2013 comes with ready-made visual representations of text, known as *building blocks*, which are available from various groups on the Insert tab. You can insert the following types of building blocks:

- **Cover page** You can quickly add a formatted cover page to a longer document such as a report by selecting a style from the **Cover Page** gallery. The cover page includes text placeholders for elements such as a title so that you can customize the page to reflect the content of the document.

  TIP You can quickly insert a blank page anywhere in a document—even in the middle of a paragraph—by positioning the cursor and then clicking the Blank Page button in the Pages group on the Insert tab.

- **Header and footer** You can display information on every page of a document in regions at the top and bottom of a page by selecting a style from the **Header** or **Footer** gallery. Word displays dotted borders to indicate the header and footer areas, and displays a **Design** tool tab on the ribbon. You can enter and format information in the header and footer by using the same techniques you do in the document body and also by using commands on the **Design** tool tab. You can have a different header and footer on the first page of a document and different headers and footers on odd and even pages.

  TIP If your document contains section breaks, each successive section inherits the headers and footers of the preceding section unless you break the link between the two sections. You can then create a different header and footer for the current section. For information about sections, see "Controlling what appears on each page" in Chapter 6, "Preview, print, and distribute documents."

- **Page number** You can quickly add headers and footers that include only page numbers and require no customization by selecting the style you want from one of the **Page Number** galleries.

- **Text box** To reinforce key concepts and also alleviate the monotony of page after page of plain text, you can insert text boxes such as sidebars and quote boxes by selecting a style from the **Text Box** gallery. The formatted text box includes placeholder text that you replace with your own.

If you frequently use a specific element in your documents, such as a formatted title-subtitle-author arrangement at the beginning of reports, you can define it as a custom building block. It is then available from the Quick Parts gallery.

SEE ALSO For information about saving frequently used text as a building block, see "Creating custom building blocks" in Chapter 16, "Work in Word more efficiently."

You can display information about the available building blocks by clicking the Quick Parts button in the Text group on the Insert tab and then clicking Building Blocks Organizer.

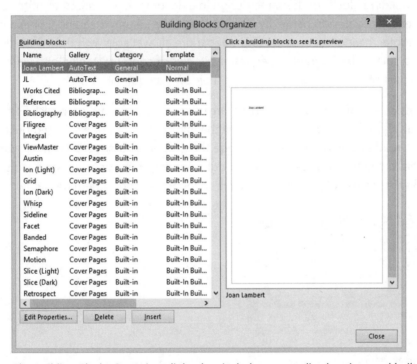

The Building Blocks Organizer dialog box includes personalized options and built-in options for design elements such as headers, footers, page numbers, tables, text boxes, and watermarks.

TROUBLESHOOTING If the screen resolution of your display is such that the Quick Parts button is displayed as a large button, it is labeled *Quick Parts*. If the button is displayed as a small, unlabeled button, its ScreenTip is *Explore Quick Parts*. For simplicity, we refer to it in this book as the *Quick Parts button*.

The left pane of the Building Blocks Organizer dialog box displays a complete list of all the building blocks available on your computer. Clicking a building block in the left pane displays a preview in the right pane, along with its description and behavior.

TIP The Building Blocks list on your computer includes AutoText entries for your user name and initials. To change either of these entries, update your information on the General page of the Word Options dialog box.

Initially the building blocks are organized by type, as reflected in the Gallery column. If you want to insert building blocks of the same design in a document, you might want to sort the list alphabetically by design name, by clicking the Name column heading. For example, a cover page, footer, header, quote box, and sidebar are all available with the Whisp design. Some elements, such as bibliographies, equations, tables of contents, tables, and watermarks, are not part of a design family and have their own unique names.

In the lower-left corner of the Building Blocks Organizer dialog box, you can click Edit Properties to display a dialog box containing all the information about a selected building block in a more readable format. You can change the properties associated with any building block in this dialog box (but be cautious about changing the properties assigned to the building blocks that came with Word; you might accidentally render them unusable).

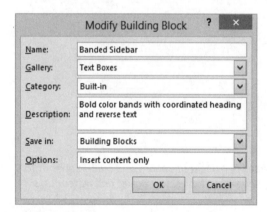

The Modify Building Block dialog box.

You can delete the selected building block from the list (and from the Building Blocks global template) by clicking Delete at the bottom of the Building Blocks Organizer dialog box, and you can insert a selected building block into the document by clicking Insert.

SEE ALSO For information about global templates, see "Creating custom styles and templates" in Chapter 16, "Work in Word more efficiently."

In this exercise, you'll add a cover page, header, and footer to a document. You'll also insert a quote box and a sidebar, and save the customized sidebar as a building block.

SET UP You need the Flyer document located in the Chapter09 practice file folder to complete this exercise. Open the document, set the zoom level to display the entire page, and then follow the steps.

1   Ensure that the cursor is at the top of the document. On the **Insert** tab, in the **Pages** group, click the **Cover Page** button to display the gallery of available cover pages.

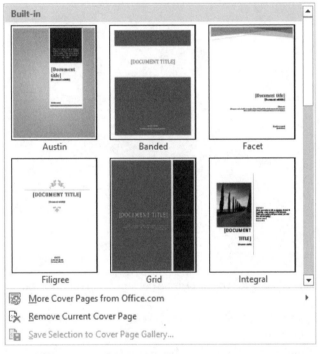

The thumbnails show the designs of the available cover pages.

TROUBLESHOOTING You might have different cover page thumbnails than we show here. We've created this exercise by using document elements that we think will be available to all readers. If the specified element isn't available on your computer, substitute another.

2   Scroll through the **Cover Page** gallery to display the available options, and then click **Semaphore** to insert the cover page at the beginning of the document. Notice that the cover page includes placeholders for the date, title, subtitle, author name, company name, and company address.

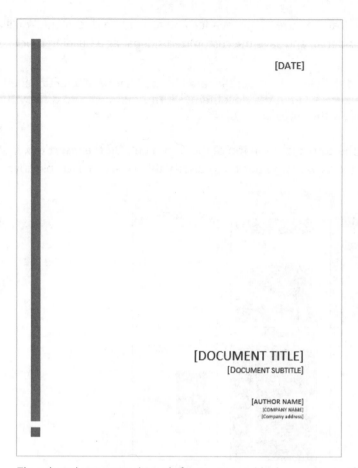

[DATE]

[DOCUMENT TITLE]
[DOCUMENT SUBTITLE]

[AUTHOR NAME]
[COMPANY NAME]
[Company address]

The selected cover page is ready for you to provide document-specific information.

TIP If any of the required information is already saved with the properties of the document into which you're inserting the cover page, Word inserts the saved information instead of the placeholders. For information about document properties, see "Preparing documents for electronic distribution" in Chapter 6, "Preview, print, and distribute documents."

3   Click the **Date** placeholder, click the arrow that appears, and then in the calendar control that appears, click **Today**.

4   Click the **Document title** placeholder, and then enter Simple Room Design. Notice as you enter the text that it appears on the page in capital letters. This is due to the character formatting applied to the style.

5   Click the **Document subtitle** placeholder, and enter Using the Room Planner tool. Notice that this text appears on the page in *small caps*—all the letters look like capital letters, but the actual capital letters are taller than the others.

6   Click the **Author name** placeholder, and begin entering your name. Partway through, Word should recognize your name from the user name information stored with the program and display a ScreenTip containing your completed name.

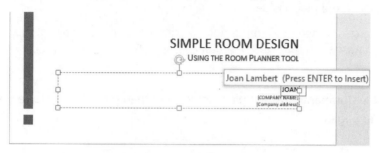

When you begin entering your name, Word recognizes you.

7   Enter the rest of your name, or if the ScreenTip appears, press **Enter** to have Word insert it for you. Then display the **Info** page of the **Backstage** view, and notice that some of the information you entered on the cover page is now visible in the **Properties** area.

Properties ▾

Size	26.9KB
Pages	3
Words	821
Total Editing Time	0 Minutes
Title	Simple Room Design
Tags	Add a tag
Comments	Add comments

Related Dates

Last Modified	10/25/2012 6:48 AM
Created	5/3/2010 1:34 PM
Last Printed	

Related People

Author  Joan Lambert

Add an author

Last Modified By   Not saved yet

Entering information in fields in the document populates the document properties.

8   At the bottom of the **Properties** area, click the **Show All Properties** link to display more properties. In the expanded list of properties, point to the text to the right of **Company** and click in the box that appears. Then enter the name of your company or organization (if you don't have one, you can use Graphic Design Institute).

9   Click the **Back** arrow above the page tabs to return to the cover page. Notice that the company name you entered in the **Properties** area now appears in place of the **Company Name** placeholder.

> **TIP** You are not restricted to the default contents of the cover page building block; you can change it in any way that you want to. Think of it as a convenient starting point.

10   Select the **Company Address** placeholder, and then press **Delete** to remove it from the cover page.

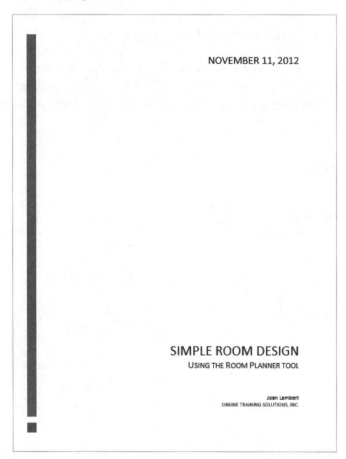

NOVEMBER 11, 2012

SIMPLE ROOM DESIGN
Using the Room Planner Tool

Joan Lambert
ONLINE TRAINING SOLUTIONS, INC.

The completed cover page, including information that is now saved with the document properties.

Now let's add headers and footers to the document. We'll use two different headers designed for odd pages and even pages, and their coordinating footers, so that when the document is printed double-sided, the headers and footers will always appear on the outside edges of the paper.

11 Scroll to the second page. Select and delete the heading **Simple Room Design**, because its function is now fulfilled by the document title on the cover page.

12 With the cursor at the beginning of page **2**, on the **Insert** tab, in the **Header & Footer** group, click the **Header** button. Scroll through the **Header** gallery, and then click the **Facet (Even Page)** header to add it to the page. Notice that although you're on the second page of the file, the header displays page number **1**. This is because the cover page is counted separately from the document pages.

> **TIP** You can mix different headers, footers, and document themes to create a document that has the look and feel you want.

13 Investigate the configuration options available on the **Design** tool tab. In the **Options** group, select the **Different Odd & Even Pages** check box, and notice that the header label changes from **Header** to **Odd Page Header**.

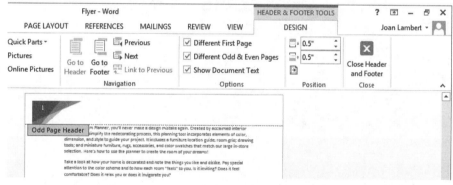

The header label helps you determine which kind of header to use.

> **TIP** In step 13, we inserted an even page header on the second page of the document, but Word now indicates that it is an odd page, because it is page number 1 of the document following the cover page. However, if we print the document double-sided, the even page header will align appropriately on the outside edge of the paper when we turn the pages.

14 In the **Navigation** group, click the **Next** button to move to the header area at the top of the page **3**. In the **Header** gallery, click the **Facet (Odd Page)** thumbnail to insert the header. Again, the seemingly incorrect page number **2** appears in the header because the document content is numbered separately from the cover page.

> **TIP** To use a numbering scheme other than arabic numerals, to number pages by chapter, or to control the starting number, click the Page Number button in the Header & Footer group, and then click Format Page Numbers. In the Page Number Format dialog box, you can select from several page numbering formats and options.

15 In the **Navigation** group, click the **Go to Footer** button to move the cursor to the footer area at the bottom of the last page of the document. In the **Header & Footer** group, click the **Footer** button, and then in the gallery, click the **Facet (Odd Page)** thumbnail to insert the footer and the associated document properties.

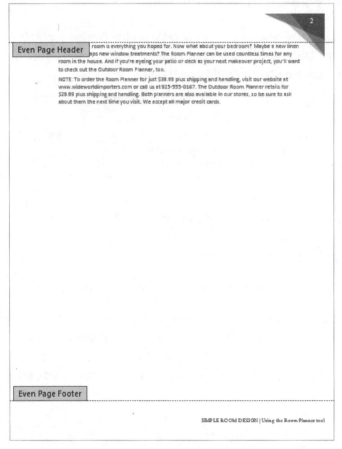

Headers and footers can include any information you want to display, including graphics.

16 In the **Navigation** group, click the **Previous** button to move to the footer area of the second page. In the **Footer** gallery, click the **Facet (Even Page)** thumbnail to insert the footer and the associated document properties. Then in the **Close** group, click the **Close Header and Footer** button.

All pages of the document other than the cover page now have a header and footer. Next, let's add a quote box to emphasize a specific phrase in the document.

17 On the **Insert** tab, in the **Text** group, click the **Quick Parts** button, and then click **Building Blocks Organizer** to open the **Building Blocks Organizer** dialog box shown at the beginning of this topic.

18 Scroll through the **Building blocks** list, previewing a few of the building blocks. Click the **Name** column heading, double-click the separator to the right of the **Name** column heading so that all the names are visible, and then scroll through the list again. Notice that page elements of the same theme are coordinated.

19 In the **Building blocks** list, click **Semaphore Quote**, and notice its position on the page shown in the preview pane. Then click **Insert** to insert the quote box in the same position on the document page and display the **Drawing Tools Format** tool tab, from which you can format the quote box contents.

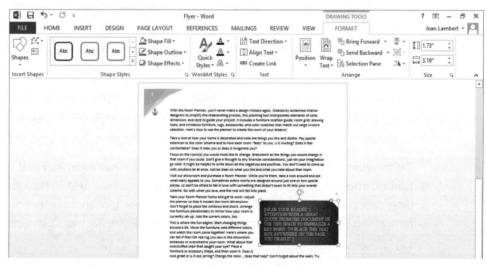

Placeholder text in the quote box tells how to enter text and move the quote box on the page.

20 Change the zoom level of the document to **100%** so that the text is legible. Select and copy the last sentence of the fourth paragraph of the document (**Go with what you love...**). Then click the placeholder in the quote box to select the placeholder text.

Drawing text boxes

If none of the predefined text-box building blocks meet your needs, you can draw and format your own text box. On the Insert tab, click Text Box, and then click Draw Text Box to activate the drawing tool. Click and drag to draw a box of the approximate size you want anywhere on the page. You can immediately start typing at the blinking cursor, and you can format the text the way you would any other text. You can format the text box shape, outline, fill, and other properties by using the commands on the Drawing Tools Format tab. Click inside a text box to edit and format the text; click the text box frame to format the text box.

When a text box has a solid border, you can reposition it by dragging it to another location or pressing the arrow keys, rotate it by dragging the rotate handle, and change its size by dragging the size handles around its frame.

You can link text boxes so that text flows from one to the next. To do so:

1   Ensure that the second text box is empty.

2   Click the first text box.

3   On the **Format** tool tab, in the **Text** group, click **Create Link**. The pointer shape changes to a pitcher.

4   Point to the second text box, and when the pointer changes to a pouring pitcher, click once.

Text boxes are not accessible to adaptive technologies, so if you want to ensure that a text reading program can access the content of your document, do not use a text box.

21   On the **Home** tab, in the **Clipboard** group, click the **Paste** arrow. Point to each of the **Paste Options** buttons to display a preview of the copied text in the quote box, and then click the **Keep Text Only** button to replace the placeholder text but retain its formatting. Notice that the quote box automatically resizes to fit its new contents.

SEE ALSO For more information about text boxes, see the sidebar "Drawing text boxes" later in this chapter.

22   Change the zoom level to display the whole page in the program window. Then scroll to the last page of the document, and click anywhere on the page.

23   On the **Insert** tab, in the **Text** group, click the **Text Box** button, scroll through the
      gallery, and click the **Facet Sidebar (Left)** thumbnail to insert the sidebar on the
      opposite side of the page from the header and footer content.

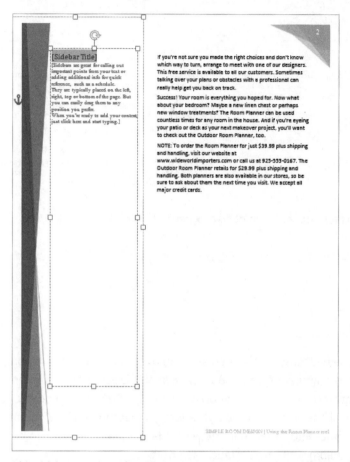

This sidebar consists of multiple overlapping text boxes and shapes.

24   Change the zoom level of the document to **100%** so that the text is legible.

25   With the **Sidebar Title** placeholder active, enter Ordering Information.

26   At the beginning of the last paragraph of the document, delete **NOTE:** (including the
      colon and following space). Then select the remainder of the paragraph, and cut the
      selected content to the Clipboard.

      KEYBOARD SHORTCUT Press Ctrl+X to cut the selected content to the Clipboard.

27 In the sidebar, click the sidebar content placeholder (not the sidebar title) to select the placeholder text. Then repeat step 21 to paste the text from the Clipboard into the sidebar and retain the sidebar formatting.

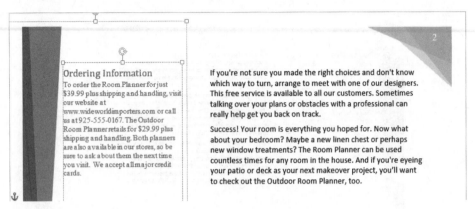

The pasted text takes on the formatting assigned to the text box.

❌ CLEAN UP Close the Flyer document, saving your changes if you want to.

Building equations

You can insert mathematical symbols, such as π (pi) or ∑ (sigma, or summation), the same way you would insert any other symbol. But you can also create entire mathematical equations in a document. You can insert some predefined equations, including the Quadratic Formula, the Binomial Theorem, and the Pythagorean Theorem, into a document with a few clicks. If you need something other than these standard equations, you can build your own equations by using a library of mathematical symbols.

SEE ALSO For information about symbols, see the sidebar "Inserting symbols" in Chapter 5, "Add simple graphic elements."

Equations are different from graphics in that they are accurately rendered mathematical formulas that appear in the document as fields. However, they are similar to graphics in that they can be displayed in line with the surrounding text or in their own space with text above and below them.

You can insert an equation from a gallery or by entering it into a box, by doing one of the following from the Symbols group on the Insert tab:

- Clicking the **Equation** *arrow* displays a gallery of commonly used equations and a menu of related commands. You can insert an equation from the gallery by clicking it, search for other predefined equations by clicking **More Equations from Office.com**, or start to build your own equation by clicking **Insert New Equation**.

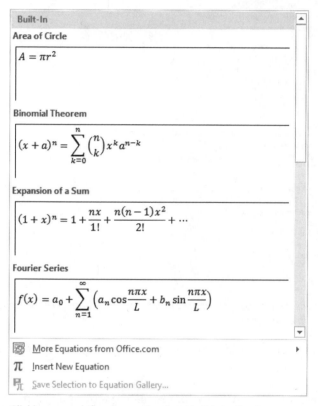

Built-In
Area of Circle

$$A = \pi r^2$$

Binomial Theorem

$$(x + a)^n = \sum_{k=0}^{n} \binom{n}{k} x^k a^{n-k}$$

Expansion of a Sum

$$(1 + x)^n = 1 + \frac{nx}{1!} + \frac{n(n-1)x^2}{2!} + \cdots$$

Fourier Series

$$f(x) = a_0 + \sum_{n=1}^{\infty} \left(a_n \cos\frac{n\pi x}{L} + b_n \sin\frac{n\pi x}{L} \right)$$

More Equations from Office.com

π Insert New Equation

Save Selection to Equation Gallery...

Clicking a predefined equation inserts it into the document at the cursor.

- Clicking the **Equation** *button* inserts a field in which you can build or enter an equation, and also displays the **Design** tool tab for equations. This tab provides access to mathematical symbols and structures such as fractions and radicals. Clicking the **Tools** dialog box launcher on the **Design** tool tab displays the **Equation Options** dialog box.

9

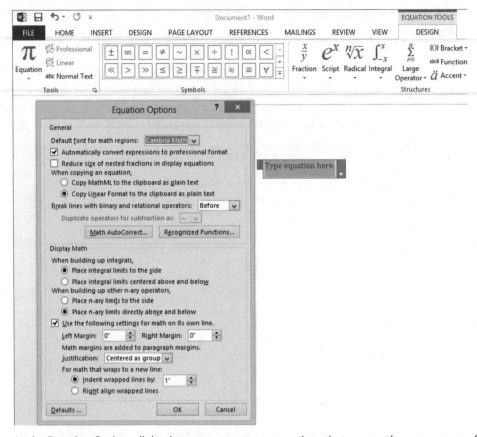

In the Equation Options dialog box, you can set many options that govern the appearance of equation expressions in a document.

After building an equation, you can add it to the Equation gallery so that it is readily available the next time you need it.

In this exercise, you'll build a simple equation for calculating a per-person price for a fishing trip, and you'll add the equation to the Equation gallery.

SET UP You need the Welcome document located in the Chapter09 practice file folder to complete this exercise. Open the document, and then follow the steps.

1   Press **Ctrl+End** to move to the end of the document.

2   On the **Insert** tab, in the **Symbols** group, click the **Equation** button to insert an equation field into the document.

3   Enter (p-3)* in the equation field.

TIP The asterisk represents a multiplication symbol.

4   On the **Design** tool tab, in the **Structures** group, click the **Fraction** button to display the **Fraction** gallery.

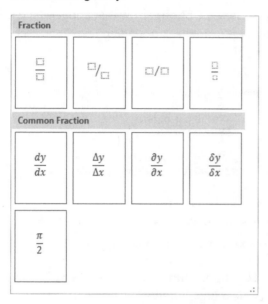

This gallery provides structures for forming fractions.

5   In the **Fraction** category, click the first thumbnail in the first row (**Stacked Fraction**) to insert structured placeholders for a simple fraction in the equation field.

Services
The following services are available to enhance your visit:

Limousine winery tour: $49.99 per person
In-home massage: $55.00 per hour
Guided fishing trips
    Full-day base cost: $575.00 for up to three people
    Half-day base cost: $325.00 for up to three people
    Each additional person: $(p-3) * \frac{\Box}{\Box}$

You can replace the placeholders within the fraction structure with alphanumeric characters or symbols.

6   Click the top box in the fraction structure, and enter b. Then click the bottom box, and enter 3.

7   Click the blank area to the right of the equation field. Then press the **Spacebar**, and enter where p is the total number of people and b is the base cost. (Include the period.) This equation subtracts 3 from the total number of people and multiplies the result by a per-person amount to calculate the cost for each additional person. Word has taken care of formatting the equation so that it looks professional.

8   Click the equation, click the **Equation Options** arrow that appears, and click **Change to Display** to set the equation off from the surrounding text. Then click away from the equation to display the result.

Services

The following services are available to enhance your visit:

Limousine winery tour:	$49.99 per person
In-home massage:	$55.00 per hour
Guided fishing trips	
Full-day base cost:	$575.00 for up to three people
Half-day base cost:	$325.00 for up to three people
Each additional person:	

$$(p - 3) * \frac{b}{3}$$

where p is the total number of people and b is the base cost

The variables in the equation are automatically formatted as italic.

9   Click the equation, click the **Equation Options** arrow, and then click **Save as New Equation** to open the **Create New Building Block** dialog box.

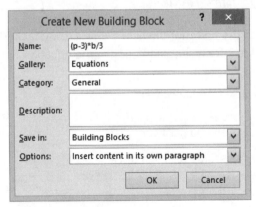

The equation is entered in the Name box.

SEE ALSO For more information about building blocks, see "Starting, entering text in, and saving documents" in Chapter 2, "Enter, edit, and proofread text."

10   In the **Name** box, replace the equation with Additional people cost. Then click **OK**.

11   Click away from the equation field to release the selection. Then on the **Insert** tab, in the **Symbols** group, click the **Equation** arrow, and scroll to the bottom of the **Equation** gallery to display your custom equation.

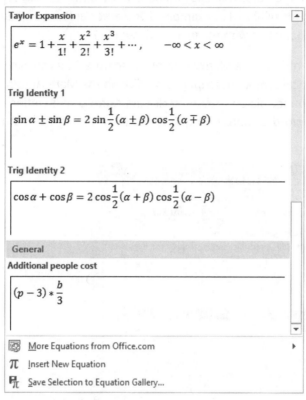

Custom equations appear in the General area of the Equation gallery.

12   Press the **Esc** key to close the gallery without making a selection.

✖ CLEAN UP Close the Welcome document, saving your changes if you want to. When you exit Word, remember to click Don't Save when you are asked whether you want to save changes to the Building Block template.

Setting mathematical AutoCorrect options

If you frequently create documents that contain mathematical formulas, you don't have to insert mathematical symbols by using the ribbon buttons. Instead, you can enter a predefined combination of characters and have Word automatically replace it with a corresponding math symbol. For example, if you enter \infty in an equation field, Word replaces the characters with the infinity symbol (∞).

This replacement is performed by the Math AutoCorrect feature. You can view all the predefined mathematical symbol descriptions by clicking the Math AutoCorrect button in the Equation Options dialog box, or by clicking AutoCorrect Options on the Proofing page of the Word Options dialog box, and then clicking the Math AutoCorrect tab.

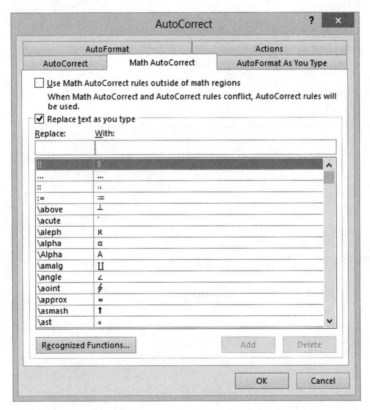

The Math AutoCorrect feature simplifies the process of inserting mathematical symbols.

TIP You can create custom Math AutoCorrect entries in the same way you create text AutoCorrect entries. For information, see "Correcting spelling and grammatical errors" in Chapter 2, "Enter, edit, and proofread text."

Key points

- A background color, texture, pattern, or picture can really give a document pizzazz, but be careful that it doesn't overwhelm the text.

- By using a watermark, you can flag every page of a document with a faint word, such as "Confidential," or a faint picture. Watermarks appear behind the text of the document, so the text can still be read.

- Word comes with predefined building blocks that you can use to quickly add graphic elements to a document.

- You can construct complex math equations in your documents and have Word display them in traditional math formats.

9

Chapter at a glance

Organize

Reorganize document outlines,
page 298

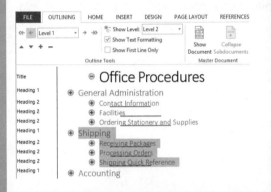

Arrange

Arrange objects on the page,
page 304

Contain

Use tables to control page layout,
page 315

Payment Schedule	
Interest Rate	3.6%
Years	3
Loan Amount	$155,000.00
Monthly Payment	$4,548.69
Cost of Loan	$163,752.79
3-Year Lease Cost	$180,000.00
Savings	$16,247.21

Payment Schedule	
Interest Rate	5.0%
Years	3
Loan Amount	$155,000.00
Monthly Payment	$4,645.49
Cost of Loan	$167,237.61
3-Year Lease Cost	$180,000.00
Savings	$12,762.39

Organize and arrange content

10

IN THIS CHAPTER, YOU WILL LEARN HOW TO

- Reorganize document outlines.
- Arrange objects on the page.
- Use tables to control page layout.

Microsoft Word 2013 provides the following tools for organizing and arranging your document's content:

- **Outlining tools** You can use these tools to control the organization of the content in a styled document. In Outline view, you can reorganize content by moving it or by promoting or demoting it.

- **Object arranging tools** You can use these tools to control the layout of objects on the page. You can precisely position objects and control their alignment and stacking order.

- **Nested tables** You can use a table to control the positions of blocks of information on the page. For example, a table with two columns and two rows can hold a set of four paragraphs, four bulleted lists, or four tables in a format in which they can be easily compared.

In this chapter, you'll first reorganize a document by working with its outline. Then you'll modify the text wrapping, position, and stacking order of multiple pictures in a document. Finally, you'll create a table to hold nested tables of information.

PRACTICE FILES To complete the exercises in this chapter, you need the practice files contained in the Chapter10 practice file folder. For more information, see "Download the practice files" in this book's Introduction.

Reorganizing document outlines

When you create a document that contains headings, you can format the headings by applying built-in heading styles that define not only formatting but also outline levels. Then it is easy to view and organize the document in Outline view. In this view, you can hide all the body text and display only the headings at and above a particular level. You can also rearrange the sections of a document by moving their headings.

SEE ALSO For information about formatting headings by using styles, see "Applying styles to text" in Chapter 3, "Modify the structure and appearance of text." For general information about styles, see "Creating custom styles and templates" in Chapter 16, "Work in Word more efficiently."

When you view a document in Outline view, the document is displayed with a hierarchical structure, and the Outlining tab appears on the ribbon.

Style area pane

A styled document, displayed in Outline view.

The indentations and symbols used in Outline view to indicate the level of a heading or paragraph in the document's structure don't appear in the document in other views or when you print it. To easily reference paragraph styles while working in Outline view, you can display the style area pane to the left of the document. This pane is available only in Draft and Outline views. By default, the style area pane is 0 inches wide, which effectively closes it. We find it useful to have the style area pane open while working in Outline view. You can set the width of the style area pane on the Advanced page of the Word Options dialog box.

You can use commands in the Outline Tools group of the Outlining tab to do the following:

- Display only the headings at a specific level and above.
- Promote or demote headings or body text by changing their level.
- Move headings and their text up or down in the document.

TIP You can click the buttons in the Master Document group to create a master document with subdocuments that you can then display or hide. The topic of master documents and subdocuments is beyond the scope of this book. For information, refer to Word Help.

When working in Print Layout view, you can display a hierarchical structure of the document headings in the Navigation pane. You can reorganize document content by dragging headings in the Navigation pane, and promote, demote, or remove sections by using commands on the Navigation pane shortcut menu. You can also display only specific heading levels in the Navigation pane by clicking that option on the shortcut menu.

In this exercise, you'll display a document in Outline view, display the style area pane, promote and demote headings, move sections, and expand and collapse the outline. Then you'll look at similar functionality that is available in the Navigation pane.

 SET UP You need the OfficeProcedures document located in the Chapter10 practice file folder to complete this exercise. Open the document, and then follow the steps.

1   On the **View** tab, in the **Views** group, click **Outline** to display the document in **Outline** view, with the **Outlining** tab at the left end of the ribbon. Notice that the **Outlining** tab is not differentiated by a colored heading as tool tabs are, because it is always available when you are in **Outline** view (not only when a specific type of content is selected).

2   In the **Backstage** view, click the **Options** page tab to open the **Word Options** dialog box.

3   In the **Word Options** dialog box, click the **Advanced** page tab. Scroll to the **Display** area (about halfway down the page), and change the **Style area pane width in Draft and Outline views** setting to 1″. Then click **OK** to return to the document.

4   On the **Outlining** tab, in the **Outline Tools** group, point to each of the unlabeled buttons to familiarize yourself with its name and purpose.

5   In the **Outline Tools** group, click the **Show Level** arrow, and then in the list, click **Level 1** to collapse the document to display only first-level headings.

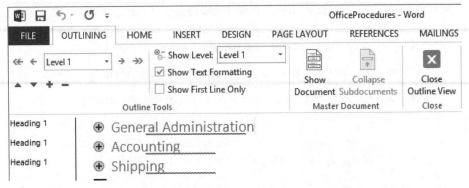

The plus sign to the left of each heading indicates that the heading has subheadings.

KEYBOARD SHORTCUT Press Alt+Shift+1 to display only first-level headings. For more information about keyboard shortcuts, see "Keyboard shortcuts" at the end of this book.

6   In the document, click anywhere in the **Accounting** heading.

7   In the **Outline Tools** group, click the **Expand** button to expand only the **Accounting** section to display its level 2 subheadings.

KEYBOARD SHORTCUT Press Alt+Shift++ to expand a section.

8   In the **Outline Tools** group, click the **Demote** button to change the **Accounting** heading to a level 2 heading. Notice that it is now at the same level as its former subheadings.

KEYBOARD SHORTCUT Press Alt+Shift+Right Arrow to demote a heading.

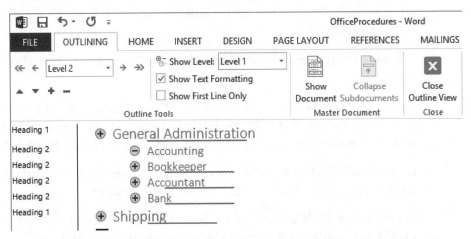

The minus sign to the left of the Accounting heading indicates that it has no subheadings.

9   On the **Quick Access Toolbar**, click the **Undo** button to return the **Accounting** heading to level 1.

10   In the **Outline Tools** group, click the **Collapse** button to display only level 1 headings.

KEYBOARD SHORTCUT Press Alt+Shift+- to collapse a heading.

11   Click the **Demote** button to revert the **Accounting** heading to level 2. Then click the **Expand** button to expand the **Accounting** section. Because its subheadings were hidden when you demoted the heading, the subheadings have also been demoted, to level 3, to maintain the hierarchy within the section.

The style of the Accounting heading changes to Heading 2, and the style of its subheadings changes to Heading 3.

12   Click the **Collapse** button to hide the subheadings of the **Accounting** section, and then in the **Outline Tools** group, click the **Promote** button to change **Accounting** back to a level 1 heading.

KEYBOARD SHORTCUT Press Alt+Shift+Left Arrow to promote a heading.

13   Press **Ctrl+Home** to move to the beginning of the document. In the **Outline Tools** group, in the **Show Level** list, click **Level 2** to display all level 1 and level 2 headings in the document.

KEYBOARD SHORTCUT Press Alt+Shift+2 to display all first-level and second-level headings.

14 Click the plus sign to the left of the **Shipping** heading to select all the content in that section, and then in the **Outline Tools** group, click the **Move Up** button four times to move the **Shipping** heading and its subheadings above the **Accounting** heading.

KEYBOARD SHORTCUT Press Alt+Shift+Up Arrow to move a selected section upward in an outline.

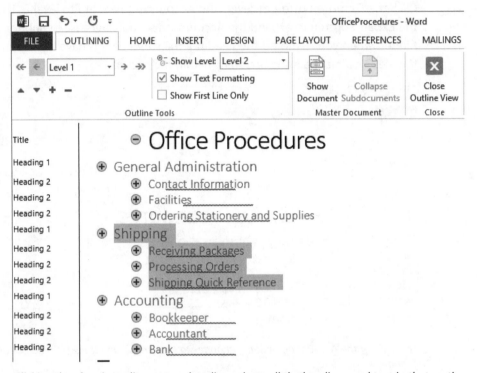

Clicking the plus sign adjacent to a heading selects all the headings and text in that section.

15 Press **Ctrl+Home** to release the selection, and then in the **Outline Tools** group, in the **Show Level** list, click **All Levels**. You can now scroll through the document to review the effects of the reorganization.

KEYBOARD SHORTCUT Press Alt+Shift+A to display all levels.

16 In the **Close** group, click the **Close Outline View** button to display the reorganized document in **Print Layout** view.

Now we'll look at ways of reorganizing a document within the Navigation pane.

17 On the **View** tab, in the **Show** group, select the **Navigation Pane** check box. Notice that the **Navigation** pane reflects the changes you made to the document structure.

18 In the **Navigation** pane, drag the **Accounting** heading up and drop it immediately above the **Shipping** heading (a bold line indicates the drop location) to move the **Accounting** section back to its original location.

19 In the **Navigation** pane, right-click any heading to display a menu of actions you can perform directly in the **Navigation** pane.

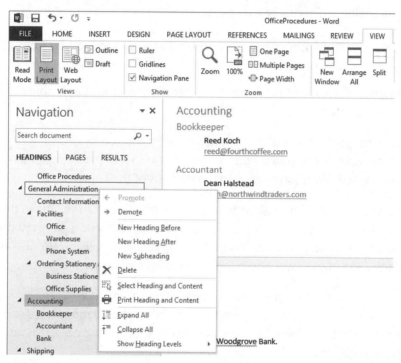

You can work with a document in the Navigation pane in much the same way you can in Outline view.

20 Experiment with the commands available on the **Navigation** pane shortcut menu.

❌ CLEAN UP Close the OfficeProcedures document, saving your changes if you want to.

10

Arranging objects on the page

You have already learned basic ways to control how text wraps around an object, such as a picture, and to position an object on the page. However, sometimes things don't work out quite the way you expect them to, especially when you are dealing with multiple objects.

TIP In the exercise for this chapter, you work with photographs, but the concepts discussed here also apply to other graphic objects, such as clip art images, diagrams, and shapes.

When you choose a text wrapping option other than In Line With Text, you can specify that an object be positioned in one of two ways:

- **Absolutely** This option positions the object at a distance you set from a margin, page, paragraph, or line.

- **Relatively** This type of positioning is determined by the relationship of the object to a margin or page.

You can take the guesswork out of setting an object's position by choosing one of nine predefined position options from the Position gallery. These options all implement square text wrapping in a specific location relative to the margins of the page.

If you use one of the position options to locate an object, you can still move the object manually by dragging it to another position on the page. Often it is easier to drag objects into position if you display an onscreen grid to align against. You can also use alignment commands to align objects with the margins and with each other.

Changing the document text after you position an object might upset the arrangement of content on the page. You can specify whether an object should move with its related text or remain anchored in its position. You can also specify whether the object should be allowed to overlap other objects.

If you insert several objects and then position them so that they overlap, they are said to be "stacked." The stacking order (which object appears on top of which) is initially determined by the order in which you inserted the objects, but it can also be determined by other factors such as the type of text wrapping assigned to each object. Provided all the objects have the same kind of text wrapping, you can change their order by selecting an object and clicking the Bring Forward or Send Backward button in the Arrange group to move the object to the top or bottom of the stack. If you click either button's arrow and then click Bring Forward or Send Backward, the object moves forward or backward in the stack one position at a time.

After you arrange objects on the page, you can use the Selection And Visibility pane to hide and show them so that you can judge each object's contribution to the whole.

In this exercise, you'll modify the text wrapping, position, and stacking order of pictures that have already been inserted into a document. Then you'll hide one of the pictures.

SET UP You need the BambooInfo document located in the Chapter10 practice file folder to complete this exercise. Open the document in Print Layout view, and then follow the steps.

1   Click the first picture on the page to select it, and then click the **Layout Options** button that appears.

From the Layout Options menu, you can quickly format the position of an object without accessing the ribbon.

10

2   In the **With Text Wrapping** area of the **Layout Options** menu, click the second icon (**Tight**). Notice that the options at the bottom of the menu become available and the **Move with text** option is selected.

3   At the bottom of the **Layout Options** menu, click the **See more** link to display the **Position** page of the **Layout** dialog box.

> **TIP** You can also open the Layout dialog box from the Format tool tab for Pictures by clicking the Position arrow in the Arrange group and then clicking More Layout Options.

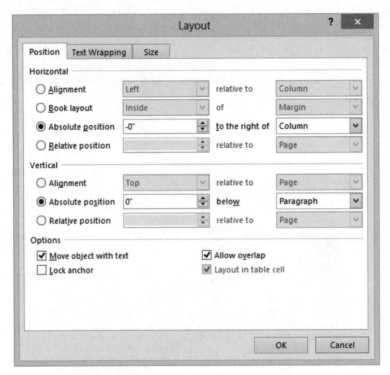

The settings here are linked to the text wrapping option you chose..

4   In the **Layout** dialog box, click the **Text Wrapping** tab. Notice that the settings reflect the selection you made on the **Layout Options** menu.

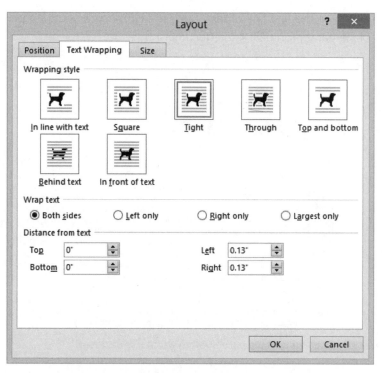

More exact positioning can be done by configuring the settings on this page.

5   In the **Distance from text** area, set both **Left** and **Right** to 0.3". Then click **OK**.

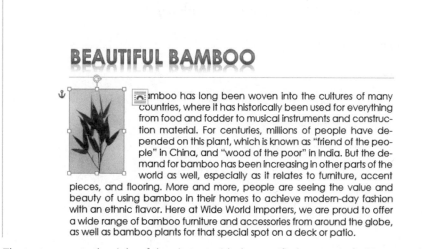

The text wraps to the right of the picture, with the specified amount of white space between the picture and the text.

6   Click anywhere in the first line of text, press the **Home** key, and then press **Enter** to insert a blank paragraph below the document title.

BEAUTIFUL BAMBOO

Bamboo has long been woven into the cultures of many countries, where it has historically been used for everything from food and fodder to musical instruments and construction material. For centuries, millions of people have depended on this plant, which is known as "friend of the people" in China, and "wood of the poor" in India. But the demand for bamboo has been increasing in other parts of the world as well, especially as it relates to furniture, accent pieces, and flooring. More and more, people are seeing the value and beauty of using bamboo in their homes to achieve modern-day fashion with an ethnic flavor. Here at Wide World Importers, we are proud to offer a wide range of bamboo furniture and accessories from around the globe, as well as bamboo plants for that special spot on a deck or patio.

The picture moves down with the paragraph to which it is attached.

7   On the **Quick Access Toolbar**, click the **Undo** button to remove the blank paragraph.

KEYBOARD SHORTCUT Press Ctrl+Z to undo the most recent action.

8   Click the picture to select it. Then on the **Format** tool tab, in the **Arrange** group, click the **Position** button to display the **Position** gallery.

The Position gallery offers several preconfigured text wrapping options.

9   In the **Position** gallery, point to each thumbnail in turn to display a live preview of its effects on the position of the picture. Then in the **With Text Wrapping** category, click the first thumbnail in the first row (**Position in Top Left with Square Text Wrapping**) to move the picture to the upper-left corner of the document.

BEAUTIFUL BAMBOO

Bamboo has long been woven into the cultures of many countries, where it has historically been used for everything from food and fodder to musical instruments and construction material. For centuries, millions of people have depended on this plant, which is known as "friend of the people" in China, and "wood of the poor" in India. But the demand for bamboo has been increasing in other parts of the world as well, especially as it relates to furniture, accent pieces, and flooring. More and more, people are seeing the value and beauty of using bamboo in their homes to achieve modern-day fashion with an ethnic flavor. Here at Wide World Importers, we are proud to offer a wide range of bamboo furniture and accessories from around the globe, as well as bamboo plants for that special spot on a deck or patio.

The picture is now aligned with the top and left page margins.

10   In the document title, click to position the cursor to the left of **Beautiful**, and then press **Enter** to insert a blank paragraph above the title. Notice that the picture does not move down with the title.

11   Click the picture, and then click the **Layout Options** button that appears. Notice that the **Fix position on the page** option is now selected instead of the **Move with text** option. The picture is no longer anchored to the paragraph.

12   At the bottom of the **Layout Options** menu, click the **See more** link to display the **Position** page of the **Layout** dialog box. Notice that the **Horizontal** and **Vertical** settings have changed to **Alignment** and **relative to Margin**.

10

TIP When pictures have a text wrapping setting other than In Line With Text, you can use the options on the Align menu to align multiple objects horizontally or vertically. You can also distribute selected objects equally between the first and last objects in the selection. Understanding how these options work takes practice. It is a good idea to test various settings with multiple objects to review the results. Remember, the Undo button is your ally!

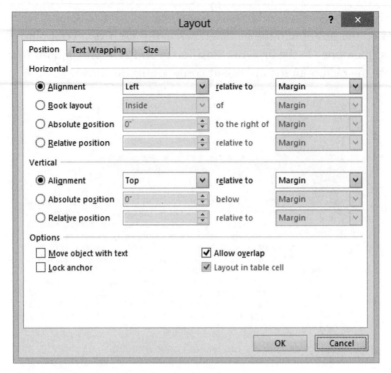

The picture is now anchored to the margins.

13   Click **Cancel** to close the dialog box without making any changes.

       Now we'll format the second picture.

14   Click the second bamboo picture, display the **Position** gallery, and in the **With Text Wrapping** category, click the third thumbnail in the first row (**Position in Top Right with Square Text Wrapping**) to send the picture to the upper-right corner of the page.

       TIP Selecting one of the predefined Position options is a quick way of both setting text wrapping and breaking the relationship of the picture with the text.

15   On the **Format** tool tab, in the **Arrange** group, click the **Align Objects** button to display the **Align** menu.

The Align menu provides easy access to all the alignment options.

16 On the **Align** menu, click **Grid Settings** to open the **Grid and Guides** dialog box.

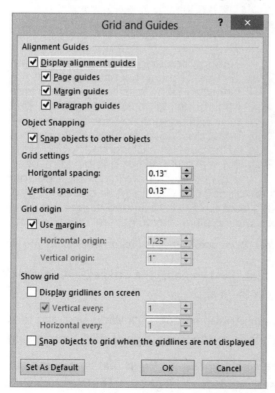

You can specify the location and functionality of the onscreen alignment guides and grid.

17 In the **Grid settings** area, set both **Horizontal spacing** and **Vertical spacing** to 0.25". In the **Show grid** area, select the **Display gridlines on screen** check box. Then click **OK** to fill the text column with a grid of quarter-inch squares.

18 Drag the selected picture down and to the left until it sits three squares from the top margin and three squares from the left margin, overlapping the first picture. Notice as you drag that the picture snaps to the grid.

> **TIP** To move a picture without snapping to the grid, hold down the Ctrl key while pressing an arrow key. The picture moves in tiny increments.

19 Click the third picture in the document, click the **Layout Options** button that appears, and click the first thumbnail in the **With Text Wrapping** category (**Square**). Drag the picture up and to the right until it sits six squares from the top margin and six squares from the left margin, overlapping the second picture. The text wraps on both sides of the picture, which makes it quite difficult to read (even if the grid weren't there).

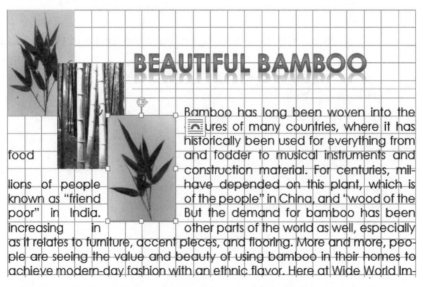

Using the predefined alignment options doesn't always produce the results you want.

20 With the third picture selected, press and hold the **Ctrl** key, and then click the first and second pictures to select them also.

21 On the **Format** tool tab, in the **Arrange** group, click **Wrap Text**, and then click **More Layout Options** to display the **Text Wrapping** page of the **Layout** dialog box.

22 In the **Wrapping style** area, click **Tight**. In the **Wrap Text** area, click **Right only**. In the **Distance from text** area, set both **Left** and **Right** to 0.3". Then click **OK** to rewrap the text to the right of and below the group of pictures.

You can apply alignment options to multiple objects at the same time.

23   Click away from the pictures and then click only the second picture. In the **Arrange** group, click **Bring Forward** to position the selected picture on top of the others.

24   In the **Arrange** group, click the **Align Objects** button, and click **View Gridlines** to turn them off. Then click away from the picture to display the results.

BEAUTIFUL BAMBOO

Bamboo has long been woven into the cultures of many countries, where it has historically been used for everything from food and fodder to musical instruments and construction material. For centuries, millions of people have depended on this plant, which is known as "friend of the people" in China, and "wood of the poor" in India. But the demand for bamboo has been increasing in other parts of the world as well, especially as it relates to furniture, accent pieces, and flooring. More and more, people are seeing the value and beauty of using bamboo in their homes to achieve modern-day fashion with an ethnic flavor. Here at Wide World Importers, we are proud to offer a wide range of bamboo furniture and accessories from around the globe, as well as bamboo plants for that special spot on a deck or patio.

The final result is artistic and elegant.

Now we'll experiment with the Selection pane.

25   Click the third picture to activate the **Format** tool tab. In the **Arrange** group, click the **Selection Pane** button to open the **Selection** pane, which identifies the three objects on this page. The eye icon to the right of each picture indicates that it is currently visible on the page.

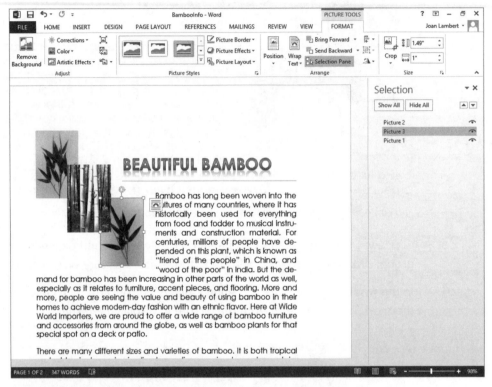

You can manage objects from the Selection pane.

26   At the top of the **Selection** pane, click the **Hide All** button to hide the pictures in the document. The eye icons change to small horizontal lines to indicate that the pictures are hidden. Notice that the text in the document flows naturally as though the pictures weren't there.

27   Click the bar icons adjacent to **Picture 1** and **Picture 2** to redisplay only those pictures.

Hiding a picture reformats the document content as though the picture doesn't exist.

28   Close the **Selection** pane.

❌ CLEAN UP Close the BambooInfo document, saving your changes if you want to.

Using tables to control page layout

Most people are accustomed to thinking of a table as a means of displaying data in a quick, easy-to-grasp format. But tables can also serve to organize content in creative ways. For example, suppose you want to display two tables next to each other. The simplest way to do this is to first create a page-width table that has only one row and two columns, and then insert one of the tables you want to display in the first cell and the other table in the second cell. When the outer table borders are hidden, these nested tables appear side by side.

Consultation Fees

Location	Hourly
In home	$50.00
Phone	$35.00
In store	$40.00

Trip Charges

Distance	Fee
0-10 miles	No charge
11-20 miles	$10.00
Over 50 miles	$20.00

These headings and tables are nested within the cells of a one-row, two-column table.

As with regular tables, you can create a nested table in one of three ways:

- From scratch

- By formatting existing information

- By inserting Microsoft Excel data

And just like with other tables, you can format a nested table either manually or by using one of the ready-made table styles.

TIP You can use tables to organize a mixture of elements such as text, tables, charts, and diagrams. For more information, see Chapter 4, "Organize information in columns and tables."

If you are designing your document with accessibility in mind, be aware that screen readers and other assistive devices access the content linearly—from left to right, row by row—whereas you might expect a person looking at the table to read its content from top to bottom, column by column. Some screen readers have a table reading mode that can help to ameliorate this problem, so if you're arranging content by using a simple table layout, this won't present as much of an issue (although the content meaning might still be less clear than when presented in normal text or in a list). If you create a fancy table layout that includes cells of varying heights and widths, with some merged cells and some split cells, it's likely that the screen reader will access and deliver the content out of order. Keep this in mind if you're intending to deliver your content in an electronic format, and certainly if your organization is required to adhere to accessibility standards.

In this exercise, you'll first create a table, and then you will nest and format two tables within the original table.

 SET UP You need the Loan workbook, the DeliveryTruckPurchase document, and the LoanComparisons document located in the Chapter10 practice file folder to complete this exercise. Open the Loan workbook in Excel, and open the DeliveryTruckPurchase document in Word. Then open the LoanComparisons document, and follow the steps.

1   Press **Ctrl+End** to position the cursor at the end of the document.

2   On the **Insert** tab, in the **Tables** group, click the **Table** button. In the **Insert Table** gallery, click the second box in the first row (**2x1 Table**) to insert a two-column page-width table in the document.

MEMO

From: Garth Fort
To: Robin Counts
Date: November 12, 2012
Re: Loan comparisons

Below is a comparison of two loans for delivery vehicles.

You can arrange content side by side within this basic table structure.

3   On the **View** tab, in the **Window** group, click the **Switch Windows** button, and then click **DeliveryTruckPurchase**.

4   Scroll to the bottom of the page, and click anywhere in the **Payment Schedule** table. On the **Layout** tool tab, in the **Table** group, click **Select**, and then click **Select Table**.

5   On the **Home** tab, in the **Clipboard** group, click the **Copy** button to copy the selected table to the Microsoft Office Clipboard.

> **KEYBOARD SHORTCUT** Press Ctrl+C to copy the selected content to the Clipboard.

6   Switch to the **LoanComparisons** document, right-click the left table cell, and then below **Paste Options**, click the **Nest Table** button to insert the table you copied into the cell and adjust the height of the container table to fit the nested table.

7   On the **Windows Taskbar**, click the **Microsoft Excel** button and then, if necessary, click the **Loan** workbook. On **Sheet 1** of the **Loan** workbook, select cells **A1:B8**, and then copy the selected cells to the Clipboard.

8   Switch back to the **LoanComparisons** document, click the right table cell, and then on the **Home** tab, in the **Clipboard** group, click the **Paste** button to insert the worksheet data as a nested table in the cell.

> **KEYBOARD SHORTCUT** Press Ctrl+V to paste the most recently copied content from the Clipboard.

10

Using tables to control page layout   **317**

Below is a comparison of two loans for delivery vehicles.

Payment Schedule	
Interest Rate	3.6%
Years	3
Loan Amount	$155,000.00
Monthly Payment	$4,548.69
Cost of Loan	$163,752.79
3-Year Lease Cost	$180,000.00
Savings	$16,247.21

Payment Schedule	
Interest Rate	5.0%
Years	3
Loan Amount	$155,000.00
Monthly Payment	$4,645.49
Cost of Loan	$167,237.61
3-Year Lease Cost	$180,000.00
Savings	$12,762.39

Nested tables inserted from a Word document and an Excel worksheet.

9   Point to the container table, and then click the table selector that appears just outside of its upper-left corner to select the table. (Be sure you select the container table and not the nested table.)

10   On the **Design** tool tab, in the **Borders** group, click the **Borders** arrow, and then click **No Border** to remove the borders from the container cells.

11   Click anywhere in the left table, click the table selector that appears, and then press **Ctrl+Spacebar** to clear the formatting brought over from the original table source.

12   On the **Design** tool tab, in the **Table Style Options** group, ensure that the **Header Row** and **Total Row** check boxes are selected, and clear the other check boxes.

13   In the **Table Styles** gallery, click the thumbnail of the table style you want to apply to the nested table. (We used **Grid Table 5 Dark – Accent 1**.)

14   Repeat steps 11 through 13 to format the right table, perhaps using a similar table style with a different color. (We used **Grid Table 5 Dark – Accent 6**.) Then click away from the tables to display the results.

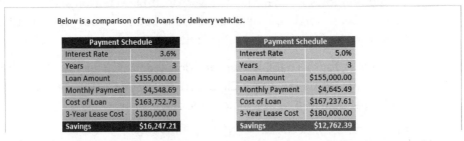

Although invisible, the container table provides the structure to display these two tables.

✖ CLEAN UP Close the LoanComparisons document, saving your changes if you want to. Then close the DeliveryTruckPurchase document and the Loan workbook.

Key points

- If you take the time to apply heading styles to a document, you can use the document's outline to rearrange its sections, either in Outline view or in the Navigation pane.

- You can position an object in relation to the text that surrounds it and in relation to other objects on the page.

- By using tables in creative ways, you can place information in non-linear arrangements for easy comparison or analysis.

10

Chapter at a glance

Save

Save Word documents in other formats,
page 322

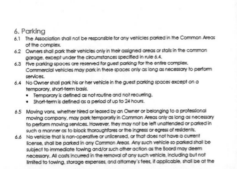

Design

Design accessible documents,
page 329

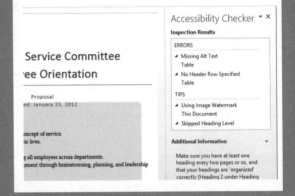

Create

Create and modify web documents,
page 333

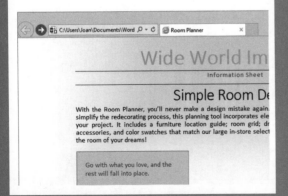

Publish

Create and publish blog posts,
page 342

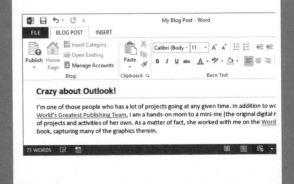

Create documents for use outside of Word

11

IN THIS CHAPTER, YOU WILL LEARN HOW TO

- Save Word documents in other formats.
- Design accessible documents.
- Create and modify web documents.
- Create and publish blog posts.

You can distribute documents that you create in Microsoft Word 2013 in several ways. You can print a hard copy of the document and give it to someone, provide an electronic copy of the file to someone, present the document online, or post its contents to a blog. Although Word is a "word-processing program" it also provides you with the tools you need to share your words with the world!

In Chapter 6, "Preview, print, and distribute documents," we looked at the processes of preparing a document for printing or electronic distribution, printing a document, and sharing a document file. In this chapter we'll look at the ways in which you can distribute information from a Word document in other formats or to people who are not running Word 2013. We'll also discuss some of the design decisions you might want to consider to ensure that your document content is accessible to people with disabilities and to electronic readers.

Sometimes you'll create a document in Word 2013 and then want to send it to someone who doesn't have Word 2013 installed on his or her computer. You can save a document created by using Word 2013 in several other file formats.

If you plan to distribute a document electronically but want to ensure that the document appears exactly the same to the recipients as it does to you, you can save the document in Portable Document Format (PDF) or XML Paper Specification (XPS) format. When people view or print the PDF or XPS file, no matter what computer or what printer they use, the pages appear just as they do when printed from your computer on your printer.

One way of distributing the information in your documents is by converting them to web-pages and posting them online for people to read. The Internet has become a major part of our everyday lives. We use it to research topics, shop, check the news, and find out how our favorite sports team is doing. It's also a great publishing tool if you are trying to reach a broad audience. For example, your organization might want to publish an online newsletter to provide information while advertising its goods or services. Or if you have a blog (short for *web log*), you can use the built-in Word tools to create and post articles.

In this chapter, you'll first save a document in a different file format. You'll experiment with the new PDF-editing functionality. Then you'll preview a document in Web Layout view, save the document as a webpage, and make any adjustments necessary for optimum pres-entation in a web browser. Finally, you'll learn how to use Word to create a blog post.

PRACTICE FILES To complete the exercises in this chapter, you need the practice files contained in the Chapter11 practice file folder. For more information, see "Download the practice files" in this book's Introduction.

Saving Word documents in other formats

When you save a Word document, the default file format is the Word 2013 .docx format. Although the file extension is the same, Word 2013 recognizes a difference between .docx files saved in Word 2013 and .docx files saved in Word 2010 or Word 2007. A Word 2013 .docx file can be opened and edited in Word 2010 or Word 2007 on a computer running Windows, or in Word 2011 or Word 2008 on a Mac, but if it is saved in one of those pro-grams, the next time you open it in Word 2013 it will be displayed in Compatibility View.

A .docx file can't be opened in Word 2003 or an earlier version of Word unless the person using that version of Word installs the Microsoft Office Compatibility Pack for Word, Excel, and PowerPoint File Formats, which is available for free from the Microsoft Download Center at *download.microsoft.com*. If you want to ensure that recipients running older ver-sions of Word can open and edit a file that you create in Word 2013, you can save the file in the .doc format, as a Word 97-2003 Document.

Export

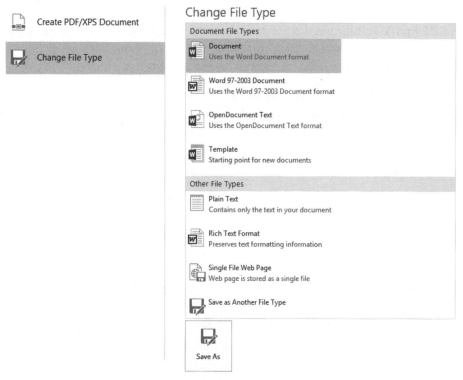

You can save Word documents in many different formats.

If you are looking for a file format that is more exotic than those listed on the Export page, click Save As Another File Type and then click the Save As button. In the Save As dialog box, you can choose from an extensive list of additional file formats, including Word Macro-Enabled Document, Word Macro-Enabled Template, Word XML Document, Web Page, Word 97-2003 Template, Word 2003 XML Document, Strict Open XML Document, and Works 6-9 Document.

If you want to save a Word document in a format that can be opened by the widest variety of programs (including text editors that are installed with most operating systems), use one of these two formats:

- **Rich Text Format (*.rtf)** This format preserves the document's formatting.
- **Plain Text (*.txt)** This format preserves only the document's text.

If you want people to be able to view a document exactly as it appears on your screen, use one of these two formats:

- **PDF (.pdf)** This format is preferred by commercial printing facilities. Recipients can display the file in the free Microsoft Reader or Adobe Reader programs, and can display and edit the file in Word 2013 or Adobe Acrobat.

- **XPS (.xps)** This format precisely renders all fonts, images, and colors. Recipients can display the file in the free Microsoft Reader program or the free XPS Viewer program.

TIP Another way to create a PDF file or XPS file is by selecting that option when sending the document by email. For more information, see "Printing and sending documents" in Chapter 6, "Preview, print, and distribute documents."

Editing a PDF file in Word

An exciting feature of Word 2013 is the ability to edit PDF files by using all the standard Word proofing tools. To open a PDF file in Word, do one of the following:

- In **File Explorer**, right-click the file, click **Open**, and then click **Word (Desktop)**.

  TIP In Windows 8, File Explorer has replaced Windows Explorer. Throughout this book, we refer to this browsing utility by its Windows 8 name. If your computer is running Windows 7 or an earlier version of Windows, use Windows Explorer instead.

- In Word, display the **Open** page of the **Backstage** view, navigate to the file location, click the file, and then click **Open**. (In the **Open** dialog box, PDF files now fall into the category of **Word Documents**.)

Word converts the file to an editable Word document. If the file contains complicated formatting and layout, the Word version of the document might not be a perfect replica of the PDF, but most simple files convert quite cleanly.

The PDF and XPS formats are designed to deliver documents as electronic representations of the way they appear when printed. Both types of files can easily be sent by email to many recipients and can be made available on a webpage for downloading by anyone who wants them. However, the files are no longer Word documents. A PDF file can be converted to the editable Word format. An XPS file cannot be opened, viewed, or edited in Word.

When you save a Word document in PDF or XPS format, you can optimize the file size of the document for your intended distribution method—the larger Standard file size is better for printing, whereas the Minimum file size is suitable for online publishing. You can also configure the following options:

- Specify the pages to include in the PDF or XPS file.

- Include or exclude comments and tracked changes in a PDF file.

- Include or exclude non-printing elements such as bookmarks and properties.

- Select compliance, font embedding, and encryption options in a PDF file.

In this exercise, you'll save one page of a multipage document in PDF format. Then you'll edit the PDF file in Word.

→ SET UP You need the ParkingRules document located in the Chapter11 practice file folder to complete this exercise. Open the document, and then follow the steps.

1   Scroll through the document and notice that it consists of 13 sections on 9 pages. Display page **3**, and notice that it contains only section **6**. Click anywhere on page **3** to make that the active page.

2   Display the **Export** page of the **Backstage** view. With **Create PDF/XPS Document** selected in the left pane, click the **Create PDF/XPS** button.

3   In the **Publish as PDF or XPS** dialog box, verify that the **Chapter11** practice file folder appears in the **Address** bar and **PDF** appears in the **Save as Type** box. With the **Standard** option selected in the **Optimize for** area, click the **Options** button to open the **Options** dialog box.

11

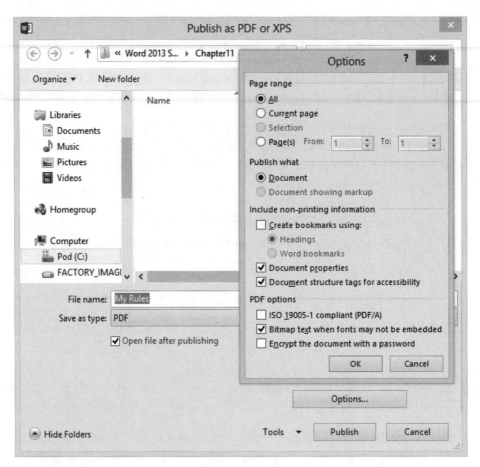

You can choose from these options to tailor the PDF file to your needs.

4   In the **Page range** area, click **Current page**. In the **Include non-printing information** area, clear the **Document properties** check box. Then click **OK**.

5   Back in the **Publish as PDF or XPS** dialog box, notice that the **Open file after publishing** check box is selected by default. In the **File name** box, enter My Rules. Then click **Publish** to save the document in PDF format and open it in Microsoft Reader or your default PDF viewer.

   TROUBLESHOOTING If you don't have a PDF viewer installed, don't worry; we're going to open the file in Word next.

6. Parking

6.1 The Association shall not be responsible for any vehicles parked in the Common Areas of the complex.

6.2 Owners shall park their vehicles only in their assigned areas or stalls in the common garage, except under the circumstances specified in rule 6.4.

6.3 Five parking spaces are reserved for guest parking for the entire complex. Commercial vehicles may park in these spaces only as long as necessary to perform services.

6.4 No Owner shall park his or her vehicle in the guest parking spaces except on a temporary, short-term basis.
- Temporary is defined as not routine and not recurring.
- Short-term is defined as a period of up to 24 hours.

6.5 Moving vans, whether hired or leased by an Owner or belonging to a professional moving company, may park temporarily in Common Areas only as long as necessary to perform moving services. However, they may not be left unattended or parked in such a manner as to block thoroughfares or the ingress or egress of residents.

6.6 No vehicle that is non-operative or unlicensed, or that does not have a current license, shall be parked in any Common Areas. Any such vehicle so parked shall be subject to immediate towing and/or such other action as the Board may deem necessary. All costs incurred in the removal of any such vehicle, including but not limited to towing, storage expenses, and attorney's fees, if applicable, shall be at the expense and risk of the owner of the vehicle. Such vehicles may be parked in the Owner's assigned stall in the common garage.

6.7 No repairs to or maintenance of any vehicle (other than washing) shall be performed in any Common Area, except in the case of an emergency and then only to the extent necessary to enable movement of the vehicle to a proper repair facility.

6.8 Any damage to property within the complex caused by any vehicle, including moving vans, commercial vehicles, and vehicles owned by guests, shall be the responsibility of the associated Owner.

6.9 Any oil stains or related problems caused by any vehicle, including moving vans, commercial vehicles, and vehicles owned by guests, shall be the responsibility of the associated Owner to clean.

6.10 Vehicle shall not exceed a speed of 10 miles an hour within the Common Area.

6.11 No dirt bikes, go-carts, or off-road vehicles shall be ridden within the complex. The riding of motorcycles shall be limited to safe ingress and egress.

11

The file opens in your default PDF viewer.

6   Notice that the PDF file contains the same content as page **3** of the original Word document. Then close the file and return to the **ParkingRules** document.

7   On the **Open** page of the **Backstage** view, navigate to the **Chapter11** practice file folder. Notice that the **My Rules** PDF file now appears in the folder with the Word documents.

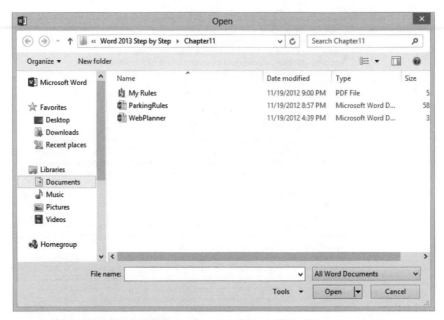

The icon that represents the default PDF viewer on your computer will precede the PDF file name.

Now let's open the PDF file in Word.

8   In the **Open** dialog box, click the **My Rules** file, and then click **Open**. Word displays a message box that provides information about the conversion process.

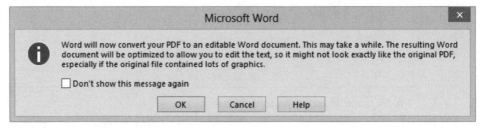

If you don't want this message box to appear again, select the check box before clicking OK.

9   In the message box, click **OK** to complete the conversion process and open the converted file in Word.

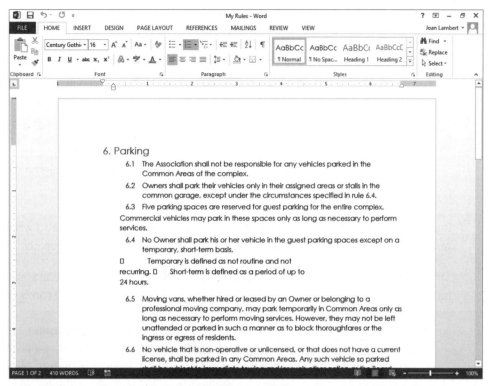

The file contains the same content as the original.

10   Scroll through the file in Word. Notice that it contains the same content as page **3** of the original Word document. However, it is now more than one page in length, and some of the formatting is not the same as in the original document or the PDF.

❌ CLEAN UP Close the My Rules and ParkingRules documents without saving your changes.

Designing accessible documents

Whenever you create a document that will be distributed electronically, particularly if it will be displayed as a webpage, think about whether its content will be accessible to all the people you want to reach. For example, consider the following:

- Not all people will display the document in Word 2013 or in the same web browser in which you preview it.

- Some people might set their default web browser font sizes larger than usual, or display their web browser content at an increased zoom level.

- Some people can't differentiate changes in color. Others might have their computers configured to display a high-contrast color scheme that changes the default colors of text so they can read it better.

- People with visual impairments might use an assistive device such as a screen reader to "read" content to them from the document or webpage.

- Web browsers might be configured to not display certain page elements.

- A slow connection might prevent the display of large images.

If you intend to publish the document on a public webpage, consider also whether the terms that your prospective viewers might search for are accessible to search engines.

There are some things you can do to make a document display more uniformly on screen (or on paper) and be more accessible to assistive devices and Internet search engines:

- Use styles to format content, rather than applying manual formatting. People can then apply a style set with large, legible fonts and high-contrast colors so the content scales to a size that is easier for them to read on screen. In addition, when you use heading styles, your viewers can easily display a document outline and navigate to specific locations in the document.

- Similarly, when specifying colors, use the theme colors so that they perform appropriately when viewers choose high-contrast themes.

- If your content includes graphics, add a caption to each image and provide alternative text (frequently referred to as *alt text*) that provides a written description of the image in the image properties. The alt text is displayed in place of the image when the image can't be displayed on screen. Also, wrap text around images by using the In Line With Text setting, so that images do not interrupt text.

  SEE ALSO For more information about alt text, see "Inserting and modifying pictures" in Chapter 5, "Add simple graphic elements."

- Do not use watermarks or specify background colors, patterns, or images that might interfere with the readability of the document content.

- Present information in text paragraphs rather than in text boxes. Content in text boxes might not be accessible to screen readers.

- To ensure that your content is accessed in the correct order, present it in text paragraphs rather than in tabbed lists or tables. If you must present information in a table, use the standard table formats—don't "draw" the table manually, merge or split cells, or nest tables. Variances in the table might cause assistive devices to incorrectly interpret the content. If your table will span multiple pages, select the option to repeat the header row so that the headers are both visible and accessible to assistive devices. Add alt text and captions to tables in the event that they are incorrectly displayed or interpreted. Avoid using tables to arrange content on pages, because assistive devices might access the content in an order other than you intend.

- When formatting hyperlinks, provide ScreenTip text.

   SEE ALSO For information about creating ScreenTips for hyperlinks, see "Linking to external resources" in Chapter 12, "Link to information and content."

To determine whether your document meets standard accessibility requirements, display the Info page of the Backstage view, click the Check For Issues button, and then click Check Accessibility to run the Accessibility Checker.

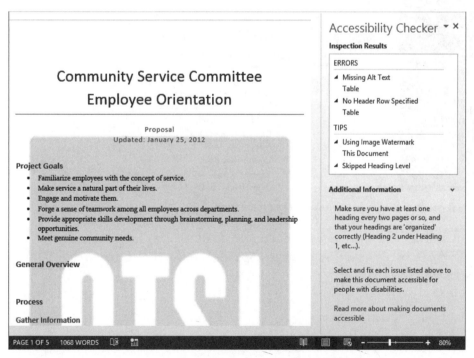

The Accessibility Checker locates content that might cause accessibility issues.

This tool checks for many common accessibility issues and provides explanations and recommendations for fixing them. You can leave the Accessibility Checker open while you work—its contents will automatically update to indicate the current issues. After you run the Accessibility Checker, information about document content issues is also shown in the Inspect Document area of the Info page of the Backstage view.

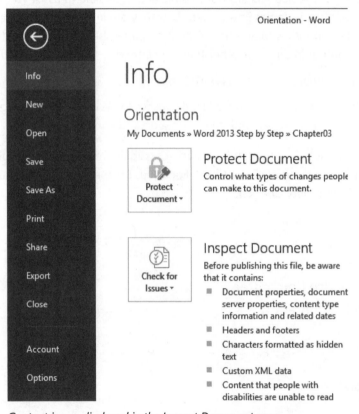

Content issues displayed in the Inspect Document area.

SEE ALSO For more information about designing documents for accessibility, run the Accessibility Checker and then click the Read More link at the bottom of the Accessibility Checker pane.

Creating and modifying web documents

You don't need to be a web designer to create a webpage. From within Word 2013, you can view a document in Web Layout view as it will appear on screen, make any necessary adjustments in Word, and then save the document as a webpage, as easily as you would save it in any other format. During the process of saving the webpage, you can assign a page title that will appear in the title bar of the viewer's web browser.

When you save a document as a webpage, Word converts the styles and formatting in the document to HTML codes, which are called *tags*. These tags tell a web browser how to display the document. During the conversion, some of the document's formatting might be changed or ignored because it is not supported by all web browsers. If that is the case, Word alerts you and gives you the option of stopping the conversion process so that you can make adjustments to the formatting to make it more compatible.

TIP In the Web Options dialog box, you can specify which browsers you anticipate will be used to view your webpages. You can also have Word make any features that are incompatible with the specified browsers unavailable .

You can save a document as a webpage in any of three formats:

- **Single File Web Page** This is the default format for saving a document as a webpage. This format embeds all the information necessary to render the webpage in one MIME-encapsulated aggregate HTML (.mhtml) file that can be distributed via email.

- **Web Page** This format saves the webpage as an .htm file with a folder of supporting files that ensure the page is rendered exactly as you want it.

- **Web Page, Filtered** This format removes any Office-specific tags from the file and significantly reduces the size of the web document and its accompanying folder of supporting files. However, it can also radically change the look of the document. For example, it might change a shaded background to a solid color, making the resulting page difficult to read.

11

After you save a document as a webpage, it is no longer a Word document. However, you can still open, view, and edit the webpage in Word, just as you would a normal document. (You can also open and edit HTML-format webpages created in other programs.) Making changes can be as basic as replacing text and adjusting alignment, or as advanced as moving and inserting graphics. When you finish modifying the webpage, you can resave it as a webpage, or save it as a regular Word document.

In this exercise, you'll check that Word is set up to create web documents that are optimized for display in Windows Internet Explorer 6 or a later version of Internet Explorer. You'll preview a document in Web Layout view and make adjustments necessary for online presentation. Finally, you'll save the document as a webpage, preview the webpage, open the webpage in Word to make some modifications, and then save and view your changes.

→ SET UP You need the WebPlanner document located in the Chapter11 practice file folder to complete this exercise. You also need a web browser. We've used Windows Internet Explorer 10; the steps might be different for other browsers and versions. Open the document, and set the zoom level to 100%. Then follow the steps.

1   Scroll through the document to observe the current layout, and then open the **Word Options** dialog box and click the **Advanced** page tab.

2   In the **General** area of the **Advanced** page, click the **Web Options** button to display the **Browsers** page of the **Web Options** dialog box.

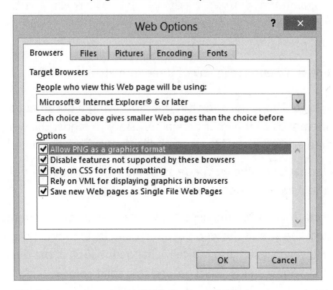

The Browsers page of the Web Options dialog box.

3   Click the **People who view this Web page will be using** arrow to view the list of browser configurations for which you will configure content. In the list, click **Microsoft Internet Explorer 6 or later**. Then in the **Options** area, ensure that all five check boxes are selected.

4   View the other pages of the **Web Options** dialog box to familiarize yourself with the kinds of settings available for your webpages. On the **Pictures** page, notice that you can specify the screen size for which you are configuring content—by default, it is set to your current screen resolution, but you can choose another screen resolution if you want to (1024 × 768 is an achievable minimum on most modern computer displays).

5   Click **OK** once to close the **Web Options** dialog box, and again to close the **Word Options** dialog box.

6   On the **View Shortcuts** toolbar in the lower-right corner of the screen, click the **Web Layout** button to display the page as it will appear in a web browser. Notice that the page margins are ignored, and the subtitle wraps onto the same line as the WordArt depiction of the company name.

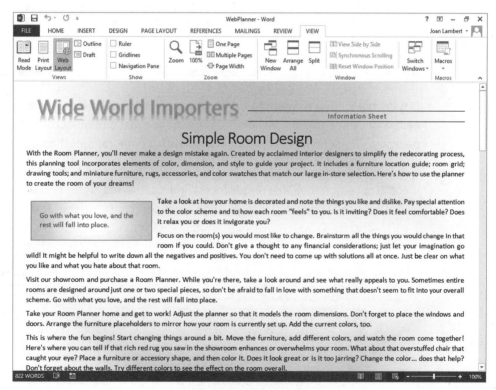

In Web Layout view, the document content fills the screen.

7   Click anywhere in the **Wide World Importers** WordArt, click the **Layout Options** button that appears, and then click the **In Line with Text** icon to move the subtitle below the WordArt.

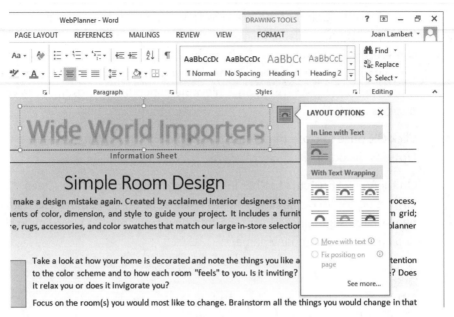

Positioning objects in line with text prevents them from interfering with other text or objects.

8   Display the hidden formatting marks, and scroll through the document further, if necessary. In the middle of the document, notice that a manual page break and blank paragraph mark force a large gap after the sixth paragraph of the document body.

9   Delete the page break and paragraph mark, and then scroll to the end of the document. Notice that the **Ordering Information** sidebar sits alone, and the graphic on which the sidebar heading is displayed covers part of the sidebar text.

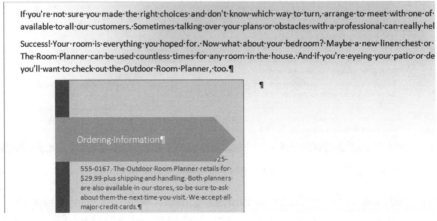

The sidebar, which really added zing to the page in Print Layout view, doesn't display gracefully in Web Layout view.

10 Hide the formatting marks. Click at the end of the last paragraph of text, press **Enter**, enter Ordering Information, and then press **Enter** to create a new blank paragraph.

11 Click anywhere on the outer edge of the sidebar to activate the container box, click the **Layout Options** button that appears, and then click the **In Line with Text** thumbnail to make all the sidebar text visible. In the sidebar, drag to select the paragraph of text.

12 On the **Home** tab, in the **Clipboard** group, click the **Copy** button to copy the text from the sidebar to the Microsoft Office Clipboard, and then position the cursor in the new blank paragraph above the sidebar and click the **Paste** button to insert the text in the new location. Click the **Paste Options** button that appears just below the pasted text, and then on the **Paste Options** menu, click the **Keep Text Only** button.

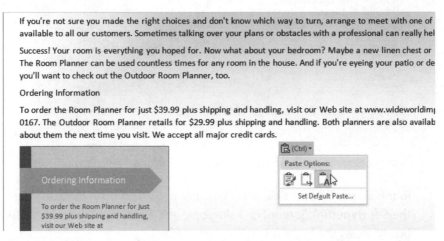

The Paste Options menu, which appears below the inserted text, offers some of the same options that are available from the Paste menu in the Clipboard group on the Home tab.

Having moved the sidebar content out into the document, we no longer need the sidebar.

13 Click the outer edge of the sidebar to select it, and then press **Delete** to remove it from the document.

14 Click anywhere in the **Ordering Information** paragraph. On the **Home** tab, in the **Style** gallery, click the **Heading 1** thumbnail to format the heading and add it to the structural elements of the document.

Now let's insert a hyperlink to the heading so that webpage viewers can easily access it.

15   Scroll to the fourth paragraph of text and select the phrase **purchase a Room Planner**. On the **Insert** menu, in the **Links** group, click **Hyperlink** to open the **Insert Hyperlink** dialog box.

KEYBOARD SHORTCUT   Press Ctrl+K to open the Insert Hyperlink dialog box. For more information about keyboard shortcuts, see "Keyboard Shortcuts" at the end of this book.

16   In the **Link to** list, click **Place in This Document**. In the **Select a place in this document** pane, click **Ordering Information**. Then click the **ScreenTip** button.

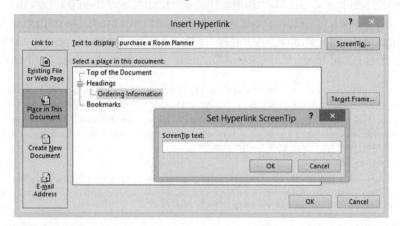

Adding a ScreenTip to hyperlinks is a best practice for accessibility purposes.

17   In the **ScreenTip text** box, enter Display ordering information. Then click **OK** in the **Set Hyperlink ScreenTip** dialog box, and again in the **Insert Hyperlink** dialog box to insert the hyperlink in the document.

Notice that the content would be easier to read if the text lines were shorter. You can accomplish this by indenting the paragraphs.

18   On the **Home** tab, in the **Editing** group, click the **Select** button, and then click **Select All**.

KEYBOARD SHORTCUT   Press Ctrl+A to select all content in the document.

19   On the **Page Layout** tab, in the **Indent** area of the **Paragraph** group, enter 1.25 in the **Left** box, enter 1.25 in the **Right** box, and then click anywhere in the document. Notice that this leaves the quote box no longer aligns with the text.

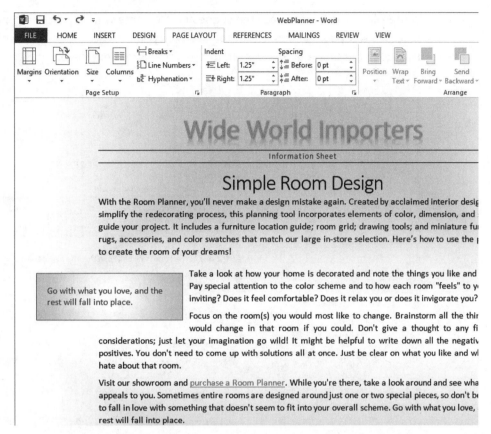

Increasing the margins decreases the width of the text area.

20 Click anywhere in the quote box, and click the **Layout Options** button that appears. On the **Layout Options** menu, click the **In Line with Text** thumbnail to position the quote box at the beginning of the **Take a look** paragraph.

21 Click to position the cursor between the quote box and the word **Take**, and press **Enter** to place the quote box on its own line.

Now that all the page elements display nicely, let's save the document as a webpage.

22 Display the **Save As** page of the **Backstage** view, and click the **Chapter11** practice file folder to open the **Save As** dialog box.

11

23 In the **File name** box, replace the suggested file name with MyWebPage (avoid spaces in webpage file names). In the **Save as type** list, click **Single File Web Page**. Then click the **Change Title** button to open the **Enter Text** dialog box.

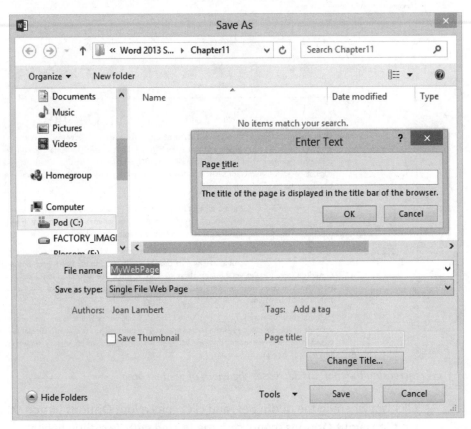

You can provide a page title that displays on the title bar in a web browser.

24 In the **Page title** box, enter Room Planner. Then click **OK** in the **Enter Text** dialog box, and **Save** in the **Save As** dialog box to create the webpage.

25 Do *not* close the Word document. Start **File Explorer**, and navigate to the **Chapter11** practice file folder. The folder now contains a file named **MyWebPage**.

26 Double-click the **MyWebPage** file to display it in your default web browser. Notice that the page title is shown on the web browser tab. Notice also that the WordArt and the gradient background of the quote box do not display correctly.

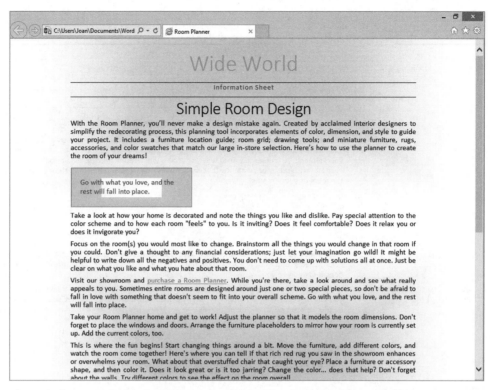

The web document looks almost the same in a web browser as it did in Web Layout view.

27 Point to the underlined text **purchase a Room Planner**, and notice that the ScreenTip appears. Then click the link to move to the **Ordering Information** section of the page.

28 Do *not* close the web browser window. Switch to the **MyWebPage** file in Word. Click the **Wide World Importers** WordArt object to select it, and then press **Delete**. Enter Wide World Importers in its place. Then select the text, click the **Font Color** arrow on the **Mini Toolbar**, and click the top orange swatch in the **Theme Colors** palette (**Orange, Accent 1**). Then in the **Font Size** list, click **36**.

29 Click the quote box to select it. On the **Format** tool tab, in the **Shape Styles** group, click the **Shape Fill** button, and then click the top blue swatch in the **Theme Colors** palette (**Ice Blue, Background 2**).

30 In the **Backstage** view or on the **Quick Access Toolbar**, click **Save**. Switch back to the web browser window, and click the **Refresh** button to display the effects of your changes.

KEYBOARD SHORTCUT Press F5 to refresh the Internet Explorer window.

11

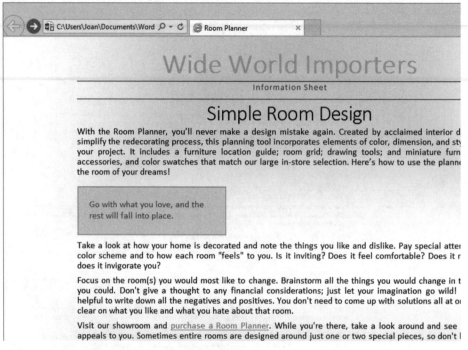

You can easily make changes to the webpage and preview the results.

❌ CLEAN UP Close your web browser and File Explorer. Then close the MyWebPage file.

Creating and publishing blog posts

Blogs used to be personal websites—online spaces where individuals expressed their opinions about anything and everything. With the evolution of social sites such as Facebook and MySpace, blogs are now less likely to be personal online diaries intended for a limited audience, such as the author's family or circle of friends, and are more likely to serve a promotional purpose. For example, they might provide news and information about an industry. Or they might offer commentary on a specific subject, such as a genre of music, a political point of view, a medical condition, or local news. Blogs may be created by individuals, or they may be part of the communication stream from a company to its customers.

Blog content consists of posts that can include text, images, and links to related blogs, webpages, and other media. You can create blog posts through your online blog provider, or you can create them in Word 2013 and publish them from Word when you're ready to. A benefit of creating a blog post in Word is that you can work offline and at your leisure, and use the Word proofing tools to ensure that your content is ready for prime time.

You can create a blog post within the Blog Post template, or in any Word document. If you use the Blog Post template, you can manage the content and publishing process from within the document, by using the tools available on the Blog Post ribbon tab.

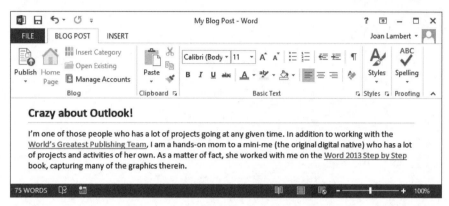

In the Blog Post template, the ribbon displays only the specialized Blog Post tab and the Insert tab.

If you don't use the Blog Post template, you can still publish the document contents to your blog by clicking Post To Blog on the Share page of the Backstage view.

If you have already set up a blog account with a blog service provider, you can register your account with Word the first time you create a blog post. If you haven't yet set up a blog account, you'll need to register with a service provider before you can publish your first post. Thereafter, Word uses your registered account information when you create or publish a blog post.

Key points

- You can save a document in a file format that allows it to be opened in other programs.

- To ensure that a document appears as you intend it to when recipients view it, you can distribute the document as a PDF or XPS file.

- You can edit PDF files in Word 2013.

- When you are creating a document, there are many simple actions you can take to ensure that it meets accessibility requirements. You can use the Accessibility Checker to identify document elements that commonly affect accessibility.

- A Word document can easily be converted to a webpage. You can review how it will look in a web browser, and edit the webpage by using Word.

- You can easily create and publish blog posts by using Word.

11

Additional
techniques

Chapter at a glance

Link

**Link to external resources,
page 348**

...er, you'll want to explore the Walla Walla music scene. This little town offe...
...al choral, funky blues, downhome country, refined chamber, rock, and pop...
...ne Walla Walla Symphony Orchestra, the oldest continuously operating syn...
...pi.

...ings, this exceptional orchestra has matured into one of the best we have l...
...est in a <u>series of outstanding conductors</u>, Maestro Yaacov Bergman continu...
...rams that challenge his musicians and his audiences. In April, we look forw...
...*una* at the orchestra's 416th concert since its...
...held in beautiful Cordiner Hall on the Whitm...
...er offerings at www.wwsymphony.org, or <u>email us</u> for more information.

> Send message to Margie's Travel
> **Ctrl+Click to follow link**

Embed

**Embed linked objects,
page 353**

R. Lee Friese	1977-1986
Cindy Egolf Sham-Rao	1986-1987
Yaacov Bergman	1987-Present

In December, we look forward to a performance of the holiday classic *The* ...
with the Eugene Ballet. The performance will be held in beautiful Cordiner...
campus. Be sure to check out this and their other offerings at www.wwsyn...
more information.

Display a timeline
of conductors

Bookmark

**Insert and link to bookmarks,
page 360**

¶10. **Building Maintenance**
10.1 The maintenance, repair, and replacement of the exterior structure of all Apartments to the
surfaces of the Apartments' perimeter walls, floors, ceilings, windows, and doors is the resp...
of the Board.
10.2 The maintenance, repair, and replacement of the interior structure of all Apartments is the
responsibility of the Owner. Such maintenance, repair, and replacement shall not interfere w...
damage the structural integrity of the Building.
10.3 The maintenance of the Building Limited Common Areas is the responsibility of the Owner...
Owners who have exclusive use of those Limited Common Areas. The repair and replaceme...
Limited Common Areas is the responsibility of the Board. Limited Common Areas include, b...
not limited to, the following:
• [Decks and patios
• Maintenance
• Repair and replacement
• Elevator shaft and equipment
• Entry lobby/elevator lobbies
• Parking areas, drive aisles, and garage fan]
10.4 The Board retains the authority to perform maintenance inspections and to require that Ow...
perform necessary maintenance of Limited Common Areas. In the event that an Owner doe...
perform the maintenance required to ensure the adequate upkeep of a Limited Common Ar...

Display

**Display document information in fields,
page 365**

Warehouse¶
The rear of the building contains the warehouse, which occupies the major portion of the buildin...
space. The warehouse is divided into four separate areas: Receiving, Shipping, Packaging, and
Inventory storage: ¶
• → The Receiving area consists of two loading docks (also used for Shipping), and a 12 x
area with racks for holding incoming packages. The racks are divided by shipping cor...

11/23/2012 4:41 PM → Office Procedures → File name: proceduresfields¶

Link to information and content

12

IN THIS CHAPTER, YOU WILL LEARN HOW TO

- Link to external resources.

- Embed linked objects.

- Insert and link to bookmarks.

- Display document information in fields.

Sometimes the information you want to convey in a document already exists in another location—either external to the document or elsewhere within the document. Rather than repeating the information or simply telling the reader where to find it, you can insert a link to the information in its original location. The reader can click the link to move to that location or to access the external resource.

If the external resource is a picture, slide, or other image that might be updated frequently, you can embed an updateable version of the image that is linked to the image storage location. Then each time you open the document, Word can check for an updated version of the image.

If the information you want to present is saved as a document property, you can insert a field that displays the property. Then if the property is updated, the document content replicates the change.

Microsoft Word 2013 has several tools that help you to link to or display information:

- **Hyperlinks** To help a reader move to a location in the same file, in another file, or on a webpage, you can add links from text or graphics to the target location.

- **Bookmarks** You can quickly return to a specific location in a document by inserting a bookmark. You can jump to a bookmarked location by selecting it from a list, and you can help a reader find information by inserting hyperlinks or cross-references to bookmarks.

- **Cross-references** To help a reader move to a related location in a document, you can insert a cross-reference. Then if the text at the location changes, you can tell Word to update the cross-reference to reflect the change.

- **Fields** Instead of entering information that is associated with a document, you can have Word insert it for you in a field. Then if the information changes, you can simply update the field to ensure that the information is current.

In this chapter, you'll first insert two different kinds of hyperlinks. You'll embed linked objects in a document and then update the external objects so that changes are reflected. Then you'll create and modify bookmarks and cross-references. Finally, you'll insert three different types of fields.

PRACTICE FILES To complete the exercises in this chapter, you need the practice files contained in the Chapter12 practice file folder. For more information, see "Download the practice files" in this book's Introduction.

Linking to external resources

Like webpages, Word documents can include hyperlinks that provide a quick way to perform tasks such as the following:

- Open another document

- Link to a website

- Download a file

- Send an email message

You insert hyperlinks into a Word document by displaying the Insert Hyperlink dialog box, specifying the type of link you want to create, and then entering an appropriate destination for that type of link.

While creating a hyperlink to a document or a webpage, called the target, you can specify whether the target information should appear in the same window or frame as the active document or in a new one. You can also make a particular setting the default for all hyperlinks.

Within a document, hyperlinks appear underlined and in the color specified for hyperlinks by the document's theme. You can jump to the target of the hyperlink by holding down the Ctrl key and clicking the link. After you click the hyperlink, its color changes to the color specified for followed hyperlinks.

To edit or remove a hyperlink, you can select it and click Hyperlink in the Links group on the Insert tab or you can right-click the selection and then click the appropriate command.

In this exercise, you'll insert and test a hyperlink to a different document. Then you'll insert, modify, and test a hyperlink that opens an email message window.

SET UP You need the VisitorGuide and Conductors documents located in the Chapter12 practice file folder to complete this exercise. You also need to have an email program configured on your computer. Open the VisitorGuide document, and then follow the steps.

1 In the second sentence of the second paragraph, select **series of outstanding conductors**. On the **Insert** tab, click the **Links** group button if necessary, and then in the **Links** group, click the **Hyperlink** button to open the **Insert Hyperlink** dialog box. Notice that on the **Link to** bar, **Existing File or Web Page** is selected.

KEYBOARD SHORTCUT Press Ctrl+K to open the Insert Hyperlink dialog box. For more information about keyboard shortcuts, see "Keyboard shortcuts" at the end of this book.

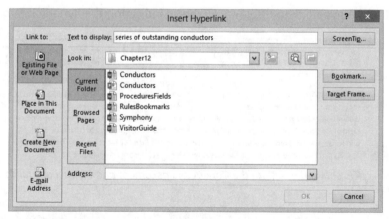

You can select the target type in the Link To bar.

TROUBLESHOOTING If the contents of the Chapter12 folder are not shown, ensure that Existing File Or Web Page is selected on the Link To bar, then click the Look In arrow, and navigate to the Chapter12 practice file folder.

12

2   In the list of file names, click (don't double-click) the **Conductors** document, and then click the **Target Frame** button to open the **Set Target Frame** dialog box. Notice that **Page Default (none)** is selected as the frame in which the document will open.

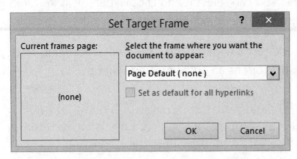

In the Set Target Frame dialog box, you can change the window in which the hyperlink target will be displayed.

3   In the **Select the frame where you want the document to appear** list, click **New window**. Then click **OK**.

4   Click **OK** to close the **Insert Hyperlink** dialog box and insert a hyperlink from the selected text in the **VisitorGuide** document to the **Conductors** document. The hyperlink is indicated by an underline and the color assigned to hyperlinks by the document's theme.

5   Point to the hyperlink to display a ScreenTip indicating the hyperlink target.

> If you are a music lover, you'll want to explore the Walla Walla music scene. This little town offers music for everyone: ethereal choral, funky blues, downhome country, refined chamber, rock, and pop. But the jewel of them all is the Walla Walla Symph̲ ̲ ̲ ̲ ̲ ̲ ̲ ̲ ̲ ̲ ̲ ̲ ̲ ̲ ̲usly operating symphony west of the Mississippi.
>
> file:///c:\users\joan\documents\word 2013 step by step\chapter12\conductors.docx
> Ctrl+Click to follow link
>
> From humble beginnings, this exceptional ̲ ̲ ̲ ̲ ̲ ̲ ̲ ̲ ̲ ̲ ̲ ̲ ̲ ̲ ̲ ̲he best we have heard in recent years. The latest in a series of outstanding conductors, Maestro Yaacov Bergman continues to deliver inspired programs that challenge his musicians and his audiences. In April, we look forward to a night of *Flora and Fauna* at the orchestra's 416th concert since its inception in 1907. As usual, the performance will be held in beautiful Cordiner Hall on the Whitman College campus. Be sure to check out this and their other offerings on their website, or email us for more information.

The ScreenTip shows the path to the Conductors document and instructions for following the link.

6   Hold down the **Ctrl** key, and then click the hyperlink to open the **Conductors** document in a new window.

7   On the **View** tab, in the **Window** group, click the **Switch Windows** button, and then click **VisitorGuide**. Notice that the color of the hyperlink in the **VisitorGuide** document has changed to indicate that you have followed this link to its target.

Now let's create an email hyperlink.

8   In the last line of the document, select **email us**, and then on the **Insert** tab, in the **Links** group, click the **Hyperlink** button.

9   In the **Insert Hyperlink** dialog box, in the **Link to** bar, click **E-mail Address**. Notice that the dialog box changes so you can enter the information appropriate for an email hyperlink.

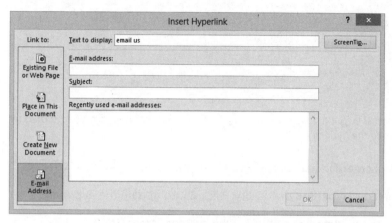

If you have previously inserted a hyperlink to an email address, it will appear in the Recently Used list, and you can easily use it again.

10   In the **E-mail address** box, enter margie@margiestravel.com. Notice that when you begin entering text in the **E-mail address** box, Word inserts *mailto:* in front of the address you enter. When a reader clicks the link, Word will start his or her default email program and open a new email message window.

11   In the **Subject** box, enter Symphony question to automatically enter this text in the **Subject** box of the new email message window.

12   Click **OK** to insert the email hyperlink in the document. Notice that the hyperlinked text is again indicated by an underline and its assigned color. Pointing to it displays information about the recipient and subject in a ScreenTip.

13   Right-click the **email us** hyperlink, and then click **Edit Hyperlink** to open the **Edit Hyperlink** dialog box with the current destination for this link in the **E-mail Address** box.

14   In the upper-right corner of the dialog box, click the **ScreenTip** button to open the **Set Hyperlink ScreenTip** dialog box.

12

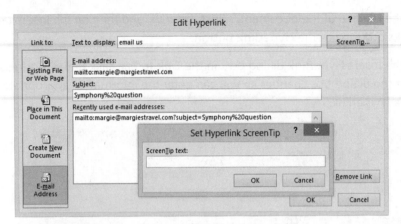

You can specify the text you want for the ScreenTip that appears when someone points to the hyperlink.

15 In the **ScreenTip text** box, enter Send message to Margie's Travel. Then click **OK**.

16 In the **Edit Hyperlink** dialog box, click **OK** to update the hyperlink.

17 Point to the hyperlink to display the custom ScreenTip.

> If you are a music lover, you'll want to explore the Walla Walla music scene. This little town offers music for everyone: ethereal choral, funky blues, downhome country, refined chamber, rock, and pop. But the jewel of them all is the Walla Walla Symphony Orchestra, the oldest continuously operating symphony west of the Mississippi.
>
> From humble beginnings, this exceptional orchestra has matured into one of the best we have heard in recent years. The latest in a series of outstanding conductors, Maestro Yaacov Bergman continues to deliver inspired programs that challenge his musicians and his audiences. In April, we look forward to a night of *Flora and Fauna* at the orchestra's 416th conce [Send message to Margie's Travel] s usual, the performance will be held in beautiful Cordiner Hall on [Ctrl+Click to follow link] Be sure to check out this and their other offerings on their website, or email us for more information.

You can provide informative ScreenTips for all kinds of hyperlinks.

18 Hold down **Ctrl**, and click the **email us** hyperlink to open a message window.

TROUBLESHOOTING If your email program isn't already running, clicking the hyperlink will cause it to start. If you have multiple email programs or profiles installed, you might be prompted to select the one you want to use.

SEE ALSO For information about the many fabulous features of Outlook 2013, refer to *Microsoft Outlook 2013 Step by Step* by Joan Lambert and Joyce Cox (Microsoft Press, 2013).

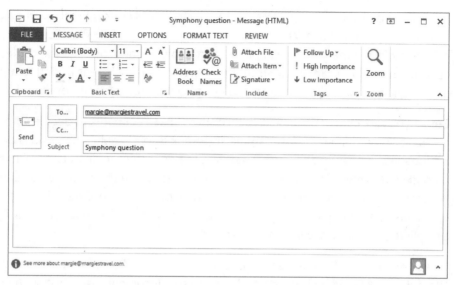

The specified email address has been inserted in the To box, and the specified description appears in the Subject box.

19   Close the message window, clicking **No** when asked whether you want to save the changes. Notice that the email hyperlink text is now the color that is assigned to followed hyperlinks by the document's theme.

❌ CLEAN UP   Close the VisitorGuide document and the Conductors document, saving your changes if you want to.

Embedding linked objects

In earlier chapters, we embedded images and tables within document content to support, reinforce, and decorate the content. Embedding content directly in a document places a static (unchanging) copy of the object in the document. If you know that a document will change, you can link to it as we did in the previous exercise. Sometimes, though, you might want to display the contents of an external object that you know might change. Rather than embedding a static copy of the content and then updating it manually whenever it changes, you can embed a linked copy and then refresh the links to ensure that the most recent content is shown. When you embed a linked copy, you can either display the full content of the embedded object so that readers can review it in the document, or provide an icon that readers click to review the content in the original program.

12

You can embed links to many types of files, including Microsoft Excel workbooks, Microsoft PowerPoint presentations, Word documents, graphics, and PDF files. Some links work a bit differently from others—for example, linking to a document displays the content in a resizable object that you can update from the shortcut menu, whereas linking to a PowerPoint presentation displays the first slide; you can play the presentation from the shortcut menu.

Before you distribute a document that contains linked elements to people who don't have access to those elements—for example, if the link is to a graphic that resides on your organization's internal server and you are sending the document to an outside recipient—it is a good idea to either disconnect the links (referred to as *breaking the links*), configure the links for manual update, or lock the links so they don't update. Otherwise, each time the recipients open the document, Word will try to automatically update the links, but won't be able to connect to the linked elements.

In this exercise, you'll embed and link to the content of a PowerPoint presentation and a Word document and embed an icon linked to the document. You'll test all the links, and then disconnect the links.

➜ SET UP You need the Symphony and Conductors documents, and the Conductors presentation, located in the Chapter12 practice file folder, to complete this exercise. Open the Symphony document, and then follow the steps.

1   Position the cursor at the beginning of the third paragraph, which starts with **Since its inception**.

    First we'll embed and link to a PowerPoint presentation.

2   On the **Insert** tab, in the **Text** group, click the **Object** arrow, and then click **Object**. In the **Object** dialog box, click the **Create from File** tab.

    TIP From the Create New page of the Object dialog box, you can insert a new worksheet, chart, presentation, slide, document, or other object into a document. You can then populate the object content by editing the inserted object.

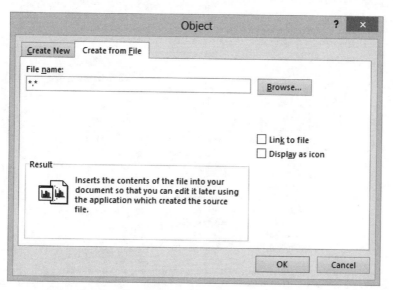

From this page you can insert the contents of a file or create a link to the file.

3   On the **Create from File** page of the dialog box, click the **Browse** button to open the **Browse** dialog box. If the **Browse** dialog box doesn't already display the contents of the **Chapter12** practice file folder, navigate to that folder. Then click the **Conductors** presentation, and click **Insert** to enter the path to the presentation in the **File name** box.

4   Select the **Link to file** check box, and then click **OK** to insert the linked presentation at the cursor. The linked presentation appears to be just another embedded image.

5   Click the linked presentation to select it. Notice that no tool tab appears on the ribbon for the linked object.

    TIP When you select a graphic object, the tools for formatting the object are usually available on a tool tab; that is not the case for linked objects. Instead, the formatting options are available from the shortcut menu.

6   Right-click the linked presentation to display the shortcut menu and tools.

12

From humble beginnings, this exceptional orchestra has matured into one of the best we have heard in recent years. The latest in a series of outstanding conductors, Maestro Yaacov Bergman continues to deliver inspired programs that challenge his musicians and his audiences.

Walla Walla Symphony Orchestra Conductors

Edgar Fischer	1907-1922
Gottfried Herbst	1922-1923
Karel Havlicek	1923-1924
Alice Reynolds Fischer	1924-1934
Victor Johnson	1934-1936
Walter Wren	1936-1940
Frank Beezhold	1940-1941, 1942-45
Nelson O. Schreiber	1941-1942
William H. Bailey	1945-1969
Jose Rambaldi	1969-1976
R. Lee Friese	1977-1986
Cindy Egolf Sham-Rao	1986-1987
Yaacov Bergman	1987-Present

Style Crop

✂ Cut
📋 Copy
📋 Paste Options:
📄 Update Link
Linked Presentation Object ▶
Insert Caption...
Borders and Shading...
Format Object...
Hyperlink...
New Comment

Since its inception in 1907, the Symphony has had only 13 conductors. Maestro Bergman has been with the Symphony for longer than any other conductor.

You can crop the inserted object, apply borders and shading, and format the display of the object.

We're not working on formatting objects in this chapter, so we won't apply any formatting as part of this exercise, but feel free to experiment with the options if you want to.

7   On the shortcut menu, click **Linked Presentation Object**, and then click **Show Link** to run the slide show. When the first slide appears, click it to move to the second slide, click again to complete the slide show, and click a third time to exit the slide show and return to the document.

Now we'll embed and link to a document.

8   Position the cursor at the beginning of the fourth paragraph, which starts with **In December**.

9   On the **Insert** tab, in the **Text** group, click the **Object** button, and then in the dialog box, click the **Create from File** tab.

10   Click the **Browse** button, and then in the **Browse** dialog box, double-click the **Conductors** document.

11   On the **Create from File** page of the **Object** dialog box, select the **Link to file** check box, and then click **OK** to insert the content of the linked document at the cursor. The linked document content appears to be an embedded image of a table.

12   Click the linked document once to select it.

Walla Walla Symphony Orchestra Conductors	
Edgar Fischer	1907-1922
Gottfried Herbst	1922-1923
Karel Havlicek	1923-1924
Alice Reynolds Fischer	1924-1934
Victor Johnson	1934-1936
Walter Wren	1936-1940
Frank Beezhold	1940-1941, 1942-45
Nelson O. Schreiber	1941-1942
William H. Bailey	1945-1969
Jose Rambaldi	1969-1976
R. Lee Friese	1977-1986
Cindy Egolf Sham-Rao	1986-1987
Yaacov Bergman	1987-Present

In December, we look forward to a performance of the holiday classic *The Nutcracker* in conjunction with the Eugene Ballet. The performance will be held in beautiful Cordiner Hall on the Whitman College

The linked document object occupies the entire width of the page.

13   Double-click the linked document to open it in Word. The title bar indicates that you're opening the original document.

TIP If you do not select Link To File in the Object dialog box, Word inserts a static copy of the document content rather than a link to the live file. Double-clicking the inserted content or icon then opens a copy of the file, rather than the original file.

Let's make a quick, obvious change to the document so we can test the results of refreshing the link.

14   In the **Conductors** document, on the **Design** tab, in the **Document Formatting** group, click **Themes** and then click **Celestial** to change the fonts and colors used in the table. Save and close the **Conductors** document to return to the **Symphony** document. Notice that the table in the **Symphony** document is still green.

15   Right-click the linked document, and then click **Update Link** to refresh the embedded image of the linked document's content and display the purple version of the table.

Now we'll insert an icon linked to the same file.

16   Press **Ctrl+End** to position the cursor at the end of the document. Repeat steps 9 and 10 to insert the path to the **Conductors** document in the **File name** box on the **Create from File** page of the **Object** dialog box.

12

17   Select the **Link to file** check box and the **Display as icon** check box. The icon that will
      be shown in the document appears in the dialog box. Click the **Change Icon** button
      that appears below the icon to display the icon options for this file type.

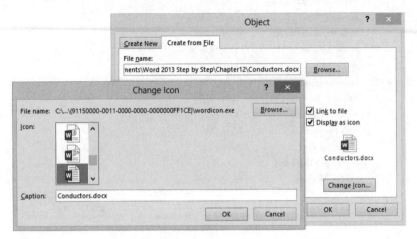

You can display the icon and text that are most appropriate for your purpose.

18   In the **Change Icon** dialog box, scroll through the **Icon** list and notice the icons you
      can use to indicate the document type to a reader. Then click the last icon in the list.

19   In the **Caption** box, replace the file name and extension with Display a timeline of
      conductors. Then click **OK** twice to close both dialog boxes and insert the icon and
      caption at the cursor.

R. Lee Friese	1977-1986
Cindy Egolf Sham-Rao	1986-1987
Yaacov Bergman	1987-Present

In December, we look forward to a performance of the holiday classic *The Nutcracker* in conjunction
with the Eugene Ballet. The performance will be held in beautiful Cordiner Hall on the Whitman College
campus. Be sure to check out this and their other offerings on their website, or email us for more
information.

Display a timeline
of conductors

A meaningful caption helps readers know what will happen when they double-click the icon.

20   Point to the icon and notice that it does not display a ScreenTip as a hyperlink would.
      Then double-click the icon to open the **Conductors** document.

21   Make changes to the **Conductors** document, then save and close it and update the links, if you want to. When you finish experimenting, right-click the icon you inserted in step 19, click **Linked Document Object**, and then click **Links**.

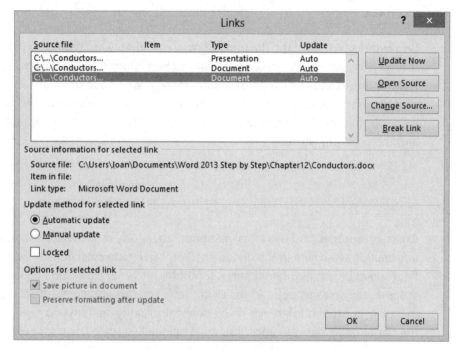

From the Links dialog box, you can manage existing linked objects.

22   Notice the various actions you can take with each of the linked objects. Click the first link (the presentation), then hold down the **Shift** key and click the last link to select all three linked objects.

23   In the **Update method for selected link** area, select the **Locked** check box to lock the links so that they do not update.

The benefit of locking the links rather than breaking them is that if at a later time you want to reconnect to the linked objects and update them in the document, you can.

24   Click **OK** in the **Links** dialog box. Then right-click the embedded icon and notice that the **Update Link** command on the shortcut menu is unavailable.

TIP To turn off automatic updating but enable the Update Link command, select the Manual Update method.

❌ CLEAN UP Close the Symphony document, saving your changes if you want to.

Inserting and linking to bookmarks

Word provides two tools that you can use to jump easily to designated places within the same document:

- **Bookmarks** Whether the document you are reading was created by you or by someone else, you can insert bookmarks to flag information to which you might want to return later. Like a physical bookmark, a Word bookmark marks a specific named place in a document. After inserting a bookmark, you can quickly jump to it by displaying the **Bookmark** dialog box, clicking the bookmark you want to locate, and then clicking **Go To**.

  TIP Another way to move to a bookmark is to display the Go To page of the Find And Replace dialog box, click Bookmark in the Go To What list, and then select the bookmark you want from the Enter Bookmark Name list.

- **Cross-references** You use cross-references to quickly move readers to associated information elsewhere in the document. You can create cross-references to headings, figures and tables, numbered items, footnotes and endnotes, and equations—Word automatically creates pointers for all of these. You can also create cross-references to manually inserted bookmarks. If you delete or modify an item you have designated as the target of a cross-reference, you must manually update the cross-reference.

SEE ALSO For information about using hyperlinks to jump to other locations, see "Linking to external resources" earlier in this chapter. For information about using the Navigation pane to jump to any paragraph styled as a heading, see "Viewing documents in different ways" in Chapter 1, "Explore Microsoft Word 2013."

In this exercise, you'll insert and navigate to bookmarks. You'll also create a cross-reference, edit the referenced item, and then update the cross-reference.

➜ SET UP You need the RulesBookmarks document located in the Chapter12 practice file folder to complete this exercise. Open the document, and then follow the steps.

1   On the **Home** tab, in the **Editing** group, click the **Find** arrow (not the button). In the **Find** list, click **Go To** to display the **Go To** page of the **Find and Replace** dialog box.

    KEYBOARD SHORTCUT Press Ctrl+G to display the Go To page of the Find And Replace dialog box.

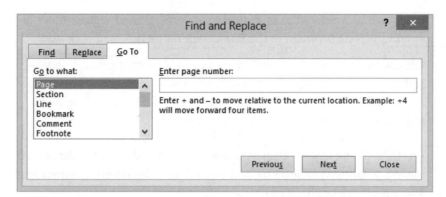

You can select the type of element and the specific element to which you want to jump.

2   With **Page** selected in the **Go to what** list, enter 5 in the **Enter page number** box. Then click **Go To**, and click **Close**.

3   If necessary, click to position the cursor to the left of the **10. Building Maintenance** heading. Then on the **Insert** tab, in the **Links** group, click the **Bookmark** button to open the **Bookmark** dialog box.

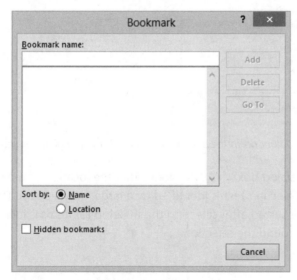

You create and manage bookmarks in this dialog box.

4   In the **Bookmark name** box, enter Maintenance. Then click **Add** to close the **Bookmark** dialog box and insert a bookmark named Maintenance into the document. The bookmark is not currently visible (even if you display hidden characters).

12

5   In section **10.3**, select the six bulleted list items. Open the **Bookmark** dialog box, enter LimitedCommon in the **Bookmark name** box, and click **Add**.

> **TROUBLESHOOTING** Bookmark names cannot contain spaces. If you enter a space and then a character, the Add button becomes inactive. To name bookmarks with multiple words, either run the words together and capitalize each word, or replace the spaces with underscores for readability.

6   Press the **Home** key to release the selection. Then display the **Advanced** page of the **Word Options** dialog box, and in the **Show Document Content** area, select the **Show Bookmarks** check box.

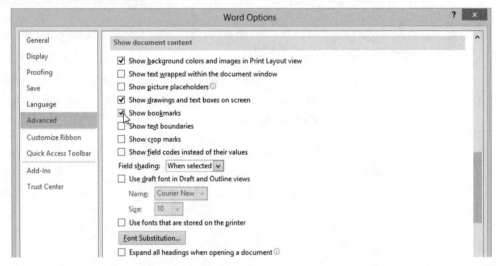

The only way to display bookmarks in the document content is by changing this setting.

7   In the **Word Options** dialog box, click **OK**. Notice that the location of the bookmark you inserted without selecting text is identified by a large, gray I-beam. The location of the bookmark you inserted after selecting the bulleted list items is identified by gray square brackets around the selection.

10. Building Maintenance

10.1 The maintenance, repair, and replacement of the exterior structure of all Apartments to the interior surfaces of the Apartments' perimeter walls, floors, ceilings, windows, and doors is the responsibility of the Board.

10.2 The maintenance, repair, and replacement of the interior structure of all Apartments is the responsibility of the Owner. Such maintenance, repair, and replacement shall not interfere with or damage the structural integrity of the Building.

10.3 The maintenance of the Building Limited Common Areas is the responsibility of the Owner or Owners who have exclusive use of those Limited Common Areas. The repair and replacement of the Limited Common Areas is the responsibility of the Board. Limited Common Areas include, but are not limited to, the following:

- Decks and patios
- Maintenance
- Repair and replacement
- Elevator shaft and equipment
- Entry lobby/elevator lobbies
- Parking areas, drive aisles, and garage fan]

The identifiers for the two types of bookmarks.

8   Press **Ctrl+Home** to move to the beginning of the document. Then display the **Go To** page of the **Find and Replace** dialog box.

9   In the **Go to what** list, click **Bookmark** to change the dialog box so that you can specify the bookmark you want to jump to. Notice that the **Enter bookmark name** list displays the name of the bookmark that comes first alphabetically.

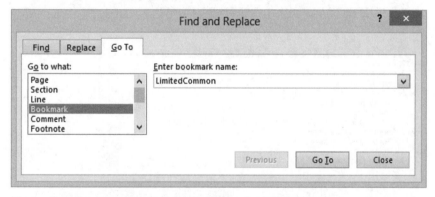

The bookmarks you created are accessible on the Go To page.

10   In the **Enter bookmark name** list, click **Maintenance**, and then click **Go To** to move to the bookmark. Notice that the dialog box remains open so that you can move among bookmarks if you want to.

Next we'll insert a cross-reference to a document section.

12

11   In the **Go to what** list, click **Heading**, and then in the **Enter heading** number box, enter **4**. Click **Go To** and then click **Close** to move to section **4**.

> **TIP** You can also jump to a bookmark by displaying the Bookmark dialog box, clicking the bookmark you want, and then clicking Go To. In the Bookmark dialog box, you can sort the bookmarks alphabetically or in the order in which they are located. To delete a bookmark, click its name, and then click Delete.

12   Click at the end of the **4.2** paragraph. Press the **Spacebar**, enter See also section, and then press the **Spacebar** again.

13   On the **Insert** tab, in the **Links** group, click the **Cross-reference** button to open the **Cross-reference** dialog box, where you can specify the type of item you want to reference and what you want the cross-reference inserted in the document to say.

14   In the **Reference type** list, click **Heading** to display all the headings in this document.

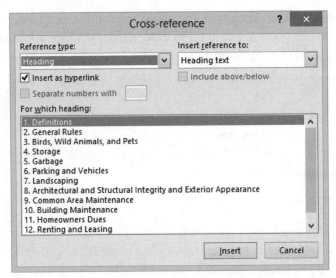

Word can identify the headings in a document only if you have applied heading styles.

15   With **Heading text** selected in the **Insert reference to** list, click **6. Parking and Vehicles** in the **For which heading** list. Then click **Insert**, and click **Close** to insert the heading text in the document. Although it's not obvious, the text has been inserted as a field.

16   Point to the inserted heading text to display a ScreenTip containing information about the cross-reference target; in this case, *Current Document*. Hold down the **Ctrl** key, and then click the cross-reference to move to the section **6** heading.

17   In the heading, delete **and Vehicles**.

18   Scroll up to section **4.2** and click (don't press the **Ctrl** key) **6. Parking and Vehicles** to select the cross-reference field.

> **TROUBLESHOOTING** Click the field; don't try to select the text.

19   Right-click the selected cross-reference, and then click **Update Field** to delete the words *and Vehicles* from the end of the cross-reference.

> **4. Storage**
> 4.1 No bicycles, tricycles, scooters, roller skates, skateboards, wagons, toys, or other personal belongings shall be stored or left in any Common Area.
> 4.2 No trailers, boats, vans, campers, house trailers, buses, or trucks shall be stored in any parking space in any Common Area. See also section 6. Parking
> 4.3 No Owner shall use his or her garage to store personal belongings in such a way that there is not enough space for his or her vehicles.
> 4.4 No Owner shall use his or her parking spaces in the common garage to store personal belongings, except that with prior written permission of the Board, bicycles may be stored in the front end of the assigned parking stall or in the Owner's unused assigned stall. Bicycles must be standing upright, by using the bicycle's own stand or in an approved type of bicycle stand. Storage of anything other than automobiles, motorcycles, and bicycles in the common garage may be a violation of fire code and subject to citation and fines by the Bellevue Fire Department.

The cross-reference reflects the change you made to the target heading.

20   Hold down **Ctrl**, and click the cross-reference to jump to the associated heading.

❌ CLEAN UP Turn off the display of bookmark identifiers by displaying the Advanced page of the Word Options dialog box and clearing the Show Bookmarks check box in the Show Document Content area. Then close the RulesBookmarks document, saving your changes if you want to.

Displaying document information in fields

When you insert a hyperlink into a document, you are actually inserting a Hyperlink field. A field is a placeholder that tells Word to supply specified information or to perform a specified action in a specified way.

Word inserts fields to control certain processes, such as the creation of a table of contents or the merging of a form letter with a data source. You can use fields to insert information that can be updated with the click of a button if the information changes. You can't enter a field in your document; instead, you must tell Word to insert the field you want. You do this by clicking the Quick Parts button in the Text group on the Insert tab and then clicking Field to display the Field dialog box.

12

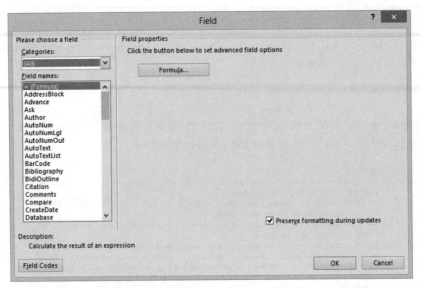

The Field dialog box provides a comprehensive list of all the available fields. In this dialog box, you can also set options that refine the field.

Each field consists of a set of curly braces containing the field name and any required or optional instructions or settings. These settings, called switches, refine the results of the field—for example, by formatting it in a particular way. When you insert a field from the Field dialog box, you can click Field Codes in the lower-left corner of the dialog box to display the field's syntax. Selecting a field and then clicking Options in the lower-left corner displays the Field Options dialog box, in which you can add general and specific optional settings to the field code. Different fields have different field options—some have only general options, whereas others have multiple types of switches.

Inserting some types of fields requires advanced knowledge of the fields and how to control them. However, some fields are very easy. For example, to insert today's date or the current time in a document, you simply click the Date & Time button (the ScreenTip says *Insert Date and Time*) in the Text group on the Insert tab to display the Date And Time dialog box and select the format you want to use. To insert the information as regular text, click OK. If you want to be able to update the date or time, insert the information as a field by selecting the Update Automatically check box. Word then inserts a field matching the format you selected and retrieves the date or time from your computer's internal calendar or clock.

TIP After Word inserts the field, the field results are shown; for example if you insert a File-Size field, the size of the file is shown. To display the field code that tells Word to insert the file size, either click the field to select it and press Alt+F9, or right-click the field and click Toggle Field Codes.

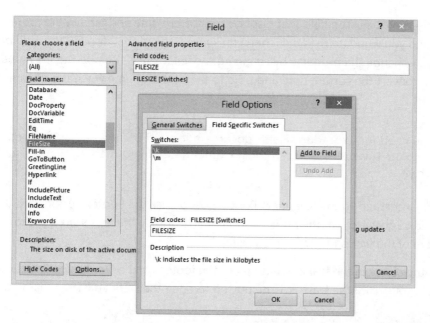

Descriptions in the Field and Field Options dialog boxes guide you in defining the field.

TIP You can insert other types of date and time fields, such as a PrintDate field or an Edit-Time field. Insert a date or time field in the usual way, right-click the field, and then click Edit Field to display the Field dialog box. Then change the Categories setting to Date And Time, and in the Field Names list, click the field you want. (Clicking a field in the list displays a brief description, so it is easy to choose the one you want.) When you click OK, the information corresponding to the field type you specified is shown in the document.

By default, date and time fields are updated every time you open a document. You can prevent this by selecting the field and pressing Ctrl+F11 to lock the field; press Ctrl+Shift+F11 to unlock it again. If a field is not locked, you can click it and then click the Update button that appears above it or press the F9 key to update it with the most current information.

Another type of field you might want to insert in a document—for example, in its header or footer—is one that contains a document property, such as the author, title, or last modification date. This type of information is easily inserted by clicking the Quick Parts button, pointing to Document Property, and then clicking the property you want. If you insert the field and then you edit the contents of the field in the document, the change is carried over to the list of properties displayed on the Info page in Backstage view.

SEE ALSO For information about document properties, see "Preparing documents for electronic distribution" in Chapter 6, "Preview, print, and distribute documents."

12

In this exercise, you'll insert a field that displays the current date and time in the footer of a document, and you'll update the field. Then you'll insert a field that displays the Title property, and you'll change the property by changing the field. You'll also add the file name. Finally, you'll convert the current date and time to the date and time when the document was last saved.

SET UP You need the ProceduresFields document located in the Chapter12 practice file folder to complete this exercise. Open the document, display formatting marks, and then follow the steps.

1   On the **Insert** tab, in the **Header & Footer** group, click the **Footer** button, and then click **Edit Footer** to dim the primary content and display the footer area at the bottom of the first page of the document.

2   With the cursor in the blank paragraph of the footer, on the **Design** tool tab, in the **Insert** group, click the **Date & Time** button to open the **Date and Time** dialog box.

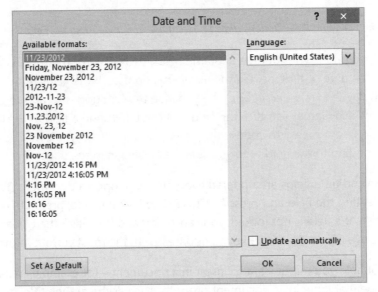

You can specify the date and/or time format you want.

3   In the **Available formats** list, click the first format that includes both the date and the time.

4   Select the **Update automatically** check box, and then click **OK** to insert the current date and time in the selected format in the document footer.

5   Press the **Tab** key. On the **Design** tool tab, in the **Insert** group, click the **Quick Parts** button, click **Document Property**, and then click **Title** to insert a field for the **Title** property of the document.

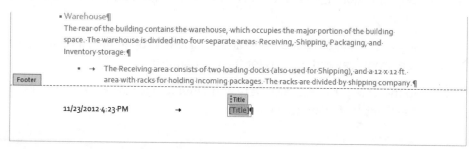

The Title property of this document is currently blank.

6   With the **Title** property active, enter Office Procedures. Then press the **Right Arrow** key to release the selection.

7   Display the **Info** page of the **Backstage** view. Notice that in the **Properties** area, the **Title** property has been set to **Office Procedures**.

Properties ˅

Size	90.9KB
Pages	7
Words	1824
Total Editing Time	91 Minutes
Title	Office Procedures
Tags	Add a tag
Comments	Add comments

The Title property on the Info page reflects the change you made in the document footer.

8   Above the top of the page tabs, click the **Back** arrow to return to the document.

9   With the cursor at the end of the document title in the footer, press the **Tab** key, enter File name: (including the colon), and press the **Spacebar**.

10 On the **Design** tool tab, in the **Insert** group, click the **Quick Parts** button, and then click **Field** to open the **Field** dialog box.

11 In the **Field names** list, click **FileName**. In the **Format** list, click **Lowercase**. Then click **OK** to insert a lowercase version of the file name at the end of the footer.

12 Save the document. Notice that at the left end of the footer, the date and time still reflect the moment when you inserted that field.

12

13   Click the **Date And Time** field, and then click the **Update** button that appears to update the time to reflect the current time.

Let's configure the field to reflect the date and time when the document was last saved.

14   Right-click the field, and then click **Edit Field** to open the **Field** dialog box and display the properties and options for the current field.

15   In the **Categories** list, click **Date and Time** to filter the **Field names** list to display only the fields that relate to dates and times.

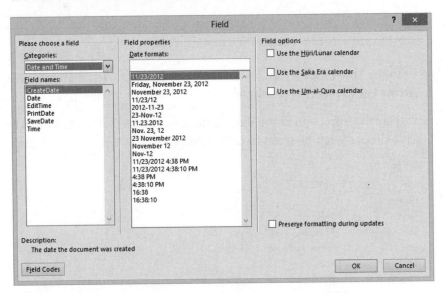

By default, a document contains four date fields and two time fields.

16   In the **Field names** list, click **SaveDate**, and in the **Date formats** list, click the first format that combines the date and time (the same format you selected in step 3).

17   Select the **Preserve formatting during updates** check box, and click **OK**.

18   Save the document. Then right-click the field, and click **Update Field** to update the time to reflect the most recent save.

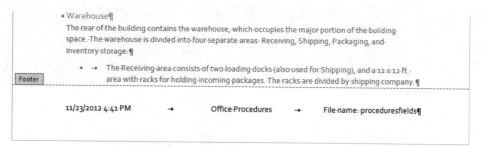

The information in this footer is supplied by three fields.

✖ CLEAN UP Hide formatting marks, then close the ProceduresFields document, saving your changes if you want to.

Key points

- Documents can contain hyperlinks to webpages, files, or email addresses, and cross-references to locations within a document.

- Flagging information with a bookmark makes it easy to look up the information later.

- You can link to documents, presentations, workbooks, and other objects and display the linked content or an icon linked to the content. Updating the links in the document displays the most recent version of the linked object.

- You can save information with a document as a property and insert the properties in fields to display and format the information in a specific way.

12

Chapter at a glance

Footnotes

Insert and modify footnotes and endnotes, page 374

Moving to a New Home

Bamboo plants grow best in a moderately acidic loamy soil. Bamboo is natively a forest plant, and grows best when mulch[1] is kept over the roots and rhizomes. Bamboo can be planted any time of the year in areas with mild climates. A newly planted bamboo requires frequent and liberal watering, twice a week or more often during hot or windy weather.

To control spread of any of the running bamboo varieties, dig a trench[2] that is at least 30 inches wide and 30 inches deep around the area that you want the newly planted bamboo to occupy. Line the trench with a polyethylene bamboo barrier, and fill the lined trench with gravel. Tightly compact the soil next to the barrier to discourage deep rhizome growth.

[1] Grass makes a good mulch, because it's high in nitrogen and silica, as do chipped trees, bark, and straw.
[2] Examine the trench each fall to determine whether any rhizomes have tried to cross it. If so, cut them off.

Contents

Create and modify tables of contents, page 378

Contents

Indexes

Create and modify indexes, page 388

Index

A

administrative businesses, 1

B

businesses, 1
Bylaws, 1, 7

C

carpenter shops, 1
Common Area
  alterations, 4
  landscaping, 3

Bibliographies

Add sources and compile bibliographies, page 394

Bibliography

American Bamboo Society. (2010). Retrieved from www.americanbamboo.org/BooksOnBamboo.html
Miller, L., & Miller, H. (2012). *Bamboo, Family Style*. Lucerne Publishing.
Nelson, J. (2013). *Big Bad Bamboo*. Litware, Inc.

Reference content and content sources

13

IN THIS CHAPTER, YOU WILL LEARN HOW TO

- Insert and modify footnotes and endnotes.

- Create and modify tables of contents.

- Create and modify indexes.

- Add sources and compile bibliographies.

When you want to ensure that information in a complicated document is readily available to readers, you can rely on the following Microsoft Word reference tools to do the job:

- **Footnotes and endnotes** You can provide supporting information without interrupting the flow of the primary content by inserting the information in footnotes at the bottom of the relevant pages or endnotes at the end of the document.

- **Table of contents** You can provide an overview of the information contained in a document and help readers locate topics by compiling a table of contents that includes page numbers or hyperlinks to each heading.

- **Index** You can help readers locate specific information by inserting index entry fields within a document and compiling an index of keywords and concepts that directs the reader to the corresponding page numbers.

- **Information sources and a bibliography** You can appropriately attribute information to its source by inserting citations into a document. Word will then compile a professional bibliography from the citations.

In this chapter, you'll first insert and modify footnotes and endnotes. You'll create and update a table of contents. Then you'll mark index entries in a document and compile an index. Finally, you'll enter source information, insert citations, and compile a bibliography.

PRACTICE FILES To complete the exercises in this chapter, you need the practice files contained in the Chapter13 practice file folder. For more information, see "Download the practice files" in this book's Introduction.

Inserting and modifying footnotes and endnotes

When you want to make a comment about a statement in a document—for example, to explain an assumption or cite the source for a different opinion—you can enter the comment as a footnote or an endnote. Doing so inserts a number or symbol called a *reference mark*, and your associated comment appears with the same number or symbol, either as a footnote at the bottom of the page or as an endnote at the end of the document or document section. In most views, footnotes or endnotes are divided from the main text by a note separator line.

By default, footnote reference marks use the *1, 2, 3* number format, and endnote reference marks use the *i, ii, iii* number format.

To change the number format of footnotes or endnotes:

1   On the **References** tab, click the **Footnotes** dialog box launcher to open the **Footnote and Endnote** dialog box.

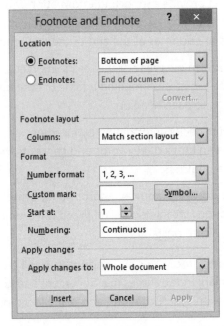

You can change the numbering format before or after you create footnotes or endnotes.

2   In the **Location** area of the **Footnote and Endnote** dialog box, click **Footnotes** or **Endnotes** to indicate the element you want to modify.

3   In the **Format** area, click the **Number format** arrow, and then click the number format you want to use.

4   With **Whole document** shown in the **Apply changes to** box, click **Apply** to change all footnotes or endnotes to the new number format.

In this exercise, you'll move peripheral information from the body of a document into endnotes and then convert the endnotes to footnotes.

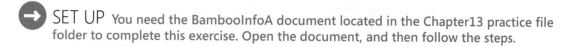 SET UP You need the BambooInfoA document located in the Chapter13 practice file folder to complete this exercise. Open the document, and then follow the steps.

1   In the first paragraph below the heading **Moving to a New Home**, select the entire sentence that begins **Grass makes a good mulch**.

2   On the **Home** tab, in the **Clipboard** group, click the **Cut** button to move the selection from the document to the Microsoft Office Clipboard.

KEYBOARD SHORTCUT Press Ctrl+X to move the selected content to the Clipboard. For more information about keyboard shortcuts, see "Keyboard shortcuts" at the end of this book.

3   In the second sentence of the paragraph, click to insert the cursor immediately after the word **mulch**.

4   On the **References** tab, in the **Footnotes** group, click the **Insert Endnote** button to create a numbered endnote following the text on page **2**.

KEYBOARD SHORTCUT Press Alt+Ctrl+F to insert a footnote or Alt+Ctrl+D to insert an endnote.

5   With the cursor in the endnote area, on the **Home** tab, in the **Clipboard** group, click the **Paste** button to insert the cut sentence as the endnote.

KEYBOARD SHORTCUT Press Ctrl+V to paste the most recently cut or copied content from the Clipboard.

13

Keeping Bugs at Bay

Mites

Bamboo mites, not to be confused with spider mites, cause stippling with yellowish centers throughout the leaf of the plant. With magnification, you can see the webbing and the mites themselves on the underside of the leaves, which is where they prefer to suck the juice from. The main problem with mites is visual. For minor infestations, it's possible to control by spraying with insecticidal soap or an approved miticide.

Mealy Bugs

These can be an occasional problem on clumping varieties of bamboo, and can be controlled by injecting dimethoate directly in the culm. If you prefer not to use this method, you can try submersing the entire plant (assuming it is potted) in water for 12-24 hours; long enough to kill the bugs but not long enough to harm the plant. Because bamboo is native to floodplains, the plants are able to tolerate immersion fairly well.

---

[i] Grass makes a good mulch, because it's high in nitrogen and silica, as do chipped trees, bark, and straw.

Endnotes use a lowercase Roman numeral number format.

6   Scroll up to page **1**. Notice that a corresponding number appears in the document at the location where you had inserted the cursor.

7   In the second paragraph below the heading **Staying Healthy**, select the text beginning with the word **examine** and extending through the period at the end of the paragraph. Cut the selected content to the Clipboard.

8   Below the heading **Moving to a New Home**, in the sentence that begins **To control spread**, click to position the cursor immediately after the word **trench**. On the **References** tab, in the **Footnotes** group, click the **Insert Endnote** button to insert a second endnote.

9   Paste the cut content from the Clipboard into the second footnote, and capitalize the letter **e** at the beginning of the new endnote.

10 Scroll to the bottom of page **1** and position the cursor in the selection area to the left of the paragraph that begins **If you dig a trench**. Click once or twice to select the paragraph, and then press **Delete** to remove the sentence fragment from the document.

11 At the end of page **1**, in the sentence that begins with **Bamboo mites**, select the text beginning with the comma after **mites** and extending through the next comma. Then press **Delete**.

12 In the **Footnotes** group, click the **Insert Endnote** button to insert a third endnote. Enter **Do not confuse bamboo mites with spider mites, which can severely damage plants.**

Because the endnotes are not on the same page as their reference marks, readers must turn the page or scroll to display the related content. Let's position the notes on the same page as their reference marks.

13 On page **2**, drag to select the three endnotes. Right-click the selection, and then click **Convert to Footnote** to change endnotes **i**, **ii**, and **iii** to footnotes **1**, **2**, and **3**.

Moving to a New Home

Bamboo plants grow best in a moderately acidic loamy soil. Bamboo is natively a forest plant, and grows best when mulch[1] is kept over the roots and rhizomes. Bamboo can be planted any time of the year in areas with mild climates. A newly planted bamboo requires frequent and liberal watering, twice a week or more often during hot or windy weather.

To control spread of any of the running bamboo varieties, dig a trench[2] that is at least 30 inches wide and 30 inches deep around the area that you want the newly planted bamboo to occupy. Line the trench with a polyethylene bamboo barrier, and fill the lined trench with gravel. Tightly compact the soil next to the barrier to discourage deep rhizome growth.

Staying Healthy

Do not rake or sweep the bamboo leaves from under the plant, as they provide an effective mulch to keep the soil soft and moist.

Stake tall and slender bamboos.

In the spring, excessive yellowing of the leaves and leaf drop are normal for the growth cycle.

---

[1] Grass makes a good mulch, because it's high in nitrogen and silica, as do chipped trees, bark, and straw.
[2] Examine the trench each fall to determine whether any rhizomes have tried to cross it. If so, cut them off.

The footnotes appear on the same page with their reference marks.

14 Scroll to page **2**. Notice that footnote **3** appears at the bottom of the page instead of at the end of the text where the endnote was located.

❌ CLEAN UP Close the BambooInfoA document, saving your changes if you want to.

13

Creating and modifying tables of contents

When you create a long document that includes headings, such as an annual report or a catalog that has several sections, you might want to add a table of contents to the beginning of the document to give your readers an overview of the document content and help them navigate to specific sections. In a document that will be printed, you can indicate with a page number the page where each heading is located. If the document will be distributed electronically, you can link each entry in the table of contents to the corresponding heading in the document so that readers can jump directly to the heading with a click of the mouse.

By default, Word expects to create a table of contents based on paragraphs within the document that you have formatted with the standard heading styles: Heading 1, Heading 2, and so on. (Word can also create a table of contents based on outline levels or on fields that you have inserted in the document.) When you tell Word to create the table, Word identifies the table of contents entries and inserts the table at the cursor as a single field. You can modify the elements on which Word bases the table at any time, and update the table with a single click to reflect your changes.

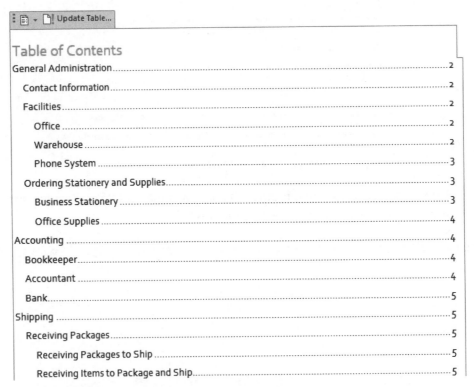

The table of contents is a field that can be updated.

SEE ALSO For information about applying styles, see "Applying styles to text" in Chapter 3, "Modify the structure and appearance of text."

The Table Of Contents controls are available from the References tab. In the Table Of Contents gallery, you can select from three standard table options:

- **Automatic Table 1** This option inserts a table of contents that has the heading *Contents* and includes all text styled as Heading 1, Heading 2, or Heading 3.

- **Automatic Table 2** This option inserts a table of contents that has the heading *Table of Contents* and includes all text styled as Heading 1, Heading 2, or Heading 3.

- **Manual Table** This option inserts a table of contents that has the heading *Table of Contents* and includes placeholders that are not linked to the document content.

The formatting of the entries in a table of contents is controlled by nine levels of built-in TOC styles (TOC 1, TOC 2, and so on). By default, Word uses the styles that are assigned in the template attached to the document. If you want to use a different style, instead of clicking one of the three options in the Table Of Contents gallery, you can click Custom Table Of Contents below the gallery to display the Table Of Contents dialog box, where you can choose from several formats, such as Classic, Fancy, and Simple.

After you create a table of contents, you can format it manually by selecting text and then applying character or paragraph formatting or styles.

If you change a heading in the document or if edits to the text change the page breaks, the easiest way to update the table of contents is to click the Update Table button and have Word do the work for you. You have the option of updating only the page numbers, or if you have changed, added, or deleted headings, you can update (re-create) the entire table.

In this exercise, you'll first insert a simple table of contents for a document based on heading styles, and then create a custom table of contents. You'll alter the document by changing page breaks, and then you'll update the table of contents to reflect your changes.

 SET UP You need the ProceduresContents document located in the Chapter13 practice file folder to complete this exercise. Open the document, and then follow the steps.

1   Click to position the cursor at the left end of the **General Administration** heading. On the **References** tab, in the **Table of Contents** group, click the **Table of Contents** button to display the **Table of Contents** menu.

13

Built-In

Automatic Table 1

Contents
Heading 1 1
  Heading 2 1
    Heading 3 1

Automatic Table 2

Table of Contents
Heading 1 1
  Heading 2 1
    Heading 3 1

Manual Table

Table of Contents
Type chapter title (level 1) 1
  Type chapter title (level 2) 2
    Type chapter title (level 3) 3
Type chapter title (level 1) 4
  Type chapter title (level 2) 5
    Type chapter title (level 3) 6

  📰   <u>M</u>ore Tables of Contents from Office.com   ▶

  📄   <u>C</u>ustom Table of Contents...

  📝   <u>R</u>emove Table of Contents

  📑   <u>S</u>ave Selection to Table of Contents Gallery...

The colors and fonts in the gallery reflect the document theme.

2   In the **Table of Contents** gallery, click **Automatic Table 1**. Then press **Ctrl+Home** to return to the beginning of the document and display the inserted table of contents.

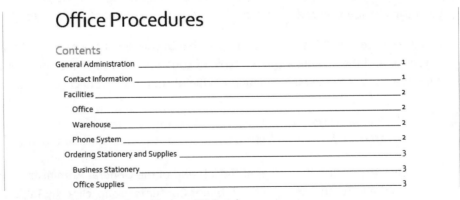

Office Procedures

Contents
General Administration _____ 1
  Contact Information _____ 1
  Facilities _____ 2
    Office _____ 2
    Warehouse_____ 2
    Phone System _____ 2
  Ordering Stationery and Supplies _____ 3
    Business Stationery_____ 3
    Office Supplies _____ 3

Each heading level is assigned its own TOC style.

Now we'll create a custom table of contents.

3 On the **Table of Contents** menu, click **Remove Table of Contents**.

4 Click at the right end of the **Office Procedures** title, and then press **Enter** to start a new paragraph.

5 In the new paragraph, enter Table of Contents. Select the new paragraph, and then on the **Mini Toolbar**, click the **Bold** button.

6 Press the **Right Arrow** key to position the cursor at the left end of the **General Administration** heading. On the **Insert** tab, in the **Pages** group, click the **Page Break** button. Then press the **Up Arrow** key to position the cursor at the left end of the empty page-break paragraph.

   KEYBOARD SHORTCUT Press Ctrl+Enter to insert a page break.

7 On the **References** tab, in the **Table of Contents** group, click the **Table of Contents** button, and then on the menu, below the gallery, click **Custom Table of Contents** to open the **Table of Contents** dialog box.

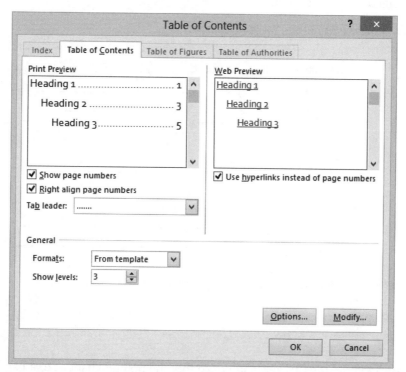

The dialog box displays previews of the table of contents formatting in documents that are prepared for print or online delivery.

13

8   In the **General** area of the **Table of Contents** page, click the **Formats** arrow. Notice that you can choose from **Classic**, **Distinctive**, **Fancy**, **Modern**, **Formal**, and **Simple** formats. In the list, click **Classic**. The samples in the **Print Preview** and **Web Preview** boxes immediately reflect the format change.

> **TIP** The TOC styles reflect the document theme and are based on the Body font of the theme. Each style has specific indent and spacing settings. If you create a table of contents based on the document template, you can customize the TOC styles during the creation process. With Formats set to From Template in the General area of the Table Of Contents dialog box, click Modify. The Style dialog box opens, displaying the nine TOC styles. You can modify the font, paragraph, tabs, border, and other formatting of these styles the same way you would modify any other style. For information about creating styles, see "Creating custom styles and templates" in Chapter 16, "Work in Word more efficiently."

9   In the **Tab leader** list, click the underscore leader option. Then click **OK** to insert the modified table of contents.

10   Point to any entry in the table of contents.

GENERAL ADMINISTRATION	2
Contact Information	2
Facilities _ Current Document	3
Office _ Ctrl+Click to follow link	3
Warehouse	3
Phone System	3
Ordering Stationery and Supplies	4
Business Stationery	4
Office Supplies	4
ACCOUNTING	6
Bookkeeper	6
Accountant	6
Bank	6

Hyperlink navigation functionality is built into the table of contents.

> **SEE ALSO** For more information about linking to other parts of a document, see "Inserting and linking to bookmarks" in Chapter 12, "Link to information and content."

11   Press and hold the **Ctrl** key, and notice that the pointer changes to a hand. Click any entry in the table of contents to move directly to that heading. Then press **Ctrl+Home** to return to the beginning of the document.

12 Display formatting marks, and then scroll to page **2**. Click in the selection area to the left of the page break, and then press the **Delete** key to delete the page break and move the **Facilities** heading to page **2**.

13 Click at the end of **Facilities**, press the **Spacebar**, and then enter Information to make the heading similar to the one that comes before it.

14 Scroll to the next manual page break, on page **3**, and delete it to move the **Ordering Stationery and Supplies** heading to that page.

15 Delete the manual page break on page **5** to move the **Shipping** heading to that page, and then delete the manual page break on page **6** to move the **Processing Orders** heading to that page.

16 Press **Ctrl+Home** to return to the beginning of the document. Click anywhere in the table to select it (do not press the **Ctrl** key).

> **TIP** The table of contents is contained in one large field, and clicking anywhere in it selects the entire field. For information about fields, see "Displaying document information in fields" in Chapter 12, "Link to information and content."

17 On the **References** tab, in the **Table of Contents** group, click the **Update Table** button to open the **Update Table of Contents** dialog box.

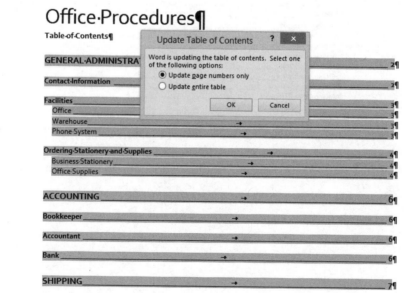

If headings or page breaks change, you can easily update the table of contents.

18   In the dialog box, click the **Update entire table** option, and then click **OK** to update the headings and page numbers displayed in the table of contents.

19   Drag in the selection area to select all the lines of text in the table of contents.

TROUBLESHOOTING You need to drag to select the actual text of the table of contents, not just click to select the field.

20   On the **Home** tab, in the **Paragraph** group, click the **Line and Paragraph Spacing** button, and click **Remove Space Before Paragraph** to remove the extra vertical space in the table of contents. Then press **Ctrl+Home** to release the selection and display the results.

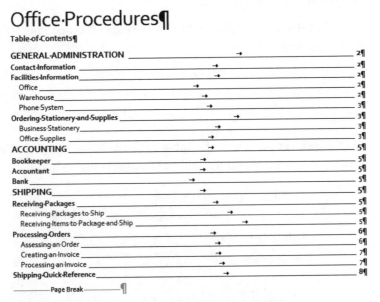

The styles and indentation in the table reflect the heading levels in the document.

❌ CLEAN UP Close the ProceduresContents document, saving your changes if you want to.

Tables of authorities

If a legal document contains items such as regulations, cases, and statutes that are identified as legal citations, you can tell Word to create a table of authorities. In the table, citations are categorized as cases, statutes, rules, treatises, regulations, or other authorities.

Word uses the citations to create this type of table the same way it uses headings to create a table of contents and captions to create a table of figures. You must insert a citation for each legal reference you want to include, and then generate the table.

To create a table of authorities:

1   Select the legal reference that you want to mark with a citation. On the **References** tab, in the **Table of Authorities** group, click the **Mark Citation** button to open the **Mark Citation** dialog box.

    KEYBOARD SHORTCUT Press Alt+Shift+I to open the Mark Citation dialog box.

2   In the **Short citation** box, edit the citation to reflect the way you want it to appear in the table.

3   The default category is **Cases**. If you want to change the category, display the **Category** list, and click the category that applies to the citation.

4   To mark one citation, click **Mark**. To mark all citations that match the selected citation, click **Mark All**. Word inserts hidden field codes in the document that identify the citation.

5   Repeat steps 1 through 4 for each legal reference you want to mark.

    TIP You can leave the Mark Citation dialog box open to facilitate the marking of citations.

    After you insert all the citations, create the table of authorities.

6   Position the cursor where you want to insert the table of authorities, and then on the **References** tab, in the **Table of Authorities** group, click the **Insert Table of Authorities** button to open the **Table of Authorities** dialog box.

7   In the **Category** list, click the category of citations that you want to appear in the table, or click **All** to include all categories.

8   Select formatting options for the table, and then click **OK** to insert the table of authorities.

13

Tables of figures

If a document includes figures or tables, you can easily create a table of figures so that readers can locate and quickly navigate to them.

Table of Figures

A table of figures generated for this chapter.

A table of figures is built from the tools in the Captions group on the References tab of the ribbon. You must insert a caption for each figure or table you want to include, and then generate the table.

To create a table of figures:

1   Select the first figure or table you want to caption. On the **References** tab, in the **Captions** group, click the **Insert Caption** button to open the **Caption** dialog box.

    TIP The number *1* in the Caption box is a field that reflects the graphic's position in the figure sequence. This number is automatically updated when you add or delete captions.

You can accept or modify the default caption.

2 If you want to change the label shown in the **Caption** box (the default is *Figure*), in the **Label** list, click **Table** or **Equation**; or click **New Label**, enter the label you want, and then click **OK**.

3 In the **Caption** box, click to the right of the label and number, press the **Spacebar**, enter the caption, and then click **OK** to add the caption to the document. Alternatively, you can add only the label as the caption, and then edit the caption in the Word document.

4 Repeat steps 1 through 3 for each figure or table you want to include in the table of figures.

   After you insert all the captions, create the table of figures.

5 Position the cursor where you want to insert the table of figures, and then on the **References** tab, in the **Captions** group, click **Insert Table of Figures** to open the **Table of Figures** dialog box, which looks similar to the **Table of Contents** dialog box.

6 If you want to display a different label in the table of figures than in the actual caption, or not display the label at all, make your selection in the **Caption Label** list.

7 If you want to create the table of figures using a format other than the default for the template, click the format you want in the **Formats** list.

8 Select any additional options you want, and then click **OK** to insert the table of figures.

Creating and modifying indexes

To help readers find specific concepts and terms that they might not be able to readily locate by looking at a table of contents, you can include an index at the end of a document. Word creates an index by compiling an alphabetical listing with page numbers based on index entry fields that you mark in the document. As with a table of contents, an index is inserted as a single field.

TIP You don't need to create indexes for documents that will be distributed electronically, because readers can use the Navigation pane to findthe information they need. For more information, see "Finding and replacing text" in Chapter 2, "Enter, edit, and proofread text."

In the index, an entry might apply to a word or phrase that appears on one page or is discussed on several pages. The entry might have related subentries. For example, in the index to this book, the main index entry *text effects* might have below it the subentries *applying* and *live preview of*. An index might also include cross-reference entries that direct readers to related entries. For example, the main index entry *text wrapping breaks* might be cross-referenced to *line breaks*. You can use cross references to direct readers to index terms they might not think of when looking for specific information.

To insert an index entry field into the document, you select the text you want to mark, and click the Mark Entry button in the Index group on the References tab. In the Mark Index Entry dialog box that opens, you can do the following:

- Use the selected text as is, modify the entry, or add a subentry.

- Format the entry—for example, to make it appear bold or italic in the index—by right-clicking it, clicking **Font**, and then clicking the options you want; or by using keyboard shortcuts.

- Designate the entry as a cross-reference, one-page entry, or page-range entry.

- Specify the formatting of this entry's page number.

KEYBOARD SHORTCUT Press Alt+Shift+X to open the Mark Index Entry dialog box.

After you set the options in the dialog box the way you want them, you can insert an index entry field adjacent to the selected text by clicking Mark, or adjacent to every occurrence of the selected text in the document by clicking Mark All. The Mark Index Entry dialog box remains open to simplify the process of inserting multiple index entry fields, so you don't have to click the Mark Entry button for each new entry. You can move the dialog box off to the side so that it doesn't block the text you're working with.

TIP When building an index, you should choose the text you mark carefully, bearing in mind the terms that readers are likely to look up. For example, one reader might expect to find information about cell phones by looking under *cell*, whereas another might look under *mobile*, another under *phones*, and another under *telephones*. A good index will include all four entries.

Index entry fields are formatted as hidden; they are not visible unless you display formatting marks and hidden characters. When the index entry field is visible, it appears in the document enclosed in quotation marks within a set of braces, with the designator *XE* and a dotted underline.

To create an index based on the index entries in a document, you position the cursor where you want the index to appear and then click the Insert Index button in the Index group on the References tab. The Index dialog box opens, and you can then specify the following:

- Whether the index formatting should use styles from the current template or be based on one of four predefined formats that you can preview in the **Print Preview** box.

- Whether page numbers should be right-aligned, and if so, whether they should have dotted, dashed, or solid tab leaders.

- Whether the index should be indented, with each subentry on a separate line below its main entry, or run-in, with subentries on the same line as the main entries.

- The number of columns you want.

When you click OK in the Index dialog box, Word calculates the page numbers of all the entries and subentries, consolidates them, and inserts the index as one field in the specified format at the specified location in the document.

TIP If you make changes to a document that affect index entries or page numbering, you can update the index by clicking it and then clicking the Update Index button in the Index group on the References tab. You can also right-click the index and then click Update Field.

You can edit the text of the index generated from the entries, but the changes you make are not permanent; regenerating the index restores the original entries. It is more efficient to edit the text within the quotation marks in the index entry fields. To delete an index entry, you select the entire hidden field and then press the Delete key. You can move and copy index entries by using the techniques you would use for regular text.

13

TIP Dragging through any part of an index entry field that includes one of the enclosing braces selects the entire field.

In this exercise, you'll first mark a few index entries and a cross-reference entry. Then you'll create and format an index, delete an index entry from the document, and update the index.

 SET UP You need the RulesIndex document located in the Chapter13 practice file folder to complete this exercise. Open the document, display hidden text, and then follow the steps.

1   In the first bulleted list item, select the word **Declaration**. Then on the **References** tab, in the **Index** group, click the **Mark Entry** button to open the **Mark Index Entry** dialog box. Notice that the selected word has already been entered in the **Main entry** box.

2   Drag the dialog box by its title bar to the upper-right corner of the screen. Then, in the dialog box, click **Mark All** to insert index entry fields adjacent to every occurrence of the word *Declaration* in the document.

     TIP If this document contained instances of the word *declaration* starting with a lower-case *d*, those would not be marked with index entries, because their capitalization does not match the selected word.

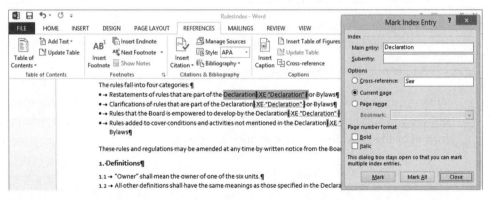

You can edit, format, add a subentry to, and otherwise adjust the index entry in this dialog box.

3   In the first bulleted list item, select the word **Bylaws**. Click the title bar of the **Mark Index Entry** dialog box to activate the dialog box and enter the selected text in the **Main entry** box. Then click **Mark All**.

4   In section **2.1**, select the word **professional**. Click the dialog box title bar to activate the dialog box and enter the selected text in the **Main entry** box. In the **Main entry** box, click at the right end of **professional**, press the **Spacebar**, enter businesses, and then click **Mark**.

5   In section **2.1**, select and mark **administrative businesses**. Without leaving the dialog box, delete the word **administrative** from the **Main entry** box, and then click **Mark** to add a third index entry to the paragraph.

6   In section **2.4**, select the words **hobby shop**. Click the dialog box title bar, and in the **Main entry** box, add an **s** to **shop** to make it **shops**. Then click **Mark**. Repeat this step to mark **carpenter shop** (as **carpenter shops**) and add a third index entry in the paragraph for **shops**.

> **TIP** Index entries will appear in the index exactly as they appear in the Mark Index Entry dialog box. For consistency, make all nouns lowercase and plural except proper nouns and those of which only one exists.

7   In section **4.3**, select the word **garage**, change the entry in the **Mark Index Entry** dialog box to garages, and click **Mark All**. Without leaving the dialog box, in the **Options** area, select the **Cross-reference** option. Notice that the cursor moves to the space after the word **See** in the adjacent box.

8   Without moving the cursor, enter also parking. Select the word **also**, press **Ctrl+I** to make it italic, and then click **Mark** to insert a cross-reference to the **parking** index entry adjacent to the word **garage**.

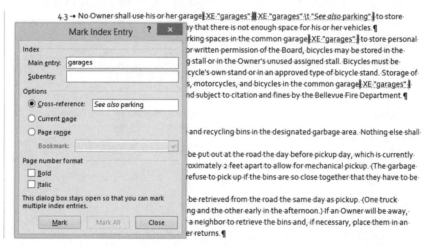

The cross-references in the document reflect your entries in the Mark Index Entry dialog box.

9   In section **7.2**, select the words **Common Area**, and click the dialog box title bar. Enter landscaping in the **Subentry** box, and click **Mark** to insert an index entry with the entry and subentry separated by a colon.

13

10   In section **8.2**, mark the words **Common Area** with a subentry of alterations. Then close the **Mark Index Entry** dialog box.

Now we'll generate the index from the index entries.

11   Press **Ctrl+End** to move to the end of the document, press **Enter** to create a new paragraph, and then press **Ctrl+Enter** to insert a page break and move the cursor to the top of the new page.

12   In the new paragraph, enter Index, and press **Enter**.

13   Select the **Index** paragraph. On the **Mini Toolbar**, click the **Styles** button and then click the **Heading 1** thumbnail.

14   Press the **Right Arrow** key to move to the empty paragraph.

15   On the **Home** tab, in the **Paragraph** group, click the **Show/Hide ¶** button to hide formatting marks, fields, and content that is formatted as hidden.

> **IMPORTANT** When hidden content is visible, the document might not be paginated correctly. Always turn off the display of formatting marks and hidden characters before creating an index.

16   On the **References** tab, in the **Index** group, click the **Insert Index** button to open the **Index** dialog box.

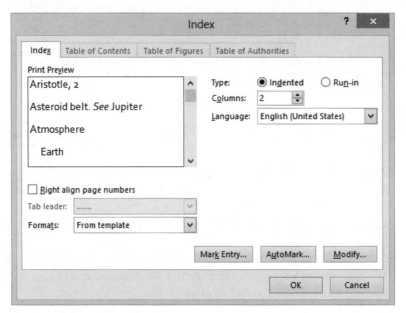

You can configure the settings in this dialog box to tailor the look of the index.

17   Change the **Columns** setting to **1**. In the **Formats** list, click **Fancy**. Then click **OK** to compile a short index based on the index entries you just marked.

Index

A

administrative businesses, 1

B

businesses, 1
Bylaws, 1, 7

C

carpenter shops, 1
Common Area
   alterations, 4
   landscaping, 3

D

Declaration, 1, 7

G

garages, 2, 3, 4, 5, *See also* parking

This index is formatted in one column with the page numbers adjacent to their index entries.

TIP You can experiment with the available index options by clicking Insert Index, selecting other column and formatting options, clicking OK, and then clicking Yes when Word asks whether you'd like to replace the index.

18   Display formatting marks and hidden characters so that you can see the index entry fields in the document, and then scroll up to section **4.3**.

Let's delete the cross-reference entry from this section, because we don't have an index entry for *parking*.

19   Select the entire cross-reference entry following **garage**, and press the **Delete** key.

TROUBLESHOOTING If you find it hard to select only this entry, try pointing to the right of the closing brace (}) and dragging slightly to the left.

20   Press **Ctrl+End** to move to the end of the document, and then click anywhere in the index to select its field.

21   Hide formatting marks and hidden characters. Then on the **References** tab, in the **Index** group, click the **Update Index** button to remove the deleted cross-reference.

✖ CLEAN UP Close the RulesIndex document, saving your changes if you want to.

13

Adding sources and compiling bibliographies

Many types of documents that you create might require a bibliography that lists the sources of the information that appears or is referenced in the document. You can use the Source Manager to help you keep track of sources you use while researching a document, and to ensure that you reference them in the proper format. Whether your sources are books, periodicals, websites, or interviews, you can record details about them and then select a common style guide, such as the *Chicago Manual of Style*, to have Word automatically list your sources in that style guide's standard format.

There are two ways to cite sources:

- You can enter all the sources into the **Source Manager** and then insert citations from the **Source Manager** into the document.
- You can create sources as you need to insert citations.

No matter which method you use to enter the source information, Word stores the sources in a separate file on your computer's hard disk so that you can cite them in any document you create. You can view this Master List and select which sources will be available to the current document from the Source Manager dialog box.

After you enter citations in a document, you can easily compile their sources into one of two types of lists by clicking the Bibliography button in the Citations & Bibliography group on the References tab, and then clicking Bibliography, References, or Works Cited on the Bibliography menu to insert the source list with that heading. Alternatively, you can click Insert Bibliography at the bottom of the menu to insert the source list without a heading. The type of bibliography you use is usually specified by the organization or person for whom you are preparing the document, such as your company, your instructor, or the publication in which you intend to publish the document.

When you compile a bibliography, Word inserts it at the cursor as one field. You can edit the text of a bibliography, but if the source information changes, it is more efficient to edit the source in the Source Manager and then update the bibliography the same way you would update a table of contents or index.

TIP You can update a bibliography by clicking the bibliography and then clicking the Update Citations And Bibliography button that appears above the field. If you used the Insert Bibliography command to compile the source list, the Update Citations And Bibliography button does not appear when you click the field. In that case, you can update the bibliography by right-clicking anywhere in the field and then clicking Update Field.

In this exercise, you'll enter information for a couple of sources, insert citations for existing sources, add a new source, compile a bibliography, and then change the bibliography format.

➡ SET UP You need the BambooInfoB and BambooBibliography documents located in the Chapter13 practice file folder to complete this exercise. Open the BambooInfoB document, and then follow the steps.

1 On the **References** tab, in the **Citations & Bibliography** group, click the **Style** arrow, and then click **Chicago** to specify that any sources you create and citations you insert will be formatted according to the *Chicago Manual of Style* rules.

2 In the **Citations & Bibliography** group, click the **Manage Sources** button to open the **Source Manager** dialog box.

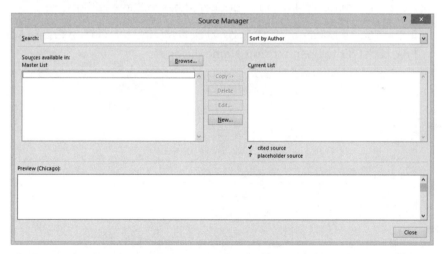

The Source Manager accumulates sources from all documents, so if other documents already contain citations, their source information might appear here.

3 In the **Source Manager** dialog box, click **New** to open the **Create Source** dialog box. Notice that **Book** is selected in the **Type of Source** list.

Now let's create a source for a book. (This isn't a real book; we're making it up.)

4   In the **Bibliography Fields for Chicago** area, enter Nelson, Jeremy in the **Author** box, Big Bad Bamboo in the **Title** box, 2013 in the **Year** box, and Litware, Inc. in the **Publisher** box.

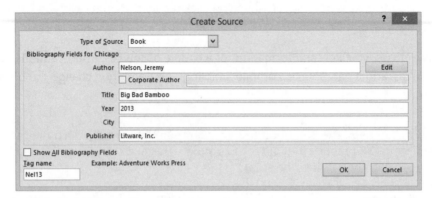

Word creates a tag name based on the author's last name and the book's year of publication.

5   Click **OK** to add the book to the **Source Manager**. Notice that it appears in the **Master List** and in the **Current List**, which is the list of sources that can be used in this document.

Next, let's create a source for a book that has multiple authors.

6   In the **Source Manager** dialog box, click **New**, and then in the **Create Source** dialog box, click **Edit** to open the **Edit Name** dialog box.

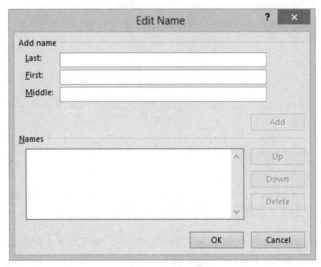

If a source has more than one author, create a multiple-name entity from this dialog box.

7   In the **Add name** area, enter Miller in the **Last** box, enter Lisa in the **First** box, and then click **Add** to enter **Miller, Lisa** in the **Names** box.

8   To specify a co-author, enter Miller in the **Last** box, enter Harry in the **First** box, click **Add**, and then click **OK**.

9   In the **Create Source** dialog box, enter Bamboo, Family Style in the **Title** box, 2012 in the **Year** box, and Lucerne Publishing in the **Publisher** box. Then click **OK** to add the new source to the **Master List** and the **Current List**.

10 In the **Source Manager** dialog box, click **Close**.

11 Open the **BambooBibliography** document, and on the **References** tab, in the **Citations & Bibliography** group, click **Manage Sources** to open the **Source Manager** dialog box. Notice that the two sources you created in the **BambooInfoB** document appear in the **Master List** but not in the **Current List**, meaning that they are not available for use in this document.

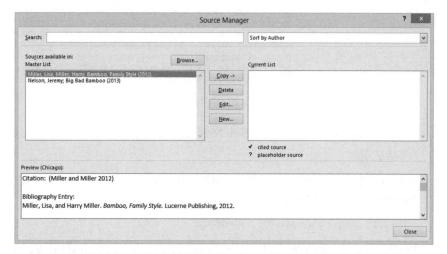

You can select the sources in the Master List that you want to be available for a particular document.

12 With the **Miller** source selected in the **Master List** box, click **Copy** to copy that source to the **Current List** box so that it is available in this document. Then copy the **Nelson** source to the **Current List** box, and click **Close**.

13 In the last line of the first paragraph after the heading, click to position the cursor immediately to the right of **Big Bad Bamboo**. In the **Citations & Bibliography** group, click the **Insert Citation** button to display the list of available sources.

13

Only the sources from the Current List appear on the Insert Citation menu.

14   On the **Insert Citation** menu, click **Nelson, Jeremy** to insert the source in the document.

15   Repeat steps 13 and 14 to insert a **Miller and Miller** source reference after the **Bamboo, Family Style** book title.

      Now let's create a source for a webpage.

16   In the same paragraph, click immediately to the right of **Entire books**. In the **Citations & Bibliography** group, click the **Insert Citation** button, and then in the list, click **Add New Source** to open the familiar **Create Source** dialog box.

17   In the **Type of Source** list, click **Web site**.

18   In the **Name of Web Page** box, enter American Bamboo Society. In the **Year** box, enter 2010. In the **URL** box, enter www.americanbamboo.org/BooksOnBamboo.html. Then click **OK** to insert the source in parentheses at the insertion point.

BEAUTIFUL BAMBOO

Bamboo has long been woven into the cultures of many countries, where it has historically been used for everything from food and fodder to musical instruments and construction material. For centuries, millions of people have depended on this plant, which is known as "friend of the people" in China, and "wood of the poor" in India. But the demand for bamboo has been increasing in other parts of the world as well, especially as it relates to furniture, accent pieces, and flooring. More and more, people are seeing the value and beauty of using bamboo in their homes to achieve modern-day fashion with an ethnic flavor. Entire books (American Bamboo Society 2010) have been written on the subject, including *Big Bad Bamboo* (Nelson 2013) and *Bamboo, Family Style* (Miller and Miller 2012).

Information stored in the Source Manager is used to create the citations in the specified format (in this case, the Chicago Manual of Style, Fifteenth Edition format).

19 In the **Citations & Bibliography** group, click the **Manage Sources** button. In the **Source Manager** dialog box, the new source appears in both the **Master List** and the **Current List**.

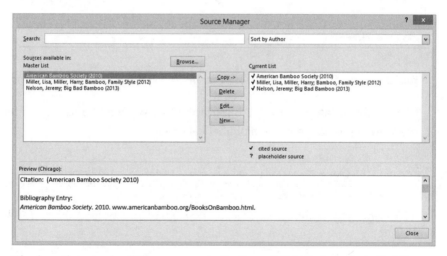

Check marks precede all three sources in the Current List box to indicate that the sources have been cited in the current document.

20 Close the **Source Manager** dialog box, and then press **Ctrl+End** to move to the end of the document.

13

21 In the **Citations & Bibliography** group, click **Bibliography** to display the **Bibliography** menu.

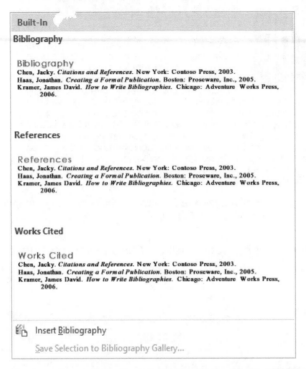

You can choose from three built-in styles or insert a bibliography with no heading.

22 In the **Built-In** category, click **Bibliography** to insert a bibliography containing all the citations in the document in alphabetical order.

Bibliography

American Bamboo Society. 2010. www.americanbamboo.org/BooksOnBamboo.html.
Miller, Lisa, and Harry Miller. *Bamboo, Family Style.* Lucerne Publishing, 2012.
Nelson, Jeremy. *Big Bad Bamboo.* Litware, Inc., 2013.

A bibliography formatted to meet the specifications of the Chicago Manual of Style Fifteenth Edition.

23 In the **Citations & Bibliography** group, display the **Style** list, and click **APA** to reformat the bibliography and citations to meet the style specifications of the *Publication Manual of the American Psychological Association, Sixth Edition.*

Bibliography

American Bamboo Society. (2010). Retrieved from
       www.americanbamboo.org/BooksOnBamboo.html
Miller, L., & Miller, H. (2012). *Bamboo, Family Style.* Lucerne Publishing.
Nelson, J. (2013). *Big Bad Bamboo.* Litware, Inc.

It's easy to reformat sources and citations to meet different style specifications.

TIP You don't have to select the bibliography to apply this change; you can do it from anywhere in the document.

❌ CLEAN UP Close the BambooInfoB and BambooBibliography documents, saving your changes if you want to.

Key points

- You can move peripheral information from the body of a document to footnotes at the bottom of each page or endnotes at the end of the document.

- A table of contents provides an overview of the topics covered in a document and lets readers navigate quickly to a topic.

- After marking index entries for key concepts, words, and phrases, you can use the Insert Index command to tell Word to compile an index.

- Word can keep track of sources and compile a bibliography of cited sources based on the style of your choosing.

13

Chapter at a glance

Prepare

**Prepare main documents,
page 411**

«AddressBlock»¶

¶

«GreetingLine»¶

I·want·to·take·a·moment·to·thank·you·for·your·continued·support·of·Wide·World·Importers.·Becaus
loyal·customers·like·you·come·back·year·after·year,·we·are·still·growing·steadily·and·the·future·look
brighter·than·ever.¶

As·you·know,·we·will·celebrate·our·10ᵗʰ·anniversary·in·March.·In·honor·of·that·occasion,·we·are·hold
a·special·*Mad·March*·sale!·Everything·in·the·store·will·be·20%·off·throughout·the·month,·and·select
specials·will·be·offered·each·day.·Please·pick·up·one·of·our·promotional·flyers·th
next·time·you·visit·the·store·for·a·complete·schedule·of·these·special·offerings.¶

«FirstName»,·for·even·greater·savings,·be·sure·to·bring·this·letter·with·you·when·you·shop.·Identify
yourself·as·a·VIP·Customer·by·presenting·the·letter·to·your·salesperson·at·the·time·of·your·purchas
and·you·will·receive·an·additional·5%·off·your·total·bill.¶

Merge

**Merge main documents and data sources,
page 415**

Dan Wilson
1234 Editorial Way
Harvest, WA 10004

Dear Dan,

I want to take a moment to thank you for your continued support of Wide World Importers. Becaus
loyal customers like you come back year after year, we are still growing steadily and the future look
brighter than ever.

As you know, we will celebrate our 10ᵗʰ anniversary in March. In honor of that occasion, we are hol
a special *Mad March* sale! Everything in the store will be 20% off throughout the month, and select
specials at higher discounts will be offered each day. Please pick up one of our promotional flyers th
next time you visit the store for a complete schedule of these special offerings.

Dan, for even greater savings, be sure to bring this letter with you when you shop. Identify yourself
VIP Customer by presenting the letter to your salesperson at the time of your purchase, and you wi
receive an additional 5% off your total bill.

Send

**Send personalized email messages to
multiple recipients, page 419**

🔄 Reply 🔄 Reply All 🔄 Forward

Sat 11/24/2012 10:25 AM
Joan Lambert
Welcome to Wide World Importers!

To   'ben@wingtiptoys.com'

Hello, Ben:

Thank you for your recent visit to our store. It
was a pleasure to be able to answer your
decorating questions and offer suggestions. As
you requested, we have added your name to our
online mailing list. You will be receiving our
monthly newsletter, as well as advance notice of
upcoming shipments and in-store events.

You can also visit our website at
www.wideworldimporters.com for a schedule of
events, links to online decorating resources,

Create

**Create and print labels,
page 423**

Isabel·Martins¶   Garth·Fort¶
7899·38th·St.¶   5678·Ford·Ave.¶
Tucker,·NJ·90025¶   Planter,·WA·10002¶
¤   ¤

Carol·Troup¶   Toby·Nixon¶
456·South·Rd.¶   987·Hard·Rock·Way¶
Harvest,·WA·10004¶   Potential,·DE·97540¶
¤   ¤

¶   ¶
¤   ¤

Work with mail merge

IN THIS CHAPTER, YOU WILL LEARN HOW TO

- Prepare data sources.

- Prepare main documents.

- Merge main documents and data sources.

- Send personalized email messages to multiple recipients.

- Create and print labels.

Many organizations communicate with their customers or members by means of letters, newsletters, and promotional pieces that are sent to everyone on a mailing list. The easiest way to generate a set of documents that are identical except for certain information—such as the name, address, and greeting of a letter—is to use a process called mail merge. If you have a list of potential recipients stored in a consistent format, you can use the mail merge process to easily produce a set of documents, email messages, or mailing labels.

The mail merge process combines static information stored in one document with variable information stored in another document, as follows:

- **Main document** This document contains the static text that will appear in all the merged documents. It also contains placeholders—called merge fields—that display the variable information.

- **Data source** This is a structured document, such as a Microsoft Word table, Excel worksheet, Access database table, or Outlook contact list, that contains sets of information—called records—in a predictable format. You can use an existing data source, or you can create a new one as part of the mail merge process.

You can use the Mail Merge wizard to merge a main document with a data source in easy steps. The first step is to select the document type, which can be a letter, an email message, envelopes, labels, or a directory. The type you select determines the subsequent steps. When you have some experience with mail merge, you can manually merge documents, to create a personalized item for each record in the data source.

You can merge the main document and data source into a new document, with each merged document separated from the next by a page break. You can then personalize the merged documents before printing them, and you can save the document for later use. If you don't need to edit or save the merged documents, you can merge the main document and data source directly to the printer or to an email message.

In this chapter, you'll use the Mail Merge wizard in Word 2013 to guide you through the process of creating a form letter. You'll select a data source, add a record to it, sort it, and filter it. You'll then add merge fields for an address and greeting line to an existing form letter, preview the merged data, exclude recipients from the merge, merge the letters into a new document, and save the merged file. You'll also set up and send a merged email message. Finally, you'll create and print mailing labels.

PRACTICE FILES To complete the exercises in this chapter, you need the practice files contained in the Chapter14 practice file folder. For more information, see "Download the practice files" in this book's Introduction.

Preparing data sources

The first step in the mail merge process is to either specify an existing data source or create one. The data source consists of a matrix of rows and columns. Each row contains one record, such as the complete name and address of a customer, and each column contains a particular type of information—called a field—such as the first name of all the customers. In the first row of the data source, each field is identified by its column heading—called a field name.

	A	B	C	D	E	F
1	FirstName ▼	LastName ▼	Address1 ▼	City ▼	State ▼	PostalCode ▼
2	Isabel	Martins	7899 38th St.	Tucker	NJ	90025
3	Garth	Fort	5678 Ford Ave.	Planter	WA	10002
4	Dan	Wilson	1234 Editorial Way	Harvest	WA	10004
5	Carol	Troup	456 South Rd.	Harvest	WA	10004
6	Toby	Nixon	987 Hard Rock Way	Potential	DE	97540

The data source stores information in a structured way.

TIP Because the field names are also used as the merge fields in the main document, they cannot contain spaces. To make the field names readable with no spaces, capitalize each word, as in PostalCode, or replace the spaces with underscores, as in Last_Name.

If the data source contains many records and it changes frequently, you might want to create it in a program designed for working with large amounts of data, such as Excel or Access. You can also use the contacts list from Outlook. If the data source contains only a few records and it won't be updated often, you can create it in Word, either as a table or as a list with each field separated by a tab. Or you can create it as part of the mail merge process.

What if you want to create merge documents for only a subset of the data in the data source? For example, you might have mail-order customers from all over the United States but want to send an announcement about a store sale only to customers with addresses in your state. After you specify the data source, you can do the following:

- Filter the data source to create merged documents for only some of its data.

- Create a query (a set of selection criteria) to extract only the information you're interested in—for example, all the postal codes for your state.

- Sort the data source—for example, in postal code order for a bulk mailing.

When you use a filter or a query, all the data remains in the data source, but only the data that meets your specifications is used for the mail merge.

In this exercise, you'll open a document that you want to send to multiple people (the main document) and use the Mail Merge wizard to select the list of recipients (the data source). After you add information for a new recipient (a record) to the data source, you'll sort and filter it.

IMPORTANT We will work through the mail merge process in the exercises in this topic and in the two following topics. You must complete the exercises in sequence. Be sure to read the Set Up paragraphs of each exercise closely to ensure that you can successfully complete the exercises.

SET UP You need the AnniversaryLetter document and CustomerList workbook located in the Chapter14 practice file folder to complete this exercise. Open the AnniversaryLetter document, and then follow the steps.

1   On the **Mailings** tab, in the **Start Mail Merge** group, click the **Start Mail Merge** button, and then click **Step-by-Step Mail Merge Wizard** to open the **Mail Merge** pane.

14

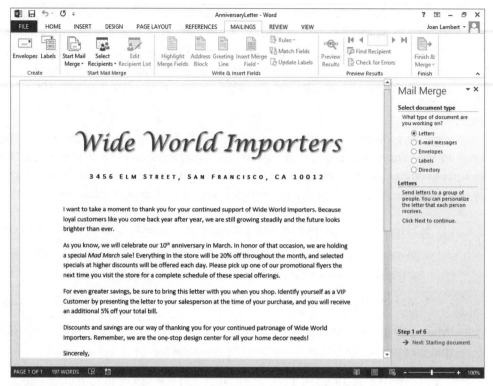

You can create a mail merge letter from a source document in six steps.

2   With **Letters** selected as the document type, at the bottom of the **Mail Merge** pane, click **Next: Starting document**.

Step 2 of the wizard requires you to select a starting document. We will use the currently active document.

3   With **Use the current document** selected in the **Step 2** pane, click **Next: Select recipients**.

Step 3 of the wizard requires you to select a data source. We will use the CustomerList workbook.

4   With **Use an existing list** selected in the **Step 3** pane, click **Browse** to open the **Select Data Source** dialog box.

5   Navigate to the **Chapter14** practice file folder, and double-click the **CustomerList** workbook to open the **Select Table** dialog box. Notice that the workbook contains only one table.

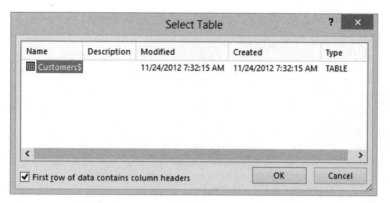

If a workbook contains multiple tables, you must select the one that contains the mail merge data.

6   With **Customers$** selected in the **Select Table** dialog box, click **OK** to open the **Mail Merge Recipients** dialog box.

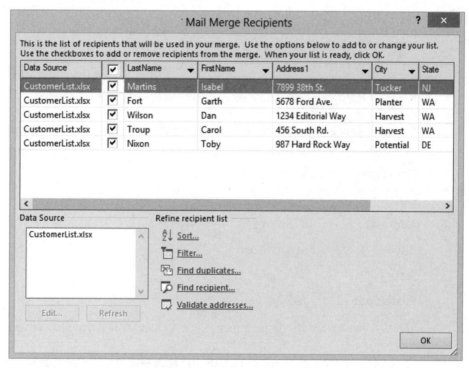

The dialog box displays all the records contained in the data source.

Now we'll modify the data source.

7   In the **Data Source** box, click **CustomerList.xlsx**, and then click **Edit** to open the **Edit Data Source** dialog box.

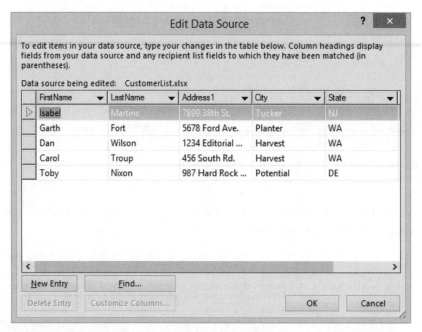

You can modify the source data before performing the mail merge operation.

8   Click the **New Entry** button, and then enter the following information, pressing **Tab** to move from field to field:

FirstName	Max
LastName	Stevens
Address1	678 Pine St.
City	Agriculture
State	WA
PostalCode	10003

TIP You can add multiple records by clicking New Entry after you enter each record.

9   Click **OK**, and then click **Yes** to update the recipient list. Notice that the new record appears below the original records in the **Mail Merge Recipients** dialog box.

Now we'll modify the order in which the mail merge process accesses the data source records.

10 In the **Refine recipient list** area, click **Sort** to display the **Sort Records** page of the **Filter and Sort** dialog box.

11 Click the **Sort by** arrow to display the sort criteria, which are the same as the field names in the selected data source.

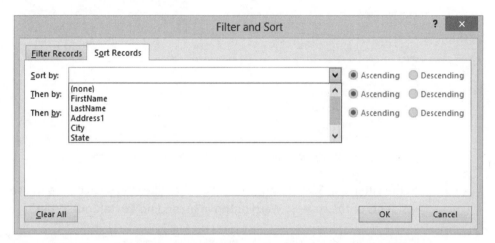

You can sort the records by up to three fields, each in ascending or descending order.

12 Scroll to the bottom of the **Sort by** list, and click **PostalCode**. Then with **Ascending** selected, click **OK** to return to the **Mail Merge Recipients** dialog box, which now displays the recipients in order by postal code.

TIP You can also sort data in the Mail Merge Recipients dialog box by clicking the arrow to the right of the field you want to sort on and then clicking Sort Ascending or Sort Descending.

13 Scroll to the right end of the recipients list, and verify that the records are sorted in ascending order by the **PostalCode** field. Then in the **Refine recipient list** area, click **Filter** to display the **Filter Records** page of the **Filter and Sort** dialog box.

TIP You can also open the Filter And Sort dialog box by clicking the arrow to the right of any field name and then clicking Advanced.

14

14　In the **Field** list, click **State** to display the default **Equal To** criterion in the **Comparison** box. In the **Compare to** box, enter WA (the postal abbreviation for *Washington*).

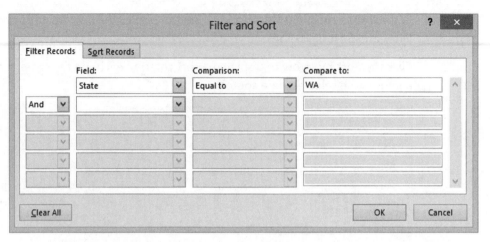

You can choose to merge only records that match specific criteria.

15　In the **Filter and Sort** dialog box, click **OK** to filter the source data to use only residents of the state of Washington in ascending **PostalCode** order.

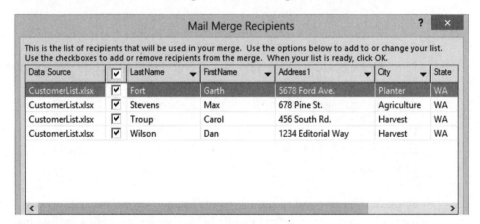

The records for customers who do not live in Washington are hidden and will be excluded from the merge process.

16　Click **OK** to close the **Mail Merge Recipients** dialog box and complete step 3 of the **Mail Merge** wizard.

✖ CLEAN UP Save the AnniversaryLetter document as MyLetter, and leave it open for the next exercise.

Preparing main documents

One type of main document commonly used in the mail merge process is a form letter. This type of document typically contains merge fields for the name and address of each recipient along with text that is the same in all the letters. In the form letter, each merge field is enclosed in « and » characters, which are called chevrons—for example, «AddressBlock».

If you have already written the letter, you can insert the merge fields during the merge process; if you haven't written the letter, you can write it as part of the process. Either way, you first enter the text that will be common to all the letters and then insert the merge fields that will be replaced by the variable information from the data source.

> **TIP** If you need to stop before you finish the merge process, you can save the form letter to retain the work you have done so far. You can then open the form letter and resume from where you left off. Because you have specified a data source for the form letter, you will be asked to confirm that you want to reattach the same data source.

14

You can insert merge fields in two ways:

- From the **Mail Merge** pane in step 4 of the **Mail Merge** wizard
- By clicking buttons in the **Write & Insert Fields** group on the **Mailings** tab

Either way, clicking Address Block or Greeting Line opens a dialog box in which you can refine the fields' settings, whereas clicking individual fields inserts them with their default settings.

«FirstName», for even greater savings, be sure to bring this letter with you when you shop. Identify yourself as a VIP Customer by presenting the letter to your salesperson at the time of your purchase, and you will receive an additional 5% off your total bill.

You can insert a merge field anywhere in the main document.

TIP To save the form letter without any mail merge information, click Start Mail Merge in the Start Mail Merge group on the Mailings tab, and then click Normal Word Document.

In this exercise, you'll modify an existing form letter by adding merge fields for a standard address, an informal greeting line, and the recipient's first name.

SET UP This exercise uses the MyLetter document to which you attached the CustomerList table as the data source in the previous exercise. With the document open, follow the steps.

TROUBLESHOOTING If you didn't complete the previous exercise, you should do so now. If you closed the document at the end of the previous exercise, open it and click Yes when Word asks whether you want to attach the data source to the document. Then click the Start Mail Merge button in the Start Mail Merge group on the Mailings tab, and click Step-by-Step Mail Merge Wizard to display the Step 3 pane.

1 At the bottom of the **Mail Merge** pane, click **Next: Write your letter**.

2 In the document, display hidden formatting marks and notice the empty paragraphs above the body of the letter.

3 Position the cursor in the first empty left-aligned paragraph. Then, in the **Mail Merge** pane, click **Address block** to open the **Insert Address Block** dialog box.

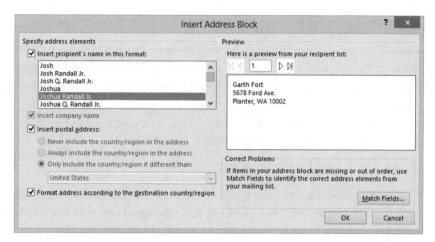

You can refine the format of the fields that make up the Address Block merge field.

4   Click **OK** to accept the default settings and insert the «**AddressBlock**» merge field into the document. When you merge the form letter with the data source, Word will substitute the individual name and address elements for this merge field.

We'll begin the letter with a personalized greeting.

5   Press the **Enter** key twice, and then in the **Mail Merge** pane, click **Greeting line** to open the **Insert Greeting Line** dialog box.

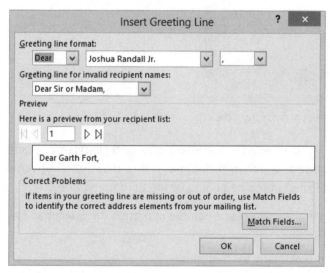

You can specify the greeting you want to use in the merged letters.

14

6　　In the list displaying formats for the recipient name, click **Joshua**.

7　　In the **Preview** area, click the **Next** button three times to view the greeting line for each of the recipients in the linked data source. Then click **OK** to close the **Insert Greeting Line** dialog box and insert the «**GreetingLine**» merge field into the document. When you merge the form letter with the data source, Word will replace this merge field with the word **Dear** and a space, followed by the information in the **FirstName** field, followed by a comma.

Now we'll personalize the letter content.

8　　Click to position the insertion point at the beginning of the third paragraph of the letter, which begins with **For even greater savings**. Then in the **Mail Merge** pane, click **More items** to open the **Insert Merge Field** dialog box.

You can insert individual fields from the data source.

9　　With **Database Fields** selected in the **Insert** area, and **FirstName** selected in the **Fields** box, click **Insert**, and then click **Close**. Notice that the «**FirstName**» merge field has been inserted at the beginning of the third paragraph.

10　　Without moving the cursor, enter a comma and press the **Spacebar**. Then change **For** to for.

The form letter is now ready for merging.

Wide World Importers.

3456 ELM STREET, SAN FRANCISCO, CA 10012 ¶

¶

«AddressBlock» ¶

¶

«GreetingLine» ¶

I want to take a moment to thank you for your continued support of Wide World Importers. Because loyal customers like you come back year after year, we are still growing steadily and the future looks brighter than ever. ¶

As you know, we will celebrate our 10th anniversary in March. In honor of that occasion, we are holding a special *Mad March* sale! Everything in the store will be 20% off throughout the month, and selected specials at higher discounts will be offered each day. Please pick up one of our promotional flyers the next time you visit the store for a complete schedule of these special offerings. ¶

«FirstName», for even greater savings, be sure to bring this letter with you when you shop. Identify yourself as a VIP Customer by presenting the letter to your salesperson at the time of your purchase, and you will receive an additional 5% off your total bill. ¶

Discounts and savings are our way of thanking you for your continued patronage of Wide World Importers. Remember, we are the one-stop design center for all your home decor needs! ¶

Sincerely, ¶

The form letter contains three merge fields.

❌ CLEAN UP Save the MyLetter document, and leave it open for the next exercise.

Merging main documents and data sources

After you specify the data source you want to use and enter merge fields in the main document, you can preview the merged documents and then perform the actual merge. You can further filter the source data during the preview process. When you're ready, you can either send the merged documents directly to the printer or you can merge them into a new document. If you merge to a new document, you have another chance to review and, if necessary, edit the merged documents before sending them to the printer.

In this exercise, you'll preview merged letters, exclude recipients from the merge, merge the letters into a new document, and then save the merged file.

14

SET UP This exercise uses the MyLetter document that you prepared in the previous exercises. With the document open, follow the steps.

TROUBLESHOOTING If you didn't complete the previous exercise, you should do so now. If you closed the document at the end of the previous exercise, open it and click Yes when Word asks whether you want to attach the data source to the document. Click the Start Mail Merge button in the Start Mail Merge group on the Mailings tab, and click Step-by-Step Mail Merge Wizard to display the Step 3 pane.

1 In the **Mail Merge** pane, click **Next** until the **Step 5** pane is displayed.

2 Hide formatting marks and, if necessary, adjust the view until the address block, greeting line, and third paragraph are all displayed at the same time. Word displays a preview of how the personalized letter will look when merged with the data source.

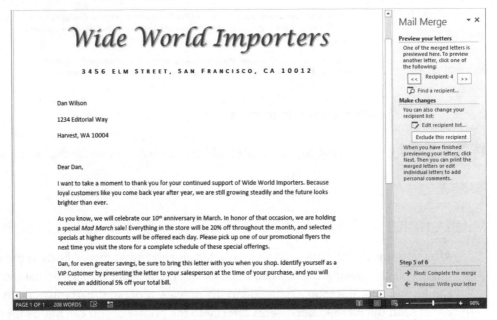

You can preview how the personalized letters will look before you proceed with the merge.

3 In the **Preview your letters** area of the **Mail Merge** pane, click the **Previous Record** button three times to preview all the letters.

TIP You can also preview the next or previous documents by clicking the Next Record or Previous Record button in the Preview Results group on the Mailings tab. You can jump to the first merged document by clicking the First Record button or to the last merged document by clicking the Last Record button.

4   To exclude the displayed recipient (**Garth Fort**) from the merge, click the **Exclude this recipient** button in the **Make changes** area of the **Mail Merge** pane.

Now we'll tidy up the address block by modifying the paragraph formatting of the merge field.

5   In the document, drag to select all three lines of the address block. Then on the **Home** tab, in the **Paragraph** group, click the **Line and Paragraph Spacing** button, and click **Remove Space After Paragraph** to move the address lines together.

6   Click away from the selection and preview the letters again. Then at the bottom of the **Mail Merge** pane, click **Next: Complete the merge**.

7   In the **Merge** area of the **Mail Merge** pane, click **Edit individual letters** to open the **Merge to New Document** dialog box.

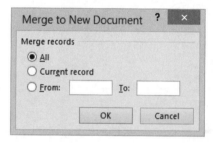

You can choose to merge only some of the currently selected records.

8   With the **All** option selected, click **OK** to create a document named **Letters1** that contains a personalized copy of the form letter for each of the selected records.

9   If necessary, click the **Print Layout** button on the **View Shortcuts** toolbar to display the letters as individual pages.

10 On the **Quick Access Toolbar**, click the **Save** button to open the **Save As** dialog box so that you can save the new document with a more specific name.

KEYBOARD SHORTCUT Press Ctrl+S to save files. For more information about keyboard shortcuts, see "Keyboard shortcuts" at the end of this book.

11 Navigate to the **Chapter14** practice file folder, enter My Merged Letters in the **File name** box, and then click **Save** to save the new document in the specified folder.

✖ CLEAN UP Close the My Merged Letters document. Then close the MyLetter document, saving your changes if you want to.

14

Printing envelopes

You can print an envelope based on an address in a document. To do so, follow these steps:

1   In the document, select the lines of the address. (Do not select any blank lines above or below the address.)

2   On the **Mailings** tab, in the **Create** group, click the **Envelopes** button to open the **Envelopes and Labels** dialog box.

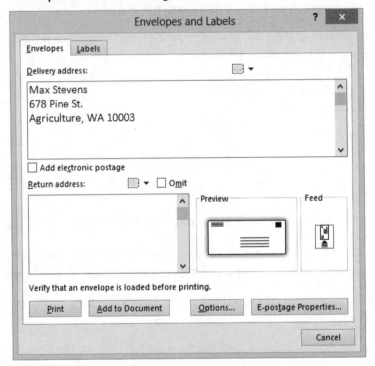

You can edit the delivery address and enter a return address.

TIP You can save time by storing the return address with your user information. In the General area of the Advanced page of the Word Options dialog box, enter the return address in the Mailing Address box, and click OK. The address then appears by default as the return address in the Envelopes And Labels dialog box. If you want to use envelopes with a preprinted return address, you must select the Omit check box to avoid duplication.

3   **Size 10** is the default envelope size. If you want to select a different envelope size, click **Options**, make your selection, and then click **OK**.

In the Envelope Options dialog box, you can also specify the feed method (horizontally or vertically and face up or face down), and the font and font size of both the address and the return address.

If you have electronic postage software installed on your computer, you can include electronic postage.

4   Insert an envelope in the printer, and then click **Print**.

Alternatively, you can click Add To Document to have Word insert the address in the format required for an envelope on a separate page at the beginning of the current document.

Sending personalized email messages to multiple recipients

When you want to send the same information to all the people on a list—for example, all your customers, or all the members of a club or your family—you don't have to print letters and physically mail them. Instead, you can use mail merge to create a personalized email message for each person in a data source. As with a form letter that will be printed, you can either use the Mail Merge wizard or use the buttons on the Mailings tab to insert merge fields into the form message. These merge fields will be replaced with information from the specified data source.

If you are using the wizard, be sure to click E-mail Messages in step 1. If you are not using the wizard, you can specify the list of email addresses you want to send the message to by clicking the Select Recipients button in the Start Mail Merge group on the Mailings tab. In either case, you have three options:

- Create an entirely new list of recipients by entering their contact information.
- Use an existing list of recipients stored outside of Outlook.
- Select recipients from an Outlook contacts list.

You can quickly add merge fields to a form message by using the buttons in the Write & Insert Fields group. Many email messages need only a greeting line. Because email messages tend to be less formal than printed letters, you might want to start the messages with a custom greeting rather than one of the predefined greeting options (Dear and To).

14

In this exercise, you'll open an existing form message, create a short mailing list, add a custom greeting line merge field, and then complete the merge.

SET UP You need the ThankYouEmail document located in the Chapter14 practice file folder to complete this exercise. You also need to have an email account configured in Outlook if you want to send the messages. Open the document, and then follow the steps.

1 On the **Mailings** tab, in the **Start Mail Merge** group, click the **Select Recipients** button, and then in the list, click **Type a New List** to open the **New Address List** dialog box.

You can create a data source as part of the mail merge process.

2 Click to position the cursor in the **First Name** field. Enter Andrea, press the **Tab** key, enter Dunker in the **Last Name** field, and press **Tab** until you reach the **E-mail Address** field (the last field in the table). Then enter andrea@consolidatedmessenger.com.

3 Click **New Entry**, and then add Judy Lew, with the email address judy@lucernepublishing.com.

TIP If you have several email addresses to add to the list, you can press Tab in the last field of the last entry, instead of clicking New Entry each time.

4 Repeat step 3 to add Ben Miller, with the email address ben@wingtiptoys.com, and then click **OK** to open the **Save Address List** dialog box, which is very similar to the **Save As** dialog box.

5 Navigate to the **Chapter14** practice file folder, enter My Email Data Source in the **File name** box, and then click **Save** to save the data source in the specified location as a database.

Now we'll insert the merge field in the main document.

6 Position the cursor at the beginning of the **ThankYouEmail** document. On the **Mailings** tab, in the **Write & Insert Fields** group, click the **Greeting Line** button to open the **Insert Greeting Line** dialog box.

7 In the first box in the **Greeting line format** area, drag to select **Dear** and then enter Hello followed by a comma and a space. In the second list, click **Joshua**. In the third list, click **:** (the colon).

8 In the **Preview** area, click the **Next** button twice to preview the greetings as they will appear in the email messages.

9 Click the **First** button to return to the first record, and then click **OK** to insert the **«GreetingLine»** merge field at the top of the form message.

«GreetingLine»

Thank you for your recent visit to our store. It was a pleasure to be able to answer your decorating questions and offer suggestions. As you requested, we have added your name to our online mailing list. You will be receiving our monthly newsletter, as well as advance notice of upcoming shipments and in-store events.

You can also visit our website at www.wideworldimporters.com for a schedule of events, links to online decorating resources, articles on furniture care, and more.

Contact us at customerservice@wideworldimporters.com, or call (925) 555-0167, for answers to all your decorating questions.

Regards,
Florian Stiller
President

Wide World Importers

3456 ELM STREET, SAN FRANCISCO, CA 10012

If you want to edit the custom greeting, right-click the merge field and then click Edit Greeting Line.

14

10   On the **Mailings** tab, in the **Preview Results** group, click the **Preview Results** button to display a preview of the first message. Click the **Next Record** button twice to preview the messages for other recipients. Then click the **Preview Results** button again to turn off the preview.

11   In the **Write & Insert Fields** group, click the **Highlight Merge Fields** button to identify the merge fields in the document with a gray highlight. There is only one merge field in this document.

Finally, we'll merge the data source and main document directly to email messages.

12   In the **Finish** group, click the **Finish & Merge** button, and then in the list, click **Send Email Messages** to open the **Merge to E-mail** dialog box.

You set up the email message header information and format in this dialog box.

13   In the **Message options** area, verify that **Email_Address** is selected in the **To** list, enter Welcome to Wide World Importers! in the **Subject line** box, and verify that **HTML** is selected in the **Mail format** list.

14   Click **OK** in the dialog box to send the email messages, or click **Cancel** to not send them.

TIP Your email program might require that you log in or manually send the messages. If you are using Outlook, a copy of each sent message appears in your Outlook Sent Items folder. If you plan to send a large number of messages, you might want to turn off the saving of sent messages.

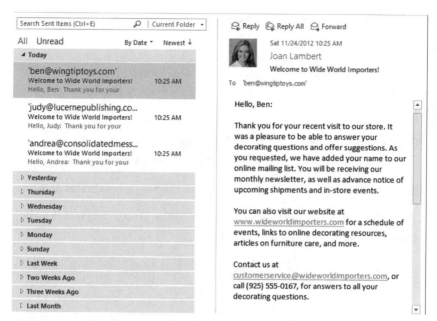

If you send the messages, you can locate them in your Sent Items folder.

❌ CLEAN UP Close the ThankYouEmail document, saving your changes if you want to.

Creating and printing labels

Most organizations keep information about their customers or clients in a worksheet or database that can be used for several purposes. For example, the address information might be used to send billing statements, form letters, and brochures. It might also be used to print sheets of mailing labels that can be attached to items such as packages and catalogs.

To create sheets of mailing labels, you first prepare the data source and then prepare the main document by selecting the brand and style of labels you plan to use. Word creates a table with cells the size of the labels on a page the size of the label sheet, so that each record will print on one label on the sheet. You insert merge fields into the first cell as a template for all the other cells. When you merge the main document and the data source, you can print the labels or create a new label document that you can use whenever you want to send something to the same set of recipients.

14

In this exercise, you'll create mailing labels. and then print the labels to proofread them.

→ SET UP You need the CustomerList workbook located in the Chapter14 practice file folder to complete this exercise. You also need an active printer connection if you want to print the labels. Open a new, blank document, display formatting marks, and then follow the steps.

1   On the **Mailings** tab, in the **Start Mail Merge** group, click the **Start Mail Merge** button, and then click **Step-by-Step Mail Merge Wizard**.

2   In the **Mail Merge** pane, click **Labels**, and then click **Next: Starting document**.

3   With **Change document layout** selected in the **Step 2** pane, click **Label options** to open the **Label Options** dialog box.

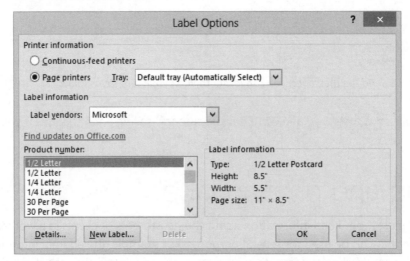

Every label is different. You need to specify the print method, the manufacturer and/or type, and the product number so that Word can set up the labels correctly.

4   In the **Label information** area, ensure that the **Label vendors** setting is **Microsoft**.

TIP When you create and print labels, purchase the label blanks that fit your size requirements, and then select the vendor and product number of those labels in the Label Information area. If the label vendor and product number you need aren't already available in the lists, click the Find Updates On Office.com link to download other available label configurations.

5   In the **Product number** box, select the second **30 Per Page** setting, which has labels with a **Height** of 1" and a **Width** of 2.63". Then click **OK** to insert a table that fills the first page of the main document.

TROUBLESHOOTING The results are visible only when formatting marks are displayed.

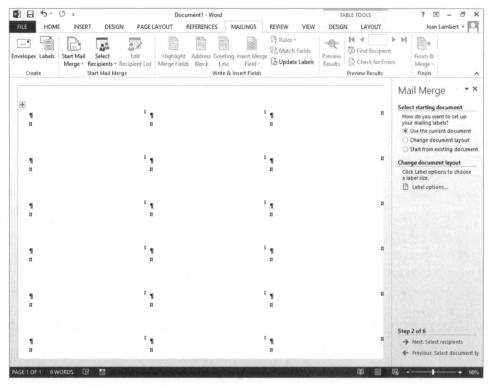

Word creates a 30-cell table that meets the label specifications.

6   At the bottom of the **Mail Merge** pane, click **Next: Select recipients**.

7   With **Use an existing list** selected, click **Browse**, navigate to the **Chapter14** practice file folder, double-click the **CustomerList** workbook, and then in the **Select Table** dialog box, click **OK**.

      SEE ALSO For more information about selecting, sorting, and filtering recipients, see "Preparing data sources" earlier in this chapter.

8   In the **Mail Merge Recipients** dialog box, click **OK** to insert a **«Next Record»** merge field in all the cells in the main document other than the first cell.

9   At the bottom of the **Mail Merge** pane, click **Next: Arrange your labels**, and then ensure that the left edge of the main document is visible.

10   With the cursor positioned in the first cell, click **Address block** in the **Merge your labels** area of the **Mail Merge** pane.

14

11 In the **Insert Address Block** dialog box, click **OK** to accept the default settings to insert an **«AddressBlock»** merge field into the first cell.

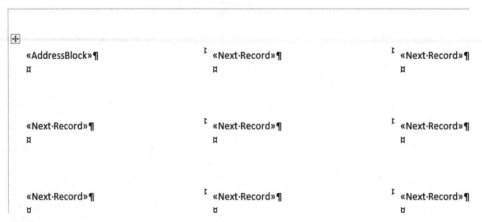

The merge fields in the first cell of the table will be used as a template for all the other cells.

SEE ALSO For more information about modifying merge fields, see "Preparing main documents" earlier in this chapter.

12 In the **Replicate labels** area of the **Mail Merge** pane, click **Update all labels** to copy the **«AddressBlock»** merge field to the other cells.

13 At the bottom of the **Mail Merge** pane, click **Next: Preview your labels** to display the data source content in place of the merge fields.

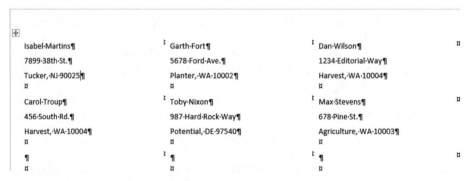

The six labels, as they will appear after the merge.

Now we'll merge the data source and main document into a new document that contains the labels.

14   At the bottom of the **Mail Merge** pane, click **Next: Complete the merge**. Then in the **Merge** area of the **Mail Merge** pane, click **Print**.

You have the opportunity to exclude records from the merge before printing the labels.

15   With the **All** option selected in the **Merge to Printer** dialog box, click **OK**.

16   In the **Print** dialog box, verify that the name of the printer you want to use to print the labels appears in the **Name** box, and then click **OK** to print the labels. The labels are printed on regular paper on the printer you selected. If you want to print on label sheets, insert the sheets in the printer's paper tray or manual feed location before clicking **OK** in the **Print** dialog box.

❌ CLEAN UP Close the label document, saving it if you want to.

Key points

- The mail merge process works by combining static information in a main document with variable information in a data source.

- The main document can be any type of document, such as a letter, email message, envelope or label template, or a directory or catalog.

- The data source is organized into sets of information, called records, with each record containing the same items, called fields.

- You insert placeholders, called merge fields, into the main document to tell Word where to merge items from the data source.

- You don't have to use all the records in a data source for a mail merge. You can filter the data and exclude specific records.

- You can send the mail merged results directly to your printer, to email, or to a new document that you can edit and save.

14

Chapter at a glance

Comment

Add and review comments,
page 430

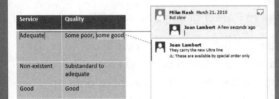

Track

Track and manage document changes,
page 434

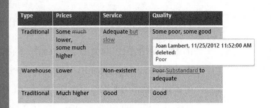

Protect

Password-protect documents,
page 442

MyLoans
My Documents » Word 2013 Step by Step » Chapter15

Protect Document
A password is required to open this document.

Control

Control changes,
page 446

Collaborate on documents

15

IN THIS CHAPTER, YOU WILL LEARN HOW TO

- Add and review comments.

- Track and manage document changes.

- Compare and merge documents.

- Password-protect documents.

- Control changes.

- Coauthor documents.

In today's workplace, many documents are developed collaboratively by a team of people or undergo a review process of some sort. You might be the lead author of some documents that are reviewed by your colleagues and managers, and you might be a reviewer of other documents. With Microsoft Word 2013, you can easily collaborate on the development of documents.

These days, most documents are reviewed on the screen rather than on paper printouts. With Word, it's easy to edit documents on-screen without losing track of the original text, and it's easy to accept or reject changes. You can also make comments, ask questions, and respond to comments made by others. If you send a document out for review and then receive several copies with changes and suggestions back from different people, you can merge the different versions into one file to simplify the process of reviewing and accepting or rejecting changes.

Even better, if your organization uses Microsoft SharePoint for collaboration, multiple people can work in a document that is stored on the SharePoint site at the same time. When you are creating a large document that requires input from several people, this method of collaboration can really save time.

Sometimes you'll want other people to review a document but not change it. You can prevent other people from making changes to a document by assigning a password to it. You can also specify that only certain people are allowed to make changes, and what types of formatting and content changes are allowed.

In this chapter, you'll first review, add, delete, and hide comments in a document. You'll track changes that you make to a document, and then accept and reject changes. You'll have Word compare and merge three versions of the same document. Then you'll set and remove a password and set up editing and formatting restrictions. Finally, we'll discuss how multiple people can work simultaneously in a document that is saved on a SharePoint site.

PRACTICE FILES To complete the exercises in this chapter, you need the practice files contained in the Chapter15 practice file folder. For more information, see "Download the practice files" in this book's Introduction.

Adding and reviewing comments

When reviewing a document, you can insert notes, called comments, to ask questions, make suggestions, or explain edits. To ensure that all the reviewing tools are available, review documents in Print Layout view. To insert a comment, you select the text to which you want the comment to refer, click the New Comment button in the Comments group on the Review tab, and enter what you want to say in the Comments balloon that appears. Word automatically adds your name to the comment.

Comments are displayed differently depending on the Display For Review setting you choose. Word 2013 has three Display For Review settings: Simple Markup (the default), All Markup, and No Markup. When all markup is shown, Word displays a balloon in the markup area outside the right margin next to the line of text that has the comment. You can display comments in several ways:

- Pointing to a balloon highlights the comments on that line in the color associated with that particular comment's author.

- Clicking the balloon displays the comments on that line.

- Right-clicking highlighted text and then clicking **Edit Comment** displays only the comment for that text.

You can work with comments in the following ways:

- To review comments, scroll through the document, or click the **Next** or **Previous** button in the **Comments** group to jump from balloon to balloon.

- To edit a comment, click the balloon and use normal editing techniques.

- To delete a comment, click its balloon and then click the **Delete** button in the **Comments** group or right-click the balloon and then click **Delete Comment**.

- To respond to a comment, you can simply add text to the existing comment balloon, or in Word 2013 you can now click the response icon in the balloon and then enter your additional comments. Note that if you use the second method, your responses will be displayed in a separate comment balloon to reviewers who use earlier versions of Word.

- If the complete text of a comment isn't visible in its balloon, view it in its entirety by clicking the **Reviewing Pane** button to display the **Revisions** pane. To change the size of the pane, point to its border, and when the pointer changes to a double-headed arrow, drag the border. To close the **Revisions** pane, click its **Close** button, or click the **Reviewing Pane** button again.

  TIP In addition to displaying comments, the Revisions pane displays all the editing and formatting changes made to a document in Track Changes, with the number of each type of change summarized at the top of the pane. For information about Track Changes, see the next topic in this chapter.

- Turn off the display of comment balloons by clicking the **Show Markup** button in the **Tracking** group and then clicking **Comments**.

- If multiple people have reviewed a document and you want to display only the comments of a specific person, click the **Show Markup** button, click **Reviewers**, and then click the name of any reviewer whose comments you don't want to display.

In this exercise, you'll show and review comments in a document, add and respond to comments, delete one that is no longer needed, and then hide the remaining comments.

 SET UP You need the CompetitiveAnalysisA document located in the Chapter15 practice file folder to complete this exercise. Display the document in Print Layout view, and then follow the steps.

1 On the **Review** tab, in the **Tracking** group, ensure that the **Display for Review** box displays **Simple Markup**. If comment balloons are not visible next to the paragraph and table in the document, click the **Show Markup** button, and if **Comments** does not have a check mark to its left in the list, click it.

2 On the **Review** tab, in the **Comments** group, click the **Next** button to display the first instance of commented text in the document.

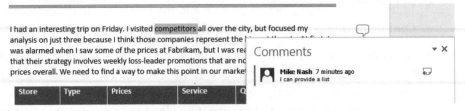

I had an interesting trip on Friday. I visited competitors all over the city, but focused my analysis on just three because I think those companies represent the ║... ╢... At first, I was alarmed when I saw some of the prices at Fabrikam, but I was rea╢ that their strategy involves weekly loss-leader promotions that are no prices overall. We need to find a way to make this point in our market╢

Comments ▾ ✕

Mike Nash 7 minutes ago
I can provide a list

Store	Type	Prices	Service	Q...

In Simple Markup view, only the active comment balloon is expanded.

TIP If a document contains both comments and tracked changes, clicking the Next or Previous button in the Changes group on the Review tab moves sequentially among both elements, whereas clicking the Next or Previous button in the Comments group moves only among comments.

3   In the **Comments** group, click the **Next** button to display the next comment.

4   In the **Tracking** group, in the **Display for Review** list, click **All Markup** to display the full comments in the markup area.

5   In the table, point to **Adequate** to display a ScreenTip with information about who inserted the comment and when.

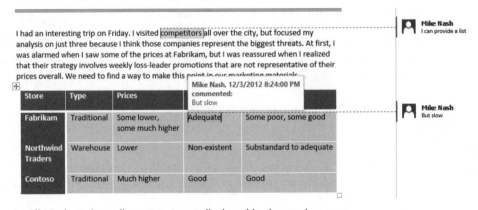

I had an interesting trip on Friday. I visited competitors all over the city, but focused my analysis on just three because I think those companies represent the biggest threats. At first, I was alarmed when I saw some of the prices at Fabrikam, but I was reassured when I realized that their strategy involves weekly loss-leader promotions that are not representative of their prices overall. We need to find a way to make this point in our marketing materials.

Mike Nash, 12/3/2012 8:24:00 PM
commented:
But slow

Store	Type	Prices			
Fabrikam	Traditional	Some lower, some much higher	Adequate	Some poor, some good	
Northwind Traders	Warehouse	Lower	Non-existent	Substandard to adequate	
Contoso	Traditional	Much higher	Good	Good	

Mike Nash
I can provide a list

Mike Nash
But slow

In All Markup view, all comments are displayed in the markup area.

6   In the last column of the same row, select the words **some good**, and then in the **Comments** group, click the **New Comment** button to highlight the selection and display a new balloon in the markup area.

7   In the comment balloon, enter They carry the new Ultra line.

8   In the markup area, click the comment balloon linked to the word **competitors**, and then in the **Comments** group, click the **Delete** button.

Next we'll experiment with another view of comments and use two different techniques to respond to comments.

9   In the **Tracking** group, click the **Reviewing Pane** button to open the **Revisions** pane on the left side of the program window.

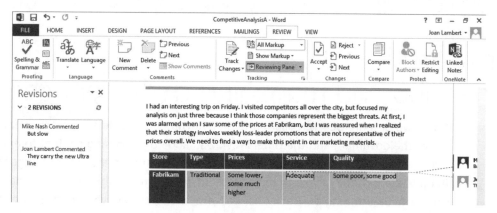

The Revisions pane shows the two remaining comments. If the document contained other revisions, they would also be shown here.

TIP You can click the Reviewing Pane arrow and then click Reviewing Pane Horizontal to display the pane across the bottom of the page.

10   In the **Revisions** pane, click at the right end of the second comment, press **Enter**, enter your initials and a colon (:), press the **Spacebar**, and then enter Ultra products are available by special order only to add the new text to the original comment.

11   Click the **Close** button in the upper-right corner of the **Revisions** pane. Then position the document so the right edges of the comment balloons are displayed.

12   Point to the comment balloon associated with **Adequate**, and then click the **Reply to Comment** button that appears in the upper-right corner of the balloon to insert a response within the comment.

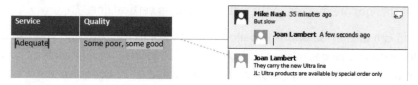

The response comment is labeled with your name.

13   In the response comment, enter **If you had been a real customer, would you have left?**

Lastly, we'll hide the comments.

14   In the **Tracking** group, in the **Show Markup** list, click **Comments** to hide the comments in the document.

❌ CLEAN UP Close the CompetitiveAnalysisA document, saving your changes if you want to.

Tracking and managing document changes

When two or more people collaborate on a document, one person usually creates and "owns" the document and the others review it, adding or revising content to make it more accurate, logical, or readable. In Word, reviewers can turn on the Track Changes feature so that the revisions they make to the document are recorded without the original text being lost. (Note that turning on Track Changes affects only the active document, not any other documents that might also be open.)

To turn on Track Changes, you click the Track Changes button in the Tracking group on the Review tab. You then edit the text as usual.

TIP If you want to know whether Track Changes is turned on when the Review tab is not displayed, right-click the status bar and then click Track Changes on the Customize Status Bar menu. Word then adds a Track Changes button to the status bar that you can click to turn the feature on and off.

By default, your revisions appear in a different color from the original text, as follows:

- Insertions are inserted in the text in your assigned color. Insertions are underlined, and deletions are crossed out (the formatting is called strikethrough).

- Formatting changes appear in balloons in the markup area.

- All changes are marked in the left margin by a vertical line.

- You can display deletions in balloons instead of in the text, and you can display formatting changes in the text instead of in balloons. Simply click the **Show Markup** button in the **Tracking** group on the **Review** tab, click **Balloons**, and then click the options you want.

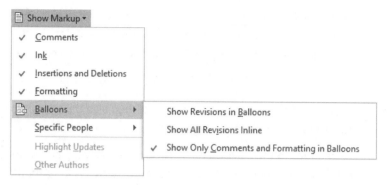

You can specify whether you want revisions to be displayed in the text or in balloons.

TIP The colors used for revisions are controlled by the settings in the Track Changes Options dialog box, which you can display by clicking the Tracking dialog box launcher.

You can display a ScreenTip identifying the name of the reviewer who made a specific change, and when the change was made, by pointing to a revision or balloon. The reviewer name is taken from the user information stored with the user account. You can change the stored user information for your user account from the Word Options dialog box, which you can open either from the Backstage view or by clicking the Tracking dialog box launcher and clicking Change User Name in the Track Changes Options dialog box.

TROUBLESHOOTING If you're signed in to Word with a Microsoft account, Word tracks revisions by the name associated with your Microsoft account. Changing your user information affects revision tracking only when you aren't signed in with a Microsoft account.

By using the commands available on the Review tab, you can work with revisions in the following ways:

- To track changes without showing them on the screen, hide the revisions by clicking the **Display for Review** arrow in the **Tracking** group and clicking **No Markup** in the list. To display the revisions again, click **All Markup** in the **Display for Review** list. You can also display the original version, with or without revisions.

- When revisions are visible in the document, select which types of revisions you want to display from the **Show Markup** list in the **Tracking** group—for example, you can display only comments or only insertions and deletions. You can also display or hide the revisions of specific reviewers from this list.

- Move forward or backward from one revision or comment to another by clicking the **Next** or **Previous** button in the **Changes** group.

- Incorporate a selected change into the document and move to the next change by clicking the **Accept** button in the **Changes** group. Click the **Reject** button to remove the selected change, restore the original text, and move to the next change.

  TIP You can also right-click the change and then click Accept or Reject.

- Accept or reject all the changes in a block of text, such as a paragraph, by selecting the block and clicking the **Accept** or **Reject** button.

- Accept all the changes in the document by clicking the **Accept** arrow and then clicking **Accept All Changes**. Reject all the changes at once by clicking the **Reject** arrow and then clicking **Reject All Changes**.

- Accept or reject only certain types of changes or changes from a specific reviewer by displaying only the changes you want to accept or reject, clicking the **Accept** or **Reject** arrow, and then clicking **Accept All Changes Shown** or **Reject All Changes Shown** in the list.

In this exercise, you'll turn on change tracking, edit the document, and accept and reject changes.

 SET UP You need the CompetitiveAnalysisB document located in the Chapter15 practice file folder to complete this exercise. Open the document, and then follow the steps.

1   On the **Review** tab, in the **Tracking** group, click the **Track Changes** button (not its arrow). Notice that the button color changes to blue to indicate that **Track Changes** is turned on. Any changes that you make now will be indicated in the document as revisions.

    KEYBOARD SHORTCUT Press Ctrl+Shift+E to turn on change tracking. For more information about keyboard shortcuts, see "Keyboard shortcuts" at the end of this book.

2   In the **Display for Review** list, click **All Markup**. In the **Show Markup** list, click **Balloons**, and ensure that **Show Only Comments and Formatting in Balloons** is selected.

3   Display the table. In the **Prices** column of the **Fabrikam** row, in the phrase **Some much lower**, double-click the word **much**, and then press the **Delete** key. Notice that Word indicates with strikethrough formatting that you deleted the word.

4   In the **Service** column of the **Fabrikam** row, position the insertion point after the word **Adequate**, press the **Spacebar**, and then enter but slow to insert the new text in the same color as the deletion.

5 In the **Quality** column of the **Northwind Traders** row, select the word **Poor**, and then enter Substandard to show this one change as both a deletion and an insertion. Then point to the deleted word **Poor** to display an informative ScreenTip.

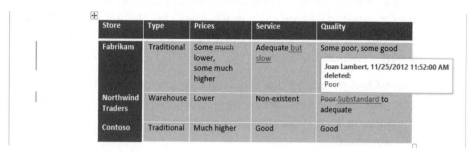

A vertical line in the left margin draws your attention to revisions. Revision ScreenTips display information about the change.

Let's look at a few other views of tracked changes.

6 In the **Tracking** group, click **Show Markup**, click **Balloons**, and then click **Show Revisions in Balloons** to remove the deletions from the text and display them in the right margin.

Store	Type	Prices	Service	Quality	
Fabrikam	Traditional	Some lower, some much higher	Adequate but slow	Some poor, some good	Joan Lambert Deleted: much
Northwind Traders	Warehouse	Lower	Non-existent	Substandard to adequate	Joan Lambert Deleted: Poor
Contoso	Traditional	Much higher	Good	Good	

The text is less cluttered if you display deletions in balloons.

7 In the **Tracking** group, click **Show Markup**, click **Balloons**, and then click **Show All Revisions Inline** to restore the inline revision indicators and remove the balloons.

8 In the **Tracking** group, in the **Display for Review** list, click **No Markup** to hide the revisions and display the document as it would appear if all the changes were accepted.

9 In the **Display for Review** list, click **Simple Markup** to indicate the presence of tracked changes only by displaying user-specific color-coded vertical lines in the left margin.

Now we'll review and process the tracked changes.

10   In the **Display for Review** list, click **All Markup** to redisplay the tracked changes. Then press **Ctrl+Home** to move to the beginning of the document.

11   In the **Changes** group, click the **Next** button to select the first change in the document—the deleted word **much**. Then click the **Accept** button (not its arrow) to accept the change, remove the revision and associated balloon, and move to the next change (**but slow**).

12   In the **Changes** group, click the **Reject** button (not its arrow) to remove the inserted text, and because there are no more changes in this row of the table, to also remove the adjacent vertical bar from the left margin, and then move to the next change (**Substandard**).

      TIP You can click the Accept or Reject arrow to display a menu of actions associated with the command, including not moving to the next change, processing all changes of that type, and turning off change tracking after processing the change.

13   In the **Changes** group, click the **Accept** button to implement the deletion, and then click the same button again to implement the insertion. Word then displays a message box telling you that there are no more changes in the document.

14   Click **OK** to close the message box.

15   In the **Tracking** group, click the **Track Changes** button to stop tracking changes made to the active document.

❌ CLEAN UP Change the balloon setting to the one you like best. Then close the CompetitiveAnalysisB document, saving your changes if you want to.

Comparing and merging documents

Sometimes you might want to compare several versions of the same document. For example, if you have sent a document out for review by colleagues, you might want to compare their edited versions with the original document.

Instead of comparing multiple open documents visually, you can tell Word to compare the documents and merge the changes into one document. Even if the changes were not made with Track Changes turned on, they are recorded in the merged document as revisions. From within that one document, you can view all the changes from all the reviewers or view only those from a specific reviewer.

In this exercise, you'll first merge three versions of the same document. You'll then evaluate and resolve the differences between the versions.

→ SET UP You need the Service, ServiceCP, and ServiceTA documents located in the Chapter15 practice file folder to complete this exercise. Open the Service document, and then follow the steps.

1   On the **Review** tab, click the **Compare** group button if necessary, and then in the **Compare** group, click **Combine** to open the **Combine Documents** dialog box.

> **TIP** Click the Compare option to the differences between two documents in a third document. The documents being compared are not changed.

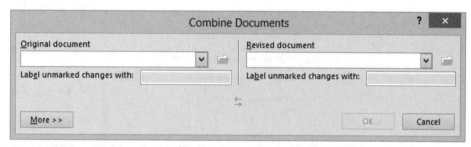

You select the two documents you want to combine in this dialog box.

2   In the **Original document** list, click **Service**. Then enter your name in the **Label unmarked changes with** box.

> **TROUBLESHOOTING** If the Service document doesn't appear in the list, click the Browse button to the right of the list, navigate to the Chapter15 practice file folder, and then double-click the file.

3   In the **Revised document** list, click **ServiceCP**. Ensure that Chris Preston appears in the associated **Label unmarked changes with** box.

4   If the dialog box isn't already expanded, click the **More** button in the lower-left corner of the dialog box. Then in the **Comparison settings** area, verify that all the check boxes are selected.

5   In the **Show changes** area, ensure that **Original document** is selected below **Show changes in**. Then click **OK** to compare the two documents and mark the differences in a merged version of the document, which is displayed in the center pane. The **Revisions** pane is displayed on the left, and the two documents being compared are displayed on the right.

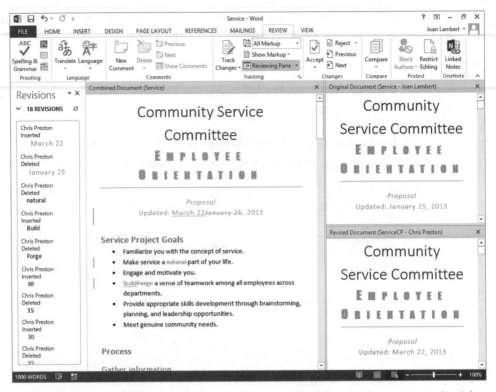

The document in the center pane combines the changes from the two documents on the right, and the Revisions pane provides details about the changes.

TROUBLESHOOTING If the Revisions pane is not open, click the Reviewing Pane button in the Tracking group on the Review tab. If the source documents are not displayed, click the Compare button, click Show Source Documents, and then click Show Both.

TIP If you compare documents that contain conflicting formatting, a message box will ask you to confirm which document's formatting should be used.

Now we'll compare a third version of the document to the first two versions.

6   With the first two combined documents displayed, click **Combine** in the **Compare** group to display the **Combine Documents** dialog box.

7   In the **Original document** list, click **Service**. In the **Revised document** list, click **ServiceTA** and ensure that Terry Adams appears in the associated **Label unmarked changes with** box. Then click **OK** to add the changes from the **ServiceTA** version of the document to those of the other two versions.

8   In the center pane, scroll through the document to review all the revisions, and then in the **Revisions** pane, scroll through the individual revisions.

9   In the **Tracking** group, click the **Show Markup** button, click **Specific People**, and then click **Chris Preston** to remove the change tracking markup from the revisions made in the **ServiceCP** document.

10 In the **Show Markup** list, click **Specific People**, and then click **All Reviewers** to redisplay all the revisions.

    Before accepting changes in the document, we must resolve conflicting changes.

11 In the **Revisions** pane, below **Chris Preston Deleted**, right-click **January** and then click **Accept Deletion**. Click any other changes in the **Revisions** pane to display that location in the three document panes.

12 Click to position the cursor in the document in the center pane. In the **Changes** group, click the **Accept** arrow, and then in the list, click **Accept All Changes**.

13 Close the **Revisions** pane, and then close the two windows on the right side of the screen.

    TIP The next time you combine documents, the Revisions pane and the source windows will be closed. You can open the Revisions pane by clicking the Reviewing Pane button in the Tracking group on the Review tab, and you can open the source windows by clicking Show Source Documents in the Compare list and then clicking the option you want.

❌ CLEAN UP Close the Service document, saving your changes if you want to.

Managing document versions

Word automatically saves a temporary copy of your open documents every 10 minutes. Autosaved versions of the document are displayed in the Manage Versions area of the Info page of the Backstage view. You can work with documents in this area in the following ways:

- You can display previous versions of a document by clicking the version you want to display.

- You can identify changes between versions by clicking the **Compare** button on the yellow information bar at the top of the previous version of the file.

- You can roll back to a previous document version by clicking the **Revert** button on the information bar.

- You can display autosaved versions of all documents by clicking the **Manage Versions** button.

You can change the autosave frequency on the Save page of the Word Options dialog box.

Password-protecting documents

Sometimes, you might want only certain people to be able to open and change a document. The easiest way to exercise this control is to assign a password to protect the document. Word then requires that the password be entered correctly before it will allow the document to be opened and changed.

You can assign a password to a document from the Info page of the Backstage view or when saving the document. Word offers two levels of password protection:

- **Unencrypted** The document is saved in such a way that only people who know the password can open it, make changes, and save the file. People who don't know the password can open a read-only version. If they make changes and want to save them, they have to save the document with a different name or in a different location, preserving the original.

- **Encrypted** The document is saved in such as way that people who do not know the password cannot open it at all.

In this exercise, you'll set an unencrypted password for a document and then test the document's security by entering an incorrect password. You'll open a read-only version of the document and then reopen it with the correct password. You'll remove the unencrypted password protection from the document and then set an encrypted password.

➡ SET UP You need the Loans document located in the Chapter15 practice file folder to complete this exercise. Open the document, and then follow the steps.

1 Display the **Save As** page of the **Backstage** view, and in the **Current Folder** area, click the **Chapter15** practice file folder.

2 In the **Save As** dialog box that opens, change the name in the **File name** box to My Loans.

3 At the bottom of the dialog box, click **Tools**, and then in the list, click **General Options** to open the **General Options** dialog box.

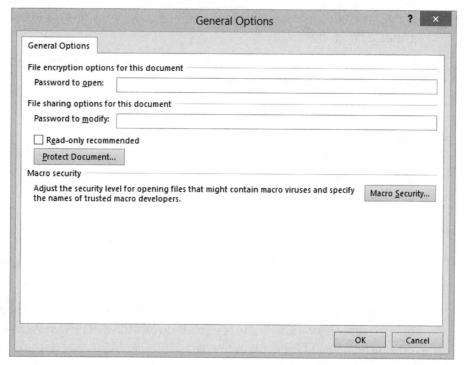

Assigning a password to open a document encrypts the document; assigning a password to modify the document does not encrypt it.

15

TIP If you want people to be able to read the document's contents but you don't expect them to change the document, you can select the Read-Only Recommended check box to tell Word to display a message suggesting that the document be opened as read-only. Then click OK to close the General Options dialog box without assigning a password.

4   In the **Password to modify** box, enter P@ssw0rd. Then click **OK**. Notice that as you enter the password, dots appear instead of the characters to keep the password confidential.

> **IMPORTANT** Don't use common words or phrases as passwords, and don't use the same password for multiple documents. After assigning a password, make a note of it in a safe place. If you forget it, you won't be able to open the password-protected document.

5   In the **Confirm Password** dialog box, enter P@ssw0rd in the **Reenter password to modify** box, and then click **OK** to set the password.

6   In the **Save As** dialog box, click **Save** to save a copy of the original document that is protected from change.

7   Close the **My Loans** document. Then open it from the **Chapter15** practice file folder. Word displays the **Password** dialog box.

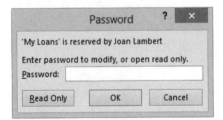

You must enter the password or open the document as read-only.

8   Enter password (all lowercase) in the **Password** box, and then click **OK**. Word displays a message telling you that you entered an incorrect password.

9   Click **OK** in the message box. Then in the **Password** dialog box, click **Read Only** to open a read-only version of the **My Loans** document. Notice that Word opens the document in **Read Mode**; this is the default view for read-only documents.

10 Close the document, and then reopen it. This time, in the **Password** dialog box, enter P@ssw0rd, and then click **OK** to open an editable version of the document.

Now we'll remove the password protection.

11 Display the **Save As** page of the **Backstage** view, and in the **Current Folder** area, click the **Chapter15** practice file folder. At the bottom of the **Save As** dialog box, in the **Tools** list, click **General Options**.

12 In the **General Options** dialog box, select the contents of the **Password to modify** box, press **Delete**, and then click **OK**.

13 In the **Save As** dialog box, click **Save**.

Now we'll encrypt the document and require a password to open it.

14 Display the **Info** page of the **Backstage** view. Click the **Protect Document** button, and then click **Encrypt with Password** to open the **Encrypt Document** dialog box.

After the password is assigned, you will no longer be able to open the document without it.

15 In the **Encrypt Document** and **Confirm Password** dialog boxes, enter P@ssw0rd in the **Password** box and click **OK**.

The protected status of the document is displayed on the Info page of the Backstage view.

16   Close the **My Loans** document, saving your changes, and then reopen it. Test the document's security by trying to open it with an incorrect password.

17   If you want to remove the password encryption, open the **My Loans** document by using the P@ssw0rd password. On the **Info** page of the **Backstage** view, in the **Protect Document** list, click **Encrypt with Password**. In the **Encrypt Document** dialog box, delete the password from the **Password** box, and then click **OK**.

❌ CLEAN UP Close the My Loans document, saving your changes if you want to.

Controlling changes

Sometimes you'll want people to be able to open and view a document but not make changes to it. Sometimes you'll want to allow changes, but only of certain types. For example, you can specify that other people can insert comments in the document but not make changes, or you can require that people track their changes.

To prevent anyone from introducing inconsistent formatting into a document, you can limit the styles that can be applied. You can select the styles individually, or you can implement the recommended minimum set, which consists of all the styles needed by Word for features such as tables of contents. (The recommended minimum set doesn't necessarily include all the styles used in the document.)

You can protect a document from unauthorized changes by specifying formatting and editing restrictions in the Restrict Editing pane. There are two ways to display this pane:

- On the **Info** page of the **Backstage** view, click the **Protect Document** button, and then click **Restrict Editing**.
- On the **Review** tab, in the **Protect** group, click the **Restrict Editing** button.

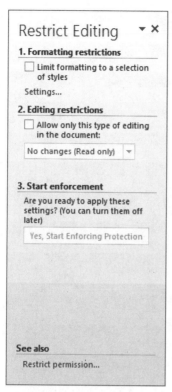

You specify the changes that are allowed in the document in this pane.

In this exercise, you'll set editing and formatting restrictions to selectively allow modifications to a document.

SET UP You need the ProceduresRestricted document located in the Chapter15 practice file folder to complete this exercise. Open the document, and then follow the steps.

1   On the **Review** tab, in the **Protect** group, click the **Restrict Editing** button.

2   In the **Formatting restrictions** area of the **Restrict Editing** pane, select the **Limit formatting to a selection of styles** check box, and then click the **Settings** link to open the **Formatting Restrictions** dialog box.

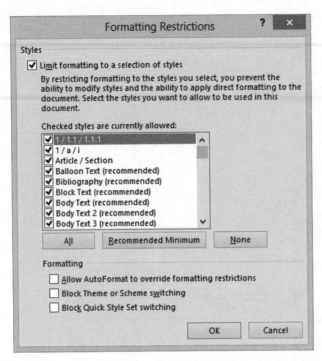

All the available styles are currently allowed.

3   Scroll through the **Checked styles are currently allowed** list to view the styles in the template attached to the open document, including styles that are available but not currently in use.

4   Below the list, click the **Recommended Minimum** button. Then scroll through the list again. All the selected styles are designated by the word **recommended**.

The recommended set does not include some of the styles used in the document, so we'll add the other styles to those that are allowed.

5   Toward the top of the list, select the **Address** check box. Then scroll through the list, and select the **BulletList1** and **BulletList2** check boxes.

6   In the **Formatting** area, select the **Block Theme or Scheme switching** and the **Block Quick Style Set switching** check boxes. Then click **OK** to implement the restricted set of styles.

Word displays a message stating that the document might contain formatting or styles that aren't allowed.

7   In the message box, click **Yes** to remove the other formatting and styles. This causes the telephone number and other indented paragraphs to revert to the **Normal** style.

8   In the **Editing restrictions** area of the **Restrict Editing** pane, select the **Allow only this type of editing in the document** check box. Then in the associated list, click **Tracked changes**.

9   In the **Start enforcement** area of the **Restrict Editing** pane, click **Yes, Start Enforcing Protection** to open the **Start Enforcing Protection** dialog box.

People who don't know the password can't turn off the restrictions.

10   Without entering a password, click **OK**. Notice that the **Restrict Editing** pane now provides information about actions permitted while the restrictions are in place.

11   Display the **Home** tab, and notice that many of the buttons in the **Font** and **Paragraph** groups are unavailable.

12   Display the **Review** tab, and point to the **Track Changes** button.

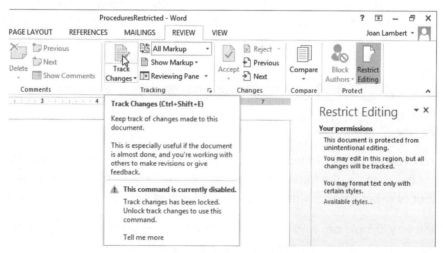

The Track Changes button has been disabled; all changes will be tracked.

13   In the document title, double-click the word **Office**, and enter Operations. Notice that your change is marked as a revision. Any edits you make will be recorded, and because the **Track Changes** button is unavailable, you cannot turn it off.

❌ CLEAN UP Close the ProceduresRestricted document, saving your changes if you want to.

Coauthoring documents

Whether you work for a large organization or a small business, you might need to collaborate with other people on the development of a document. No matter what the circumstances, it can be difficult to keep track of different versions of a document produced by different people. If you store a document in a shared location such as a Microsoft SharePoint site, multiple people can use Word to work in the document simultaneously.

After you save a document to a shared location, you can open it and indicate that you want to edit it, without first checking it out. You can work on the version that is stored on the site just as you would a document on your computer. When another contributor begins making changes to the file stored on the site, Word alerts you to that person's presence by displaying an icon on the taskbar, and a list of people currently editing the document on the Info page of the Backstage view. You can send an email message or instant message to the document editors from this location.

Word keeps track of changes that people make in the document and indicates which paragraphs are currently being edited and by whom. You can update your copy of the document to reflect other people's changes, and share your changes with other people, by saving the document or clicking the Updates Available notification on the status bar.

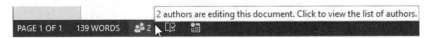

Clicking the Number Of Authors Editing status bar indicator displays a list of the people currently editing the document

Recent changes are indicated by colored text. If each person working in the document tracks his or her changes, the tracked changes remain available so that the document owner can accept or reject changes when the team has finished working on the document.

In this way, people can work efficiently on a document whether they are in the same office building, on the other side of town, or in a different time zone.

Restricting who can do what to documents

If rights management software is installed on your computer, you can control who can view and work with your documents. If you have this capability, a Restrict Permission By People option appears in the list displayed when you click the Protect Document button in the Permissions area of the Info page. Clicking Restrict Permission By People and then Restricted Access displays the Permission dialog box. In this dialog box, you can click Restrict Permission To This Document and then allow specific people to perform specific tasks, such as opening, printing, saving, or copying the document. When this protection is in place, other people cannot perform these tasks. The assigned permissions are stored with the document and apply no matter where the file is stored.

Before you can work on a document to which access has been restricted, you must verify your credentials with a licensing server. You can then download a use license that defines the tasks you are authorized to perform with the document. You need to repeat this process with each restricted document.

Key points

- You can merge multiple versions of a document so that the changes in all versions are recorded in one document.

- You can insert comments in a document to ask questions or explain suggested edits.

- When you collaborate on a document, you can record the revisions you make to the document without losing the original text.

- If only specific people should work on a document, you can protect it with a password. You can also restrict what people can do to it.

- Multiple people can simultaneously edit a document that is stored on a SharePoint site.

Chapter at a glance

Style

Create custom styles and templates,
page 454

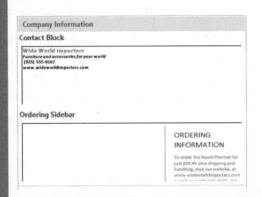

Build

Create custom building blocks,
page 472

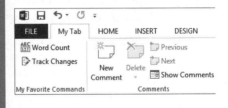

Modify

Change default program options,
page 478

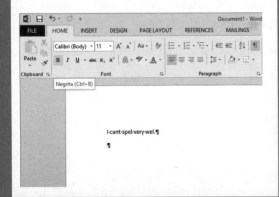

Command

Customize the ribbon,
page 494

Work in Word more efficiently

IN THIS CHAPTER, YOU WILL LEARN HOW TO

- Create custom styles and templates.

- Create custom building blocks.

- Change default program options.

- Customize the Quick Access Toolbar.

- Customize the ribbon.

If you use Microsoft Word 2013 only occasionally, you might be perfectly happy creating new documents by using the wide range of tools we have already discussed in this book. And you might be comfortable with the default working environment options and behind-the-scenes settings. However, if you create a lot of documents of various types, you might want to streamline the document development process or change aspects of the program to make it more suitable for the kinds of documents you create.

In this chapter, you'll learn to create custom styles, templates, and building blocks, which can greatly enhance document development efficiency. You'll explore the Word Options dialog box and experiment with some of the ways in which you can customize the program. Then you'll modify the Quick Access Toolbar and the ribbon to put the tools you need for your daily work at your fingertips.

PRACTICE FILES To complete the exercises in this chapter, you need the practice files contained in the Chapter16 practice file folder. For more information, see "Download the practice files" in this book's Introduction.

Creating custom styles and templates

When you want to quickly create an effective, visually coordinated document, you can build on work that you or your co-workers have already done by saving an existing document with a new name and then customizing it to suit the current purpose. However, if you frequently create the same type of document, such as a monthly or quarterly report, one of the most efficient ways to generate the document is to base it on a *template* that already contains the text, character and paragraph styles, page formatting, and graphic elements that you generally use in that type of document.

When it comes to maximizing your efficiency while creating documents in Word, styles and templates are among the most powerful tools available to you. Entire books have been written about them; this discussion can only scratch the surface. We'll talk about templates first to provide some context; then we'll discuss styles.

Creating and attaching templates

Although most Word users rarely need to concern themselves with the fact, all Word documents are based on templates. New blank documents are based on the built-in Normal template, which defines paragraph styles for regular text paragraphs, a title, and different levels of headings. It also defines a few character styles that you can use to change the look of selected text. These styles appear in the Styles pane and are also available in the Styles gallery on the Home tab. You can apply these template styles to format the content in the document.

SEE ALSO For information about applying styles, see "Applying styles to text" in Chapter 3, "Modify the structure and appearance of text."

Depending on the types of documents you create and the organization for which you create them, it might be quite realistic for you to work happily in the Normal template for the entire length of your word-processing career. However, many other templates are available when you're working in Word 2013. Most are for specific types of documents, and many are pre-populated with text, tables, images, and other content that you can modify to fit your needs. A few of the templates are installed on your computer with Word. Many more templates are maintained on the Microsoft Office website, but you can locate and use them directly from within Word (provided you have an Internet connection). You can create a document based on one of these templates from the Start screen or from the New page of the Backstage view.

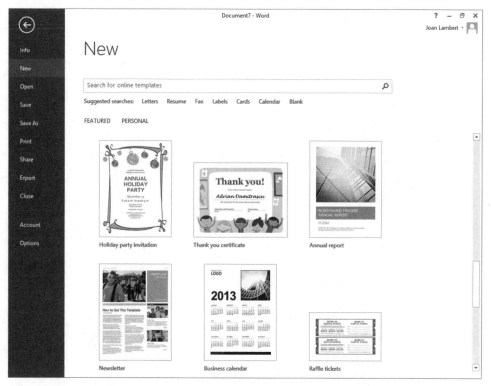

Featured templates on the New page of the Backstage view when working online.

TIP Featured and Personal appear at the top of the New page only after you configure a personal templates folder. More information is available later in this topic.

The templates available on the New page vary depending on whether you're working online or offline.

- When you're working online (that is, when your computer has an active Internet connection, whether or not you're using it to do anything else), the **New** page displays thumbnails of featured templates. These vary based on the season; for example, they might include holiday-specific or season-specific templates for creating announcements, invitations, and newsletters. The search box at the top of the page is active; you can enter a search term to display related online templates, or click a category below the search box to display online templates in that category.

- When you're working offline, the **New** page displays only templates that are stored on your computer. These include any templates that you have already used, as well as a selection of letter, newsletter, report, and resume templates. The search box is unavailable (you can only search the offline templates by scrolling through the thumbnails on the **New** page).

New

Search for online templates

FEATURED   PERSONAL

Origin letter

Origin report

Origin resume

Red and black letter

Red and black report

Annual
Report
FY 2014

[Report Title]

Student report

Content on the New page of the Backstage view when working offline.

Word document templates contain elements such as the following:

- **Formatting** Most templates contain formatting information, which in addition to styles can include page layout settings, backgrounds, themes, and other types of formatting. A template that contains only formatting defines the look of the document; you add your own content.

- **Text** Templates can also contain text that you customize for your own purposes. For example, if you base a new document on an agenda template from Office.com, the text of the agenda is already in place, and all you have to do is customize it. Sometimes, a document based on a template displays formatted text placeholders surrounded by square brackets—for example, [Company Name]—instead of actual text. You replace a placeholder with your own text by clicking it and then typing the replacement. If you don't need a placeholder, you simply delete it.

- **Graphics, tables, charts, and diagrams** Templates can contain ready-made graphic elements, either for use as is or as placeholders for elements tailored to the specific document.

- **Building blocks** Some templates make custom building blocks, such as headers and footers or a cover page, available for use with a particular type of document. They might also include AutoText, such as contact information or standard copyright or privacy paragraphs.

  SEE ALSO For information about working with building blocks, see "Inserting pre-formatted document parts" in Chapter 9, "Add visual elements," and "Creating custom building blocks" later in this chapter.

- **Custom tabs, commands, and macros** Sophisticated templates might include custom ribbon tabs or toolbars with commands and macros that are specific to the purposes of the template. A macros is a recorded series of commands that allows a user to perform a process with the click of a button. The topic of macros is beyond the scope of this book; for information, refer to Word Help.

  TIP Word 2013 template files have one of two file name extensions, depending on their content. Those that contain macros have the .dotm file name extension; those that don't contain macros have the .dotx extension.

When you base a new document on a template, that template is said to be *attached* to the document. The styles defined in the attached template appear in the Styles pane so that you can easily apply them to any content you add to the document. You can change the document template by attaching a different one. You can also load templates as *global templates* to make their contents available in all documents that you work on. Two global templates are automatically loaded by Word—the Normal template and the Building Blocks template—but you can load others. For example, your organization might have a Custom Building Blocks template containing corporate-themed document parts that it wants you to use in all documents.

TIP If the designation *(Compatibility Mode)* appears in the title bar when you create a document based on a template, it indicates that the template was created in an earlier version of Word. Usually this will have no effect on your use of the template, but bear in mind that certain Word functionality is disabled in Compatibility Mode. To upgrade a document to Word 2013, click the Convert button on the Info page of the Backstage view.

If none of the templates that come with Word or that you download from Office.com meets your needs, you can create your own template. You can distribute the custom template to other people as well. By doing so, you can ensure that documents you and your co-workers create adhere to a specific set of styles or are based on the same content.

Creating a custom template is easy—you simply create a document containing the content, styles, and settings that you want, and then save it as a document template (a .dotx file) rather than as a document (a .docx file). You can save a custom template with text in it, which is handy if you create many documents with only slight variations. Or you can delete the text so that a new document based on the template will open as a blank document with the set of predefined styles available to apply to whatever content you enter.

You can save a custom template anywhere and then browse to and double-click the file name to open a new document based on the template. However, if you save the template in your default Personal Templates folder, it will be available when you click Personal at the top of the New page of the Backstage view.

TIP In earlier versions of Office, the default Templates location was a hidden folder stored at C:\Users\<*user name*>\AppData\Roaming\Microsoft\Templates. Word 2013 allows you to choose your own Personal Templates folder from the Save page of the Backstage view.

In Chapter 3, "Modify the structure and appearance of text," we discuss how to assign formats and outline levels to content by applying styles, and how to change the appearance of styled content by using style sets. Although style sets provide a quick and easy way to change the look of an existing document, there might be times when you want to attach an entirely different template to a document. For example, you might attach a company-specific template that contains a defined set of styles permitted in corporate communications.

You attach a template from the Developer tab, which by default is hidden. To display the Developer tab, open the Word Options dialog box, display the Customize Ribbon page, and in the Customize The Ribbon pane displaying the main tabs, select the check box to the left of Developer.

To attach a different template to an open document and reset the document styles to the template styles, follow these steps:

1   On the **Developer** tab, in the **Templates** group, click **Document Template** to display the **Templates** page of the **Templates and Add-ins** dialog box.

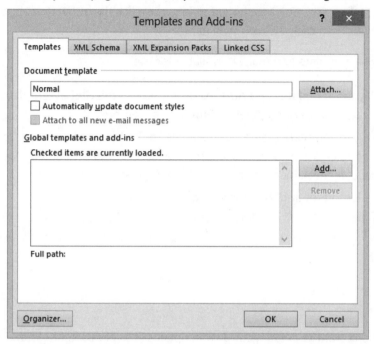

From this page, you can attach a document template or load a global template.

2   In the **Document template** area, click **Attach** to open the **Attach Template** dialog box. Navigate to the template you want to attach, and then double-click it to enter the path to the template in the **Document template** box.

3   In the **Templates and Add-ins** dialog box, select the **Automatically update document styles** check box, and then click **OK** to attach the new template and update the document styles.

If the styles in the new template have the same names as the styles in the original template, the formatting associated with the styles will change when you attach the new template. If the styles have different names, you can quickly restyle the document content by using commands available from the Styles pane. To replace the styles attached to content:

■ In the **Styles** pane, point to the old style name, click the arrow that appears, and click **Select All.** Then click the new style name.

To load a global template and make it available for use:

1 Display the **Templates and Add-ins** dialog box. In the **Global templates and add-ins** area, click **Add** to open the **Add Template** dialog box.

2 In the **Add Template** dialog box, navigate to the template you want to load, and then double-click it to enter the template name in the **Global templates and add-ins** pane. A check mark indicates that the template is active.

3 In the **Templates and Add-ins** dialog box, click **OK**.

TIP You can deactivate a global template (but keep it available for future use) by clearing its check box, and you can unload it by selecting it in the list and clicking Remove.

Creating and modifying styles

Even if you don't want to create your own templates, it's very useful to know how to create and modify styles. When you apply direct character formatting or paragraph formatting, you affect only the selected characters or paragraphs. If you change your mind about how you want to format a particular document element, you have to change the formatting manually everywhere it is applied. When you format characters or paragraphs by applying a style, you can change the way all of those characters or paragraphs look simply by changing the style definition. With one change in one place, you can completely change the look of the document.

You already know that when you create a blank document, it is based on the Normal template. Initially, the Normal template displays only a limited number of styles in the Styles gallery, but in fact it contains styles for just about every element you can think of. Although they are available, these styles aren't actually used unless you apply the style or add the corresponding element to the document. For example, nine paragraph styles are available for an index, but none of them is used until you create and insert an index in the document. You can access the unused styles and then manually apply them to characters and paragraphs in these ways:

- Clicking the **Styles** dialog box launcher displays the **Styles** pane. By default, the pane shows only the recommended styles in the document. Clicking **Options** at the bottom of the pane opens the **Style Pane Options** dialog box.

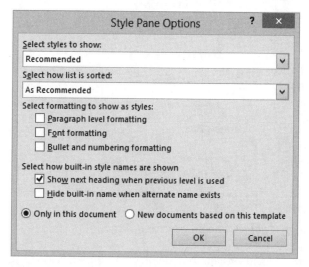

You can specify which styles should be shown and how.

By selecting **All Styles** in the **Select Styles to Show** list and **Alphabetical** in the **Select How List Is Sorted** list, you can display all the available styles (from all templates and global templates) in alphabetical order. You can then apply a style from the **Styles** pane by clicking it. If you prefer to display a preview of each style so that you can sort through styles visually, you can do so by selecting the **Show Preview** check box at the bottom of the pane.

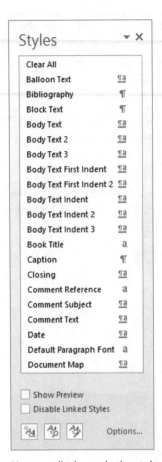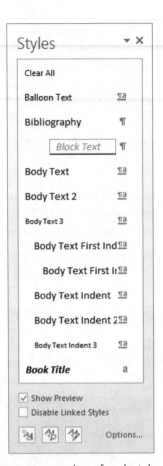

You can display only the style names, or a preview of each style.

TIP Selecting the Show Preview check box displays style names in the formatting assigned to the style. Pointing to a style displays its formatting specifications.

■ Clicking **Apply Styles** at the bottom of the **Styles** gallery on the **Home** tab opens the **Apply Styles** dialog box. If you don't have room to display the entire **Styles** pane, you can keep theis dialog box open while you work and apply or reapply styles from here.

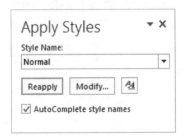

The Style Name box displays the style applied to the active selection.

Selecting a different style from the **Style Name** list applies it to the active paragraph or selected text. The **Style Name** list displays the same set of styles that are in the **Styles** pane; that is, if the pane shows only the styles in use, so does the **Style Name** list.

■ Right-clicking a style in the **Styles** pane, or pointing to the style and clicking the arrow that appears, and then clicking **Add to Style Gallery** adds the style to the **Styles** gallery on the **Home** tab of the ribbon.

There are three major types of styles, identified in the Styles pane by icons:

■ **Paragraph** These styles can include any formatting that can be applied to a paragraph. They can also include character formatting. Paragraph styles are applied to the entire paragraph containing the cursor. In the **Styles** pane, a paragraph style is identified by a paragraph mark to the right of its name.

■ **Character** These styles can include any formatting that can be applied to selected text. They are applied on top of the character formatting defined for the paragraph style. Like direct character formatting, character styles are applied to selected text; to apply them to an entire paragraph, you must select it.

■ **Linked** These styles are hybrids. If you click in a paragraph and then apply the style, the style is applied to the entire paragraph like a paragraph style. If you select text and then apply the style, the style is applied to the selection only.

> **TIP** Two additional style types, Table and List, are reserved for styles for those document elements.

The simplest way to customize the look of a document is to modify an existing style in one of the following ways:

■ Apply the style to a paragraph or selected text, and adjust the formatting so that the paragraph or selection looks the way you want it. Then update the style definition with the new formatting by right-clicking the style in the **Styles** gallery, or by clicking the arrow to the right of the style in the **Styles** pane, and then clicking **Update** *<style>* **to Match Selection**.

■ Right-click the style in the **Styles** gallery and click **Modify**; click the arrow to the right of the style in the **Styles** pane; or display the style name in the **Apply Styles** dialog box and click **Modify**. Then in the **Modify Style** dialog box, change the settings in the **Formatting** area to achieve the look you want.

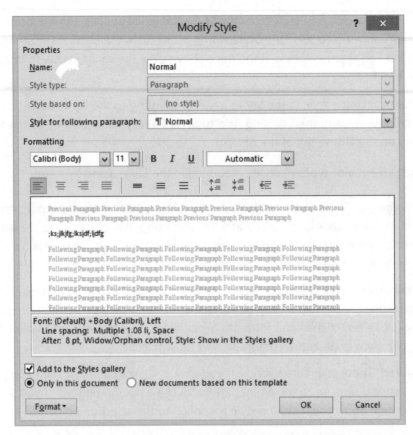

You can adjust the formatting definition of any style by changing the settings in this dialog box.

If you modify the existing styles, you can save the new style definitions as a style set. (Each new style must have the same name as its corresponding existing style.) Clicking Save As A New Style Set below the Style Set gallery on the Design tab opens the Save As A New Style Set dialog box, where you name the set. Without changing the storage location, click Save to save the style set in the QuickStyles folder. You can then make the style set accessible to any document by selecting it from the Style Set gallery.

SEE ALSO For information about switching style sets, see "Applying styles to text" in Chapter 3, "Modify the structure and appearance of text."

If you want to create a style rather than redefine an existing one, you apply the formatting you want for the style to a paragraph or selection and then click Create A Style below the Styles gallery on the Home tab, or click the New Style button at the bottom of the Styles pane, to open the Create New Style From Formatting dialog box.

Create New Style from Formatting   ?   ✕

Name:

Style1

Paragraph style preview:

Style1

| OK | Modify... | Cancel |

The Paragraph Style Preview box displays the formatting applied to the style name.

If you want to refine the definition of the new style, clicking Modify expands the dialog box so that it resembles the Modify Style dialog box. (You can go directly to the expanded dialog box by clicking the New Style button at the bottom of the Styles pane.) There you can specify the style name and type and all formatting for the style. If you are building on an existing style, you can select that style in the Style Based On list and then specify the formatting differences rather than defining the style from scratch. If you are creating the style as part of a new template, you can make the style part of the template instead of only part of the current document.

After you create the styles you want, you can remove those you don't want from the Styles gallery. by right-clicking the style in the gallery and clicking Remove From Style Gallery. The styles will still be available in the Styles pane, and you can add them back to the Styles gallery at any time by clicking the arrow to the right of the style in the pane and then clicking Add To Style Gallery. To remove a style from the Styles pane, click the arrow to the right of the style, click Delete or Revert To *<style>*, and then click Yes to confirm the deletion.

TIP The Delete command appears on the menu only for styles that aren't based on other styles. The Revert To command appears for styles that are based on other styles. You cannot delete a built-in style, but if you have modified it, you can revert it back to its original formatting.

In this exercise, you'll set up a location for personal templates, create a document based on a predefined Word template, modify the document, and save it as a personal template. You'll create a document based on the personal template. Then you'll modify the styles in an existing document, create new styles, personalize the Styles gallery, and save the document as a personal template.

→ SET UP You need the AuthorsBlank document located in the Chapter16 practice file folder, and an active Internet connection, to complete this exercise. Start Word, but don't open the document yet. Just follow the steps.

1   If you haven't previously configured a default personal templates folder, display the **Word Options** dialog box by clicking **Options** in the **Backstage** view. On the **Save** page of the **Word Options** dialog box, in the **Default personal templates location** box, enter the path to the folder in which you'd like to store templates that you create. If you don't already have a location in mind, copy the **Default local file location** path from the box above, and add Templates to the end. Then click **OK** to save the setting.

2   On the **New** page of the **Backstage** view, below the search box, click the **Fax** category to display thumbnails of facsimile message cover sheets.

   TIP After you configure a personal templates folder, Featured and Personal appear at the top of the New page. Clicking these links switches between displaying the featured templates and displaying the contents of your personal templates folder.

3   Scroll through the list, click a template that you like (we chose the **Basic Fax Cover** template), and then in the preview window, click **Create** to download the template, create a new fax cover page document based on the selected template, and fill in the information about you that Word has stored.

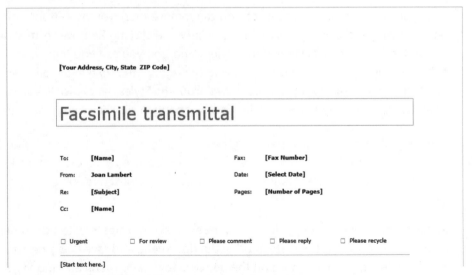

The fax cover page has placeholders for the text you need to supply.

4   Replace at least one placeholder with your own contact information. (Imagine that you're filling in the template with all the information that would be the same for each fax that you send.) Then make any formatting changes you want.

5   In the **Backstage** view, click the **Save As** page tab. In the left pane of the **Save As** page, click **Computer**, and then in the right pane, click the **Browse** button to open the **Save As** dialog box.

6   In the **Save as type** list, click **Word template**. Notice that the folder path in the **Address** bar changes to display your default personal templates folder.

7   In the **File name** box, enter My Fax Template. Then click **Save**.

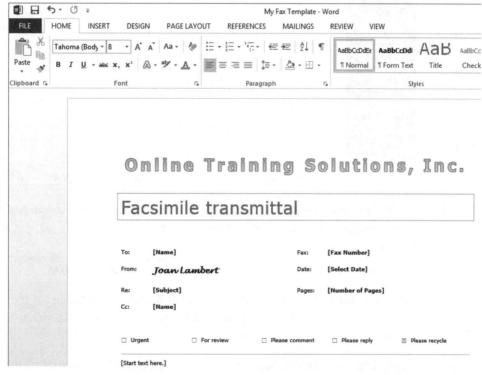

The new file name is shown in the title bar, but there is no indication that this is a template rather than a regular document.

8   In the **Backstage** view, click **Close** to close the template without quitting Word.

9   On the **New** page of the **Backstage** view, above the thumbnails, click **Personal** to display the contents of your personal templates folder.

TIP If you create a lot of your own templates, you can organize them by storing them in subfolders of your personal templates folder. You can create subfolders either by browsing to your personal templates folder in File Explorer and clicking the New Folder button, or by clicking the New Folder button in the Save As dialog box.

New

Search for online templates   🔎

Suggested searches: Letters   Resume   Fax   Labels   Cards   Calendar   Blank

FEATURED   PERSONAL

My Fax Template

The customized template is available when you display personal templates on the New page.

10   In the **Personal** templates list, click the **My Fax Template** thumbnail. Notice that
Word creates a new document based on your custom template without displaying
a preview pane.

Now we'll modify an existing document and save it as a template.

11   Open the **AuthorsBlank** document from the **Chapter16** practice file folder, and
then (if the **Styles** pane isn't open) click the **Styles** dialog box launcher to display
the **Styles** pane.

12   At the bottom of the **Styles** pane, click the **Options** link to open the **Style Pane
Options** dialog box.

13   In the **Select styles to show** list, click **In current document**. In the **Select how list
is sorted** list, click **Alphabetical**. Then click **OK**.

14   In the document, click **Select** and then **Select All** in the **Editing** group, or press
Ctrl+A, to select all the text in the document. With the text selected, set the font
to **Tahoma**.

15   Select the title and first heading, and change the font color to the first purple swatch
in the **Theme Colors** gallery (**Purple, Accent 4**).

16 Select the first paragraph below the **Author1** heading, and set the font size to **12** points.

17 Click anywhere in the **About the Authors** heading. In the **Styles** pane, point to (don't click) the active **Title** style, click the arrow that appears, and then click **Update Title to Match Selection** to change the font face and font color settings assigned to the style.

Now let's change the style so that the color of the line below the title coordinates with the font color of the title.

18 In the **Styles** pane, point to **Title**, click the arrow that appears, and then click **Modify** to open the **Modify Styles** dialog box. In the lower-left corner of the dialog box, click **Format** to display a list of formatting elements that can be modified for the style.

You can modify as many aspects of a style as you can of the document text.

19   On the **Format** menu, click **Border** to display the **Borders** page of the **Borders and Shading** dialog box. In the **Borders and Shading** dialog box, click the **Color** arrow and then in the **Theme Colors** palette, click the darkest purple swatch (**Purple, Accent 4, Darker 50%**). In the **Preview** area, click the existing blue border to change its color. Then click **OK** in both dialog boxes.

Now let's update the other styles we changed earlier.

20   Click anywhere in the **Author1** heading. In the **Styles** pane, right-click the active **Heading 1, h1** style, and then click **Update Heading 1 to Match Selection**. Notice that the formatting of the other two headings changes to match that of **Author1**. (Imagine the time savings of doing this in a document that has two dozen headings!)

21   Click anywhere in the **<paragraph1>** paragraph, and then update the **Normal** style to match the selection and update the remainder of the document content.

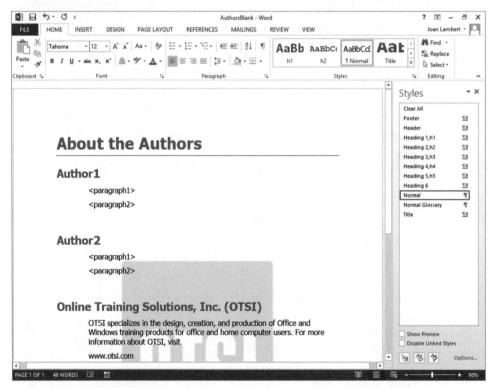

Updating a style changes the formatting of any paragraphs to which the style is applied.

22 Select the last paragraph in the document (the **Copyright** paragraph). Using the commands on the **Mini Toolbar**, change the font size to **9** points, and make the selection bold, underlined, and purple.

23 With the **Copyright** paragraph selected, in the **Styles** group, click the **More** button and then on the **Styles** menu, below the **Style** gallery, click **Create a Style** to open the **Create New Style from Formatting** dialog box.

24 In the **Name** box, replace **Style1** with Copyright, and then click **Modify** to expand the dialog box to display options for modifying the new style.

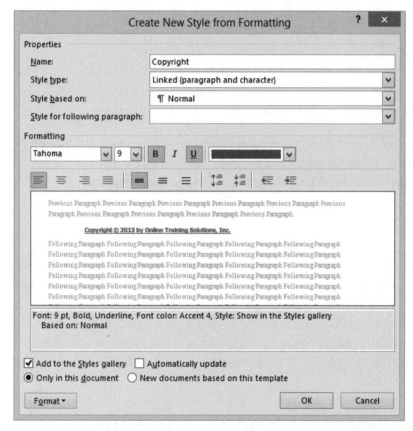

Because the Style Type is set to Linked, you will be able to apply this style to entire paragraphs or to only selected text.

25 At the bottom of the expanded dialog box, select the **New documents based on this template** option and then click **OK** to make the new style available to other documents that you create based on the **Normal** template.

26 Expand the **Styles** gallery to verify that the new style appears in the gallery.

The new style in the Styles gallery.

27 Repeat steps 5 through 7 to save the document as a template named **My Author Template** in your personal templates folder. Then verify that the template appears in the **Personal** area of the **New** page of the **Backstage** view.

✕ CLEAN UP Close the My Author Template file.

TIP If you want to make changes to the content or formatting that is part of an existing template, you must open the template file instead of creating a document based on the template. To edit a template, you can either display the contents of the folder that contains the template, right-click the template file, and then click Open, or display the Open page of the Backstage view, navigate to the template location, select the template, and click Open. Then in the Open dialog box, set the file type to Word Templates, navigate to your Templates folder, and double-click the template.

Creating custom building blocks

A building block is a document element that is saved in the Building Blocks global template. A building block can be as straightforward as a word, or as complicated as a page full of formatted elements. Many building blocks are provided with Word 2013, including professionally designed page elements such as cover pages, headers and footers, and sidebars; and content elements such as bibliographies, common equations, Quick Tables, and watermarks. You can use these building blocks to assemble or enhance a document.

SEE ALSO For information about working with building blocks to insert document elements such as cover pages, headers, footers, and page numbers, see "Inserting preformatted document parts" in Chapter 9, "Add visual elements."

You can save information and document elements that you use frequently as custom building blocks so that you can easily insert them into documents. A custom building block can be a simple phrase or sentence that you use often, or it can include multiple paragraphs, formatting, graphics, and so on. You need to create the element exactly as you want it only one time; then you can save it as a building block and use it confidently wherever you need it. You insert a custom building block into a document from the Quick Parts gallery on the Quick Parts menu.

To create a building block, you create and select the item you want to save, click Save Selection To Quick Parts Gallery on the Quick Parts menu, and assign a name to the building block. You can then insert the building block at the cursor by entering the building block name and pressing F3, or by displaying the Quick Parts gallery and clicking the thumbnail of the building block you want. Or you can insert it elsewhere by right-clicking the thumbnail in the gallery and then clicking one of the specified locations.

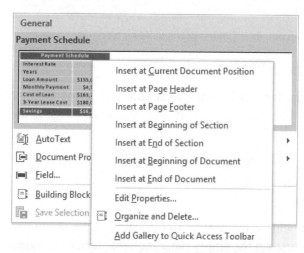

You can insert a custom building block by selecting a location from a list.

IMPORTANT When you exit Word after saving a custom building block, Word prompts you to save changes to the template in which you stored the building block. If you want the building block to be available for future documents, click Save; otherwise, click Don't Save.

In this exercise, you'll save information as building blocks in a custom category, insert the building block content in other documents, and then delete the building blocks.

SET UP You need the Bamboo and RoomFlyer documents located in the Chapter16 practice file folder to complete this exercise. Open the Bamboo document, and then follow the steps.

1   Select the first four lines of information at the top of the document.

2   On the **Insert** tab, in the **Text** group, click the **Quick Parts** button, and then click **Save Selection to Quick Part Gallery** to open the **Create New Building Block** dialog box.

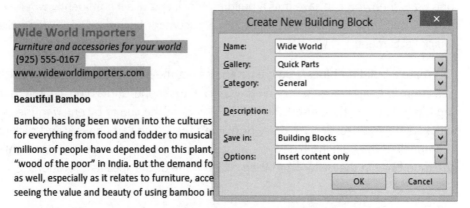

Word suggests text from the selection as the name of the building block.

3   In the **Name** box, enter Contact Block.

4   Click the **Category** arrow, and then click **Create New Category**. In the **Create New Category** dialog box, enter Company Information in the name box, and then click **OK**.

5   In the **Create New Building Block** dialog box, retain the default selections in the other fields, and then click **OK** to add the selection to the **Quick Parts** gallery and the **Building Blocks** template.

6   Open the **RoomFlyer** document. At the bottom of the right column of the cover page, click to position the cursor in the empty paragraph that follows **Call now to order!**

7   Enter Contact Block, and then press **F3** to replace the building block name with the four lines of text from the **Bamboo** document. Notice that the color of the company name changes, from orange to red, to reflect the theme colors of the destination document.

16

SIMPLE ROOM DESIGN

The building block picks up the formatting information from the document into which you insert it.

8   Display page **3** of the **RoomFlyer** document. Click the **Ordering Information** heading to activate the text box, and then click the text box that forms the sidebar to select it. On the **Insert** tab, in the **Text** group, click the **Quick Parts** button, and then click **Save Selection to Quick Part Gallery**.

9   In the **Create New Building Block** dialog box, enter Ordering Sidebar in the **Name** box, select **Company Information** from the **Category** list, enter Sidebar with ordering information in the **Description** box, and then click **OK**.

   TIP To save changes to a custom building block, modify the building block in the document and then save it to the Quick Parts gallery with the same name as the original, and then click Yes when Word prompts you to indicate whether you want to redefine the building block.

   Now we'll insert the building block we created in one document into another.

10   Display the **Bamboo** document. On the **Insert** tab, in the **Text** group, click the **Quick Parts** button. Notice that both building blocks are now available in the **Company Information** category.

The building blocks in the Quick Parts gallery reflect the color scheme of the current document.

TIP The Quick Parts gallery displays only the building blocks you create. The built-in building blocks are available from other galleries, such as the Cover Page gallery.

11   In the **Quick Parts** gallery, click **Ordering Sidebar** to insert the building block content as a sidebar on the current page. You can now update the information to reflect the ordering of bamboo furniture rather than the Room Planner.

Wide World Importers
Furniture and accessories for your world
(925) 555-0167
www.wideworldimporters.com

Beautiful Bamboo

Bamboo has long been woven into the cultures of many countries, where it has historically been used for everything from food and fodder to musical instruments and construction material. For centuries, millions of people have depended on this plant, which is known as "friend of the people" in China,

ORDERING
INFORMATION

To order the Room Planner for just $39.99 plus shipping and handling, visit our website, at www.wideworldimporters.com or call us at 925-555-0167. We accept all major credit cards.

Custom building blocks make it easy to insert specific text and objects in any document.

12   In the **Text** group, on the **Quick Parts** menu, click **Building Blocks Organizer**. In the **Building Blocks Organizer** dialog box, click the **Template** heading to bring your custom building blocks to the top of the list. Then click **Ordering Sidebar** one time to view the custom building block in the preview pane.

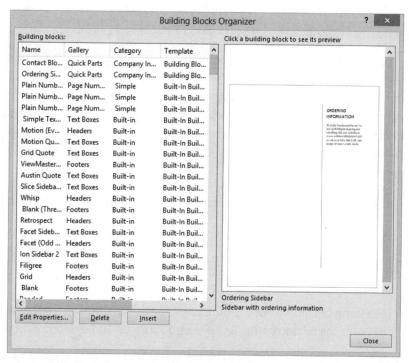

Custom building blocks are stored in the Building Blocks template, and built-in building blocks are stored in the Built-In Building Blocks template.

TIP Modifying a built-in building block saves a copy of it in the Building Blocks template and retains the unchanged original in the Built-In Building Blocks template.

Now we'll delete the custom building blocks to revert to the default set.

13 In the **Building Blocks Organizer** dialog box, click the **Delete** button and then click **Yes** when Word prompts you to indicate whether you want to delete the selected building block.

14 Repeat step 13 to delete the **Contact Block** building block. Then close the **Building Blocks Organizer** dialog box.

❌ CLEAN UP Close the Bamboo and RoomFlyer documents, saving your changes if you want to. If Word prompts you to indicate whether you want to save changes to the Building Blocks template, click Don't Save.

Changing default program options

In earlier chapters, we mentioned that you can change settings in the Word Options dialog box to customize the Word environment in various ways. For example, we told you how to create AutoCorrect entries, how to adjust the save period for AutoRecover information, and how to recheck the spelling and grammar of a document. After you work with Word for a while, you might want to refine more settings to tailor the program to the way you work. Knowing which settings are where in the Word Options dialog box makes the customizing process more efficient.

In this exercise, you'll open the Word Options dialog box and explore several of the available pages.

 **SET UP** You don't need any practice files to complete this exercise. With a blank document open, follow the steps.

1   On the **Home** tab, in the **Font** group, point to the **Bold** button to display a ScreenTip that includes the button name, its keyboard shortcut, and a description of its purpose.

> **SEE ALSO** For information about keyboard shortcuts, see "Keyboard shortcuts" at the end of this book.

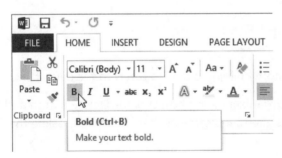

A default ScreenTip.

2   Click the **File** tab to display the **Backstage** view, and click **Options** to display the **General** page of the **Word Options** dialog box.

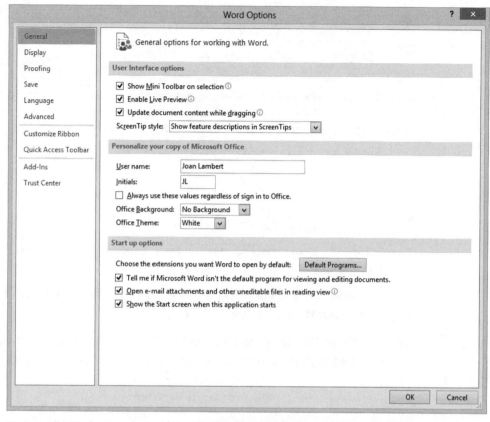

You can disable features such as the Mini Toolbar and the Live Preview of styles from this page.

3   In the **User Interface options** area, in the **ScreenTip style** list, click **Don't show feature descriptions in ScreenTips**.

4   In the **Personalize your copy of Microsoft Office** area, verify that the **User name** and **Initials** are correct, or change them to the way you want them to appear. In the **Office Background** list, click **Stars**. In the **Office Theme** list, click **Dark Gray**.

    TIP Changing any of the settings in the Personalize Your Copy Of Microsoft Office area in any Microsoft Office 2013 program changes it in all the programs.

5   Click **OK** to close the **Word Options** dialog box. Notice that the title bar is now a dark gray color that displays a pattern of stars.

6   In the **Font** group, point to the **Bold** button to display the ScreenTip, which now includes only the button name and its keyboard shortcut.

In the Dark Gray color scheme, the File tab and status bar in all Office 2013 programs are black.

7   In the document, enter I cant spel verry wel. Then press **Enter**.

I cant spel very wel.

The spelling and grammar checking utilities mark three of the words for review, and the AutoCorrect function changes verry to very.

You can control the functionality that Word uses from the Word Options dialog box. We'll leave this text here for now and look at it again later.

8   Open the **Word Options** dialog box, and click the **Display** page tab to display options for adjusting how documents look on the screen and when printed.

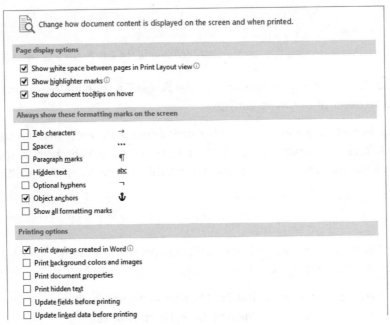

The Display page of the Word Options dialog box.

9   In the **Always show these formatting marks on the screen** area, select the **Show all formatting marks** check box.

10   Click the **Proofing** page tab to display options for adjusting the **AutoCorrect** settings and for refining the spell-checking and grammar-checking processes.

SEE ALSO For information about AutoCorrect and checking spelling, see "Correcting spelling and grammatical errors" in Chapter 2, "Enter, edit and proofread text."

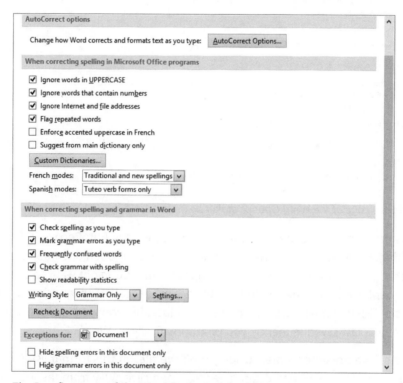

The Proofing page of the Word Options dialog box.

11   In the **Exceptions for** area, select the **Hide spelling errors in this document only** and **Hide grammar errors in this document only** check boxes.

12   Click the **Save** page tab to display options for saving, editing, and sharing documents.

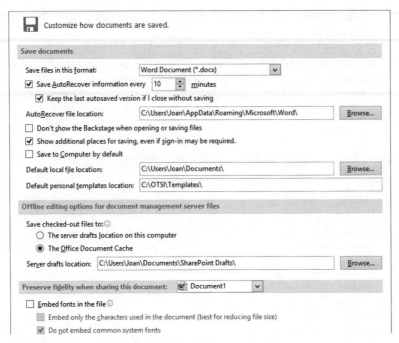

The Save page of the Word Options dialog box.

An important setting to notice on this page is the Save AutoRecover Information Every setting. By default, Word saves a backup copy of your open documents every 10 minutes. If you are working on important documents, you might want to autosave more frequently. If Word unexpectedly shuts down, it recovers the most recently saved version when it next starts, so you can only lose the work you've done since the document was last saved (either by you or automatically by Word).

13   In the **Save documents** area, display the **Save files in this format** list. Notice the many formats in which you can save files. Then click away from the list to close it.

TIP If you want to save all documents by default as a certain file type, choose that file type here. If you want to save only one document in a format that is compatible with earlier versions of the program, choose that file type in the Save As Type list of the Save As dialog box.

14   Select the **Save to Computer by default** check box to have Word choose **Computer** as the default location on the **Save As** page, instead of your Microsoft SkyDrive.

Notice that the Default Personal Templates Location reflects the location you set earlier in this chapter.

15   Click the **Language** page tab to display options for setting the editing, display, Help, and ScreenTip languages.

As with some of the options that you set on the General page of the Word Options dialog box, the options you set on the Language page apply to all the Office programs installed on your computer.

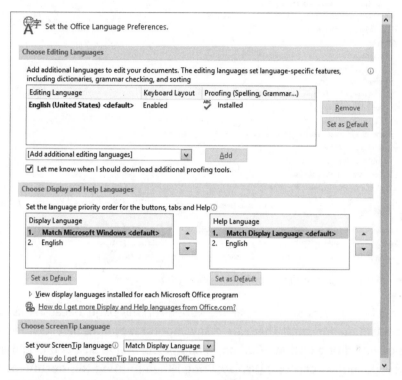

The Language page of the Word Options dialog box.

16   In the **Set your ScreenTip language** list, click **Spanish (Spain) [español]**.

17   Click the **Advanced** page tab to display options related to editing document content; displaying documents on screen; printing, saving, and sharing documents; and a variety of others. Although these options are labeled **Advanced**, they are the ones you're most likely to want to adjust to suit the way you work.

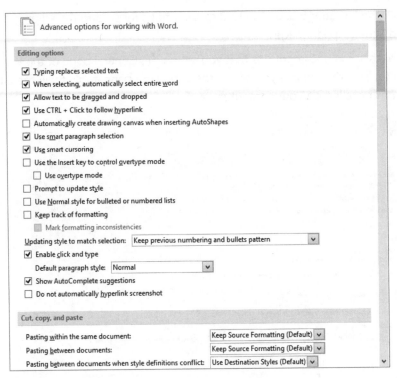

The Advanced page of the Word Options dialog box.

18 Take a few minutes to explore all the options on this page, because this is where you'll find the fun stuff! There are many important options here, divided into sections including **Editing options; Cut, copy, and paste; Image Size and Quality; Chart; Show document content; Display; Print; When printing this document; Save; Preserve fidelity when sharing this document; General; Layout options for;** and **Compatibility options for**.

> **TIP** The File Locations and Web Options buttons at the bottom of the General area allow you to change the default locations of various types of files and adjust the default settings for converting a document to a webpage. For information about converting a Word document to a webpage, see "Creating and modifying web documents" in Chapter 11, "Create documents for use outside of Word."

Some of the options can be set for the current document (the default) or for all new documents. These options have a drop-down list in the section title bar.

19 In the **Display** area, set **Show this number of Recent Documents** to **6** (the default number of documents to display is 25). Select the **Quickly access this number of**

Recent Documents check box, and set it to **3** (the default is 4). Then set **Show this number of unpinned Recent Folders** to **3** (the default is 5).

20   Skipping over the **Customize Ribbon, Quick Access Toolbar**, and **Add-Ins** pages, which we discuss later in this chapter, click the **Trust Center** page tab to display links to information about privacy and security.

21   In the **Microsoft Word Trust Center** area, click **Trust Center Settings** to open the **Trust Center** dialog box. From this dialog box, you can control the actions Word takes in response to documents that are provided by certain people or companies, that are saved in certain locations, or that contain ActiveX controls or macros.

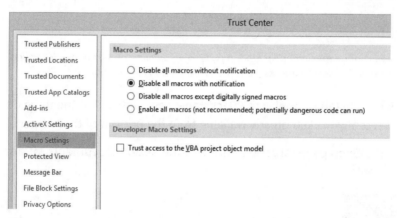

The Macro Settings page of the Trust Center dialog box.

22   Review each of the pages of the **Trust Center** dialog box, because there will very likely be settings here that you want or need to configure either now or in the future. Then click **Cancel** to return to the **Word Options** dialog box.

23   In the **Word Options** dialog box, click **OK** to save the changes you've made and return to the document.

Now let's review the effects of your changes.

24   On the document page, notice that the formatting marks are visible, and squiggly underlines no longer indicate possible spelling or grammar errors in the sentence you entered. Point to the **Bold** button, and notice that the ScreenTip says **Negrita**.

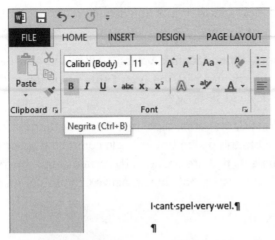

I·cant·spel·very·wel.¶

¶

You can change the ScreenTip language, turn off spelling and grammar checking, and turn on formatting marks from the Word Options dialog box.

25 Click the **File** tab to display the **Backstage** view. Notice that the three documents you most recently worked on are available from the bottom of the left pane.

26 Click the **Open** page tab, and notice that the **Recent Documents** list displays only six documents.

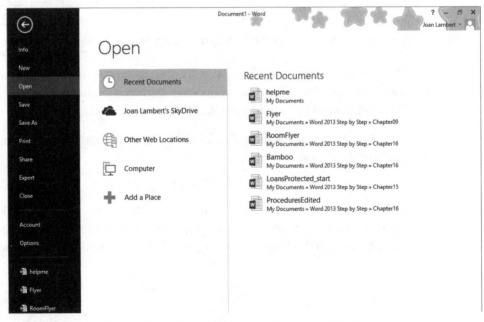

You can customize the way that files and folders are displayed in the Backstage view.

27   Click the **Save As** page tab, and notice that **Computer** is selected in the left pane, and the **Recent Folders** list displays only three folders, plus the **My Documents** and **Desktop** folders (these system folders are always in the list and are not counted among the unpinned folders).

> **TIP** If you have any pinned folders, they will also be shown. To pin a folder to the list, point to the folder name and then click the pushpin icon that appears.

28   In the **Backstage** view, click **Options** to return to the **Word Options** dialog box. Reverse any changes that you don't want to keep in your working environment, and then click **OK** to close the dialog box and save your changes.

> **TIP** We changed the Office background back to No Background and the Office theme to White so as to not clutter up the screen shots in other exercises. We also reset the ScreenTip, ScreenTip language, formatting marks, and file and folder display settings.

✖ CLEAN UP Close the document without saving your changes.

Customizing the Quick Access Toolbar

By default, buttons representing the Save, Undo, and Redo commands appear on the Quick Access Toolbar. If you regularly use a few commands that are scattered on various tabs of the ribbon and you don't want to switch between tabs to access the commands, you might want to add them to the Quick Access Toolbar so that they're always available to you.

> **TIP** If you have upgraded to Word 2013 from Word 2003 or an earlier version, you might have identified a few commands that no longer seem to be available. A few old features have been abandoned, but others that people used only rarely have simply been pushed off to one side. If you sorely miss one of these sidelined features, you can make it a part of your Word environment by adding it to the Quick Access Toolbar or to the ribbon. You can find a list of all the commands that do not appear on the ribbon but that are still available in Word by displaying the Quick Access Toolbar or Customize Ribbon page of the Word Options dialog box and then clicking Commands Not In The Ribbon in the Choose Commands From list.

16

There are three ways to add commands to the Quick Access Toolbar:

- From the **Customize Quick Access Toolbar** menu that appears when you click the button at the right end of the **Quick Access Toolbar**. Some of the most common commands, including the popular **Quick Print** command, are available from this list.

- By right-clicking a command on the ribbon and then clicking **Add to Quick Access Toolbar**. You can add any type of command this way; you can even add a drop-down list of options or gallery of thumbnails.

- From the **Quick Access Toolbar** page of the **Word Options** dialog box. On this page, you can customize the **Quick Access Toolbar** in the following ways:

  - You can define a custom **Quick Access Toolbar** for all documents, or you can define a custom **Quick Access Toolbar** for a specific document.

  - You can add any command from any group of any tab, including tool tabs, to the toolbar.

  - You can display a separator between different types of buttons.

  - You can move commands around on the toolbar until they are in the order you want.

  - You can reset everything back to the default **Quick Access Toolbar** configuration.

After you add commands to the Quick Access Toolbar, you can reorganize them and divide them into groups to simplify the process of locating the command you want.

As you add commands to the Quick Access Toolbar, it expands to accommodate them. If you add a lot of commands, it might become difficult to view the text in the title bar, or all the commands on the Quick Access Toolbar might not be visible, defeating the purpose of adding them. To resolve this problem, you can move the Quick Access Toolbar below the ribbon by clicking the Customize Quick Access Toolbar button and then clicking Show Below The Ribbon.

In this exercise, you'll add commands to the Quick Access Toolbar for all documents, then organize and test the commands.

SET UP You need the Agenda document located in the Chapter16 practice file folder to complete this exercise. Open the document, and then follow the steps.

1　On the **Home** tab, in the **Font** group, right-click the **Text Highlight Color** arrow, and then click **Add to Quick Access Toolbar** to add the command and gallery to the toolbar.

2　At the right end of the **Quick Access Toolbar**, click the **Customize Quick Access Toolbar** button.

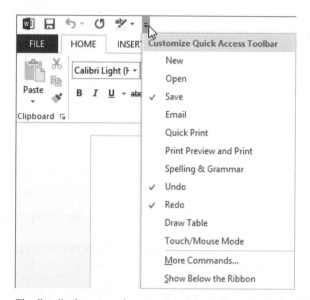

The list displays popular commands; check marks indicate those that are currently displayed.

3　On the **Customize Quick Access Toolbar** menu, click **Spelling & Grammar** to add that button to the toolbar.

4　On the **Customize Quick Access Toolbar** menu, click **More Commands** to display the **Quick Access Toolbar** page of the **Word Options** dialog box. Available commands are shown on the left, and the commands currently displayed on the **Quick Access Toolbar** are shown on the right.

You can filter the available commands by choosing a category from the list on the left.

5   In the **Choose commands from** list, click **File Tab**. In the left list, click **E-mail as PDF Attachment**. Then click the **Add** button to add the command to the list on the right.

6   In the **Choose commands from** list, click **View Tab**. In the list on the left, double-click **Open the Navigation Pane** to add the command to the list on the right.

7   In the **Choose commands from** list, click **Developer Tab**. Scroll to the bottom of the list, and double-click **Templates** to add the command to the list on the right.

TIP The Developer tab isn't displayed on the ribbon by default. If you use only one or two commands from that tab, you can add them to the Quick Access Toolbar rather than cluttering up the ribbon with an additional tab.

Now we'll organize the commands on the Quick Access Toolbar.

8   In the list on the right, click **Redo**. Then at the top of the list on the left, double-click **<Separator>** to insert a separator after the selected command.

9   In the list on the right, click **Open the Navigation Pane**. Click the up arrow to the right of the list three times to position the command just below the separator. Then in the list on the left, double-click **Separator**.

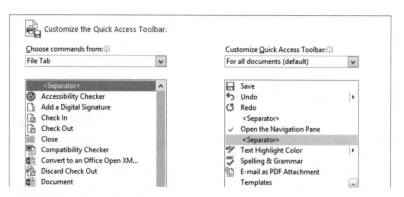

The arrows to the right of the Text Highlight Color and Templates commands indicate that clicking these buttons on the Quick Access Toolbar will display additional options.

TIP To create a Quick Access Toolbar that is specific to the active document, click the arrow at the right end of the box below Customize Quick Access Toolbar, and then click For *<name of document>*. Then any command you select will be added to that specific toolbar instead of the toolbar for all documents.

10 Click **OK** to close the **Word Options** dialog box. The **Quick Access Toolbar** now includes the default buttons and the additional commands you've added.

Now we'll display the Quick Access Toolbar in a more convenient location.

11 On the **Customize Quick Access Toolbar** menu, click **Show Below the Ribbon** to move the **Quick Access Toolbar** close to the document content.

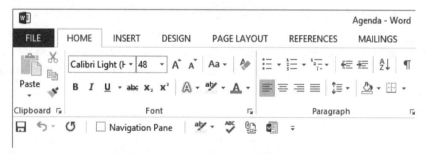

The customized Quick Access Toolbar is at your service!

Now let's experience how much more efficient it is to work with commands on the Quick Access Toolbar rather than the ribbon. You can perform each of these actions from another area of the user interface, but you can perform them with fewer clicks from the Quick Access Toolbar.

12 On the **Quick Access Toolbar**, select the **Navigation Pane** check box.

13   In the **Navigation** pane, click **Preliminaries**. In the document, select the first high-lighted paragraph, **Proof of notice of meeting**. On the **Quick Access Toolbar**, click the **Text Highlight Color** arrow, and then click **No Color** to remove the yellow high-light from the selection. Notice that the **No Color** option becomes the default for the **Text Highlight Color** button.

14   Select the next highlighted paragraph, and on the **Quick Access Toolbar**, click the **Text Highlight Color** button to remove the yellow highlight from the selection.

15   On the **Quick Access Toolbar**, click the **Spelling & Grammar** button to proof the document; click **OK** in the message box that appears when the process completes.

16   Experiment with any other **Quick Access Toolbar** options you want to. Then display the **Quick Access Toolbar** page of the **Word Options** dialog box, click **Reset**, and click **Reset only Quick Access Toolbar**.

17   In the **Reset Customizations** message box, click **Yes** to return the **Quick Access Toolbar** to its default contents. Then click **OK** to close the **Word Options** dialog box.

❌ CLEAN UP Close the Navigation pane and move the Quick Access Toolbar above the ribbon if you want to. Then close the Agenda document, saving your changes if you want to.

Using add-ins

Add-ins are utilities that add specialized functionality to a program (but aren't full-fledged programs themselves). Word uses two primary types of add-ins: COM add-ins and Word add-ins. The first type uses the Component Object Model to create utilities that extend the functionality of Office programs. The second type includes templates that incorporate sophisticated functionality such as macros.

There are several sources of add-ins:

- You can purchase add-ins from third-party vendors—for example, you can pur-chase an add-in that augments the ability to work with numbers in tables.

- You can download free add-ins from the Microsoft website or other websites.

- When you install a third-party program, it might also install an add-in to allow it to communicate with Office programs. For example, certain non-Microsoft programs install add-ins that enable the program to send content as an email message attachment.

You can view and manage installed add-ins from the Add-Ins page of the Word Options dialog box.

Your Add-Ins page will likely contain different add-ins in the Active, Document Related, and Disabled categories.

To unload an add-in, click the add-in category in the Manage list and then click Go to open the Add-Ins dialog box. In the dialog box, clear the check box of the add-in you want to unload. This removes the add-in from memory but keeps its name in the list. To permanently remove an add-in from the list, click the add-in name, and then click Remove. (This completely deletes the add-in, so be sure you want to do so before you click the button.)

IMPORTANT Be careful when downloading add-ins from websites other than those you trust. Add-ins are executable files that can easily be used to spread viruses and otherwise wreak havoc on your computer. For this reason, default settings in the Trust Center intervene when you attempt to download or run add-ins.

Customizing the ribbon

Even if Word 2013 is the first version of Word you have ever worked with, you will by now be accustomed to working with commands represented as buttons on the ribbon. The ribbon was designed to make all the commonly used commands visible, so that people could more easily discover the full potential of the program. But many people use Word to perform the same set of tasks all the time, and for them, the visibility of buttons (or even entire groups of buttons) that they never use is just another form of clutter.

Would you prefer to display fewer commands, not more? Or would you prefer to display more specialized groups of commands? Well, you can. Clicking Customize Ribbon in the left pane of the Word Options dialog box displays the Customize Ribbon page.

The Customize Ribbon page of the Word Options dialog box.

On this page, you can customize the ribbon in the following ways:

- You can hide an entire tab.

- You can remove a group of commands from a tab. (The group is not removed from the program, only from the tab.)

- You can move or copy a group of commands to another tab.

- You can create a custom group on any tab and then add commands to it. (You cannot add commands to a predefined group.)

- You can create a custom tab. For example, you might want to do this if you use only a few commands from each tab and you find it inefficient to flip between them.

Don't be afraid to experiment with the ribbon to come up with the configuration that best suits the way you work. If at any point you find that your new ribbon is harder to work with rather than easier, you can easily reset everything back to the default configuration.

IMPORTANT Although customizing the default ribbon content might seem like a great way of making the program yours, we don't recommend doing so. A great deal of research has been done about the way that people use the commands in each program, and the ribbon has been organized to reflect the results of that research. If you modify the default ribbon settings, you might end up inadvertently hiding or moving commands that you need. Instead, consider the Quick Access Toolbar to be the command area that you customize and make your own. If you add all the commands you use frequently to the Quick Access Toolbar, you can hide the ribbon and have extra vertical space for document display (this is most convenient when working on a smaller device). Or if you really want to customize the ribbon, do so by gathering your most frequently used commands on a custom tab, and leave the others alone.

In this exercise, you'll add a custom tab to the ribbon, add groups of commands to the tab, and change the position of the tab on the ribbon. You'll move groups of commands from one tab to another, and hide tabs. Then you'll reset the ribbon to its default state.

 SET UP You don't need any practice files to complete this exercise. With a blank document open, follow the steps.

1   With the **Home** tab active, display the **Word Options** dialog box, and then click the **Customize Ribbon** page tab.

   TIP To quickly display the Customize Ribbon page of the Word Options dialog box, right-click anywhere on the ribbon other than in a gallery, and then click Customize The Ribbon.

2   On the **Customize Ribbon** page, click the **New Tab** button to insert a new custom tab below the active **Home** tab in the right pane.

TIP You can clear the check box of any tab other than the File tab to hide that tab. (You can't hide the File tab.)

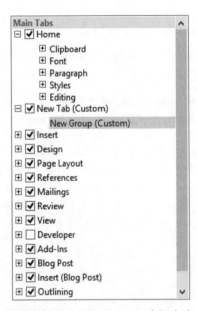

By default, a new custom tab includes an empty custom group.

3   Click **New Tab (Custom)** and then click the **Rename** button. In the **Rename** dialog box, replace **New Tab** with My Tab, and then click **OK** to rename the tab.

4   Click **New Group (Custom)** and then click the **Rename** button to open a **Rename** dialog box that includes icons.

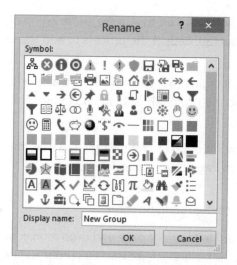

The icon you choose for your group is displayed on the group button when the ribbon is not wide enough to display the group.

5   In the **Rename** dialog box, click an icon that you like (naturally, we chose the happy face) and replace **New Group** with My Favorite Commands. Then click **OK**.

Now we'll add some commands to the custom group.

6   In the **Choose commands from** list, click **Main Tabs**. Then in the list, click the plus sign adjacent to **Review** to display the groups that are predefined for this tab, and click the plus sign adjacent to **Proofing** to display the commands in that group. In the **Proofing** group, click **Word Count**, and then click **Add** to add the command to your custom tab.

7   Expand the **Tracking** group, expand the **Track Changes** menu group, and then add the **Track Changes** command to your custom tab.

8   Click the **Comments** group, and then click **Add** to add the entire group of commands after the custom group on the new tab. Repeat the process to add the **Changes** group to the custom tab.

For the purposes of this exercise, imagine that you have added all the Review tab commands you will ever use to your custom tab, and you no longer need the Review tab.

9   In the right pane, clear the **Review** check box to remove the tab from the ribbon. Then click the plus sign adjacent to **Page Layout** to display the groups of commands on that tab.

Now let's modify the custom tab contents and position.

10   Drag the **Page Setup** group upward in the right pane and drop it on your custom tab, after the **Changes** group. (A thick black line indicates its progress.) Repeat this process to move the **Paragraph** and **Arrange** groups to follow the **Page Setup** group. Then clear the **Page Layout** check box to hide the now-empty tab.

11   In the right pane, click **My Tab**. Click the up arrow one time to move your custom tab above the **Home** tab in the list.

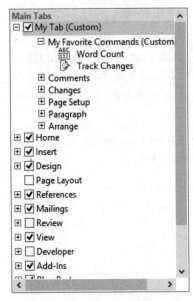

The order from top to bottom in the pane determines the order from left to right on the ribbon.

12   Click **OK** to close the **Word Options** dialog box and display the results. **My Tab** appears at the left end of the ribbon, immediately following the **File** tab. The **Page Layout** and **Review** tabs are missing from the ribbon.

13   Click **My Tab** to display the contents of your custom tab.

The custom tab includes your custom group and the groups you added from other sources.

14   If the program window is maximized, restore it. Then drag the right edge of the window to the left, to narrow the window until the ribbon can no longer display the groups.

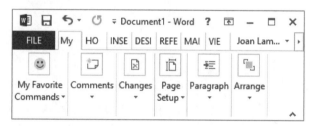

The group icon you chose appears on the group button.

15   Display the **Customize Ribbon** page of the **Word Options** dialog box. In the lower-right corner, click the **Reset** button, and then click **Reset all customizations**. In the message box asking you to confirm that you want to delete all ribbon and **Quick Access Toolbar** customizations, click **Yes**.

16   Click **OK** to close the **Word Options** dialog box.

❌ CLEAN UP   Close the document without saving your changes.

Customizing the status bar

You can easily add or remove indicators from the status bar by right-clicking any blank area of the status bar and then, on the Customize Status Bar menu, clicking the indicator you want to add or remove.

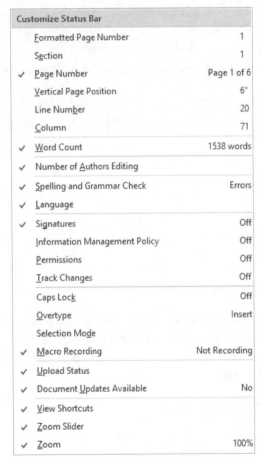

Customize Status Bar	
Formatted Page Number	1
Section	1
✓ Page Number	Page 1 of 6
Vertical Page Position	6"
Line Number	20
Column	71
✓ Word Count	1538 words
✓ Number of Authors Editing	
✓ Spelling and Grammar Check	Errors
✓ Language	
✓ Signatures	Off
Information Management Policy	Off
Permissions	Off
Track Changes	Off
Caps Lock	Off
Overtype	Insert
Selection Mode	
✓ Macro Recording	Not Recording
✓ Upload Status	
✓ Document Updates Available	No
✓ View Shortcuts	
✓ Zoom Slider	
✓ Zoom	100%

On the Customize Status Bar menu, a check mark indicates a control that is currently shown or will be shown when related information is available.

Key points

- The Word environment is flexible and can be customized to meet your needs.

- You can create styles and templates to speed up the work of formatting a document. Styles and templates ensure that formatting is consistent within a document and between documents.

- You don't have to enter and proof the same text over and over again. Instead, save the text as a building block and insert it with a few mouse clicks.

- Most of the settings that control the working environment are available from the pages of the Word Options dialog box.

- You can provide one-click access to any Word 2013 command by adding a button for it to the Quick Access Toolbar, either for all documents or for one document.

- You can customize the ribbon to put precisely the document development tools you need at your fingertips.

16

Glossary

accessible content Content that is optimized for consumers with disabilities and for assistive devices such as electronic readers.

add-in A utility that adds specialized functionality to a program but does not operate as an independent program.

aspect ratio The ratio of the width of an image to its height.

attribute An individual item of character formatting, such as size or color, that determines how text looks.

AutoCorrect A feature that automatically detects and corrects misspelled words and incorrect capitalization. You can add your own AutoCorrect entries.

AutoShape One of a wide array of predrawn shapes provided by Word to assist you with creating more complex pictures.

background The colors, shading, texture, and graphics, that appear behind the text and objects in a document.

balloon In Print Layout view or Web Layout view, a box that shows comments and tracked changes in the margins of a document, making it easy to review and respond to them.

bar chart A chart with bars that compares the quantities of two or more items.

blog A frequently updated online journal or column. Blogs are often used to publish personal or company information in an informal way. Short for *web log*.

bookmark A location or section of text that is electronically marked so that it can be returned to at a later time. Like a physical bookmark, a Word bookmark marks a specific location in a document. You can quickly display a specific

bookmark from the Go To page of the Find And Replace dialog box.

building block Frequently used text saved in a gallery, from which it can be inserted quickly into a document.

caption Descriptive text associated with a figure, photo, illustration, or screen shot.

category axis The axis used for plotting categories of data in a chart. Also called the *x-axis*.

cell A box formed by the intersection of a row and column in a worksheet or a table, in which you enter information.

cell address The location of a cell, expressed as its column letter and row number, as in *A1*.

character formatting Formatting you can apply to selected typographical characters.

character spacing The distance between characters in a line of text. Can be adjusted by pushing characters apart (expanding) or squeezing them together (condensing).

character style A combination of any character formatting options identified by a style name.

chart area A region in a chart object that is used to position chart elements, render axes, and plot data.

chevron A small control or button that indicates that there are more items than can be displayed in the allotted space. You click the chevron to display the additional items. Also the « and » characters that surround each merge field in a main document; also known as *guillemet characters*.

Click and Type A feature that allows you to double-click a blank area of a document to position the cursor in that location, with the appropriate paragraph alignment already in place.

clip art Pre-made images that are distributed without copyright. Usually cartoons, sketches, illustrations, or photographs.

Clipboard A storage area shared by all Microsoft Office programs where cut or copied items are stored.

column Either the vertical arrangement of text into one or more side-by-side sections or the vertical arrangement of cells in a table.

column break A break inserted in the text of a column to force the text below it to move to the next column.

column chart A chart that displays data in vertical bars to facilitate data comparison.

comment A note or annotation that an author or reviewer adds to a document. Word displays the comment in a balloon in the margin of the document or in the Reviewing pane.

contextual tab See *tool tab*.

cross-reference entry An entry in an index that refers readers to a related entry.

cursor A representation on the screen of the input device pointer location.

cycle diagram A diagram that shows a continuous process.

data marker A customizable symbol or shape that identifies a data point on a chart. Data markers can be bars, columns, pie or doughnut slices, dots, and various other shapes and can be various sizes and colors.

data point An individual value plotted in a chart.

data series Related data points that are plotted in a chart. One or more data series in a chart can be plotted. A pie chart has just one data series.

data source A file containing variable information, such as names and addresses, that is merged with a main document containing static information.

demoting In an outline, changing a heading to body text or to a lower heading level; for example, changing from Heading 5 to Heading 6. See also *promoting*.

desktop publishing A process that creates pages by combining text and objects, such as tables and graphics, in a visually appealing way.

destination file The file into which a linked or embedded object or mail merge data is inserted. When you change information in a destination file, the information is not updated in the source file. See also *source file*.

diagram A graphic in which shapes, text, and pictures are used to illustrate a process, cycle, or relationship.

dialog box launcher On the ribbon, a button at the bottom of some groups that opens a dialog box with features related to the group.

digital signature Data that binds a sender's identity to the information being sent. A digital signature may be bundled with any message, file, or other digitally encoded information, or transmitted separately. Digital signatures are used in public key environments and provide authentication and integrity services.

Document Inspector A tool that automates the process of detecting and removing all extraneous and confidential information from a document.

Draft view A document view that displays the content of a document with a simplified layout.

drag-and-drop editing A way of moving or copying selected text by dragging it from one location to another.

dragging A way of moving objects by selecting them and then, while the selection device is active (for example, while you are holding down the mouse button), moving the selection to the new location.

drawing canvas A work area for creating pictures in Word. The drawing canvas keeps the parts of the picture together, helps you position the picture, and provides a framelike boundary between your picture and the text on the page.

drawing object Any graphic you draw or insert that can be changed and enhanced. Drawing objects include AutoShapes, curves, lines, and WordArt.

drop cap An enlarged, decorative capital letter that appears at the beginning of a paragraph.

embedded object An object that is wholly inserted into a file. Embedding the object, rather than simply inserting or pasting its contents, ensures that the object retains its original format. If you open the embedded object, you can edit it with the toolbars and menus from the program used to create it.

endnote A note that appears at the end of a section or document and that is referenced by text in the main body of the document. An endnote consists of two linked parts, a reference mark within the main body of text and the corresponding text of the note. See also *footnote*.

Extensible Markup Language (XML) A format for delivering rich, structured data in a standard, consistent way. XML tags describe the content of a document, whereas HTML tags describe how the document looks. XML is extensible because it allows designers to create their own customized tags.

field A placeholder that tells Word to supply the specified information in the specified way. Also, the set of information of a specific type in a data source, such as all the last names in a contacts list.

field name A first-row cell in a data source that identifies data in the column below.

file format The structure or organization of data in a file. The file format of a document is usually indicated by the file name extension.

filtering Displaying files or records in a data source that meet certain criteria; for example, filtering a data source so that you display only the records for people who live in a particular state. Filtering does not delete files, it simply changes the view so that you display only the files that meet your criteria.

font A graphic design applied to a collection of numbers, symbols, and characters. A font describes a certain typeface, which can have qualities such as size, spacing, and pitch.

font effect An attribute, such as superscript, small capital letters, or shadow, that can be applied to a font.

font size The height (in points) of a collection of characters, where one point is equal to approximately 1/72 of an inch.

font style The emphasis placed on a font by using formatting such as bold, italic, underline, or color.

footer One or more lines of text in the bottom margin area of a page in a document, typically containing elements such as the page number and the name of the file. See also *header*.

footnote A note that appears at the end of a page that explains, comments on, or provides references for text in the main body of a document. A footnote consists of two linked parts, a reference mark within the main body of the document and the corresponding text of the note. See also *endnote*.

formatting See *character formatting* and *paragraph formatting*.

formula A sequence of values, cell references, names, functions, or operators in a cell of a table or worksheet that together produce a new value. A formula always begins with an equal sign (=).

gallery A grouping of thumbnails that display options visually.

graphic Any piece of art used to illustrate or convey information or to add visual interest to a document.

grayscale The spectrum (range) of shades of black in an image.

gridlines In a table, thin lines that indicate the cell boundaries. Table gridlines do not print when you print a document. In a chart, lines that visually carry the y-axis values across the plot area.

group On a ribbon tab, an area containing buttons related to a specific document element or function.

grouping Assembling several objects, such as shapes, into a single unit so that they act as one object. Grouped objects can easily be moved, sized, and formatted.

header A line, or lines, of content in the top margin area of a page in a document, typically containing elements such as the title, page number, or name of the author. See also *footer*.

hierarchy diagram A diagram that illustrates the structure of an organization or entity.

hyperlink A connection from a hyperlink anchor such as text or a graphic that you can follow to display a link target such as a file, a location in a file, or a website. Text hyperlinks are usually formatted as colored or underlined text, but sometimes the only indication is that when you point to them, the pointer changes to a hand.

Hypertext Markup Language (HTML) A markup language that uses tags to mark elements in a document to indicate how web browsers should display these elements to the user and how they should respond to user actions.

hyphenating Splitting a word that would otherwise extend beyond the right margin of the page.

icon A small picture or symbol representing a command, file type, function, program, or tool.

indent marker A marker on the horizontal ruler that controls the indentation of text from the left or right margin of a document.

index A list of the words and phrases that are discussed in a printed document, along with the page numbers they appear on.

index entry A field code that marks specific text for inclusion in an index. When you mark text as an index entry, Word inserts an XE (Index Entry) field formatted as hidden text.

index entry field The XE field, including the braces ({ }), that defines an index entry.

justifying Making all lines of text in a paragraph or column fit the width of the document or column, with even margins on each side.

keyboard shortcut Any combination of keystrokes that can be used to perform a task that would otherwise require a mouse or other pointing device.

landscape The orientation of a picture or page where the width is greater than the height.

legend A key in a chart that identifies the colors and names of the data series or categories that are used in the chart.

line break A manual break that forces the text that follows it to the next line. Also called a *text wrapping break*.

line graph or line chart A type of chart in which data points in a series are connected by a line.

link See *hyperlink*; *linked object*.

linked object An object that is inserted into a document but that still exists in the source file. When information is linked, the document can be updated automatically if the information in the original document changes.

list diagram A diagram in which lists of related or independent information are visually represented.

Live Preview A feature that temporarily displays the effect of applying a specific format to the selected document element.

mail merge The process of merging information into a main document from a data source, such as an email address book or database, to create customized documents, such as form letters or mailing labels.

main document In a mail merge operation in Word, the document that contains the text and graphics that are the same for each version of the merged document.

manual page break A page break inserted to force subsequent information to appear on the next page.

margin The blank space outside the printing area on a page.

matrix diagram A diagram that shows the relationship of components to a whole.

merge field A placeholder in a document that is replaced with variable information from a data source during the merge process.

Microsoft Office Clipboard See *Clipboard*.

Navigation pane A pane that displays an outline of a document's headings, or thumbnails of a document's pages, and allows you to jump to a heading or page in the document by clicking it. Also provides content search capabilities.

nested table A table inserted into a cell of a table that is being used to arrange information on a page.

object An item, such as a graphic, video clip, sound file, or worksheet, that can be inserted into a document and then selected and modified.

orientation The direction—horizontal or vertical—in which a page is laid out.

orphan The first line of a paragraph printed by itself at the bottom of a page.

Outline view A view that shows the headings of a document indented to represent their level in the document's structure.

palette A collection of color swatches that you can click to apply a color to selected text or an object.

paragraph In word processing, a block of text that ends when you press the Enter key.

paragraph formatting Formatting that controls the appearance of a paragraph. Examples include indentation, alignment, line spacing, and pagination.

paragraph style A combination of character formatting and paragraph formatting that is named and stored as a set. Applying the style to a paragraph applies all the formatting characteristics at one time.

path A sequence of folders (directories) that leads to a specific file or folder. A backslash is used to separate each folder in a Windows path, and a forward slash is used to separate each directory in an Internet path.

PDF Portable Document Format, a fixed-layout file format in which the formatting of the document appears the same regardless of the computer on which it is displayed.

picture A photograph, clip art image, illustration, or another type of image created with a program other than Word.

picture diagram A diagram that uses pictures to convey information, rather than or in addition to text.

pie chart A round chart that shows the size of items in a single data series, proportional to the sum of the items.

plot area In a two-dimensional chart, the area bounded by the axes, including all data series. In a three-dimensional chart, the area bounded by the axes, including the data series, category names, tick-mark labels, and axis titles.

point The unit of measure for expressing the size of characters in a font, where 72 points equals 1 inch.

pointing to Pausing the mouse pointer or other pointing device over an on-screen element.

Portable Document Format See *PDF*.

portrait The orientation of a picture or page where the page is taller than it is wide.

post A message published on a blog, discussion board, or message board.

Print Layout view A view of a document as it will appear when printed; for example, items such as headers, footnotes, columns, and text boxes appear in their actual positions.

process diagram A diagram that visually represents the ordered set of steps required to complete a task.

promoting In an outline, changing body text to a heading, or changing a heading to a higher-level heading. See also *demoting*.

pull quote Text taken from the body of a document and showcased in a text box to create visual interest.

pyramid diagram A diagram that shows foundation-based relationships.

query Selection criteria for extracting information from a data source.

Quick Access Toolbar A small, customizable toolbar that displays frequently used commands.

Quick Style A collection of character and paragraph formatting that makes formatting documents and objects easier. Quick Styles appear in the Quick Styles gallery and are organized into ready-made Quick Style sets that are designed to work together to create an attractive and professional-looking document.

Quick Table A table with sample data that you can customize.

Read Mode A document view that displays a document in a simplified window with minimal controls, at a size that is optimized for reading documents on a computer screen. Previously referred to as Full Screen Reading view or Reading Layout view.

read-only A setting that allows a file to be read or copied, but not changed or saved. If you change a read-only file, you can save your changes only if you give the document a new name.

record A collection of data about a person, a place, an event, or some other item. Records are the logical equivalents of rows in a table.

reference mark The number or symbol displayed in the body of document when you insert a footnote or endnote.

relationship diagram A diagram that shows convergent, divergent, overlapping, merging, or containment elements.

revision A change in a document.

ribbon A user interface design that organizes commands into logical groups that appear on separate tabs.

saturation In color management, the purity of a color's hue, moving from gray to the pure color.

screen clipping An image of all or part of the content displayed on a computer screen. Screen clippings can be captured by using a graphics capture tool such as the Screen Clipping tool included with Office 2013 programs.

ScreenTip A note that appears on the screen to provide information about the program interface or certain types of document content, such as proofing marks and hyperlinks within a document.

section break A mark you insert to show the end of a section. A section break stores the section formatting elements, such as the margins, page orientation, headers and footers, and sequence of page numbers.

selecting Highlighting text or activating an object so that you can manipulate or edit it in some way.

selection area An area in a document's left margin in which you can click and drag to select blocks of text.

series axis The optical axis that is perpendicular to the x-axis and y-axis, usually the "floor." Also called the *z-axis*.

sizing handle A small circle, square, or set of dots that appears at the corner or on the side of a selected object. You drag these handles to change the size of the object horizontally, vertically, or proportionally.

SmartArt graphic A predefined set of shapes and text used as a basis for creating a diagram.

soft page break A page break that Word inserts when the text reaches the bottom margin of a page.

source file A file that contains information that is linked, embedded, or merged into a destination file. Updates to source file content are reflected in the destination file when the data connection is refreshed.

stack A set of graphics that overlap each other.

status bar A program window element, located at the bottom of the program window, that displays indicators and controls.

status bar indicator A notification on the status bar that displays information related to the current program.

style Any kind of formatting that is named and stored as a set. See also *character style*, *paragraph style*, *Quick Style*, and *table style*.

style area pane A pane that can be displayed along the left side of a document on the screen in Draft or Outline view and that displays the assigned paragraph style of the adjacent paragraph.

subentry An index entry that falls under a more general heading; for example, *Mars* and *Venus* might be subentries of the index entry *planets*.

switch In a field, a setting that refines the results of the field; for example, by formatting it in a particular way.

tab A tabbed page on the ribbon that contains buttons organized in groups.

tab leader A repeating character (usually a dot or dash) that separates text before the tab from text or a number after it.

tab stop A location on the horizontal ruler that indicates how far to indent text or where to begin a column of text.

tabbed list A list that arranges text in simple columns separated by left, right, centered, or decimal tab stops.

table One or more rows of cells commonly used to display numbers and other items for quick reference and analysis. Items in a table are organized in rows and columns.

table of authorities A list of the references in a legal document, such as references to cases, statutes, and rules, along with the numbers of the pages on which the references appear.

table of contents A list of the headings in a document, along with the numbers of the pages on which the headings appear.

table of figures A list of the captions for pictures, charts, graphs, slides, or other illustrations in a document, along with the numbers of the pages on which the captions appear.

table style A set of formatting options, such as font, border style, and row banding, that are applied to a table. The regions of a table, such as the header row, header column, and data area, can be variously formatted.

target A file, location, object, or webpage that is displayed from a link or hyperlink.

template A file that can contain predefined formatting, layout, text, or graphics, and that serves as the basis for new documents with a similar design or purpose.

text box A container that contains text separately from other document content.

text wrapping The way text wraps around an object on the page.

text wrapping break A manual break that forces the text that follows it to the next line. Also known as a *line break*.

theme A set of unified design elements that combine color, fonts, and effects to provide a professional look for a document.

thumbnail A small representation of an item, such as an image, a page of content, or a set of formatting, usually obtained by scaling a snapshot of it. Thumbnails are typically used to provide visual identifiers for related items.

tick-mark A small line of measurement, similar to a division line on a ruler, that intersects an axis in a chart.

tool tab A tab containing groups of commands that are pertinent only to a specific type of document element such as a picture, table, or text box. Tool tabs appear only when relevant content is selected.

value axis The axis used for plotting values in a chart. Also called the *y-axis*.

View Shortcuts toolbar A toolbar located at the right end of the status bar that contains tools for switching between views of document content and changing the display magnification.

watermark A text or graphic image on the page behind the main content of a document.

Web App See *Word Web App*.

web browser Software that interprets HTML files, formats them into webpages, and displays them. A web browser, such as Internet Explorer,

can follow hyperlinks, respond to requests to download files, and play sound or video files that are embedded in webpages.

Web Layout view A view of a document as it will appear in a web browser. In this view, a document appears as one page (without page breaks); text and tables wrap to fit the window.

webpage A World Wide Web document. A webpage typically consists of an HTML file, with associated files for graphics and scripts, in a particular folder on a particular computer. It is identified by a Uniform Resource Locator (URL).

widow The last line of a paragraph printed by itself at the top of a page.

wildcard character A keyboard character that can be used to represent one or many characters when conducting a search. The question mark (?) represents a single character, and the asterisk (*) represents one or more characters.

word processing The writing, editing, and formatting of documents in a program designed for working primarily with text.

Word Web App An app that you can use to review and edit a document stored in a shared location in your web browser.

word wrap The process of breaking lines of text automatically to stay within the page margins of a document or within window boundaries.

WordArt object A text object you create with ready-made effects and to which you can apply additional formatting options.

x-axis The axis used for plotting categories of data in a chart. Also called the *category axis*.

y-axis The axis used for plotting values in a chart. Also called the *value axis*.

z-axis The optical axis that is perpendicular to the x-axis and y-axis, usually the "floor." Also called the *series axis*.

Keyboard shortcuts

Throughout this book, we provide information about how to perform tasks quickly and efficiently by using keyboard shortcuts. This section presents information about keyboard shortcuts that are built in to Microsoft Word 2013 and Microsoft Office 2013, and about custom keyboard shortcuts.

TIP In the following lists, keys you press at the same time are separated by a plus sign (+), and keys you press sequentially are separated by a comma (,).

Word 2013 keyboard shortcuts

This section provides a comprehensive list of keyboard shortcuts built into Word 2013. The list has been excerpted from Word Help and formatted in tables for convenient lookup.

Perform common tasks

Action	Keyboard shortcut
Create a nonbreaking space	Ctrl+Shift+Spacebar
Create a nonbreaking hyphen	Ctrl+Shift+Hyphen
Make letters bold	Ctrl+B
Make letters italic	Ctrl+I
Make letters underlined	Ctrl+U
Decrease font size one value	Ctrl+Shift+<
Increase font size one value	Ctrl+Shift+>
Decrease font size 1 point	Ctrl+[
Increase font size 1 point	Ctrl+]
Remove paragraph or character formatting	Ctrl+Spacebar
Copy the selected text or object	Ctrl+C
Cut the selected text or object	Ctrl+X
Paste text or an object	Ctrl+V
Refine paste action (Paste Special)	Ctrl+Alt+V
Paste formatting only	Ctrl+Shift+V

Action	Keyboard shortcut
Undo the last action	Ctrl+Z
Redo the last action	Ctrl+Y
Open the Word Count dialog box	Ctrl+Shift+G

Work with documents and webpages

Create, view, and save documents

Action	Keyboard shortcut
Create a new document	Ctrl+N
Open a document	Ctrl+O
Close a document	Ctrl+W
Split the document window	Alt+Ctrl+S
Remove the document window split	Alt+Shift+C or Alt+Ctrl+S
Save a document	Ctrl+S

Find, replace, and browse through text

Action	Keyboard shortcut
Open the Navigation pane (to search the document)	Ctrl+F
Repeat a Find action (after closing the Find And Replace dialog box)	Alt+Ctrl+Y
Replace text, specific formatting, and special items	Ctrl+H
Go to a page, bookmark, footnote, table, comment, graphic, or other location	Ctrl+G
Switch between the last four places that you have edited	Alt+Ctrl+Z
Open a list of browse options	Alt+Ctrl+Home
Move to the previous browse object (set in browse options)	Ctrl+Page Up
Move to the next browse object (set in browse options)	Ctrl+Page Down

Switch to another view

Action	Keyboard shortcut
Switch to Print Layout view	Alt+Ctrl+P
Switch to Outline view	Alt+Ctrl+O
Switch to Draft view	Alt+Ctrl+N

Work in Outline view

Action	Keyboard shortcut
Promote a paragraph	Alt+Shift+Left Arrow
Demote a paragraph	Alt+Shift+Right Arrow
Demote to body text	Ctrl+Shift+N
Move selected paragraphs up	Alt+Shift+Up Arrow
Move selected paragraphs down	Alt+Shift+Down Arrow
Expand text under a heading	Alt+Shift+Plus sign
Collapse text under a heading	Alt+Shift+Minus sign
Expand or collapse all text or headings	Alt+Shift+A
Hide or display character formatting	The slash (/) key on the numeric keypad
Show the first line of body text or all body text	Alt+Shift+L
Show all headings with the Heading 1 style	Alt+Shift+1
Show all headings up to the Heading n style	Alt+Shift+9
Insert a tab character	Ctrl+Tab

Work in Read Mode

Action	Keyboard shortcut
Go to the beginning of the document	Home
Go to the end of the document	End
Go to page n	n, Enter
Exit Read Mode	Esc

Print and preview documents

Action	Keyboard shortcut
Print a document	Ctrl+P
Display the Print page of the Backstage view	Alt+Ctrl+I
Move around the preview page when zoomed in	Arrow keys
Move by one preview page when zoomed out	Page Up or Page Down
Move to the first preview page when zoomed out	Ctrl+Home
Move to the last preview page when zoomed out	Ctrl+End

Review documents

Action	Keyboard shortcut
Insert a comment	Alt+Ctrl+M
Turn change tracking on or off	Ctrl+Shift+E
Close the Reviewing pane if it is open	Alt+Shift+C

Work with references, footnotes, and endnotes

Action	Keyboard shortcut
Mark a table of contents entry	Alt+Shift+O
Mark a table of authorities entry (citation)	Alt+Shift+I
Mark an index entry	Alt+Shift+X
Insert a footnote	Alt+Ctrl+F
Insert an endnote	Alt+Ctrl+D

Work with webpages

Action	Keyboard shortcut
Insert a hyperlink	Ctrl+K
Go back one page	Alt+Left Arrow
Go forward one page	Alt+Right Arrow
Refresh	F9

Edit and move text and graphics

Delete text and graphics

Action	Keyboard shortcut
Delete one character to the left	Backspace
Delete one word to the left	Ctrl+Backspace
Delete one character to the right	Delete
Delete one word to the right	Ctrl+Delete
Cut selected content to the Microsoft Office Clipboard	Ctrl+X
Undo the last action	Ctrl+Z
Cut selected content to the Spike	Ctrl+F3

Copy and move text and graphics

Action	Keyboard shortcut
Open the Clipboard	Press Alt+H to move to the Home tab, and then press F,O
Copy selected text or graphics to the Clipboard	Ctrl+C
Cut selected text or graphics to the Clipboard	Ctrl+X
Paste the most recent addition or pasted item from the Clipboard	Ctrl+V
Move text or graphics once	F2 (then move the cursor and press Enter)
Copy text or graphics once	Shift+F2 (then move the cursor and press Enter)
When text or an object is selected, open the Create New Building Block dialog box	Alt+F3
When a building block—for example, a SmartArt graphic—is selected, display the shortcut menu that is associated with it	Shift+F10
Copy the header or footer used in the previous section of the document	Alt+Shift+R

Insert special characters

Action	Keyboard shortcut
A field	Ctrl+F9
A line break	Shift+Enter
A page break	Ctrl+Enter
A column break	Ctrl+Shift+Enter
An em dash	Alt+Ctrl+Minus sign
An en dash	Ctrl+Minus sign
An optional hyphen	Ctrl+Hyphen
A nonbreaking hyphen	Ctrl+Shift+Hyphen
A nonbreaking space	Ctrl+Shift+Spacebar
The copyright symbol	Alt+Ctrl+C
The registered trademark symbol	Alt+Ctrl+R
The trademark symbol	Alt+Ctrl+T
An ellipsis	Alt+Ctrl+Period
An AutoText entry	Enter (after the ScreenTip appears)

Insert characters by using character codes

Action	Keyboard shortcut
Insert the Unicode character for the specified Unicode (hexadecimal) character code. For example, to insert the euro currency symbol (€), enter 20AC, and then hold down Alt and press X	The character code, Alt+X
Find out the Unicode character code for the selected character	Alt+X
Insert the ANSI character for the specified ANSI (decimal) character code For example, to insert the euro currency symbol, hold down Alt and press 0128 on the numeric keypad	Alt+ the character code (on the numeric keypad)

Select text and graphics

Action	Keyboard shortcut
Select text and graphics	Hold down Shift and use the arrow keys to move the cursor

Extend a selection

Action	Keyboard shortcut
Turn extend mode on	F8
Select the nearest character	F8+Left Arrow or Right Arrow
Increase the size of a selection	F8 (press once to select a word, twice to select a sentence, and so on)
Reduce the size of a selection	Shift+F8
Turn extend mode off	Esc
Extend a selection one character to the right	Shift+Right Arrow
Extend a selection one character to the left	Shift+Left Arrow
Extend a selection to the end of a word	Ctrl+Shift+Right Arrow
Extend a selection to the beginning of a word	Ctrl+Shift+Left Arrow
Extend a selection to the end of a line	Shift+End
Extend a selection to the beginning of a line	Shift+Home
Extend a selection one line down	Shift+Down Arrow
Extend a selection one line up	Shift+Up Arrow
Extend a selection to the end of a paragraph	Ctrl+Shift+Down Arrow

Extend a selection to the beginning of a paragraph	Ctrl+Shift+Up Arrow
Extend a selection one screen down	Shift+Page Down
Extend a selection one screen up	Shift+Page Up
Extend a selection to the beginning of a document	Ctrl+Shift+Home
Extend a selection to the end of a document	Ctrl+Shift+End
Extend a selection to the end of a window	Alt+Ctrl+Shift+Page Down
Extend a selection to include the entire document	Ctrl+A
Select a vertical block of text	Ctrl+Shift+F8, and then use the arrow keys; press Esc to cancel
Extend a selection to a specific location in a document	F8+arrow keys; press Esc to cancel

Select text and graphics in a table

Action	Keyboard shortcut
Select the next cell's contents	Tab
Select the preceding cell's contents	Shift+Tab
Extend a selection to adjacent cells	Hold down Shift and press an arrow key repeatedly
Select a column	Use the arrow keys to move to the column's top or bottom cell, and then do one of the following: ■ Press Shift+Alt+Page Down to select the column from top to bottom ■ Press Shift+Alt+Page Up to select the column from bottom to top
Extend a selection (or block)	Ctrl+Shift+F8, and then use the arrow keys; press Esc to cancel selection mode
Select an entire table	Alt+5 on the numeric keypad (with Num Lock off)

Move through documents

Action	Keyboard shortcut
One character to the left	Left Arrow
One character to the right	Right Arrow
One word to the left	Ctrl+Left Arrow
One word to the right	Ctrl+Right Arrow
One paragraph up	Ctrl+Up Arrow
One paragraph down	Ctrl+Down Arrow
One cell to the left (in a table)	Shift+Tab
One cell to the right (in a table)	Tab

Action	Keyboard shortcut
Up one line	Up Arrow
Down one line	Down Arrow
To the end of a line	End
To the beginning of a line	Home
To the top of the window	Alt+Ctrl+Page Up
To the end of the window	Alt+Ctrl+Page Down
Up one screen (scrolling)	Page Up
Down one screen (scrolling)	Page Down
To the top of the next page	Ctrl+Page Down
To the top of the previous page	Ctrl+Page Up
To the end of a document	Ctrl+End
To the beginning of a document	Ctrl+Home
To a previous revision	Shift+F5
Immediately after opening a document, to the location you were working in when the document was last closed	Shift+F5

Move around in a table

Action	Keyboard shortcut
To the next cell in a row	Tab
To the previous cell in a row	Shift+Tab
To the first cell in a row	Alt+Home
To the last cell in a row	Alt+End
To the first cell in a column	Alt+Page Up
To the last cell in a column	Alt+Page Down
To the previous row	Up Arrow
To the next row	Down Arrow

Insert characters and move content in tables

Action	Keyboard shortcut
New paragraphs in a cell	Enter
Tab characters in a cell	Ctrl+Tab
Move content up one row	Alt+Shift+Up Arrow
Move content down one row	Alt+Shift+Down Arrow

Apply character and paragraph formatting

Copy formatting

Action	Keyboard shortcut
Copy formatting from text	Ctrl+Shift+C
Apply copied formatting to text	Ctrl+Shift+V

Change or resize the font

TIP The following keyboard shortcuts do not work in Read Mode.

Action	Keyboard shortcut
Open the Font dialog box to change the font	Ctrl+Shift+F
Increase the font size	Ctrl+Shift+>
Decrease the font size	Ctrl+Shift+<
Increase the font size by 1 point	Ctrl+]
Decrease the font size by 1 point	Ctrl+[

Apply character formats

Action	Keyboard shortcut
Open the Font dialog box to change the formatting of characters	Ctrl+D
Change the case of letters	Shift+F3
Format all letters as capitals	Ctrl+Shift+A
Apply bold formatting	Ctrl+B
Apply an underline	Ctrl+U
Underline words but not spaces	Ctrl+Shift+W
Double-underline text	Ctrl+Shift+D
Apply hidden text formatting	Ctrl+Shift+H
Apply italic formatting	Ctrl+I
Format letters as small capitals	Ctrl+Shift+K
Apply subscript formatting (automatic spacing)	Ctrl+Equal sign
Apply superscript formatting (automatic spacing)	Ctrl+Shift+Plus sign
Remove manual character formatting	Ctrl+Spacebar
Change the selection to the Symbol font	Ctrl+Shift+Q

View and copy text formats

Action	Keyboard shortcut
Display nonprinting characters	Ctrl+Shift+8
Review text formatting	Shift+F1 (then click the text with the formatting you want to review)
Copy formats	Ctrl+Shift+C
Paste formats	Ctrl+Shift+V

Set the line spacing

Action	Keyboard shortcut
Single-space lines	Ctrl+1
Double-space lines	Ctrl+2
Set 1.5-line spacing	Ctrl+5
Add or remove one line space preceding a paragraph	Ctrl+0 (zero)

Align paragraphs

Action	Keyboard shortcut
Switch a paragraph between centered and left-aligned	Ctrl+E
Switch a paragraph between justified and left-aligned	Ctrl+J
Switch a paragraph between right-aligned and left-aligned	Ctrl+R
Left align a paragraph	Ctrl+L
Indent a paragraph from the left	Ctrl+M
Remove a paragraph indent from the left	Ctrl+Shift+M
Create a hanging indent	Ctrl+T
Reduce a hanging indent	Ctrl+Shift+T
Remove paragraph formatting	Ctrl+Q

Apply paragraph styles

Action	Keyboard shortcut
Open the Apply Styles pane	Ctrl+Shift+S
Open the Styles pane	Alt+Ctrl+Shift+S
Start AutoFormat	Alt+Ctrl+K
Apply the Normal style	Ctrl+Shift+N

Action	Keyboard shortcut
Apply the Heading 1 style	Alt+Ctrl+1
Apply the Heading 2 style	Alt+Ctrl+2
Apply the Heading 3 style	Alt+Ctrl+3
Close the active Styles pane	Ctrl+Spacebar, C

Work with mail merge and fields

Perform mail merges

Action	Keyboard shortcut
Preview a mail merge	Alt+Shift+K
Merge a document	Alt+Shift+N
Print the merged document	Alt+Shift+M
Edit a mail-merge data document	Alt+Shift+E
Insert a merge field	Alt+Shift+F

Work with fields

Action	Keyboard shortcut
Insert a Date field	Alt+Shift+D
Insert a LIstNum field	Alt+Ctrl+L
Insert a Page field	Alt+Shift+P
Insert a Time field	Alt+Shift+T
Insert an empty field	Ctrl+F9
Update linked information in a Word source document	Ctrl+Shift+F7
Update selected fields	F9
Unlink a field	Ctrl+Shift+F9
Switch between a selected field code and its result	Shift+F9
Switch between all field codes and their results	Alt+F9
Run GoToButton or MacroButton from the field that displays the field results	Alt+Shift+F9
Go to the next field	F11
Go to the previous field	Shift+F11
Lock a field	Ctrl+F11
Unlock a field	Ctrl+Shift+F11

Use the Language bar

Action	Keyboard shortcut
Switch between languages or keyboard layouts	Left Alt+Shift
Display a list of correction alternatives	Windows logo key+C
Turn handwriting on or off	Windows logo key +H
Turn Japanese Input Method Editor (IME) on 101 keyboard on or off	Alt+~
Turn Korean IME on 101 keyboard on or off	Right Alt
Turn Chinese IME on 101 keyboard on or off	Ctrl+Spacebar

TIP The Windows logo key is available on the bottom row of keys on most keyboards.

Perform function key tasks

Function keys

Action	Keyboard shortcut
Get Help or visit Office.com	F1
Move text or graphics	F2
Repeat the last action	F4
Choose the Go To command (Home tab)	F5
Go to the next pane or frame	F6
Choose the Spelling command (Review tab)	F7
Extend a selection	F8
Update the selected fields	F9
Show KeyTips	F10
Go to the next field	F11
Choose the Save As command	F12

Shift+function key

Action	Keyboard shortcut
Start context-sensitive Help or reveal formatting	Shift+F1
Copy text	Shift+F2

Change the case of letters	Shift+F3
Repeat a Find or Go To action	Shift+F4
Move to the last change	Shift+F5
Go to the previous pane or frame (after pressing F6)	Shift+F6
Choose the Thesaurus command (Review tab, Proofing group)	Shift+F7
Reduce the size of a selection	Shift+F8
Switch between a field code and its result	Shift+F9
Display a shortcut menu	Shift+F10
Go to the previous field	Shift+F11
Choose the Save command	Shift+F12

Ctrl+function key

Action	Keyboard shortcut
Expand or collapse the ribbon	Ctrl+F1
Choose the Print Preview command	Ctrl+F2
Close the window	Ctrl+F4
Go to the next window	Ctrl+F6
Insert an empty field	Ctrl+F9
Maximize the document window	Ctrl+F10
Lock a field	Ctrl+F11
Choose the Open command	Ctrl+F12

Ctrl+Shift+function key

Action	Keyboard shortcut
Insert the contents of the Spike	Ctrl+Shift+F3
Edit a bookmark	Ctrl+Shift+F5
Go to the previous window	Ctrl+Shift+F6
Update linked information in a Word source document	Ctrl+Shift+F7
Extend a selection or block	Ctrl+Shift+F8, and then press an arrow key
Unlink a field	Ctrl+Shift+F9
Unlock a field	Ctrl+Shift+F11
Choose the Print command	Ctrl+Shift+F12

Alt+function key

Action	Keyboard shortcut
Go to the next field	Alt+F1
Create a new building block	Alt+F3
Exit Word	Alt+F4
Restore the program window size	Alt+F5
Move from an open dialog box back to the document, for dialog boxes that support this behavior	Alt+F6
Find the next misspelling or grammatical error	Alt+F7
Run a macro	Alt+F8
Switch between all field codes and their results	Alt+F9
Display the Selection And Visibility pane	Alt+F10
Display Microsoft Visual Basic code	Alt+F11

Alt+Shift+function key

Action	Keyboard shortcut
Go to the previous field	Alt+Shift+F1
Choose the Save command	Alt+Shift+F2
Display the Research pane	Alt+Shift+F7
Run GoToButton or MacroButton from the field that displays the field results	Alt+Shift+F9
Display a menu or message for an available action	Alt+Shift+F10
Select the Table Of Contents button when the Table Of Contents is active	Alt+Shift+F12

Ctrl+Alt+function key

Action	Keyboard shortcut
Display Microsoft System Information	Ctrl+Alt+F1
Choose the Open command	Ctrl+Alt+F2

Office 2013 keyboard shortcuts

This section provides a comprehensive list of keyboard shortcuts available in all Office 2013 programs, including Word.

Display and use windows

Action	Keyboard shortcut
Switch to the next window	Alt+Tab
Switch to the previous window	Alt+Shift+Tab
Close the active window	Ctrl+W or Ctrl+F4
Restore the size of the active window after you maximize it	Alt+F5
Move to a pane from another pane in the program window (clockwise direction) If pressing F6 does not display the pane that you want, press Alt to put the focus on the ribbon, and then press Ctrl+Tab to move to the pane	F6 or Shift+F6
Switch to the next open window	Ctrl+F6
Switch to the previous window	Ctrl+Shift+F6
Maximize or restore a selected window	Ctrl+F10
Copy a picture of the screen to the Clipboard	Print Screen
Copy a picture of the selected window to the Clipboard	Alt+Print Screen

Use dialog boxes

Action	Keyboard shortcut
Move to the next option or option group	Tab
Move to the previous option or option group	Shift+Tab
Switch to the next tab in a dialog box	Ctrl+Tab
Switch to the previous tab in a dialog box	Ctrl+Shift+Tab
Move between options in an open drop-down list, or between options in a group of options	Arrow keys
Perform the action assigned to the selected button; select or clear the selected check box	Spacebar
Select an option; select or clear a check box	Alt+ *the underlined letter*

Open a selected drop-down list	Alt+Down Arrow
Select an option from a drop-down list	*First letter of the list option*
Close a selected drop-down list; cancel a command and close a dialog box	Esc
Run the selected command	Enter

Use edit boxes within dialog boxes

An edit box is a blank box in which you enter or paste an entry.

Action	Keyboard shortcut
Move to the beginning of the entry	Home
Move to the end of the entry	End
Move one character to the left or right	Left Arrow or Right Arrow
Move one word to the left	Ctrl+Left Arrow
Move one word to the right	Ctrl+Right Arrow
Select or unselect one character to the left	Shift+Left Arrow
Select or unselect one character to the right	Shift+Right Arrow
Select or unselect one word to the left	Ctrl+Shift+Left Arrow
Select or unselect one word to the right	Ctrl+Shift+Right Arrow
Select from the insertion point to the beginning of the entry	Shift+Home
Select from the insertion point to the end of the entry	Shift+End

Use the Open and Save As dialog boxes

Action	Keyboard shortcut
Open the Open dialog box	Ctrl+F12 or Ctrl+O
Open the Save As dialog box	F12
Open the selected folder or file	Enter
Open the folder one level above the selected folder	Backspace
Delete the selected folder or file	Delete
Display a shortcut menu for a selected item such as a folder or file	Shift+F10
Move forward through options	Tab
Move back through options	Shift+Tab
Open the Look In list	F4 or Alt+I
Refresh the file list	F5

Use the Backstage view

Action	Keyboard shortcut
Display the Open page of the Backstage view	Ctrl+O
Display the Save As page of the Backstage view (when saving a file for the first time)	Ctrl+S
Continue saving an Office file (after giving the file a name and location)	Ctrl+S
Display the Save As page of the Backstage view (after initially saving a file)	Alt+F+S
Close the Backstage view	Esc

TIP You can use dialog boxes instead of Backstage view pages by selecting the Don't Show The Backstage When Opening Or Saving Files check box on the Save page of the Word Options dialog box. Set this option in any Office program to enable it in all Office programs.

Navigate the ribbon

1 Press **Alt** to display the KeyTips over each feature in the current view.
2 Press the letter shown in the KeyTip over the feature that you want to use.

TIP To cancel the action and hide the KeyTips, press Alt.

Change the keyboard focus without using the mouse

Action	Keyboard shortcut
Select the active tab of the ribbon and activate the access keys	Alt or F10. Press either of these keys again to move back to the document and cancel the access keys
Move to another tab of the ribbon	F10 to select the active tab, and then Left Arrow or Right Arrow
Expand or collapse the ribbon	Ctrl+F1
Display the shortcut menu for the selected item	Shift+F10
Move the focus to select each of the following areas of the window: ■ Active tab of the ribbon ■ Any open panes ■ Status bar at the bottom of the window ■ Your document	F6

Action	Keyboard shortcut
Move the focus to each command on the ribbon, forward or backward, respectively	Tab or Shift+Tab
Move among the items on the ribbon	arrow keys
Activate the selected command or control on the ribbon	Spacebar or Enter
Display the selected menu or gallery on the ribbon	Spacebar or Enter
Activate a command or control on the ribbon so that you can modify a value	Enter
Finish modifying a value in a control on the ribbon, and move focus back to the document	Enter
Get help on the selected command or control on the ribbon	F1

Undo and redo actions

Action	Keyboard shortcut
Cancel an action	Esc
Undo an action	Ctrl+Z
Redo or repeat an action	Ctrl+Y

Change or resize the font

TIP The cursor must be inside a text box when you use these shortcuts.

Action	Keyboard shortcut
Change the font	Ctrl+Shift+F
Change the font size	Ctrl+Shift+P
Increase the font size of the selected text	Ctrl+Shift+>
Decrease the font size of the selected text	Ctrl+Shift+<
Change the font	Ctrl+Shift+F

Move around in text or cells

Action	Keyboard shortcut
Move one character to the left	Left Arrow
Move one character to the right	Right Arrow

Action	Keyboard shortcut
Move one line up	Up Arrow
Move one line down	Down Arrow
Move one word to the left	Ctrl+Left Arrow
Move one word to the right	Ctrl+Right Arrow
Move to the end of a line	End
Move to the beginning of a line	Home
Move up one paragraph	Ctrl+Up Arrow
Move down one paragraph	Ctrl+Down Arrow
Move to the end of a text box	Ctrl+End
Move to the beginning of a text box	Ctrl+Home
Repeat the last Find action	Shift+F4

Move around in and work in tables

Action	Keyboard shortcut
Move to the next cell	Tab
Move to the preceding cell	Shift+Tab
Move to the next row	Down Arrow
Move to the preceding row	Up Arrow
Insert a tab in a cell	Ctrl+Tab
Start a new paragraph	Enter
Add a new row at the bottom of the table	Tab at the end of the last row

Access and use panes and galleries

Action	Keyboard shortcut
Move to a pane from another pane in the program window	F6
When a menu is active, move to a pane	Ctrl+Tab
When a pane is active, select the next or previous option in the pane	Tab or Shift+Tab
Display the full set of commands on the pane menu	Ctrl+Spacebar
Perform the action assigned to the selected button	Spacebar or Enter
Open a drop-down menu for the selected gallery item	Shift+F10
Select the first or last item in a gallery	Home or End

Action	Keyboard shortcut
Scroll up or down in the selected gallery list	Page Up or Page Down
Close a pane	Ctrl+Spacebar, C
Open the Clipboard	Alt+H, F, O

Access and use available actions

Action	Keyboard shortcut
Display the shortcut menu for the selected item	Shift+F10
Display the menu or message for an available action or for the AutoCorrect Options button or the Paste options button	Alt+Shift+F10
Move between options in a menu of available actions	Arrow keys
Perform the action for the selected item on a menu of available actions	Enter
Close the available actions menu or message	Esc

Find and replace content

Action	Keyboard shortcut
Open the Find dialog box	Ctrl+F
Open the Replace dialog box	Ctrl+H
Repeat the last Find action	Shift+F4

Use the Help window

Action	Keyboard shortcut
Open the Help window	F1
Close the Help window	Alt+F4
Switch between the Help window and the active program	Alt+Tab
Return to the Help table of contents	Alt+Home
Select the next item in the Help window	Tab
Select the previous item in the Help window	Shift+Tab
Perform the action for the selected item	Enter
Select the next hidden text or hyperlink, including Show All or Hide All at the top of a Help topic	Tab

Action	Keyboard shortcut
Select the previous hidden text or hyperlink	Shift+Tab
Perform the action for the selected Show All, Hide All, hidden text, or hyperlink	Enter
Move back to the previous Help topic (Back button)	Alt+Left Arrow or Backspace
Move forward to the next Help topic (Forward button)	Alt+Right Arrow
Scroll small amounts up or down, respectively, within the currently displayed Help topic	Up Arrow, Down Arrow
Scroll larger amounts up or down, respectively, within the currently displayed Help topic	Page Up, Page Down
Display a menu of commands for the Help window. This requires that the Help window have the active focus (click in the Help window)	Shift+F10
Stop the last action (Stop button)	Esc
Print the current Help topic If the cursor is not in the current Help topic, press F6 and then press Ctrl+P	Ctrl+P
In a Table of Contents in tree view, select the next or previous item, respectively	Up Arrow, Down Arrow
In a Table of Contents in tree view, expand or collapse the selected item, respectively	Left Arrow, Right Arrow

Creating custom keyboard shortcuts

If a command you use frequently doesn't have a built-in keyboard shortcut, or if you don't like the keyboard shortcut that is assigned to the command, you can create one either in a specific document or in a template. You can also modify the built-in keyboard shortcuts.

To manage keyboard shortcuts:

1   Display the **Customize Ribbon** page of the **Word Options** dialog box.

2   Below the **Choose commands from** pane, to the right of **Keyboard shortcuts**, click the **Customize** button.

3   In the **Customize Keyboard** dialog box, select the category containing the command for which you want to create a keyboard shortcut, and then select the command.

The Current Keys box displays any keyboard shortcut already assigned to the command.

4   Click to position the cursor in the **Press new shortcut key** box, and then press the key combination you want to use as a keyboard shortcut for the selected command.

    In the area below the Current Keys box, Word tells you whether the keyboard shortcut is currently assigned to a command or unassigned.

5   To delete an existing keyboard shortcut to make it available for reassignment, select it in the **Current keys** box, and then click the **Remove** button.

6   To assign an available keyboard shortcut to the selected command, do one of the following:

    ▪ To save the keyboard shortcut in all documents based on the current template, verify that the template name is selected in the **Save changes in** list, and then click **Assign**.

    ▪ To save the keyboard shortcut only in the current document, click the document name in the **Save changes in** list, and then click **Assign**.

7   To delete all custom keyboard shortcuts, click **Reset All**.

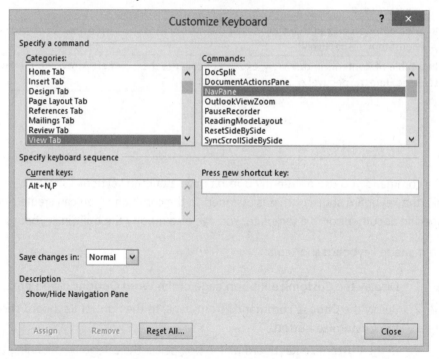

The ribbon tabs are listed in the Categories pane on the left, and the commands in the selected category are listed in the Commands pane on the right.

8   Close the **Customize Keyboard** dialog box and the **Word Options** dialog box.

Index

Numbers

B

backgrounds, 265. *See also* watermarks
    changing, 266
    colors, applying, 266
    pictures as, applying, 269
Backstage view, 7, 25, 332
    Account page, 30
    displaying, 11
    Info page, 26, 207
    New page, 27
    Open page, 28
    Print page, 194
    Save As page, 29
balloons, *defined*, 503
bar charts, 250, 503
bar tabs, setting, 121
Basic Bending Process diagram, 233
bibliographies
    creating, 394
    inserting, 394, 400
    inserting citations, 397
    selecting style guide for, 395, 401
    sources, adding, 396
    updating, 395, 401
Bing Image Search, 177
blank documents, creating, 55
blog posts, publishing, 342
blogs, *defined*, 503
blue wavy underlines, 86. *See also* spelling and
    grammar, checking
bolding text, 111
book exercises, adapting for other display settings,
    18
Bookmark dialog box, 361
bookmarks, 347
    defined, 503
    displaying, 362
    inserting, 360, 361
    jumping to, 363
    moving to, 360
    naming, 362
borders
    page, 270
    paragraph, 124, 127
    table, 165, 318

Borders And Shading dialog box, 124, 270
breaking links to embedded content, 354
breaks
    column, 146
    line, 119, 125
    section, 141
brightness, adjusting for pictures, 174
bringing objects forward, 304, 313
browsers
    configuring webpages for, 334
    opening webpages in, 340
building blocks, 66, 265
    defined, 503
    categories for, creating, 474
    creating, 472
    deleting, 278, 477
    displaying, 477
    inserting, 475
    naming, 474
    placeholders, deleting, 282
    placeholder text, replacing, 285
    previewing, 278, 285
    properties, changing, 278
    saving, 473, 475
    sorting list of, 278
    types of, 276
    viewing information on, 277
    working with, 473
Building Blocks Organizer dialog box, 277
building equations, 288
bullet symbol, changing, 132
bulleted lists
    adding items to, 131
    creating, 130, 132
    customizing, 131
    indenting, 134
    nesting, 131
    removing formatting, 131
    sorting, 135
Bullets menu, 132
buttons
    adding to Quick Access Toolbar, 488–490
    adding to ribbon tabs, 498
    arrows on, 13
    inactive, 20
    ScreenTips for, 12

C

J

jumping to hyperlink target, 348, 350
justifying text, 120, 125
    defined, 506
    in columns, 141

K

Keep Text Only button, 64
keyboard, navigating documents by using, 32,
    511–531
keyboard shortcuts, 511–531
    defined, 506
    adding symbols by using, 191
    custom, creating, 531
    editing text by using, 62
    Office, listed, 525
    Word, listed, 511

L

Label Options dialog box, 424
labels, chart, 251
    removing, 256
labels, mail merging. *See* mail merge
labels, mailing. *See* mailing labels
landscape orientation
    defined, 506
    selecting, 195, 198
languages
    default translation, changing, 80
    setting options for, 483
    translating text from/to, 78, 83
Layout dialog box, 230, 306, 309
Layout Options menu, 228, 305, 335
Layout view, switching to, 42
left indent, setting, 119, 125
legal references. *See* citations
legends, chart, 251
    defined, 506
    removing, 256

licenses for use, obtaining, 451
line breaks
    defined, 506, 510
    creating, 55
    inserting, 119, 125
line charts, 250
    defined, 506
    creating, 252
line graphs, *defined*, 506
line spacing, adjusting for pictures, 171
lines, selecting, 60
linked objects, *defined*, 506
linking objects in documents, 353
linking text boxes, 286
links. *See* hyperlinks
list diagrams, 224, 506
lists, bulleted and numbered
    adding items to, 131
    continuing sequence of, 135
    creating, 130, 132, 133
    customizing, 131
    indenting, 134
    nesting, 131
    removing formatting, 131
    sorting, 135
lists, tabbed
    converting into tables, 151
    creating, 147
    entering text for, 147
    formatting, 148
Live Preview, 14, 506
locking embedded objects, 359

M

macros
    controlling settings for, 485
    displaying, 13
magnification. *See* screen magnification; zooming
mail merge
    defined, 507
    creating mailing labels, 423

N

naming
> bookmarks, 362
> building blocks, 474

navigating
> comments, 430, 431
> documents. *See* navigating documents
> tables, in Word, 152
> tracked changes, 435
> worksheets, 248

navigating documents
> by using the cursor, 32, 34
> jumping to specific page, 360
> by using the keyboard, 32, 40
> moving to beginning, 89, 101
> by scrolling, 31

Navigation pane, 35, 72
> *defined*, 507
> displaying, 53, 491
> working with, 303

nested tables, *defined*, 507
nesting tables in Word, 315
New Address List dialog box, 420
new documents, saving, 56
new features of Word 2013, 6
New page of the Backstage view, 26, 467
Normal template, 94, 454, 461

numbered lists
> adding items to, 131
> continuing sequence of, 135
> creating, 130, 133
> customizing, 131
> indenting, 134
> nesting, 131
> removing formatting, 131

O

Object dialog box, 354

objects
> *defined*, 507
> aligning, 310
> arranging on page, 304
> bringing forward, 313
> fixing position on page, 309
> grouping, 312
> hiding all, 314
> inserting in documents, 354
> moving, 304, 312
> positioning, 335
> selecting, 308
> snapping to grid, 312
> stacking, 304
> wrapping text around, 306

Office 2013 background, choosing, 30
Office 365, 4

Office Clipboard, 61
> *defined*, 504
> viewing, 67

Office Home & Student 2013 RT, 5

Office theme, 104
> changing, 479

offline help, 46

online pictures
> finding and downloading, 177
> inserting, in documents, 170

Open dialog box, 328
Open page of the Backstage view, 27, 28

opening. *See also* opening documents
> PDF files, in Word, 324, 328
> templates, 19
> webpages, in browser, 340
> Word, 9, 18, 52
> worksheets, in Word, 246

opening documents, 19, 27, 31
> as read-only, 31
> earlier versions of, 322
> from the Backstage view, 39
> from previous Word versions, 58
> in Protected view, 31

Options dialog box (Word), 325
organization of book, ix
orientation. *See* page orientation

orphans
> *defined*, 507
> avoiding, 200

Outline view, 37, 298
> *defined*, 507
> displaying, 299

About the authors

Joan Lambert

Joan has worked in the training and certification industry for 16 years. As President of Online Training Solutions, Inc. (OTSI), Joan is responsible for guiding the translation of technical information and requirements into useful, relevant, and measurable training and certification tools.

Joan is a Microsoft Office Certified Master, a Microsoft Certified Application Specialist Instructor, a Microsoft Certified Technology Specialist, a Microsoft Certified Trainer, and the author of more than two dozen books about Windows and Office (for Windows and Mac). Joan enthusiastically shares her love of technology through her participation in the creation of books, learning materials, and certification exams. She greatly enjoys communicating the benefits of new technologies by delivering training and facilitating Microsoft Experience Center events.

Joan currently lives in a nearly perfect small town in Texas with her daughter, Trinity Preppernau, who proudly assisted with the creation of the graphics for this book.

Joyce Cox

Joyce has more than 30 years' experience in the development of training materials about technical subjects for non-technical audiences, and is the author of dozens of books about Office and Windows technologies. She is the Vice President of OTSI.

As President of and principal author for Online Press, she developed the Quick Course series of computer training books for beginning and intermediate adult learners. She was also the first managing editor of Microsoft Press, an editor for Sybex, and an editor for the University of California.

The team

This book would not exist without the support of these hard-working members of the OTSI publishing team:

- Jan Bednarczuk
- Rob Carr
- Susie Carr
- Jeanne Craver
- Kathy Krause
- Marlene Lambert
- Jaime Odell
- Jean Trenary

We are especially thankful to the support staff at home who make it possible for our team members to devote their time and attention to these projects.

Rosemary Caperton provided invaluable support on behalf of Microsoft Learning.

Online Training Solutions, Inc. (OTSI)

OTSI specializes in the design, creation, and production of Office and Windows training products for information workers and home computer users. For more information about OTSI, visit:

www.otsi.com

Microsoft

How to download your ebook

To download your ebook, go to
http://aka.ms/PressEbook
and follow the instructions.

Please note: You will be asked to create a free online account and enter the access code below.

Your access code:

> # HNXHZXW

Microsoft Word 2013 Step by Step

Your PDF ebook allows you to:

- Search the full text
- Print
- Copy and paste

Best yet, you will be notified about free updates to your ebook.

If you ever lose your ebook file, you can download it again just by logging in to your account.

Need help? Please contact:
mspinput@microsoft.com

What do you think of this book?

We want to hear from you!
To participate in a brief online survey, please visit:

microsoft.com/learning/booksurvey

Tell us how well this book meets your needs—what works effectively, and what we can do better. Your feedback will help us continually improve our books and learning resources for you.

Thank you in advance for your input!